POLITICS AND PEOPLE

The Ordeal of Self-Government in America

Politics and People

The Ordeal of Self-Government in America

ADVISORY EDITOR

Leon Stein

EDITORIAL BOARD

James MacGregor Burns

William E. Leuchtenburg

"BOSS" TWEED

THE STORY OF A GRIM GENERATION

BY

DENIS TILDEN LYNCH

ARNO PRESS

A New York Times Company

New York — 1974

Reprint Edition 1974 by Arno Press Inc.

Copyright © 1927, by Boni & Liveright, Inc.
Reprinted by permission of Dunstan W.P.Lynch,
   Administrator of the Estate of Denis Tilden Lynch

POLITICS AND PEOPLE: The Ordeal
of Self-Government in America
ISBN for complete set: 0-405-05850-0
See last pages of this volume for titles.

Manufactured in the United States of America

Library of Congress Cataloging in Publication Data

Lynch, Denis Tilden.
   "Boss" Tweed; the story of a grim generation.

   (Politics and people: the ordeal of self-government
in America)
   Reprint of the ed. published by Boni and Liveright,
New York.
   1. Tweed, William Marcy, 1823-1878. 2. New York
(City)--Politics and government--To 1898. 3. Tweed
Ring. I. Title. II. Series.
F128.47.T96L96 1974   320.9'747'103 [B]   73-19157
ISBN 0-405-05879-9

"BOSS" TWEED

WILLIAM MARCY TWEED
(From the original in the collection of The New York Historical Society.)

★ ★ ★

"BOSS" TWEED

THE STORY OF A GRIM GENERATION

BY

DENIS TILDEN LYNCH

★ ★ ★

BONI AND LIVERIGHT ★ NEW YORK

1927

To
THE MEMORY
OF
GEORGE JONES
SOMETIME EDITOR
OF
THE NEW YORK TIMES

CONTENTS

vii

ILLUSTRATIONS

"BOSS" TWEED

"BOSS" TWEED

CHAPTER I

It was the middle of the eighteenth century when a young Scotch couple landed in the City of New York. They were natives of Kelso, a town on the River Tweed, fifty-two miles southeast of Edinburgh. They had spent their honeymoon in crossing the Atlantic. The man was tall, bronzed, brawny, and broad-shouldered. He bent slightly as he trudged through the unpaved streets with the scant belongings of the pair. What weighted him down was a kit of blacksmith's tools. The couple settled in the northeastern section of the city—then a mere handful of less than 15,000 inhabitants, many of whom still spoke the language of Petrus Stuyvesant.

The young couple answered to the name of Tweed—on whose bonnie banks they were born. Their new home was immediately east of Beekman's Swamp, which lies about midway between the East River and the present City Hall. The section they selected was then, as now, known as Cherry Hill, and commanded a view of the river. To the north, where towering structures of steel and stone limn the sky to-day, farms were tilled and streams purled, and game abounded in the primitive patches of woodland. The Tweeds had two sons, Robert and Phillip, who learned their father's trade. Phillip, the older of the brothers, set up his own forge in Rutgers Street, a stone's throw from where he was born.

In Phillip Tweed we have the first printed record of the ancestors of William Marcy Tweed, the first Boss of Tammany Hall, who set a fashion for political leadership in a representative democracy. In the year 1790 we find Boss Tweed's grandfather listed in the city directory, then in its fifth year, as a blacksmith; address, Rutgers Street. No number is given. That meant little then, as Rutgers Street could be distanced by a small boy in five minutes, and malodorous rookeries, swarming like rabbit warrens, were unknown.

In the year that Phillip Tweed is first listed, his wife bore him a son, Richard. While Richard was an infant his father determined that the son must not follow the trade that the Tweeds for two generations had carried on in the new country. They had made a living, but that was all. There was a man down on John Street whose horses he shod in those days, a mechanic like himself, but a man of property and distinction. He was Thomas Ash (sometimes spelled Ashe), a chairmaker. He was Foreman of the Fire Department, and Treasurer of Tammany Hall. What blacksmith could hope for such honors? And what blacksmith could put on the tone that Ash the chairmaker could? Treasurer of Tammany Hall and Foreman in the Fire Department!

So when Richard Tweed was old enough to work, that is, when he was able to find his way about the neighborhood, he was apprenticed to a chairmaker who, like Ash, specialized in fashioning Windsor chairs. And each morning that the apprentice set forth for the shop of his master, he had held before him for example, Thomas Ash, chairmaker, man of property, Foreman of the Fire Department, and Treasurer of Tammany Hall.

Young Richard became known as one of the finest chairmakers in the city. He branched out for himself on reaching manhood, and opened a shop at 24 Cherry Street. He married one of the belles of the neighborhood, and started a home a few steps away from his shop, on the top of Cherry Hill, at No. 1 Cherry Street.

In 1819, when three children had blessed the union of Richard and Eliza Tweed, yellow fever made one of its periodical and devastating visits to the city. One of its victims was a young Virginian who had come to the city on business. He brought with him a young Negro, who, after finding his master dead, did what wealthy freemen did when fever visited New York—

fled the city. He did not have to go far to do this, as ten minutes' run in a northerly direction would place him in the open country. The young slave—now no longer a slave—ran farther than was needed or good for him. He kept running until he came to the center of Manhattan Island, where, in what is now Central Park, dwelt a motley community of lazy Indians, run-away Negroes, nondescript half-breeds, and lawless whites. One of the white men stopped him and took his good clothes, and gave him his ragged ones in exchange. Here the young runaway tarried for a year. Returning to the city by way of the Road to Boston, he turned east at one of the first streets he came to, and presently offered his services to Richard Tweed.

"What is your name?" asked the chairmaker as he leaned against a bench.

The Negro said he had none and offered to take the chairmaker's.

"No," laughed Richard Tweed, who in an aside to his assistant said: "Black as a crow, yet guileless as a dove."

Bill Dove ran errands, worked round the shop, and looked after the young Tweeds—there were four now, two boys and two girls. Two years later, on April 3, 1823, Bill Dove sprinted from the top of Cherry Hill to the chair shop to announce that William Marcy Tweed had come into the world.

This was the last of Richard Tweed's flock. Tweed senior was then but thirty-three years of age. His wife was his junior by two years. And both lived to ripe old ages. Richard himself did not attain the honors and prosperity of the boyhood model, the prosperous Thomas Ash, maker of Windsor chairs, Foreman of the Fire Department. But he did not have to wait long to see his son, William, a successful chairmaker and brush manufacturer, with two shops of his own at the age of twenty-one, and while still in his twenties, Foreman in the Fire Department, an Alderman and a Member of Congress, and had he lived a few years beyond 1860, Richard would have seen his last born one of the very rich men in the Metropolis, Boss of Tammany, master of the entire machinery of the State government, executive, legislative and judicial, the Court of

Appeals the sole exception. Judges rendered decisions dictated by Tweed. The Legislature passed or defeated measures as he willed. The Governor carried out his orders. Taxpayers filled the city treasury that Tweed might loot it. From this one source alone Tweed stole in excess of $30,000,000 in cash in less than three years—the total peculations of the Ring are not less than $45,000,000 and have been put at $200,000,000— and yet he was not satisfied. For Tweed had an unquenchable ambition. He wanted to control the Nation as he did the State.

And yet this Titan of partisan politics while living was pictured by Nast as a drunken Falstaff. And more astonishing, when dead, the earth not yet settled on his casket, before an editorial writer in *The World* called him a cheap and vulgar rogue.

The career of Tweed is a complete refutation of the tradition built upon these two impeachments.

He was a rogue, but monumental. He was never a comic figure, unless gross corruption moves to laughter. When he drank, it was never to excess. The charge that a man is a drunkard trips lightly off the tongue of the unfair partisan. Even Lincoln, a teetotaler, has been caricatured as a drunken sot. Nast, who imagined Tweed as Falstaff in his cups, was charged with the Lincoln libel. This accusation he vigorously denied. But he was proud of his concept of Tweed.

When trying to stay the tide that finally overwhelmed him, Tweed forced John Jacob Astor and five of the next richest citizens of the city to publish over their own names that Tweed and his Ring had not stolen a cent from the city treasury. No one has stolen anything. The books are faithfully kept. All is in order. The pot whitewashes the kettle. This baseless certificate of character signed by Astor and the other slaves of the Ring puts many more millions of loot in the pockets of Tweed. Tweed lets Astor defraud the people in taxes, and Astor enables Tweed to steal more money from the people.

Arrested, and held in the unprecedented bail of $1,000,000, Tweed sends for Jay Gould to go his bond. Gould obeys. Tweed is free.

One of his forerunners in Tammany on the eve of a nominating convention finds that he has lost control. He fears that an attempt to nominate his ticket by fraud may result in his death. Tweed—they called him Big Bill then because of his huge bulk—volunteers. His fearlessness, his dominating will, his matchless mastery of the mass mind is triumphant. Another victory on the side of fraud.

Later the streets of the city are running rivulets of blood. Grotesquely armed citizens clash with seasoned veterans of the Army of the Potomac. Tweed and two other cronies, unarmed, escort the trembling Governor of the State through the urban battlefields. The mobs, whom Tweed and a few others had, by covert suggestion, spurred on to the work of slaughter, desert the barricades to hail their chief. More than a thousand citizens and soldiers perish in the four days of fighting.

James Fisk, Jr., surnamed the Prince of Erie, who with Gould robbed the railroad of untold millions, and who together with him plotted the gold corner of 1869 with its disastrous Black Friday, brazenly drives down Broadway at high noon in an open carriage, accompanied by his leering harlots, plays Lucullus to President Grant and Pandar to Boss Tweed.

William Cullen Bryant has stopped creating poetry to translate Homer. The management of his paper, *The Evening Post*, is in the competent hands of the incorruptible Charles Nordhoff. The journalist does his duty to the public and savagely assails Tweed. The Boss complains. The honest newspaperman is discharged from the poet's paper.

For years Tweed, with his money, had purchased the silence of his natural critics, not only the press, but his partisan opponents. He had more than half a hundred Republican leaders on his payroll. Decent citizens who started reform movements found that their chosen leaders suddenly became advocates of Tweed.

To Tweed, money is the unfailing arbiter of human differences. This is his faith and practice. When *The Times* has the proofs of his guilt, with details showing the manner in which the city was looted, Tweed, through one of his trusted aides, offers $5,000,000 to George Jones, editor of *The Times*, to surrender the damning evidence.

Jones shatters the faith of Tweed. Some day the Fourth Estate will pay the debt it is under to this worthy craftsman.

There is no treaty for the return of escaped prisoners with Spain. Tweed flees from jail and seeks a haven in the land of the Don. An American warship brings him back, a dying man. Tweed offers to make a full confession if he is permitted to die outside prison walls. He will involve men of national prominence, some as sharers of his loot, some as beneficiaries of his election stealing, and some as sharers of the knowledge of his crimes. The interests and counsels of others had hitherto prevented his making public amend. He is now contrite, and writes:

"I am an old man, greatly broken in health, and cut down in spirits, and can no longer bear my burden, and to mitigate the prospects of hopeless imprisonment, which must speedily terminate my life, I should, it seems to me, make any sacrifice or effort."

Shakespeare gives us its parallel:

> "An old man, broken with the storms of State,
> Is come to rest his weary bones among ye;
> Give him a little earth for charity."

A Tweed, softened from the defiant Boss of five years before, who answered the talk of prosecution, and the serious threats to hang him and his friends, with the defiant snarl of a denizen of a Bowery dive:

"What are you going to do about it?"

There was historic precedent for this sneer. Cambronne of the Old Guard created it when he reached out to the gutters of faraway Paris for that Gallic monosyllable of supreme contempt, to hurl at an outraged yet admiring Europe that praised their bravery in entreating their surrender.

Tweed's proffered confession is to be a baring of all his wrongful public acts. There was the bold theft of a State election when Samuel J. Tilden was State Chairman. Tilden was not ignorant of the incriminating telegram bearing his

name that aided Tweed to steal a Governorship. Tilden had
no hand in the financial thievings of the Tweed Ring, but he
had in its debaucheries of the ballot box. And he maintained
a shameful silence while the looting of the city went on lest it
hurt his Presidential aspirations.

Tweed laughs at Tilden's ambitions, severing for all time the
friendship of these two past masters of political intrigue.
Tweed wants his own creature, Governor Hoffman, in the White
House. Fate rushes to Tilden's aid. A sleigh overturns in
a rut in Harlem, killing one of Tweed's trusted underlings.
The rut in the Harlem road is another ditch of Ohain.

Tweed's offer to confess on condition that he be let die outside prison walls was at first accepted. The Attorney General
of the State, Charles S. Fairchild, made the agreement. He
agreed to let others who aided Tweed in his great steal go
free on return of a pittance of their loot. He kept his promise
with these but broke faith with Tweed, who constantly hoped,
up to a month of his death, that his release from prison was
only a matter of a few hours.

But "the cohesive ties of public plunder"—a phrase of
Cleveland's—outweighed Tweed's zeal to make public confession
of his crimes in return for a death in a freeman's bed.

Tweed was not surprised. He knew the shifty game of politics as few ever have. He knew how even a statesman's conscience could be warped by the unquenchable thirst for place.
Tilden was a statesman. Even Tweed had to admit that of his
implacable enemy. The record cannot be denied. He must
have smiled grimly as he recalled a certain day of sorrow when
the response was:

"Statesman!"

It was Tweed's own response. He flung it in his dominating
voice at the timid prison clerk who took down his pedigree
that day the steel gates of the penitentiary closed behind him.
And thus it was entered upon the records. And when asked to
declare his religion, Tweed replied:

"I have none."

There was a mental reservation in this response. While he
refused the benefit of clergy in his last days, he sought
solace in religion. He read his Bible constantly, and believed

with the simple faith of his youth, that his guardian angels would show him the way. Sometimes he would forget the presence of the celestial visitors, and swear one of his many old-fashioned, fire-and-brimstone oaths. This was when thoughts of Tilden and Fairchild flashed across his mind.

There was one day when Tweed thought of these two men and did not curse them. That day was April 12, 1878. Did he hear the soft sobbing of Bill Dove on the street outside, now a tottering grizzled old man, and still black as a crow, and for years on Tweed's pension list? Or was it the beckoning of the two attendants that he alone saw, that stayed the curse? Said Tweed on that day—it lacked a few minutes of noon:

"I hope that Tilden and Fairchild are satisfied now."

And as the chimes in a neighboring steeple tolled the hour of twelve Boss Tweed joined his guardian angels on their homeward journey.

No other country but ours could have produced him, and no other age but his own.

CHAPTER II

In the thirty years ending with the dethronement of Tweed, and the overthrow of the Ring, New York was in the hands of corruptionists. The country as a whole fared but little better. Honest millions toiled in complete ignorance of the wrongs inflicted upon them by their chosen servants. The minority of the mass sensed what was going on. These grumbled to themselves and then lapsed back into their natural apathy. Democracy had not changed human nature.

There were many black squares in life's checkerboard of good and evil. Grotesques adorned the border. The greatest city in the New World produced an imperishable Tweed. The silent backwoods gave to the world an immortal Lincoln.

Democracy was threatened not alone by corruption of its representatives. A graver menace lurked in the forces of aristocracy.

In the shadow of the Capitol of the State of New York, nearly three decades before Tweed's first trip to Albany as a member of the State Senate, an attempt was made to revive the feudal system that had its inception here in the days of the Patroons. This effort was supported by what was inadequately called a Sheriff's posse. It was, in reality, a regiment, in arms and in numbers. Back of this posse, in fact, as well as in theory, loomed the armed forces of the State. There had been a little bloodshed before the Sheriff's forces took the field. The determined tenant-farmers rose *en masse*, armed themselves, and to the number of several thousand, went forth to meet the enemy. At the point of contact the Sheriff advanced for a parley. To have done otherwise would have meant the annihilation of his forces. The Sheriff and his men retreated. This peasant uprising is known as the War of the Helderbergs.

European monarchs noted the latent danger to their

dynasties in the survival of the republic, and plotted its destruction. They carefully nurtured the distrust of democracy shared by so many American apologists, and hoped ultimately to destroy it by force. Napoleon the Third had his counterpart in Queen Victoria.

Aristocracy and corruption occasionally made democracy smile. Before the Civil War a Southern judge was escorted to and from the court by guards wearing cocked hats and carrying naked swords. After the Reunion a judge in the North held court in the house of a courtesan. The one was done as openly as the other.

Democracy more often afforded its foes a laugh. Northern abolitionists while demanding freedom for the blacks had their housework performed by white girls—mere children of five or six years of age. The more tender-hearted when advertising for a servant specified in the want columns of the daily press that the white child must be at least ten years of age.

From ten to thirty thousand homeless boys and girls roamed the streets of New York during the day, sleeping wherever night, and hunger, and weariness, overtook them. These innocents were looked upon by the good people of the Metropolis as the pious Turk regards the stray dogs of Constantinople. Thugs and thieves and harlots were recruited from the ranks of these unfortunate children.

Houses of shame operated openly on Broadway. Newspapers denounced vice and accepted the advertisements of gamblers, prostitutes, and abortionists.

The most influential woman in New York was an abortionist. She sold the infants that survived her unholy rites. Clergymen denounced her. A bishop thundered anathema from his cathedral pulpit at this false priestess of Hera. She bided her time. Years later she retaliated by buying the ground the bishop had chosen for his new episcopal residence. And on this site she raised a temple to her cult. She could outbid him. His church was poor. She measured her wealth in seven figures.

Woman suffrage was coming to the fore. Some of its advocates preached the doctrine of free love from the same platform. The most notorious of these was ravishingly beautiful. A noted minister of the Gospel declined to preside at one of her meetings. She charged that never less than twenty of his mistresses listened to his Sunday sermons. She frankly confessed to practicing what she preached. She could not vote. But she did better. She ran for President of the United States on a feminist platform.

Devotees of democracy, at the close of this age, in a misapplied zeal, attempted to make it appear that the evils of the age, which were of steady, cumulative growth, were confined to the last ten years of the period, some dating it from the beginning of the Civil War and others from its close.

"This decline in the public tone," said the Union League, "was not confined to the vulgar and the ignorant. It affected all ranks and professions, perhaps most marked where it would naturally be least looked for and most abhorrent, in the clerical calling. No doubt, it affected injuriously many of the leaders of all parties and every school of politics; the Senate, the Bench, the Bar, and the Pulpit as well as the ranks of trade and the directors of Banks, Insurance Companies, Savings Institutions, and even the Boards of Education."

But to confine the deliberate robbery of bank depositors to a decade was to ignore the past. This form of thievery had been in New York City for a period of nearly seventy years, beginning with the advent of the last century. And political corruption is coeval with statecraft.

Further on, the same source attributes the country-wide scandals in part to "a reaction on (*sic*) the exalted patriotism that had sustained the war unto victory, partly the dreadful result of the unsettling of values, standards, habits, by the creation and use of an artificial currency that did not carry its measure in itself."

We are also told that particular period of public debauchery was caused "partly by the coming to the top of powerful men who had suddenly without the aid of any moral habits, or amenableness to any refined or gentlemanly standards, swept through the land in railroad land grabs, in mining speculations, in purchases of legislatures, in stock dilutions, in great corners on stock and grain; and who intoxicated and poisoned the once sober blood of the people, until politics had become a trade, or a gambling shop, and trade, a trial of wits."

The partial objective—an apology—is praiseworthy. The ignorance displayed is pardonable. The snobbery exhibited is pitiable.

At the time the Union League spoke, there still survived in the jargon of the day, the word *swartwout*. It meant to defraud. As a name it has been borne by many brave and illustrious men. Several of Washington's staff bore the name of Swartwout. Their American primogenitor was the distinguished Dutch Patroon of the same name. A scion of this family, Samuel Swartwout, was honored by President Jackson with the Collectorship of the Port of New York. This was in 1829. After retiring from office at the end of Jackson's second term, an investigation by his successor of the records of the office disclosed that Swartwout had stolen $1,222,705.69 from the Federal Government. He fled to Europe and escaped imprisonment.

This was the scandal of the day. Tweed was then eighteen years of age. Hold public office, steal, flee to Europe and enjoy the luxury of loot. This was the lesson preached by Samuel Swartwout.

Swartwout was but one of many of moral habits and amenableness to refined and gentlemanly standards who gave rise to the belief in the early days of the Republic that our democracy was a delusion.

In the year that Swartwout secretly departed to Europe there was coming to the fore in New York politics a young man of goodly Quaker stock. This was Fernando Wood. John Bigelow, author and statesman, knew him well. One day, during the administration of Seth Low, Bigelow was seated on one of the Colonial benches in the corridor of the City Hall, just outside the Mayor's office. Opposite him, on the wall, was a portrait of Fernando Wood. After gazing at it for a few minutes, at the deep blue eyes and patrician features, symmetrical as though chiseled by Praxiteles, Bigelow observed: "He was the handsomest man I ever saw, and the most corrupt man that ever sat in the Mayor's chair."

Wood began his first term as Mayor in 1855. His second overlapped the beginning of the great civil strife. Wood was an arch-hypocrite as well as corrupt. He obtained his start in life by purchasing three ships with money he had stolen in the course of one year from "longshoremen made drunk in his waterfront groggery." This his hired biographers, at his instigation, euphemistically called a grocery. This is permissible. For politicians, like poets, enjoy the same license. Wood ran lotteries, and was covertly leagued with the underworld. He professed sympathy with the zealous efforts of churchmen to effect reforms in public office. Wood schemed to end his career in the White House. A greater schemer opposed him. This was Tweed, who abjured hypocrisy, loathed Wood for his cant, and drove him from public office. An act which would cover a multitude of Tweed's sins were it not that his motive was chiefly his predilection for plunder.

A decade or more prior to this, while the Swartwout scandal was still the talk of the country, the notorious Police Justices Ring, which levied blackmail on offenders brought before them, was uncovered. One of the impeached jurists was a good man in the public esteem. He was noted for his charity.

Public thieving did not begin with Tweed. Nor did it die with him. It exists because of the apathy of the mass. Sometimes the mass is roused to a sense of the wrongs inflicted upon it. Invariably, it is immediately blinded by passions of racial, religious, or partisan strife, kindled by politicians. On rare occasions the mass struggles until it has effected a reform. But eventually the politician triumphs and the mass is divided and one side wars upon the other and then succumbs to inertia. The looting is resumed.

Almost every one of Tweed's associates from the beginning of his public life, played this age-old game of the politician. Tweed was an exception. He humored the prejudices of the mob when forced to recognize them. There was a great influx of European immigration beginning in the Forties. It was largely Irish and German. A large part of it settled in New York. It was here before Tweed became of age. But not until he was a power in Tammany was a German-born nominated for any important public office. He sent naturalized Germans to the State Legislature and placed them on local tickets. The Irish outnumbered the German immigrants two to one. Tweed gave the Germans everything in his power, short of the offices of Governor and Mayor.

At the zenith of his power, in 1870, the Mayor was A. Oakey Hall, the Beau Brummell of the times—"Elegant Oakey" he was called. Tweed made him. Hall was a society favorite, clubman, and litterateur. He was a man of extraordinary talents. He had been a Republican and was now a Democrat. He was now a patron of Roman Catholics. He had been a Know-Nothing. In a word, Hall was always on the side of power, which to him spelled pelf.

Tweed admired the Elegant Oakey's brilliancy of mind. His faultlessness of attire amused him. Early in March of that year Tweed whispered to Hall. The Elegant Oakey at first demurred. Tweed insisted. His word was law. The result was that the Elegant Oakey reviewed the St. Patrick's Day Parade of 1870 from a platform raised in front of the steps of City Hall, wearing an emerald green coat and vest, and adorned with a cravat of the same vivid hue.

Tweed loved a good joke.

FERNANDO WOOD

A. OAKEY HALL

CHAPTER III

TWEED's earliest boyhood recollection is associated with the discovery, not far from his home, of a spring, possessed, it was claimed, of great curative powers. He was then four years old. Young Tweed was feeling out of sorts, when the High Constable of the city, Jacob Hays, visited the shop of his father to order some chairs. The child was sitting quietly in a corner. On learning the child was not well, the High Constable recommended that a bottle of water from a newly found spring be procured. Hays assured the parental chairmaker that the waters were of greater efficacy than any from the most famous European spas. They had cured him of a complaint of many years' standing. The High Constable's suggestion was acted upon forthwith. The bottle of water cost a few cents, for the owner of the spring was making the most of it.

Tweed never recalled the incident without a laugh. He did not remember drinking the water, but the subject was a constant source of mirth in his father's house. For it was not long after the visit of High Constable Hays that the source of the healing waters was discovered, shattering the faith of many in all mineral springs. The peculiar taste of the water, which gave rise to the belief in its curative properties, was due to the overflowing of vats in a nearby tannery. The antiquarian will recall the spring. It was in Jacob Street, in the old Beekman's Swamp.

After Tweed's downfall the false statement was printed in nearly every newspaper that he was an illiterate fellow. The untruth is repeated in books dealing with the period. But then even Lincoln was called an illiterate boor by James Gordon Bennett, and the famed journalist, still unsatisfied, likened him to a satyr.

Tweed had more than the average training of the youth of

his day. When little more than a toddler he was sent to a public school in Chrystie Street, near Hester. In this same school Nast received his early instruction.

During the first years of the boyhood of the future Boss, Tweed's father began to set aside a little money for the first time in his life. Five children, one after another, had kept his purse thin. The larder, always plentifully stocked, now began to know the presence of an occasional luxury. Father Tweed was proud of his youngest, and dreamed of saving enough, not only for the rainy day, but to give the boy an education superior to that afforded by the public school, one that would fit him for a place in a mercantile establishment where he could learn the business, and luck with him, branch out for himself. While the new order gave each an equal chance, the father had, observed that more than a mere ability to read and write and figure was demanded of youths reaching for the golden opportunities of commerce. Training in a school under masters who added letters to their names, would be the ideal place to send the boy, mused the chairmaker. He had just learned of such a school, where two dominies taught. The only drawback was that the school was in distant Elizabethtown, New Jersey. He knew that his wife's intense love for the boy would revolt at the thought of his leaving home But he would win her over. She wouldn't object very hard when she heard that the master and his assistant were brothers, and members of his own faith. They would give the lad a religious training that would stand him in good stead through life. He had another trump card to play—they were sons of Captain Luther Halsey, an old aristocrat, founder of the Cincinnati, and a friend of Washington. He had seen Captain Halsey with other silver-haired veterans of the Revolution on that memorable Monday in August when they welcomed back their old companion in arms, General Lafayette. He recalled the crowds at the Battery, the thundering cannon, the ringing of bells, and the frenzied cheers of the populace. Little Bill was with him. They were on the sidewalk in front of St. Paul's when the procession came up Broadway. He could not see Lafayette because they were too far back in the press on the sidewalk, and he had to hold Little Bill high over his head so that his baby eyes could see over the heads of the crowd. It was too bad that Little Bill was too young to remember the scene— soldiers and sailors with standards flying, and bands playing, and the loud huzzas.

And a day never passed that Richard Tweed did not dream of the time when he could send Little Bill to the school run by the Reverend John Taylor Halsey, and his brother, the Reverend Abraham Oothout Halsey, gentlemen both, and to boot, sons of the man who knew Lafayette and Washington.

But many more Windsor chairs must be made and sold before that dream could be realized. He must increase his output. That meant more craftsmen and more apprentices. A cartman must be hired to take the chairs to the distant settlements on the northern part of the Island. Another cartman must be hired to sell the chairs on the Long Island shore. But all that meant money, and it could not be spared out of the little that he had put aside for the rainy day, against whose coming he always fervently prayed.

Tweed the elder had two apprentices working in the shop at this time. One of them was an older brother of Little Bill. He did not have Little Bill's brains. None of his other children, Father Tweed observed whenever he heard his youngest read, or saw him do his sums, displayed the same capacity for learning, or anything approaching it. Little Bill's willingness to work surpassed theirs. This the father noted as the boy, when school was done, would visit the shop and, broom in hand, sweep up the shavings and sawdust on the floor. Were there any errands to be done? Sometimes the father humored the lad and sent him to deliver a statement of account.

If there were no errands to run Little Bill would stand outside the door of his father's shop, or their home, hoping to hear the fire alarm bells which were scattered through the city. One hung in the tower of City Hall. The flames were fought in those days by volunteers, who received no pay for their services. New York's old Volunteer Fire Department, supplanted by a paid force in 1865, was perhaps the most democratic institution in the new democracy. All that was required of a candidate was willingness, coupled, of course, with the strength and agility of youth.

Rich and poor alike eagerly sought the honor of serving, and no light task was their lot. Business men, mechanics, and professional men worked side by side in the various units of the old volunteer department.

When the alarm was sounded, the silver mounted fire engine came clattering through the streets, drawn by the long line of red-shirted volunteers, each holding the stout rope to which the apparatus was attached, running at breakneck speed. At their head, wearing a red shirt like the rest, and brandishing aloft a silver trumpet, raced their Foreman, who kept yelling constantly at his men, urging them to still mightier endeavors.

Here were romance and adventure to stir the heart of a small boy. And there was not a normal youngster in the town who did not have his particular favorite among the many units of the city's red shirts.

Little Bill Tweed's favorite was Number 33, whose headquarters were on Gouverneur Street, a few blocks from his home. Aping other boys of Cherry Hill, he wore the numerals of Number 33 on the leather binding piece on the back of his suspenders. No better "33" was intaglioed on any boy's suspenders. Tweed's father had done the work.

An event which gave even greater thrill to the small boy was the firemen's parade. Then the engines, polished till they shone like the sun, garlanded with flowers, moved at a stately pace behind their long lines of red shirts, their leaders no longer yelling, but swinging with martial tread, their silver trumpets carried peacefully at their sides.

Little Bill made frank confession that he wanted to be Foreman of Number 33 when he grew up. His father returned a pleased smile, recalling his own boyhood, with its memories of Thomas Ash, Foreman of volunteers, and Treasurer of Tammany Hall.

None could look upon these volunteers without being stirred. Italy's great liberator, Garibaldi, saw them, and borrowed their red shirt to inflame his land against tyranny.

About the time Little Bill began attending school, his father began to be troubled with shortness of breath. Climbing a flight of stairs became an effort. The chairmaker did not complain. He was big and strong, although he had to confess that at forty he could not lift weights, any more than he could climb stairs, without gasping for breath. But it was a trouble that would soon pass. He could work at the bench or lathe without feeling any ill effects. And now that Little Bill was showing such unexpected progress with his studies he worked well into the night by candle light. Money must be had for his last born's training.

So the chairmaker continued to work, continuing late at night in his shop, long after the apprentices had put aside their aprons, paying no heed to the shortness of breath that still persisted and seemed to grow worse. And he paid less heed to his wife who urged him not to overwork, saying that the boy would make his way, whether or not he went to the school of Reverend Mr. Halsey over in New Jersey. She warned her husband that he would ruin his health if he did not forget work for a time. Then too, she did not like the thought of her youngest going so far away from home. Why, the place was on the road to Philadelphia. Wasn't it nearly thirty or forty miles' travel on land after one set foot on the Jersey shore? And even if he did have the money for the boy's schooling, who would go down on the stage coach with him? It was out of the question to think that she could make the trip. She had the house to look after, and as for her husband, he could not be dragged away from the shop with a yoke of oxen on a week-day.

Richard Tweed let his wife talk on. He was too weak, and in no mood to argue with her.

That shortness of breath did not pass away. It grew worse. One morning, a week-day morning at that, he stayed in bed quite late. Then he found he could not get up. At last he let his wife send Bill Dove for the doctor. The faithful darkey, worried lest his master would die, would not leave the physician's office until he went with him.

The case was diagnosed as heart disease. Digitalis and rest were prescribed. Father Tweed did not mind what his complaint was called, or how bitter the medicine prescribed. What worried him was the enforced rest. But that was entirely out of the question. He had to work. If he did not, the chairmaking would suffer, and that would reduce his earnings, and maybe cut into his little savings, and that might mean the end of his dream of Little Bill going to that New Jersey school.

Tweed consoled himself with the thought that doctors sometimes made mountains out of molehills. He was confident that he had no serious trouble, and that he would be out of bed in a day, and equally confident that Little Bill would go to that school in New Jersey.

Richard Tweed prayed.

He was not long in bed. But when he returned to his shop he learned that he could not fool the doctor who had warned him to go slow. The chairmaker tried it, and had to take to his bed again. The doctor now talked to his patient's wife. This resulted in a long family discussion. She did most of the talking. Richard listened. The upshot of it was that Little Bill, then eleven years old, was taken from school, and put to work in his father's shop to learn the chairmaker's craft.

This time a month was spent in bed. Little Bill was an apt apprentice. Youthful apprentices in those days were also the errand boys of the establishment, and now young Tweed's ambition to go unaccompanied into distant parts of the town was gratified. He was big for his age, and even at home it was no longer the thing to call him Little Bill. And young Tweed had grown to dislike it. One day after delivering a chair to a patron of his father he learned that Little Bill, shouted by a boy of his own age, meant "fight." He came out of that fight triumphant. He had learned how to use his fists. He kept the story of his first fight to himself, but he found an unholy joy in secretly gazing at the slight abrasion on one of the knuckles of his right hand.

Young Tweed had many scraps in the first year of his apprenticeship. But as he was a strong, powerful hitter, and a good stayer, he in time could proceed through the streets on his errands without some taunting urchin calling "Little Bill" after him. More than that, his prowess with his fists was the talk of the boys of the neighborhood.

Tweed worked two years in his father's shop. He quit it, not for the school of Dominie Halsey in New Jersey, of which his father still dreamed, but to work for Isaac Fryer, a saddler and dealer in hardware, who had a store on Pearl Street, not far from Tweed's home. Young Tweed liked chairmaking. But to his father, with the dream of his last born attending school across the Hudson ever before him, the sight of the boy at the bench or lathe, was almost maddening. So when his friend, Isaac Fryer, suggested that his youngest son run errands for him, and eventually learn the business, the father readily assented. Anything to get him out of the shop. Young Tweed in his heart rebelled. Outwardly he was all acquiescence. For obedience he had learned with his prayers.

William Marcy Tweed was thirteen years of age when he began to work with Isaac Fryer, the saddler and dealer in hardware. He did not like his new job until the end of the first month when he was given his wages—a few silver coins. These he proudly brought home, and with a smile, part pride, and part bashfulness, a kindly twinkle in his grayish blue eyes, presented his earnings to his mother. She flicked away a tear that stole into her eye. The youth's smile vanished at once. No son could love a mother more. This tender affection grew with the years.

Tweed, although now only thirteen years of age, possessed the physique of a young gladiator. Boys of the neighborhood, who had taunted him only a few months before with a yahooed "Little Bill," and who were drubbed in fair fight as a consequence, now affectionately spoke of him as Big Bill. No longer did Tweed have to drop his bundle to chase a taunting youngster of his own age. Now they accompanied him on his errands, in pairs and threes, and sometimes small mobs, quarreling among themselves as to who should have the honor of carrying the bundle on Tweed's shoulder. This was Tweed's first following.

In those days New Yorkers who were particular about the water they drank, purchased it from venders who brought the water to their doors in hogsheads perched on carts. Only the poor drank the water from the old backyard well. The hogsheads were filled from wells or springs north of the City Hall. The most favored of these was the Tea Pump, famous to generations of old New Yorkers who loved a good cup of tea. Hence its name. It was considered a profanation to use its waters for any other purpose. The Tea Pump was on old Chatham Street, now Park Row, and opposite Roosevelt Street—the southern fringe of the present Chinese Quarter. Was there any subtle influence in this old Tea Pump that lured the first Celestials to settle immediately above it?

Tweed paused one evening on his way home from work to let one of the water-venders, an old man, have the right of way from his cart at the curb to the door of his customer. The gray-beard staggered as he carried the pails, filled with water, in either hand. A mischievous boy who also appeared on the scene at the same moment, threw a handful of dirt into one of the pails. Then he scampered off. Tweed ran after him, and overtaking him, shook him as a terrier would a rat. Had the water-vender been a young man, able to give chase himself, Tweed would have enjoyed a good laugh, for he was not entirely lacking in the capacity for mischief, even at this age. But his ingrained reverence for elders revolted at the sight of youth making game of old age.

Tweed, after he began work for Isaac Fryer the saddler and hardware dealer, was allowed more latitude in his spare hours. He was no longer sent to bed an hour or two after supper. Sometimes when he had the required number of pennies in his pocket, he would go to the theater, and from his seat in the pit, applaud virtue and hiss vice. More often he stayed on Cherry Hill.

To boys of nearby neighborhoods, Tweed and his companions were known as Cherry Hillers. They constituted, in a liberal interpretation of the word, a gang. Most of his companions were the seniors of Young Tweed by two or three years. None was his superior in weight or fistic prowess. The mantle of leadership fell naturally on his shoulders.

Three blocks to the north, and like Cherry, running parallel with the East River, was Henry Street. There also was a puerile solidarity which took its name from the street. Boys from many other streets gravitated to these two gangs. Both were unfavorably known throughout the East Side. There was more swing and rhythm in the name of Tweed's gang than in that of their enemy. It came easier to the tongue.

A gang, to survive, must be peaceful in its own neighborhood. Its petty offenses are invariably directed against peaceful citizens of distant streets. Piracy would never have been an honored profession if the black flag flew only on home waters.

The juxtaposition of the Cherry Hill and Henry Street gangs made them natural enemies. When they met on one of their evening forays a battle royal was inevitable. On such occasions the butcher and the vender of vegetables was spared a visitation, for after the two gangs separated, each would retire to a convenient spot to remove the tell-tale signs of scrimmage. Sometimes these chance meetings would leave bad blood. Then there would be formal challenge issued and accepted, and on the following Saturday afternoon both gangs would meet on a high spot of ground on the outskirts of the city, just east of what is now Union Square, where, as a passenger on a Broadway car swings by on old Deadman's Curve, he sees the heroic bronzes of Lincoln, Lafayette, and Washington. Here the combat would be renewed, and after a few more nose bleeds, peace would be declared. A peace no more lasting than peace among European nations.

This piece of ground, then an orchard, was sanctuary as well as battleground. For if the Cherry Hillers and the Henry Streeters met there by chance, even though they had only recently engaged in a sanguinary pummeling match, they would exchange friendly greetings. For this battlefield was also the joint retreat and picnic ground of the rival gangs. Here the pilferings of their forays of the night before were devoured the following day. This loot consisted of potatoes and pigs' tails. They were always roasted over a fire built some distance from the nearest apple tree. This was in accordance with the instructions of the owner of the orchard, who had not forgotten that he had been a boy himself. He had warned them against building fires where the flames might injure the trunk or limbs of the trees. Trespass notices were posted around the orchard. The Cherry Hillers and the Henry Streeters enforced the prohibition they alone ignored.

The pigs' tails and potatoes roasted over fires in this orchard were stolen from shops a mile or more to the south. These tiny thefts were committed with appropriate ritual. It would have been easy for the Henry Streeters, or Tweed's gang, to have obtained at home all the potatoes required for their picnics. But what is true of stolen sweets is likewise true of stolen spuds.

In purloining potatoes the boys, running in Indian file, and yelling like Comanches, would swoop down, one at a time, on a green grocer's stall. A potato to a boy was prescribed. But it was seldom that four potatoes were taken from the same stand, as the familiar war whoops meant but one thing to the lawful proprietor of the tubers, who lost no time in assuming a protecting position before his mound of potatoes.

In those days pork was the least costly of meats, as potatoes were the cheapest of vegetables. Pigs roamed the streets of New York at will, looking for stray scraps. Garbage disposal had not been added to the sciences. The unclean pig was a hygienic necessity. Pigs, when sold to butchers, were dressed, and suspended from racks outside the store, tail downward.

To deprive a suspended porker of his tail called for skill and vigilance. The butcher had to be watched from across the street. When the agreed signal was given by the scout, another member of the gang, who had been standing to one side of the shop, would quickly advance with a keen edged knife, seize the pig's tail, in one hand, and with a few hacks, sever it from the carcass.

Tweed, because of his greater strength, could cut off the pig's tail with one slash of the knife. Any boy could steal a potato.

Boys who travel in gangs learn to swear like troopers. Tweed was the most fluent of the lot. The Cherry Hill gang smoked—all save one. The exception was Tweed.

A gang leader who did not smoke!

Young Tweed worked but one year at the saddlery and hardware store of Isaac Fryer. The youth loafed around for a few days, and then his father, whose business had grown considerably in the last two years, saw the fulfillment of his dream. Big Bill was on a stage coach, a bulging portmanteau under the seat, his proud father beside him. They were on the stage coach bound for Elizabethtown, now the city of Elizabeth, where the Reverend John Taylor Halsey's boarding school for boys occupied a site on an eminence known as Chilton Hill.

Father Tweed returned to his bench quite elated at meeting the Presbyterian dominie, the son of the friend of Washington and Lafayette, who was to guide the path of his boy for another year. And what pleased him even more was his recollection of the boys who would be young Tweed's schoolmates for the next twelve months. Sons of gentlemen, every one of them no doubt . . . some of them heirs to grand estates . . . these would be his daily companions . . . and the atmosphere of the school would be bound to knock off the rough edges of the boy . . . he would return home with sufficient polish to aid him in getting a start in the world of commerce . . . he would bring back with him, which was more important still, real learning.

Big Bill returned to his home after a year at boarding school, almost as tall as his father. Little of the boy remained. His voice was a deep basso. He spoke with an assurance that carried conviction. His father had a good income now. Did he want to return to Elizabethtown for another year? No, Big Bill was satisfied. He had learned to keep books and he was anxious to find a place in some business house.

Tweed, then in his fifteenth year, found employment as a junior clerk with the Front Street tobacco merchants, J. and G. C. Alexander. For two years Tweed kept books for the Alexanders. In the meantime his father had bought an interest in the brush factory of De Berrien and Company on Pearl Street.

Tweed began keeping accounts for the brush manufacturers when he finished with the tobacconists. The head of the firm quickly realized that in Tweed there was something more than in the average youth of seventeen. Tweed had suggestions regarding the management of the factory as well as for the methods of distributing its products. Rare executive ability and capacity for organizing were displayed by Tweed even at this early age. And at the end of his second year with the brush factory in which his father owned only a minor interest, Big Bill's talents were rewarded. He was made a member of the firm. A real business man at nineteen.

Tweed lived at home. He kept good hours. And unlike many of the members of the Cherry Hill gang he led before he went to boarding school, he did not know the inside of a barroom. But if he met one of his boyhood companions on the street, Big Bill was the first to extend the hand. There was a firm, friendly grip in the handclasp, a sincere note of welcome in the greeting, and warmth in the smile, and a kindly light in the twinkling grayish-blue eyes that left a lasting impression. He had an extraordinary memory for names and faces, and he would cross the street to greet a man he had met only once before to renew the acquaintance. Men have gone far in public life with little more than the gift of amiability.

Tweed at this time had no thought of office. When he was twenty—he seemed several years older because of his mature ways and huge bulk—he gave proof of this. In the bitterly fought municipal election of 1843, when the Native Americans triumphed over Tammany and Whigs, Tweed was asked to run for Alderman on the Tammany ticket. Tweed thanked the delegation who waited upon him and said that he must decline the honor for two reasons: one, his age, and the other, his desire to stick strictly to business.

Tweed's decision to keep out of politics was partly inspired by the principal owner of the brush factory, Joseph C. Skaden. The Skadens had been friends of the Tweeds before William Marcy came into the world. At the time of his birth the Skadens lived on the west side of the town, on Chestnut Street, immediately north of Canal. If the present Howard Street were to extend westward across Broadway we could see the site of the cozy home of the Skadens in 1823. But Chestnut Street has gone with other quaint thoroughfares that grew out of the wagon roads made by the early settlers when Manhattan Island was mostly farm land and woods.

Tweed at this time valued Skaden's advice more than that of his own father. The Skadens had a daughter, Mary Jane, a charming miss of seventeen, who blushingly took Tweed's arm when he accompanied her on occasional visits to the theater. They had been childhood friends. And one evening in the spring of 1844 Tweed put on his best frilled shirt and paid a formal call to his employer. There was a directness about Tweed. And Mary Jane's father responded with equal lack of circumlocution. Then Tweed called on the girl. Moist eyes said: "Yes."

They were married by the Skadens' pastor, the Reverend Joseph H. Price, rector of St. Stephen's Episcopal Church which stood on the corner of Chrystie and Broome Streets. There was no sectarian note in Tweed's nature.

Tweed had selected a small house that would do nicely for the two of them, but this was disapproved by his father-in-law. He had a top floor that was not being used. And why shouldn't the newly wedded occupy it and thereby save a little more? The argument was unanswerable. Tweed began his married life at 193 Madison Street, less than half a mile from the house where he was born.

CHAPTER IV

ON April 9, 1844, six days after Tweed celebrated his twenty-first birthday, he cast his first vote in protest against religious and racial bigotry. Neither his race nor his religion was attacked. But intolerance was not in his faith. It was not until a few years later that municipal elections were held in November. The Native American Party, just coming into power, had nominated Fletcher Harper, one of the founders of the noted publishing house, as their candidate for Mayor. The Democrats and the Whigs nominated, as usual, their candidates for Mayor, but the Native American orators paid more heed to the Roman Catholic Bishop, the Right Reverend John Hughes, than to the Whig and Democratic mayoralty nominees. In a biography of the bishop by the Reverend Henry A. Brann, D.D., this campaign is thus treated:

"They (the Native Americans) singled out Bishop Hughes because of his prominence and aggressiveness. They misrepresented his conduct and his purposes; their newspapers attacked him daily. His controversy on the 'School Question' was distorted into an attempt to drive the Bible out of the public schools. He was accused of leading an Irish Catholic party in an attempt to get control of the government. . . . The 'Native American' orators and some of the newspapers, denounced him as an ambitious foe of republican institutions and a satellite of the Pope. . . . Bishop Hughes advised his flock to keep quiet, and to do nothing to provoke the prejudices of the political faction which was abusing the name of 'American.' . . . On the night of the municipal election in 1844, a mob of over a thousand 'Native Americans,' yelling, groaning, cursing, and bearing 'No Popery' banners, marched through the sixth and the fourteenth, then called the 'Irish' wards of the city. Yet so docile to the bishop's advice were the people of his faith, though naturally an impulsive and pugnacious race, that not one of them resented the insult."

CHAPTER V

WHEN Tweed became of age, the people of the city had enjoyed the privilege of electing their own Mayor for a matter of ten years. This concession to the voters was wrung from the reluctant lawmakers at Albany, who from the beginning of the Republic had striven with might and main, by legislative enactment, to create a ruling class. Those who had advocated this direct election reform were the extreme radicals of the day. In an earlier decade other extremists, after years of agitation, forced the landed gentry and their representatives in the Legislature to abolish the unjust law that limited suffrage to the propertied class. With it went the barbarous medievalism which permitted a man to be thrown into jail for the period of his natural life—if the money due, no matter how small, remained unpaid and the debtor obdurate.

But it was in the camp of their hereditary enemy that the tenant-farmer, the mechanic and the laborer found their most effective advocates. The sons of these die-hard Tories, who hated the feudal survivals as their fathers cherished them, pleaded the cause of their unfortunate and inarticulate compatriots.

The leading protagonist of the proletariat movement was Robert Dale Owen whose ardor was looked upon with high disfavor by his own class. In 1829, Owen, who inspired the formation of the Mechanics' Party, startled the aristocracy of the country with his daring denunciation of the privileged class and his audacious advocacy of the rights of the people. These doctrines he embodied in resolutions adopted by the Mechanics' Party—also known as the Workingmen's Party— at their meeting in New York City on October 19 of that year.

One of the demands of this assembly was the creation of an educational system "equally open to all." A free college for the sons of the poor was in the mind of Owen. But he dared urge this only by inference. It would have smacked too much of demagoguery to have espoused openly higher learning for the masses.

The newspapers, almost without exception, denounced the new party as bent on the destruction of the Republic. The mechanics and laborers who enrolled under its banner were dubbed deluded tools of the designing Owen and his associates.

The Mechanics' Party was stigmatized as hostile to the morals of the people. Mordecai M. Noah was one of the first Jews to edit a newspaper in the city. The ticket placed in the field by the Mechanics' Party, in opposition to the two major parties, was attacked as infidel by Noah in the columns of the now defunct *Courier and Enquirer*.

The mechanics and laborers polled a vote that astonished the Democrats and Whigs and elected one of their candidates to the lower branch of the State Legislature. It was obvious that a good number of Whig and Democratic workers, who dared not join the new party, secretly voted its ticket.

These successes at the polls of the recently-enfranchised inspired the uprising of the tenant-farmers who lived on the Rensselaer Manor, twenty-four miles square, a Dutch grant, which extended on both sides of the Hudson River in the Counties of Rensselaer and Albany. This, the only peasant rebellion in the history of the Republic, occurred in the year Tweed finished school. The immediate cause of the revolt was the attempt, in 1840, of the heirs of Stephen Van Rensselaer to extort enormous rents from the farmers in this rich agricultural region, larger than many a European principality.

Then tenants refused to pay. Most of them, and their ancestors for generations back, had been paying rents, and in many instances the sums paid exceeded many times the actual value of the land. Several clashes occurred between the rebellious tenants and the rent collectors of the Van Rensselaers. Then the sons of the last of the Dutch Patroons enlisted the aid of the Sheriff, who swore in several hundred deputies, armed them with shotguns and muskets, and proceeded to collect the rents.

The tenant-farmers, their hired men and grown sons assembled to the number of several thousand. All were well armed and mounted.

They met the Sheriff and his force and invited them to return from whence they came, rent rolls, rifles, shotguns and all.

The Sheriff obeyed.

That doughty Whig and brilliant diarist, Philip Hone, who served as Mayor of New York from 1825 to 1826, in discussing the revolt of the tenant-farmers, voiced the sentiments of the old order. Said Hone:

"A most outrageous revolt has broken out among the tenants of the late patroon, General Van Rensselaer, in the neighborhood of Albany, of a piece with the vile disorganizing spirit which overspreads the land like a cloud, and daily increases in darkness. The tenants of the manor of Rensselaer, which is in extent from twenty to forty miles (*sic!*), having waited for the decease of their respected proprietor, the late patroon, have now risen *en masse,* and refuse to pay their rent to his son Stephen, to whom that portion of the estate of his father has been bequeathed, except upon their own terms, and at their own good pleasure. They have enjoyed their leases for so many years, upon terms so easy, and have been treated with so much lenity, that they have brought themselves to believe that the lands belonged to them. Since the death of General Van Rensselaer they have had meetings, and resolved that in a land of liberty there is no liberty for landlords; that no man has a right to own more land than his neighbor, and that they have paid so little rent heretofore that it is not worth while to pay any hereafter; and that master Stephen, with as good a title by inheritance as any known to the laws of the State, shall neither have his land nor the income of it. This outrageous proceeding of the Rensselaerwickers has occasioned great consternation in Albany. The sheriff resorted to the ancient process of summoning the *posse comitatus;* the citizens were ordered out to march against the rioters; several hundred went, and met the enemy in the disputed territory. The sheriff, with seventy followers, went forward in advance; but finding them armed and mounted to the number of several thousands, determined to resist, and swearing by Dunder and

Plixsen (*sic!*) that they would pay no more, nor surrender their farms to the rightful owner, he returned to the main body of his forces, faced to the right about, and marched back to Albany.

"This is alarming, certainly, but nothing more than a carrying-out of the Loco-Foco [Democratic] principles of the people of the State—those principles which prevailed in this city at the late election—to the support of which the members-elect of the Legislature are pledged, and from which the councils of the State have been lately saved by the greater virtue of the country, but which must, in a short time (perhaps the very next year), sweep away all the wise restraints of law and justice, and cause the destruction of individual rights. Let it come, if come it must; the evil will be remedied some time or other; but this fair dream of Republicanism will be dissipated by its cure."

The fair dream of Republicanism was to survive greater shocks than this. The interests of the Van Rensselaers to the land were declared by the Court of Appeals some twelve years later never to have existed. It was a popular verdict, if not a just one. The tenant-farmers acknowledged the rights of the Van Rensselaers to buy the land. The Van Rensselaers insisted on being lords of the Manor. To have upheld them would have revived feudalism. A democratic tribunal could not do that.

Actually there was no difference in the control of the two major parties of the day. While it is true that the local Democratic organization had, for years prior to the abolishment of the debtors' prison and the annulment of the property distinction in the suffrage law, made gestures in favor of the end of these abuses, Tammany was as much in the hands of the proprietors of manorial estates and other advocates of the old order as the Whigs. In election frauds, each was equally culpable. One of the most brazen ballot box debaucheries was the Gubernatorial election of 1838, when the Whigs fraudulently carried the city for William H. Seward.

The success of the Mechanics' Party made the Whigs foam at the mouth. They continued their denunciations of its leaders as infidels and enemies of the Republic.

Tammany, seldom lacking in imagination, saw its opportunity, silenced Noah and its other journalistic spokesmen and at once began catering to the mechanics and laborers, gradually absorbing them. The Whigs tried the same game, but they started too late. Tammany had out-generaled them.

Had the same invention been displayed in time by the Whigs, the City of New York to-day would undoubtedly be as solidly Republican as Philadelphia, "the corrupt and contented." In both cities the same racial and religious groups are proportionately equal. Only in partisanship do they differ.

Tweed was a beneficiary of the political sagacity of the men who directed the successful fusing of the Mechanics' Party with, or rather its swallowing by, Tammany. Without them he could not have been Boss. Early he learned the value of their numbers on Election Day. And the sinister ways in which their strength at the polls could be increased, Tweed knew before he began to take an active interest in practical politics. He knew of the election scandals of the municipal election of 1843—the year before he cast his first vote. Then, in addition to the use of gangsters as political auxiliaries, the novelty of voting convicts was introduced.

Prisoners confined in the penitentiary on Blackwell's Island were brought over to the city the night before election in droves. They were lodged and well fed. After voting as they had been directed by their keepers the convicts were permitted to make their escape. Some of the more trusted of the convicts were assigned to electioneering in wards where they would be able to sway votes.

Tweed's entrance into politics was through the same door through which so many entered in his day—the Volunteer Fire Department.

And when Tweed turned politician, he had lost whatever illusions he had entertained regarding the science of politics. More than that, he had fixed ideas as to his future line of conduct. Politics was corrupt. He would have to be corrupt to be successful. And he was determined to succeed. His political *credo*, as recited by him before the Aldermanic Committee that made a pretense at investigating the Tweed Ring frauds after his downfall, was thus transcribed by the official stenographer:

"The fact is New York politics were always dishonest—long before my time. There never was a time when you couldn't buy the Board of Aldermen. A politician in coming forward takes things as they are. This population is too hopelessly split up into races and factions to govern it under universal suffrage, except by the bribery of patronage, or corruption."

In matters of religion, Tweed was a liberal. In politics, he was an unswerving bigot.

CHAPTER VI

In the autumn of 1848, a group of men, including clerks, artisans and business men, decided to organize a new fire engine company. One of them was Tweed. It was not Tweed's idea. Nor that of any of his associates. It was a neighborhood need, and had been discussed for months, ever since the *Black Joke*, as the old fire engine company on Gouverneur Street was known, had been disbanded. Some of the boyhood chums of Tweed, former members of his Cherry Hill gang, were among the active proponents of the new unit of red shirts. Of course there was one practical politician among them. He was John J. Reilly, who represented the district in the State Assembly. It was Reilly who invited Tweed to join the Volunteers.

Tweed still worked as bookkeeper in the brush factory in which he and his father had an interest. He was making a comfortable living. He had just moved with his family to a small two-story brick house at 48 Vandewater Street when the Member of Assembly extended the invitation to help form the new company.

If Tweed had not accepted this invitation he might never have gone into politics. But on the night of December 11, the die was cast. Little did Tweed dream when he entered the office of Andrew Maner's ink factory in Gouverneur Street, near Monroe, on that evening, that he was to leave it on the road to power, and a prison cell destined to be his last abode on earth.

There was no happier man in the room than Tweed, who smiled through his dark brown beard as he entered Maner's office. Reilly was there, and arose with a cheery "Hello, Bill!" Big Bill shook hands with the Assemblyman and the others who pressed forward to greet him. These were Joseph H. Johnson,

51

an artist; John Clapp, who worked in Poillon's shipyard;
David Smith, who had a carpenter shop just below Trinity
Church; George Demilt, a house and sign painter; George
Golder, a printer; Alfred Palmer, ship's calker; Jesse Sickles,
a printer; William A. Freeman, President of the Dry Dock
Floating Company, and a young man named Theodore Vallon.

At this meeting all present agreed to proceed with the
organization of the new engine company, and before adjournment a motion was made and carried to meet again in two
weeks over the beer saloon, known as the *Vivaramble*, at 3
Hester Street. This second meeting was chiefly for the purpose
of drafting a petition to be presented to the Common Council
for its approval and to decide upon a name. Some proposed
that the name of the company the new unit was to supplant
be chosen. But there were objections to this. For the *Black
Joke* Engine Company had earned an unsavory reputation as
an outfit of shoulder hitters, stopping on its way to a fire to
pummel a rival company which had cut in ahead of it, and
quarreling with some old foe—it had many—when the red
shirts of the city paraded on festal occasions. Then *Fredonia*
was proposed and voted down. *Eureka* met the same fate. One
of the printers proposed the name of their great American
craftsman. The meeting was about to accept this suggestion
when Tweed spoke for the first time. He recalled to his
hearers that there was an opportunity to make the engine
company the greatest in the land. He revered the name of
Franklin which had just been proposed. But that name, to
the narrow-minded, carried with it a suggestion of partisanship.
Most of those in the room were Democrats. But there would
be bound to be a Whig or two in the company, and why hurt
anybody's feelings, even unintentionally? And why not select
a name worthy of what was destined to be the most famous
unit of volunteer firemen in the city, nay, on the continent?
Why not the name identified for all time with the very discovery
of the country, that of Americus Vespucci?

Tweed won the day.

On the official records of the Fire Department the new
company was listed as *Americus Engine Company Number 6.*

Tweed gave this organization more than its name. He gave it a symbol that was to become known years later, throughout the world, as the emblem of the organization he ruled with an iron hand—the tiger. This was painted on the box of the fire engine and had been copied from a French lithograph depicting the head of a Bengal tiger, its gleaming fangs bared in a ferocious snarl.

There were seventy-five red shirts in the new company. All were chosen either because of their known experience as fire-fighters or for their huge bulk and great strength. A few of them were taller than Tweed, who tipped the beam at 270. And there was not an ounce of surplus flesh on his big bones.

Shortly after its formation, *Americus*, or *Big Six*, as it soon became known to the town because of its greater efficiency in fighting fires than any other of the crack units of the department, moved into the old quarters of the *Black Joke*. David Smith, the boss carpenter, was elected as its first Foreman. Some months later George Demilt succeeded him, and Big Bill Tweed was elected Assistant Foreman. This was in July, 1849.

Two months before, the racial feelings which had been rampant in the city for years, those bitter hatreds that gave rise to Tweed's political faith, climaxed in a gory riot.

The Native American Party had done more to stir up these feelings than any other single agency. Its membership was confined to Protestant citizens of native stock. While its particular targets in New York were the Irish and German immigrants, because of their constantly increasing numbers, it was impartial in its hate. A Native American despised an Englishman as much as he did an Irishman.

On this occasion the Native Americans and the Irish forgot their mutual antagonism and formed a compact to make common cause against an Englishman. The militia was called out to quell them. The riot ended when twenty lay dead in the streets. More than that number fell wounded, three of them dying of their injuries later. Some fell in front of the Astor Place Opera House where William C. Macready, the eminent English tragedian, was playing Macbeth. Others were hit by the bullets of the military several blocks from the scene of riot.

The police suspected Isaiah Rynders of having inspired the riot. Rynders and his thugs had been an adjunct of the Native American Party, but at this time Rynders was an ally of Tammany Hall. The police traced the delivery of the broadsides, which had inflamed the rioters, to the building opposite City Hall Park, where William Miner ràn a saloon on the street floor. Overhead was the headquarters of Rynders' Empire Club. To George W. Walling, later Chief of Police, Miner admitted that he received the handbills. But Miner denied that he gave them to Rynders. Miner, a thoroughgoing thug, said that he had surrendered to a man unknown to him the package left by the printer's devil.

One of these hate-inspiring broadsides was surreptitiously pasted on walls and boxes all over town during the night preceding the sanguinary riot. There had been a clash two nights earlier. But no one was killed at the first. This particular card which was generously distributed in the districts where the Irish immigrants lived, bore at its head, in heavy black type: "Will You Allow Englishmen to Rule This Country?"

The other broadside was distributed along the river front to sailors on ships flying the English flag. The English sailors were urged to be in Astor Place, the chief appeal to them being: "Sustain Your Countryman."

While politicians aided in stirring up the feelings of the Native Americans and the Irish against Macready, they were not responsible for the popular dislike of Macready.

The riot had its basic origin in the American people's love for Edwin Forrest, their own great interpreter of Shakespearean rôles, and the professional rivalry of Forrest and Macready. When Forrest had toured England, he and his performances were caustically criticized in the English press.

Forrest on his return to America accused Macready of having inspired the English critics to defame him. Nor did Forrest wait until he met his fellow Americans on their native heath to make known his feelings toward Macready. One night while the latter was playing Hamlet in Edinburgh, the audience was startled by a prolonged hiss from a box. They looked up and recognized the American tragedian. Forrest explained that Macready had stolen a novelty he had introduced in his portrayal of the Melancholy Dane.

But Forrest had no part in this riot although it has been hinted otherwise. The only basis for this suspicion is that Forrest was playing Macbeth at the Broadway Theater while Macready was giving a rival performance of the Thane of Cawdor in the nearby Opera House. Macready had been the center of a riot when he played in Philadelphia. Forrest was not there. When Macready appeared in New York the preceding year, friends of Forrest announced that they would drive Macready from the stage. Forrest prevented them.

The trouble started at Macready's first performance of Macbeth. That was Monday, May 7, 1849. The Opera House was thronged when the curtain rose. With Macready's entrance upon the stage hostilities commenced. For the first two acts the upper galleries contented themselves with continued groaning and hissing. The third act had scarcely started when a chair was thrown from the top gallery. It struck the stage, within two feet of Macready. He went on with his lines. This fearlessness was a signal for a shower of rotten eggs and decayed vegetables which came from all parts of the house. Oaths and vile epithets and other forms of abuse accompanied them. The police were unable to cope with the disturbance. The curtain was rung down. Several arrests were made.

Appeals by numerous prominent citizens were made the following day, all urging Macready to continue his engagement. Macready agreed to resume on Wednesday night.

The arrests of some of the rioters on Monday night would have been sufficient to prevent further trouble were it not for the work of the politicians. They inspired meetings to protest against Macready's reappearance, which was made possible by the assurances of the local authorities that all the forces of government would protect him in his rights. A riot would reflect on the administration. So let there be a riot.

When the rioters began their disturbance on Wednesday night, hundreds of policemen and special constables, sworn in for the occasion, seized the disturbers.

Macready's performance of Macbeth continued.

Then the tragedy outside commenced. The street had been torn up for the laying of pipes. The stones lay scattered about in convenient heaps. The mob hurled the paving stones through the windows of the playhouse. The police—they did not wear uniforms then—kept together in a compact mass at the main entrance to the theater. At the Sheriff's call a troop of cavalry followed by some two hundred infantrymen, turned into Astor Place from Broadway. A shower of paving stones descended upon them, striking the horses, who became unruly and bolted. The infantry were left alone in the field.

For a time the handful of infantry had things their own way, the mob retreating before them. They cleared the rear of the theater in Eighth Street, then turned down Broadway and started east on the Astor Place side, the mob falling back until it reached the entrance to the Opera House. Here the rioters stopped. The officers called upon them to disperse, warning them that they would be fired on if they did not. The response was a shower of paving stones. The order to fire was given. The first volley passed over the heads of the mob.

"They have only blank cartridges!" cried one. "Let's give it to them again!"

The mob obeyed.

The order was given to the soldiers to fire, and to fire low. Now the soldiers obeyed. More than a dozen fell at the first volley.

The mob retreated seventy-five feet to the corner of Lafayette Place. This little stretch of street, not three hundred yards in length, extended from Astor Place to Great Jones Street. It was one of the most beautiful bits of the old town. Here the Astors and other leaders of wealth and fashion erected spacious mansions, surrounded by shrubbery and flowering gardens, and shaded by trees such as Druids worshiped. But all this is gone—even the name, for when Lafayette Place extended itself downtown for a mile or so, it became a street. Here on the usually staid and silent corner the mob rallied. No one looked out on them from the darkened windows of the homes of the wealthy. Gas jets in all the outside rooms had been extinguished at the first sounds of the fusillade. The mob, in retreating, had picked up more paving stones.

A riot was not a novelty in New York. Politics and hunger had been their chief causes. One can sympathize with, while condemning, the ugly outbreaks of ignorant partisans. There is something pitiable in famished men and women sacking warehouses for food. But there is a magnificence in a mob charging armed soldiers with paving stones in the name of Melpomene. Tragedy avenging tragedy.

For a moment the opposing forces faced each other in sepulchral silence. With a shout the mob advanced, hurling its paving stones.

Another volley was fired.

The tragedy was finished.

The traditional defense of rioters was pleaded for those arrested on this occasion—that they could not be prosecuted because their acts were the natural effects of political passions. The trial destroyed this old belief.

Rynders, who was suspected by all of being one of the inciters of the riot, was often used by Tweed to perform some of the more desperate types of campaigning. Rynders would do anything for money. He was a coarse bully. Once he thrust the muzzle of a revolver against the pit of Tweed's stomach. Tweed's stare made him lower the weapon.

In those days it was the custom of the larger fire-fighting units to hold an annual dance. Before *Big Six* was a year old, it gave its first ball in the Apollo Rooms, Broadway, near Canal Street. Tweed directed the affair, as he did everything with which he had anything to do.

Johnson, the artist, one of the founders of *Big Six*, tells us that Tweed cut an imposing figure on the ballroom floor that evening. In an interview published in the *New York Herald* after Tweed's death, the artist describes Tweed as wearing a blue coat and brass buttons on that occasion, and says further:

"He was young and good looking then, with fine dark brown

hair and clear gritty eyes. He was a tip-top dancer and never wanted a partner."

Whether Mrs. Tweed was one of his partners on that evening we do not know. She was the mother of three children now, and did not wholly approve of Tweed's devotion to *Big Six*, for as Assistant Foreman he not only had to respond to all alarms and attend to a considerable amount of the routine business of the company, but had to be in frequent attendance at the engine house. And as Tweed's voluntary duties increased and kept him more and more from his family, his wife's duties increased at home, as she continued to bear him children—eight in all. Even when they had a house amply attended by servants, Mrs. Tweed remained beside the hearthstone to preside over its destinies.

Tweed had not sought the place of Assistant Foreman. It came to him in recognition of his outstanding qualities as a leader, as did the headship of the organization in 1850 when Demilt resigned as Foreman. In August of the same year, a week or so after Tweed was elected Foreman, the seventy-five red shirts under him presented him with a gold watch and chain. On the timepiece was engraved:

"To William Marcy Tweed from the members of Americus Engine Company No. 6."

This memento of these happy days was worn by Tweed when he was arrested some twenty years after.

Tweed's election as Foreman of *Big Six* made him a petty political power. There was a freemasonry among the volunteer firemen that knew no partisanship. This fraternalism was so deep-rooted that it long survived the abolition of the old non-paid force. When legislated out of existence, the volunteers had laws passed giving them an equal footing with the veterans of the wars in matters of public appointments. These acts were placed in the statute books by lawmakers who had once worn red shirts. They fought with one another. But they closed their ranks and formed an unbreakable hollow square when menaced by an outside force. *Big Six* numbered seventy-five men, each with a vote. Political mathematicians multiply by five to obtain the minimum strength of an active partisan in the ranks. This arbitrary formula—a fair one—raised the voting strength of *Big Six* to 375. Tweed was a successful business man, with a name identified with the life of the neighborhood for three generations. To cap all this, he had a personality that inspired confidence. And he was fast growing in popular esteem.

His entrance into ward politics was inescapable. The year he was chosen Foreman of *Big Six* he was nominated for Assistant Alderman for the Seventh Ward. That year the Democrats were divided among themselves. Yet Tweed's popularity was such that Thomas Woodward, his Whig opponent, won by a bare majority of 47. The vote stood: Woodward, 1,428; Tweed, 1,381.

Tweed's defeat pleased his family, although it rankled him for many weeks. His partisan friends consoled him by saying that he had made a better run than any other Democrat in the ward could have done.

A favorite sport of the volunteer firemen was to engage in water-throwing contests. These were usually held on a Saturday afternoon when the men would be enjoying a half holiday from their regular employment. Rivalry was keen at these tournaments which were conducted in the street, in front of a saloon boasting a Liberty Pole. All the pretentious beer gardens in the vicinity of a fire house went to considerable expense to obtain the tallest of pines to set before their doors. The more prosperous of these places had standing orders with local shipyards for a mast that topped their present possession.

The year Tweed was made Foreman of *Big Six*, the town had a hearty laugh at the expense of the red shirts of the entire West Side of the city. Engine company after engine company had vainly tried to throw a stream of water over the new Liberty Pole that had been raised in front of Riley's saloon on the irregular plaza formed by the junction of Franklin Street and West Broadway. The proud owner announced that he would not adorn the Liberty Pole with the

Phrygian cap until a stream of water had been thrown over its top.

After the firemen of the West Side failed, the challenge was taken up by the engine companies on the East Side. Tweed, ever with an eye for the dramatic, waited until all the rivals of *Big Six* had had their chance and failed. Not a stream of water had struck within seven feet of the top of the pole.

Tweed and his red shirts clattered out of their headquarters on Gouverneur Street on a balmy Saturday afternoon in late September. All the small boys of the neighborhood knew where their own *Big Six* was headed, and its purpose. And they raced behind the gleaming engine drawn by their seventy-five idols, at whose head ran Tweed, his face aglow, and his silver trumpet glistening encouragement to his perspiring followers.

No halt was made until the engine had been drawn west of Riley's Liberty Pole. The wind was from the Hudson River, and Tweed wanted the breeze at his back. Thousands were present to see *Big Six* succeed where its rivals had failed. While his men were making ready, Tweed scrutinized the tall pine that had defied every other engine company in the city. He had to admit that it seemed taller than any other, but then *Big Six* had cleared the tallest on the East Side by at least two feet. And other units had failed to come within spattering distance of the Phrygian cap. Tweed had little doubt of the outcome.

A cheer rose from the crowd as the stream of water left the nozzle of the hose. At the end of fifteen minutes a thundering roar of applause went up as *Big Six* ceased its efforts. Tweed and his red shirts had outdistanced their rivals, but they did not throw the stream over the top. They failed by less than three feet.

"We'll try again to-morrow afternoon at three o'clock," Tweed announced to the crowd.

"The engine won't make it," said Johnson, the artist, when *Big Six* returned to its headquarters. Johnson was Assistant Foreman of the company under Tweed.

"The men were not up to their usual mark to-day," replied Tweed.

Johnson shook his head. Men couldn't have striven harder. The fault was not theirs. They had worked the apparatus to capacity. There wasn't an engine in the town capable of the feat.

"Wait till to-morrow," said Tweed, doggedly.

Tweed did not eat at home that night. He went down to the waterfront. One of his boyhood chums accompanied him. They boarded a clipper ship where one of the crew was a brother of Tweed's companion. Fortunately he was on board. Tweed outlined his plan. It was simple. He wanted the sailor to climb Riley's Liberty Pole between two and three the following morning and saw six feet off the top. And for his labors he would receive ten dollars. A princely sum in those days. Tweed gave him five dollars on the spot, the balance to be paid the following evening at the headquarters of *Big Six*. Tweed's parting word to the sailor was to leave no evidence behind him, urging him to return after he had disposed of the sawed-off top and remove any tell-tale traces of sawdust.

The following morning the sailor's brother examined the ground and reported to Tweed that there was not a single speck of sawdust to be seen anywhere near the Liberty Pole. Highly elated, Tweed led *Big Six* in the afternoon to the scene of their defeat of the day before. The plaza was thronged. And again when *Big Six* sent the water streaming skyward, it was to the accompaniment of inspiring cheers.

In five minutes' time *Big Six* gave up the futile struggle, and Tweed quietly, yet eloquently, condemned a particular sailor-man to the nether regions. Tweed had been tricked. Of course there could be no traces of sawdust, as not an inch had been taken off the Liberty Pole. Tweed eventually laughed. He always enjoyed a good joke, even when it was on himself.

A year later Tweed met the sailor again. He demanded to know why the sailor had not played fair with him. The man of the sea calmly replied that as he had received only half of the amount he felt that he would even up the account by climbing half way up the pole. And this he had done. Tweed, amused at the coolness of the explanation, went on his way.

While Tweed was at the height of his power, nearly twenty years after the Liberty Pole incident, the sailor called on the Boss and said that misfortune had been his lot ever since he had played false. He was now down and out, and lacked even the price of the next meal.

"There," said Tweed, as he handed the sailor a five-dollar bill, "that will keep you from starving, and it squares our account. I promised you ten dollars for the job and you tricked me. Now I am going to try to make an honest man of you. Come and see me to-morrow and I will give you work."

Tweed gave the man work. We must pardon the Boss for his seemingly unctuous preachment on honesty. Tweed was sincere. The sailor had violated a cardinal tenet of Tweed's moral code. The game must be played in accordance with the rules. The sailor had cheated.

The year 1851 also gave Tweed his first intoxicating taste of public applause outside his home town. The volunteer fire-fighting system was the only method known. The name of *Big Six* was familiar to every volunteer fireman in North America. Invitations came to Tweed from all sections to visit with his red shirts. In the spring of the year that he plunged actively into the maelstrom of politics, Tweed took *Big Six* out of its headquarters, and with funds provided by himself and his friends, journeyed to the cities that clamored most for a sight of *Big Six*.

Philadelphia was first visited. Then Baltimore, and next the Capital. In the preceding July, upon the death of Zachary Taylor, Vice-President Millard Fillmore, former Comptroller of New York State, succeeded to the Presidency. Up Pennsylvania Avenue, dragging their glittering engine, bedecked with all the flowers of spring, marched the red shirts. Tweed wearing a tall beaver hat, a white fireman's coat slung nonchalantly over his arm, and his shining silver trumpet swinging at his side, proudly led the way. They halted at the White House, where President Fillmore welcomed them.

This was the only time on record that Tweed was unable to deliver a speech. He had responded elsewhere to words of welcome with volubility. But here, in the presence of the head of the Republic, he could only stammer:

"These are *Big Six* boys."

President Fillmore readily set Tweed and his boys at their ease. A newspaper correspondent smilingly asked Tweed after the reception why he had not made a speech in introducing his famous fire-fighters. Tweed returned the smile with:

"I let the boys' looks speak for themselves."

"But wouldn't any seventy-five young men in red shirts look as well?"

The smile vanished. His pride, the pride of the Metropolis, the pride of the volunteers everywhere, no different from any other company of red shirts! An image flashed through Tweed's mind. He threw it at the reporter.

"Does Croton Dam look like Niagara Falls?" asked Tweed.

Then Tweed answered his own question:

"Not by a damned sight!"

This ended all further argument. In Tweed's rejoinder we see the secret of successful political debate. Always pin the last line on your opponent.

Tweed visited Montreal and Quebec before returning home. And that he was not wanting in showmanship, another attribute of the politician, was demonstrated in the fall of the year when *Big Six* acquired a new fire engine. From friendly livery-men he borrowed eight white horses, their harness mounted in silver, hitched them to the engine, and with his red shirts acting as guard of honor, marched through the principal streets of the Seventh Ward. This could have been done in the daytime. That would have been commonplace. Tweed chose the night. Each of his stalwarts carried a torch.

Tweed accepted the nomination for Alderman in 1851 with the same reluctance that marked his nomination for Assistant Alderman the year before. Tammany, like every other Democratic organization in the North, was divided on the slavery question. The Free Soilers—those who opposed the extension of human servitude into new territory—although in the minority, were sufficiently strong to swing the Mayoralty election in favor of Caleb S. Woodhull, the Whig candidate in 1849.

The Free Soilers, regarded as heretical schismatics by the majority, were in fact an outlaw Democratic group in the city. And they acted accordingly, taking revenge on their opponents by voting the Whig ticket. Not only had their votes elected Woodhull, a lawyer and a corruptionist who masked his knavery behind a scholar's face and pretensions of reform, but they elected two-thirds of the Whig candidates to the Common Council.

After this crushing defeat, at a meeting in Tammany Hall, then on Nassau and Frankfort Streets, facing City Hall Park, W. D. Wallach, a Tammany politician of no great consequence, denounced the leaders of the organization as men of downright dishonesty, who had attained their power through the aid of bullies and loafers, and whose political course was predicated on the assumption that the people could and should be controlled by corruption and violence. This attack, made elsewhere, would have attracted little attention, but delivered in the Wigwam, it became of moment. Wallach's unanswered attack worked additional injury to the party. It was during this factional strife that Fernando Wood became a power in Tammany. Wood, aptly styled the most corrupt Mayor New York ever had, was destined to be relegated to private life by Tweed at a time when the artful Wood was confident that he had given the quietus to Tweed's political career.

Efforts to reconcile the slavery and anti-slavery factions proved unavailing. It is difficult even for corruptionists to compromise on a principle.

It was while this scissure was most pronounced that Tweed was nominated for Alderman. Tweed's ward, largely composed of workingmen, had a fair sprinkling of the employing and professional groups. These latter were almost exclusively Whigs, and controlled considerable votes. Many mechanics also voted the Whig ticket. Tammany politicians who persuaded Tweed to take the nomination, frankly informed him that while he was the only man in the ward who had the slightest chance to carry it against the Whigs, he was in for another defeat if he did not wage a more intensive campaign than he had for Assistant Alderman. The Whigs had nominated John B. Webb, a wealthy boat builder. Webb was popular not only with the business men of the district, but with the workers, for he had the reputation of paying his employees a generous wage. Tweed knew that while he could count on a certain number of fraudulent votes this would be offset by the stealing done by the Whigs.

Tweed resolved that if defeat again came his way, it would not be through any fault of his. At this time Tweed was twenty-eight years old. Yet he enjoyed the friendship of men much older, men of standing in the community. It was not because of any position he held, for all one could say of him was that he was a popular young man, of unblemished reputation, the head of a family, successful in business in a small way, and was Foreman of *Big Six*. One who did a service for him then did it unselfishly or charged it up against the unknown future.

One of Tweed's friends was Joel Blackmer, known to the well-to-do of the town as the principal of the East Broadway Seminary, a school for girls which took its name from the main thoroughfare of the Seventh Ward and which changed its name three or four years later to The Ladies' Institute. Blackmer was a Whig. He was a quiet, scholarly sort, whose interest in active politics began and ended when he cast his vote.

After Tweed had his campaign prospects evaluated by several politicians, including his old friend, Assemblyman Reilly, who was largely instrumental in forcing the nomination upon him, he called on Blackmer at the young ladies' seminary. The pedagogue received his young friend in the library. After they exchanged greetings, Tweed inquired if the schoolman was especially interested in the candidacy of Webb. Blackmer replied he was not, since he had heard that his young friend was opposing Webb. Who, he asked, acquainted with Tweed's merits, would do other than vote for him even though he were running on the Democratic ticket? Tweed blushed his thanks and returned the compliment by saying that Mr. Blackmer had more real friends than any other Whig in the Seventh Ward. He had taught the daughters of Whigs, and some of these girls had married Whigs. And these husbands and fathers of the girls whose alma mater was the East Broadway Seminary would vote for Blackmer for President even though he ran on a Democratic ticket. Blackmer smiled and shook his head. None of his Whig friends would ever vote a Democratic ticket in a national election, no matter who was on the ballot, and few could be persuaded to vote for a friend, who was not a Whig, for any office. The very point that Tweed was trying to make. And would Blackmer help him? He was facing possible defeat. He had been defeated the year before for Assistant Alderman. Then he did not care. Now he did. He was in distress. Blackmer would help him in every way possible. Tweed had his word on it.

Then Tweed shot a poser at the schoolmaster. Would he run for Alderman as an independent Whig?

This was more than Blackmer had expected. But he had given his word. He kept it, and ran for Alderman, and elected Tweed.

The vote, when counted, stood:

> Tweed, Democrat 1,384
> Webb, Whig 1,336
> Blackmer, Whig 206

Had Tweed failed to induce Blackmer to run as a stalking horse, the race would have gone to Webb, the regular choice of the Whigs, for Blackmer's vote would have been cast for Webb, thus electing the regular Whig nominee by a majority of 158. As it was, these 206 complimentary votes cast by Blackmer's friends gave Tweed the slender plurality of 48.

Tweed was now a politician. He had everything that made for success in the career on which he was launched. In the Aldermanic contest he had proven that he possessed that without which few can long remain in public life—cunning. Tweed was certain to succeed.

CHAPTER VII

THE Common Council to which Tweed was elected has gone down into history as The Forty Thieves. It was a little more brazen in its plunderings than its predecessors. Hence the fitting appellation. The Common Council at this time consisted of the Boards of Aldermen and Assistant Aldermen, of twenty members each. It was not until two years later that the latter Board was abolished and supplanted by a Board of Councilmen.

The position of Alderman in 1852 was one of considerable power. The Alderman was a petty despot. He appointed the police of his ward, from the humblest patrolman to the commander of the precinct. He granted licenses to saloons, or porter houses, as the language of the day had it. And with his associates, he awarded franchises to operate 'bus and street car lines and ferries. These grants, of course, were not valid until signed by the Mayor, and if disapproved by him, they could be repassed over his veto by the Aldermen. He enjoyed other powers that enabled him—if he were so inclined—to levy blackmail, but these were his principal sources of tainted money. He enjoyed still another privilege. He sat as a Justice in the Mayor's Court, which tribunal, now no more, tried all prisoners accused of violations at the polls.

It was this last which made offenses against the Election Law as safe as dropping money in the collection basket on Sunday. These offenses against the ballot were not confined to any party, so that the political belief of the offender never prejudiced a Justice of the Mayor's Court. Moreover, the Aldermen were practical politicians, who either connived at these frauds or were parties to them. In many cases the Aldermen were the *agents provocateurs* of the offenses charged against the culprits brought before them.

An Alderman also sat as a Judge in the criminal courts. He tried those accused of crime, and though he might be a butcher, a baker, or a candlestick maker, as an Alderman he was empowered to decide fine points of law when he ascended the judicial bench. He selected the thirty-six talesmen from which grand jurors were to be drawn, and could, and did, pack grand juries. Controlling, as he did, the tenure of office of the men who served the notices on talesmen, it was an easy matter to persuade the server to report back that a certain talesman, of unimpeachable integrity, was out of the city. And as eighteen grand jurors constituted an inquest, it was not difficult for the aldermanic supervisors of the grand jury to work in a few special pleaders when the occasion demanded it. To this extent an Alderman controlled justice where it should be most inviolate—the grand jury room: He appointed those charged with arresting and detecting lawbreakers; he supervised the selection of talesmen from whose number would be drawn the grand jurors who would determine if a felon should be tried; he sat as a judge in the trial of the accused. As a consequence, his power was feared in the blackness of the underworld, and a corrupt Alderman was a veritable Prince of Darkness.

Neither the Alderman nor Assistant Alderman received a salary. This was predicated on the aristocratic assumption that only those financially able to devote the time to these labors would and should seek an office where the sole return was in the honor of serving. The result was that the unscrupulous made the holding of these offices a highly profitable profession.

Tweed's membership in the ranks of the Board of Aldermen was only a matter of a few short weeks, for in the spring of the year we find him one of the leaders of The Forty Thieves, acting as the representative of the city in negotiating the purchase of land for a Potter's Field. The land was worth $30,000 at the very outside. Tweed successfully palmed it off on the municipality for $103,450 with the connivance and aid of Mayor Ambrose C. Kingsland, a Whig. The property, consisting of sixty-nine acres on Ward's Island, had a fair value of $50 to $800 an acre. The price to the city averaged a few cents under $1,500 an acre.

The sale of this land to the city netted the Aldermen more money than any previous grafting enterprise. The year before, 1851, the high mark had been reached when Solomon Kipp, a scion of one of the first families of old New York, paid $50,000 in bribes to the Aldermen for the Eighth Avenue and Ninth Avenue street railway franchises. One minor official was given $10,000 by the agent of the owner of the land. Another, a prison warden, received a $2,000 gratuity from the same source. How much the Aldermen received was never disclosed, as the seller, who received approximately $75,000 more than the property was worth, would not reveal what had been paid to the City Fathers. There was a reason for the reticence. The real estate operators had to continue in business and the city, while not always buying land, fixed the taxes annually. The tax appraiser wields a powerful club.

The next piece of corruption Tweed is known to have participated in was the purchase of fireworks for the celebration of the Fourth of July. This proved small pickings for the Aldermen, who authorized the purchases and on whose approval the bills were paid. The sum of $4,100 was spent by the city for Greek fire, Roman candles, pin-wheels, torpedoes and other pyrotechnical display to commemorate the seventy-sixth anniversary of the signing of the Declaration of Independence. A fair price would have been $500. This estimate is based on the fireworks bought for Randall's Island. Here the city paid $300 for explosives worth not more than $40.

The day after The Forty Thieves robbed the people in the name of patriotism, the body of Henry Clay, which had been lying in state in the City Hall, was taken to Albany, on the steamer *Santa Claus*. Even the obsequies of the noted statesman were made an occasion for defrauding the city. Exorbitant bills were rendered by tradesmen and others, the overcharges being shared among the Aldermen. The sum of $1,400 was paid for the cigars, wines and refreshments consumed on the boat and $2,500 was charged for decorating the little steamboat with strips of black and white cotton bunting and a few flags.

A little later Tweed mixed politics and bribery successfully. This occasion arose during the pendency of the application of Dr. Abraham J. Berry, Mayor of Williamsburgh, which was later annexed to the old City of Brooklyn, for a franchise to operate a ferry between New York and Williamsburgh. The Aldermen received more than $20,000 in bribes to pass the measure.

While Tweed's associates were content to vote favorably on the franchise when the tribute money was raised by Dr. Berry, Tweed, who had political ambitions that could be realized only with the aid of the Democratic leaders of the old City of Williamsburgh, declined to be influenced by money alone. John J. Hicks, associated with Dr. Berry in the application, had the money, ready to pay out in bribes, but Tweed, while anxious to get his share, also wanted to go to Congress. The Congressional district embracing the Seventh Ward, which Tweed represented in the Board of Aldermen, also included the old City of Williamsburgh. Congressional nominees were then chosen at party conventions. Tweed could easily get the New York delegates, but he had no claim on the Williamsburgh delegation. The Mayor of Williamsburgh and his friends could line up the delegation on their side of the river, and this was insisted upon by Tweed before he would permit the Aldermen to vote on the ferry franchise. When Tweed obtained the promise of the Williamsburgh delegation in the nominating convention, the franchise was approved by the Aldermen.

Mayor Kingsland, the Whig Mayor who signed the franchise, was an active participant in some of the steals. In the Catherine Street ferry grant, put through the preceding year, Kingsland, after the Aldermen received their loot, played the part of a lone highwayman and held up the applicants for the franchise until they submitted to further extortion. The Mayor, after observing to the petitioners that the rent paid to the city for the ferry was extremely low, proposed that a friend of his be permitted to buy a fifth interest in the ferry. Of course the petitioners, who had already paid out considerable sums to get the measure before the Mayor, could not say nay to the man who could approve or veto the franchise. They agreed to his proposal. Then the Mayor suggested that all could make a handsome profit by purchasing property in the vicinity of the ferry. The Mayor stressed that the land was certain to rise in value after the city widened the streets on which they bought. And after this intimate conversation in the Mayor's office in the City Hall, the franchise was signed, although other petitioners offered far better terms in the form of rental to the city.

This hold-up by Mayor Kingsland was regarded as particularly despicable by the politicians, regardless of party, as his predecessor in office, the sleek Caleb S. Woodhull, like Kingsland, a Whig, was the man who pulled the strings of the petitioning marionettes. One of them was Woodhull's brother-in-law, William Cockroft, a physician turned ironmonger. The other was George G. Taylor, brother of the Comptroller under Mayor Kingsland.

Woodhull had one of the richest law practices in the city. He was connected by blood and marriage with some of the most influential men in the community. The Woodhulls were justly proud of their distinguished ancestry, and none more than the former Mayor. A few years before his bribery of The Forty Thieves Woodhull prepared this modest sketch of his family:

"The ancestor of the family in this country is Richard Wodhull (as the name at that time and many years afterwards was spelt), who came from Northampshire, Eng., and settled at Brookhaven, L. I., where the family has been distinguished by important civil and military trusts. An ancestor, Nathaniel, served under Abercrombie, and was afterwards President of the Provincial Congress, at the adoption by that body of the Declaration of Independence, and at the same time General, commanding the brigade of Suffolk and Queens County, L. I., in which capacity he rendered important service, and died from the effects of a wound in Sept., 1776. Caleb S., born at Brookhaven, is a lawyer in this city, and has been President of the Common Council. He is a prominent

member of the Whig Party, and highly esteemed as one of our
most worthy citizens."

The first American ancestor was landed here in 1648 and
in 1666 was appointed a Justice of the Court of Assizes.
Seven years later he was commissioned magistrate for Brookhaven. Nathaniel, named in the sketch prepared by his unworthy descendant, was born in 1722. He was a distinguished
soldier long before the Revolution. As Major under Abercrombie he participated in the attack upon Crown Point and
Ticonderoga, aided Bradstreet in the assault against Fort
Frontenac, and his journal of the Montreal expedition of 1760
is familiar to students of the period.

After Taylor and Cockroft obtained the franchise, they
sold it to Woodhull for $20,000. This covered the expenses
they incurred in healing the wounded consciences of the Aldermen, and left a little over to assuage their own. Woodhull,
immediately after the franchise was transferred to him, resold
it to practical ferry operators for $30,000, netting the former
Mayor $10,000.

One of the most rapacious and dishonorable of the Aldermen
in 1851, Wesley Smith, was also a member of The Forty
Thieves. After the Catherine Street ferry grant went through,
he induced another Alderman, Charles Francis, who had
received a $500 bribe from Dr. Cockroft, to demand $3,000
additional. Smith accompanied Francis on this errand, and
eloquently supported the claim of Francis. But Cockroft was
through with bribery.

It was from Alderman Smith that Tweed received his first
lesson in the favorite legislative game of ringing the bell. This
is resorted to by lawmakers who want cash, and want it
quickly, and are not particular as to how they get it. Sometimes this is called strike legislation. But in legislative halls it
is usually spoken of as ringing the bell. It is a felicitous as
well as an expressive euphemism. When the individual or
individuals, corporation or corporations, affected by the proposed legislation, hear the alarm, they never fail to hasten to

the author of the strike bill to inquire what it will cost to kill the measure.

Tweed had been in the Board of Aldermen scarcely four months when Alderman Smith demonstrated the effectiveness of the bell ringing. Smith had a bill introduced that ostensibly aimed at saving money for the people. All strike bills on their face are highly meritorious. Smith's measure was to save money through a reduction in the fees of the Coroner. The Coroner heard the ringing of the bell. When he learned the name of the bell ringer, he called on a mutual friend. A meeting was effected between the Alderman and the Coroner. Said the Alderman: "Give me $250 and I'll kill the resolution in committee." The Coroner paid the price. The bell no longer rang—for the Coroner.

Tweed made the acquaintance of the notorious and tragic Jake Sharp that same summer. A petition for a franchise to operate a ferry from the foot of Wall Street to Montague Street, Brooklyn, was pending in the Board. One of the applicants was James B. Taylor, who two years prior, after spending $3,000 while he was seeking the privilege to operate a ferry from Grand Street, New York, to Williamsburgh, gave up the struggle when opponents of his application used money like water to defeat the grant. One of the active opponents of the Taylor application in 1850 was William Wall, a prominent citizen of Williamsburgh. Wall, in describing the contest, said that "it was the damnedest fight that was ever had in the Common Council; that it cost them from twenty to twenty-five thousand dollars."

Things were looking bright for Taylor when he applied for the Wall Street ferry franchise in 1852. He offered $10,000 to various members of The Forty Thieves, and was informed that it would cost $15,000 to get the franchise through the Board of Aldermen. To this Taylor readily assented. But the night that the agreement was reached, the Board reported out a rival petition. Both petitions offered similar terms to the city—five thousand dollars annual rental. That same day Taylor doubled the proposed yearly payments to the municipality. This $10,000 rental to the city was instantly doubled by Taylor's rival, who, it turned out, was Jake Sharp. This wily manipulator did not stop at this. Sharp increased the amount of the bribe named by Tweed and his associates in their parleys, paying The Forty Thieves $20,000 in tribute money.

How much Tweed received out of this steal was never disclosed.

About this time the corruption among the local leaders of the Whigs began to grate upon the nerves of owners of newspapers supporting the traditional foes of the Democrats. Horace Greeley, then presiding over the destinies of *The Tribune*, the leading organ of the Whigs in the nation as well as the city, protested against the bi-partisan deals, and publicly accused Whig ward committees of selling out to Tammany on Election Day.

This charge led to further scrutiny of the acts of the leaders of the Whigs and the Democrats, and their representatives in public place. Inevitably the crusaders struck the corrupt Common Council where sinister bi-partisan deals were not confined to Election Day, but began on the first day of January and ended on the last day of December. Before the summer was over, Tweed and his colleagues were subjected to a heavy and constant attack by part of the press. Some newspapers defended The Forty Thieves.

Tweed, now a recognized leader in the Board, counseled silence until the fall campaign approached. It would be time enough then to answer their critics if their foes had not tired, or the people had failed to react favorably to the attacks. Tweed thoroughly understood the mass mind. Then there was another reason why Tweed did not want to engage in any controversy with the assailants of The Forty Thieves just then. There was that promise of the Williamsburgh Mayor and his associates to be fulfilled. He had the delegation from New York committed to his candidacy for Congress, but the Williamsburgh delegates were yet to be lined up. Tweed, although a tyro in politics, had sufficient experience to know that a political promise is valueless until it is made good. But Williamsburgh played fair, and Tweed was nominated for Congress in due course. Then he took the stump in defense of

the Board of Aldermen and beguiled a majority of his
audiences into believing that disappointed office seekers had
inspired an unjust attack on him and the other members of
The Forty Thieves.

The attacks on The Forty Thieves were partly offset by the
Democrats in naming Jacob A. Westervelt for Mayor. Westervelt was wealthy, a successful shipbuilder, a churchman, and
possessed other attributes that appealed to independent voters.
It was also a Presidential year, and Franklin Pierce, the
nominee of the Democrats, whose biography is thus epitomized:
"born on Friday, inaugurated on Friday, died on Friday," also
lent considerable strength to the local and State tickets.
Fraud was rampant in both the Democratic and Whig ranks.
The Whigs plotted a most gigantic election steal. They had
printed 80,000 ballots for distribution among the Democrats
who were to be instructed to cast them as the official ballots of
their party. But the Whig plot was discovered in time, and
the fraudulent tickets, which did not bear the name of a single
Democrat, were confiscated by the Tammanyites in the quaint
old Middle Dutch Church in Nassau Street, then, and for many
years thereafter, the Post Office. The undeniable proofs of the
Whig conspiracy to steal the election were carried with pomp
and ceremony up Nassau Street to its head, where the Wigwam
stood.

This attempt by the Whigs to steal the election attracted
many votes to the Democrats, who made a clean sweep of the
city on Election Day, when both parties resorted to the grossest
frauds. Ballot boxes were stuffed, violence was common, and
repeaters journeyed in gangs. Some repeaters voted as often
as twenty times in the course of the day.

Tweed was twenty-nine years old when he was elected a
Member of the House of Representatives from the Fifth New
York Congressional District. The new Congressman-elect did
not take his seat in the national Legislature until December,
1853. After his election to Congress, Tweed resumed his
highly profitable labors in the Common Council where he sat
until January 1, 1854, serving in the dual rôle of municipal

and national legislator until his two-year aldermanic term expired.

While Tweed was making his campaign for Congress, he managed to spare time to meet with other members of The Forty Thieves to perfect plans to put through three of the biggest steals in the closing days of the year.

One of these was the Broadway street car franchise, fraught with drama and tragedy. Untold thousands were spent to put this grab through, although, as it later turned out, the bribes were wasted in this case. A second was the sale of city land, known as the Gansevoort Market property. Here the Aldermen divided between $40,000 and $75,000 in bribes. In the Third Avenue Railroad steal $30,000 was shared among The Forty Thieves. All three were passed by the Board of Aldermen in the month of December, and in the Third Avenue grant, we find that Tweed's share represented not less than one-tenth of the total bribery fund, or $3,000, and possibly as much as one-sixth, or $5,000. Even the smaller sum in itself reveals the prominent part he took in these transactions, as well as the high value placed on his sinister services.

The principal beneficiary of this steal was Myndert Van Schaick, a wealthy old Knickerbocker, of eminent respectability, and the first president of the Third Avenue Railroad, with its sordid background of crooked finance. Another grantee was Elijah F. Purdy, a Grand Sachem of Tammany when the title carried with it the political leadership of the organization. Purdy, then powerful, recognized the master in Tweed, and voluntarily helped him in his upward climb. Horace M. Dewey, a lawyer, was also one of the petitioners. He was the almoner of the group. He stood loyally by Tweed two years later, roundly perjuring himself, swearing that moneys traced from him to Tweed were innocent loans, and escaping prosecution when asked if he had given bribes to any member of The Forty Thieves by taking refuge in his constitutional privilege to decline to answer on the ground that it would tend to criminate him.

As early as the Third Avenue steal, Tweed was so hard pressed for time that he was forced to engage assistants in his

work of plunder. One so employed was Andrew Stevens, a
ne'er-do-well relation of Tweed's wife.

Three other grantees of the Third Avenue Railroad were S.
Benson McGown, James W. Flynn, and Patrick McElroy.
These three confessed to the manner in which the franchise was
passed by the Common Council, naming Tweed as the leader
of The Forty Thieves. Tweed answered these charges in an
affidavit that went further afield from the truth than was
required. But Tweed did not believe in doing things by halves.
As this was the first time that Tweed replied to a specific charge
of corruption, his affidavit for that reason alone is interesting.
But there is an added interest in it. For it reveals the demagogic tone that Tweed had acquired. The document reads:

"*City and County of New York*, ss:—WILLIAM M. TWEED, being
duly sworn, deposes and says as follows: I was Alderman of the
Seventh Ward, from the first Monday of January, 1852, to 1st day
of January, 1854; I have read the depositions of S. Benson Mc-
Gown, James W. Flynn and Patrick McElroy; the information
stated in the deposition of McGown, stated to have been given to
him by Horace M. Dewey, that Dewey and his associates in the
grant for the Third avenue railroad, paid to me five thousand dollars to get the grant through the Board of Aldermen is utterly
untrue.

"I never received, directly or indirectly, from any person or persons whomsoever, the said sum of money or any money, promise, or
thing whatever, to get the grant through the Board of Aldermen,
or to influence my vote or action in any respect in relation to said
grant, and everything contained in the said deposition to the contrary, is untrue; the information alleged in the deposition of
Patrick McElroy, as given to him by Horace M. Dewey, that he
had promised to give me either six or eight thousand dollars, for
procuring the grant of the Third avenue railroad, is utterly untrue;
he never, directly or indirectly, promised me either of the said
sums, or any money or consideration whatever, for procuring the
grant, or for my vote or action in any of the proceedings relating
to the same; and everything mentioned to the contrary in the last
mentioned deposition, is utterly untrue.

"The statement made in the deposition of James W. Flynn, that
he thought Mr. Dewey told him that he had promised me three

thousand dollars to get the grant through the Board of Aldermen,
I have read; I never directly or indirectly, was so promised by
Mr. Dewey, nor did he at any time to me, make any remark, or
use any words, or convey any idea to that effect, and everything
contained in Mr. Flynn's deposition to the contrary, is utterly
untrue.

"I have heard read the deposition of Horace M. Dewey; I
have at various times borrowed money from Mr. Dewey, varying
from two hundred dollars to one thousand dollars, which amounts
I have always repaid him within one week, and I do not now owe
him anything; these are the only transactions I have had with him,
and they had no reference whatever to the grant of the Third avenue
railroad.

"I have no knowledge that any member of the late Common
Council or officer of the city government, had received any money
whatever to influence his official action; in my own proceedings,
I have been influenced only from a sense of duty."

No lawyer wrote the last phrase: "in my own proceedings, I
have been influenced only from a sense of duty." In this muted
blare of brasses, at once defiant and appealing, we see the
subtler side of the swayer of mobs.

In the sale of Gansevoort Market property there was not a
single feature which could be seized upon by the most ardent
and skillful pleader of The Forty Thieves. Here was land,
fronting on the North or Hudson River, for which the city was
offered $300,000 and which the Aldermen proposed selling for
$160,000. It was so bold and daring a steal, manifestly inde-
fensible, that when it reached Mayor Kingsland for approval,
even he could not bring himself to the point of signing the
resolution. In a franchise theft, the gullible could be led into
believing, for the time being at least, that the rejected higher
offers were made by persons who for one reason or another
would not be able to live up to the terms of the contract. But
in a mere real estate transaction which involved nothing save
the exchange of a deed for cash, no specious arguments could
be offered in justification of the steal. The Mayor, with a
knowing wink, disapproved the measure, which the Aldermen
repassed over the Mayor's veto. On Christmas Eve the
property was conveyed to the first of the several dummies, one

of them a Governor of the Alms-House. In a few weeks title was vested in the real principal in the deal, James B. Taylor, who up to this time had had ill-luck in his efforts to corrupt the Aldermen, generally being outbid by some more generous giver. Ten years later another Common Council committed the city to buy back this same property for $533,437.50. And the second time that the city was swindled on this particular piece of real estate, the Councilmen again had to override a Mayor's veto.

The Forty Thieves were now so thoroughly discredited that their final act of the year, which included open defiance of a Supreme Court injunction, was but a fitting climax. They had made large profits letting contracts to favorites, awarding $600,000 to Russ and Reid for paving the Bowery with a surface that proved so worthless that it had to be ripped up not long after it was laid. During the latter part of the year a portion of the press hammered away at the Aldermen for contemplating a grant to run street cars on Broadway. Much of the opposition to the proposal, which was inherently sound, was inspired by Alexander T. Stewart, the richest merchant in the United States, whose store at Broadway and Chambers Street was one of the sights of the town.

It was the first structure of marble erected on Broadway, and the people proudly called it The Marble Palace. Stewart emigrated to this country from Ireland the year Tweed was born. He had been educated at Trinity College. His first year here he taught school. Then he entered a small mercantile business in which he had acquired a slight interest. His partner died soon after, and at the age of twenty-two the young Irishman, with little knowledge of the business, found himself its head. He had inherited some property in his native land, and made a trip there, returning with a large stock of Irish lace. Fashionable New York raved over the exquisite handiwork of Stewart's countrywomen, and marveled at his low prices. This was the start of his fortune. When The Forty Thieves took office, Stewart was worth more than $10,000,000. He was the largest land owner in the city of New York.

The Merchant Prince, as he was called, fearful that street cars would keep his fashionable patrons from driving their carriages to his store, organized a formidable opposition to the laying of tracks on Broadway. There were five petitions including that of Jake Sharp. Four of the offers were highly advantageous to the city, and were sponsored by men of standing. The most favorable of these came from Thomas E. Davies, who shared with Stewart and Astor the distinction of owning the largest amount of land in the city. Davies, who on emigrating from England in the early part of the century, had engaged in the distilling of whiskey and finding it not profitable, moved to New York in 1830, where his success in the real estate field was most spectacular for more than twenty years. Much of his success was due to his association with J. L. and S. Joseph, who preceded the first August Belmont as the American agents of the Rothschilds. In the month of December, 1852, Davies was one of the wealthiest men in the country. And he continued to add to his store. The proposal of Davies was that for each five-cent fare collected he would give one cent to the city. Jake Sharp had a bid before the Aldermen that was in every respect a grab. The compensation offered the city in return for the grant was little more than a gesture. But the wily Jake atoned for his neglect of the taxpayers by paying attention to their representatives, dealing with them through Tweed. The merchant Stewart was novel then in the ways of persuading lawmakers to see things his way, or he might have blocked the passage of the resolution by outbidding Sharp. For Stewart, in the quarter of a century fight that he had made against replacing the old stages with the more modern horse cars, spent upwards of half a million dollars before his gold and guile had to give way, like all things, to progress. But the Aldermen ignored the bids of Davies and others, and passed the resolution granting to Jake Sharp the privilege of laying tracks on Broadway, from the South Ferry to Fifty-ninth Street, and to operate cars thereon. This was during the Christmas season. No sooner was the measure on the desk of Mayor Kingsland than Stewart marched across the street to the City Hall, a large and influential delegation of merchants and other citizens of prominence at his back, and forced the Mayor to veto the grab. The Mayor was denounced to his face by Tweed for his cowardice in going back on his private pledge to sign the measure. But there was a way out. This Tweed conceded, and angrily added that there was no thanks or anything else due Kingsland, for the suggestion.

It was common knowledge that Tweed and his associates, to keep faith with Jake Sharp, who had already dealt with them generously, and who had made promises of more when the road was in operation and earnings coming in, intended repassing the measure over the Mayor's veto. No secret was made of their intentions, and Tweed let it be known that the vetoed resolution would be repassed at the last session of the year. Stewart now had the support of the unsuccessful bidders, and at a conference of lawyers it was decided to apply to the courts for an injunction. Justice Campbell granted the application, which was duly served on the Board, enjoining it from taking further action on the measure. This restraining order was served on the Board before it met on December 28. Tweed and several of the Aldermen took counsel among themselves. They conferred in the office of Oscar W. Sturtevant, a young lawyer, who lived with his family in one of the old mansions on Murray Street a few steps west of the City Hall. All were agreed that the injunction was a usurpation of the legislative powers of the Board, and none more so than Sturtevant, who was highly respected by the members of his profession, not only for his legal attainments, but for his gentle qualities. Whatever qualms were entertained by his associates were dissipated by the arguments made by the indignant Sturtevant, who dictated a resolution to be offered to the Board when it was convened. With this document in his possession, Sturtevant strode up Broadway from his office in Fulton Street, and as he ascended the marble steps of the City Hall, Tweed walked at his side. Behind him stalked grim tragedy.

The Aldermanic Chamber was thronged when Richard F. Compton, president of the Board, called the meeting to order. The murmur of voices instantly ceased as Alderman Sturtevant rose and announced that he offered a resolution and moved its adoption. A page scurried to his side, and a moment later the clerk was reading. The document set forth that thirty thousand citizens had signed a petition urging the substitution of street cars for stages on Broadway. This was true. There was popular demand for improved transit facilities, and when that part of the resolution was reached which answered the inference of corruption made in applying for the injunction, there was an outburst of applause. This passage read:

"The Common Council have an equal authority to suspect and impute improper motives to any intended judicial decision of any Judge, and consequently arrest his action on the Bench, as such Judge has in regard to the legislative action of the Common Council."

There was another full measure of handclapping when Sturtevant, with fine irony, attacked the injunction. This went:

"If the assumption be submitted to, that a Judge, without color of law or jurisdiction, can exercise the prerogative of directing and controlling municipal legislation of the City, by issuing an injunction prohibiting the Mayor, Aldermen, and Commonalty of New York from performing a legislative act supposed by him to be probably about to be performed, the next natural step of judicial usurpation will be to arrest and veto, in similar manner, the legislation of the State or that of Congress on any Judge's opinion of constitutionality, expediency, or motive, at the close of a session when all business of importance is usually completed."

Tweed, the moment the clerk ceased reading, jumped to his feet and seconded the resolution.

The resolution was carried and then the original measure awarding the franchise to Jake Sharp was brought before the Board.

S. L. H. Ward, one of the four Aldermen who had opposed the grant when it was first considered, was recognized. He then proceeded to read the injunction of Justice Campbell.

Tweed, his face flushed with anger, vibrantly demanded:

"Is that directed to you?"

"I have the floor," retorted Ward.

"Well," said Tweed, who did not care to dispute a fact, but who was determined on speaking then and there, "when the people of the Seventh Ward elected me as their representative, they gave me the right to think for them, and they have not delegated that right to Mr. Justice Campbell. Mr. Justice Campbell might issue an injunction to stay the Executive, but the members of the Board of Common Council must think for themselves. I never will permit Mr. Justice Campbell or Mr. Anybody Else to direct me how to think or vote, and will continue to do my own thinking and voting despite injunctions or any other papers."

Alderman Ward had by this time resumed his seat and made no further attempt to read the injunction. When Tweed had voiced his defiance of court orders, Sturtevant made an elaborate defense of the grant, and asserted that nothing had yet appeared which shook the ground on which the ordinance was first adopted, and volunteered that he courted full investigation, judicial or otherwise, of the reason for the action of the Board, collectively and individually.

The speech of Sturtevant won a convert, A. A. Denman, a dealer in building materials, who said that he had at first opposed the measure, but now was convinced that street cars on Broadway would prove of great service to the community.

"Amidst ten thousand rumors," he continued, "it is time that the rights and position of the Common Council were definitely determined."

Tweed again took the floor. He argued that the terms and conditions imposed on the grantee would prove of greater public advantage than the payment of moneys offered by the other applicants. This untruth voiced, Tweed said, and with no denying, that the street cars would afford greater comfort and convenience to the people, particularly the working classes, such—he proudly proclaimed—as were his constituents. He then assailed that portion of the press that impugned the motives of the Common Council.

"Public opinion as expressed by these journals is only the echo of the dollars of the property holders," said Tweed.

Alderman Ward sneered at Tweed's pretensions to speak for workingmen.

"That," retorted Tweed menacingly, "is the language of a blackguard."

One of his colleagues seized Tweed's coattails. The presiding officer rapped for order. The blows of the gavel had a quieting effect. After a little more debate the court injunction was ignored, and the measure passed over the Mayor's veto. The vote was 15 to 3. Two of the Aldermen did not vote.

But court injunctions, whether just or unjust, cannot be disobeyed with impunity. The fifteen whose votes gave Jake Sharp the coveted right to run street cars on the main artery of the city were cited before Justice Campbell. Tweed and thirteen others were fined $200 each. This was nothing. They paid and left the court smiling. But not so Sturtevant. He was fined $350, and sentenced to fifteen days in prison. Sturtevant made a courtly bow to the court as he heard the unexpected sentence. It broke his heart. The disgrace of imprisonment told on his sensitive spirit. Neither family nor friends could cheer him. From the day he came out of jail he avoided meeting his old acquaintances, and made no new ones. He wandered about alone. One day his brooding ended when he fell lifeless to the floor in the lobby of the Old Astor House.

The defiance of the courts placed the Common Council in a worse light than ever. There was a hue and cry for the prosecution of the culprits, bribers and bribed. The demand was an old one.

Let them shout. They would soon weary of it. But to the amazement of Tweed and his associates, the February grand jury had taken it upon itself to investigate the rumors of corruption, which Alderman Denman had placed at the prodigious figure of ten thousand. The Aldermen had been asleep at the switch. Fearing no danger, they had let that grand jury be selected from a list of honest talesmen. But let them indict. There still remained friendly courts and it would be easy to pack a petit jury.

Two days before the end of the life of the February grand jury, the precise date is February 25, 1853, the inquest was adjourned because an important witness, who could involve Tweed and several other Aldermen, refused to answer the question: "Did you ever offer a bribe to any member of the Common Council?" This witness was directed to appear in the grand jury room the following morning.

Tweed learned of the situation as soon as the inquest recessed. There was little that went on behind the closed doors where the county inquisitors sat that he did not know. He knew there was only one reason why the refractory witness had been summoned to appear before the body he had defied. That was to have the question repeated, and again meeting with a refusal to answer, the grand jurors would instruct the district attorney to go before the Court of Sessions and request that the witness be instructed to answer. Tweed knew that the entire press of the city would be represented in the court on the occasion, as the investigation of The Forty Thieves was being reported daily. The Court would need some moral support. So Tweed decided to supply it.

When court was convened on the morning of February 25, Tweed sat in a front row bench. Ranged alongside of him were other members of The Forty Thieves. Others of the band sat behind them. Judge Beebe sat in the presiding judge's bench. Flanking him on either side were two more Judges. These three constituted the Court of Sessions.

The district attorney, on hand as was expected, repeated to the Court the question that had been propounded in the grand jury room, complained of the witness's refractoriness, and asked that he be directed to answer.

While the district attorney was speaking Tweed kept his grayish blue eyes riveted on the two Judges who sat on either side of Judge Beebe. Ordinarily Tweed would have sworn by their loyalty. But the Press—it was always spelled with a capital then—was well represented, friendly and hostile alike, and the clamor of the latter was beginning to wear on the Aldermen, some of whom had even talked of fleeing to Canada.

Judge Beebe ordered that the witness should answer the question. The Judge did not hold with the dictum that it is the duty of those on whom a judicial task is imposed to meet reproach and not court popularity. But Lord Eldon was a consummate ass. Beebe would be popular at any price. The majority was clamoring for such a ruling. That was enough for him. Tweed had anticipated the decision. But Beebe was not the whole court. His two associates, or at least one of them, would have to concur in the order to give it force. What would they do? Tweed never took his eyes off these two Judges. It seemed an age before either of them spoke. One of them, in a hoarse whisper, took issue with Judge Beebe, and found an echo from the other extreme of the bench. Now that they had broken their silence, Tweed ceased staring at them. There was no further need. They had ruled that the witness need not answer the question. Judge Beebe was outvoted, two to one. Majorities control in a democracy. Tweed smiled. There was a scornful turn at the corners of his full-lipped mouth.

These two Judges who saved the day were William J. Brisley and John Doherty. The latter was a wily lawyer. Brisley was a stone cutter and shamelessly corrupt. Both were members of The Forty Thieves. Although their motives were wrong, their interpretation of the law was right. At the time they would have as readily decided that the end of the world had come. It is true that an appeal could be taken from the ruling of the court, that is, the decision of Aldermen Brisley and Doherty. But that would take more than a day. And the February grand jury would adjourn *sine die* within the next twenty-four hours. Therefore, an appeal would be in vain. And as for the March grand jury, Tweed had already taken steps to prevent another hostile inquest from getting under way. He and Alderman W. H. Cornell, a butcher, would supervise the selection of the talesmen. Enough damage had been done by the February panel. It indicted two Aldermen. But that was something that could be attended to later. Meanwhile bribe givers must be seen and given courage. Tweed thought of everything. He was never accused of lacking invention.

The ruling of the Aldermen-Judges came in for a great deal of censure. The presence of Tweed and his associates in

the court when the decision was rendered was justly criticized
in speech and editorial. On the day following the decision of
Brisley and Doherty, the following, typical of the journalistic
attacks, appeared in *The Tribune:*

"Do honest men unite in trained bands to awe courts and frown
down witnesses? Do honest men stand culprit-like at the doors
of Grand Jury rooms? Do honest Judges insist upon deciding
questions in which they are personally interested? If no bribe
has been received (not merely offered) how foolish in the Aldermen
to smother a document from the Grand Jury which would blow to
the winds all the charges of corruption, silence the thunders of the
Press, and establish the purity of the Common Council beyond the
reach of malice. If honest, why object to having it known?"

It is to be regretted that Greeley did not always remain a
journalist. His political pretensions sometimes stilled his voice
when the public weal needed it most. His thirst for place did
more. It made him purblind to the plunderings of the
politicians.

But Greeley and other spokesmen of the people demanded
more than the prosecution of the Aldermen. They urged that
the Common Council be shorn of some of its powers. These
demands assumed definite shape at a public meeting a week
after the February grand jury ended its labors. On this night
there was born the City Reform Party, and Peter Cooper,
whose philanthropy is perpetuated in the free institute of learning bearing his name, was elected President of the new organization. No novice in politics was this man of affairs. Back
in 1828 he had served as an Assistant Alderman. In those
days the Common Council elected the Mayor. It was not
until six years thereafter that the people were entrusted with
choosing their own Chief Executive.

Cooper had been one of those who had fought hardest for a
full measure of self-government for the city, yet he joined with
other well-meaning but mistaken reformers in a formal demand
on the Legislature to retake from the Common Council, that
essentially local privilege—the granting of local franchises.
It is such hysterical outbursts that have hampered and ham-

strung the efforts of municipal reformers the country over, fastening more firmly the hold of the filcher on the public funds.

The sentiments of the meeting were voiced by James W. Gerard, whose penchant for politics has been transmitted to his posterity. This particular Gerard and his brother William are among the few whose affluence gave them a place in a pamphlet published in 1845, entitled: "Wealth and Biography of the Wealthy Citizens of New York City, Comprising an Alphabetical Arrangement of Persons Estimated to be worth $100,000 and Upwards." Of James W. Gerard the booklet says: "A lawyer of great eminence and son of an auctioneer. He married an heiress of Philadelphia." Gerard voiced a vigorous imagery in homely phrase. In his address to the City Reform Party he said:

"Around the City Hall, round your Bureau Departments, round the meetings of your Common Council, you see a brood of leeches and bloodsuckers attacking the very vitals of your city. I never moved among these but I felt the atmosphere tainted. There have been hangers-on there for years and years, seeking the reward of party and political exertion, not however, for one party more than another, and troops of relations have swarmed there, and there have been men too who have grown rich and fat upon the public treasury."

Gerard urged that honest men, irrespective of party, be nominated for political office, saying: "On the altar of our municipal government let us sacrifice our party organizations, feelings, and principles."

Resolutions embodying the proposed reforms were offered by Henry J. Raymond, who had founded *The New York Times* eighteen months before. Prior to that he had been Greeley's chief editorial assistant. There was never any love between Raymond and Greeley, and the latter showed his scorn for his former associate by omitting Raymond's speech on the thin pretext of lack of space, in the otherwise complete report of the reform meeting that appeared in *The Tribune* the following morning. When Raymond had announced his intention to

HORACE GREELEY

REV. HENRY WARD BEECHER

start *The Times,* Greeley served the following notice upon the carriers of his journal:

"A new daily paper is to be issued in a few days, and any carrier of the *Tribune* who interests himself in said paper, in getting up routes, etc., prejudicial to the interests of the *Tribune,* will forfeit his right of property in the *Tribune* route. We give this notice now, that all who do so may know that they do it at the peril of losing their route on the *Tribune.*"

Raymond more than evened the score by depriving Greeley of three of his editors, the assistant foremen of the press and the composing rooms, a dozen good writers, and some of his circulation. This last was most galling to Greeley. A decade or so before the meeting Greeley had written: "Better a dinner of herbs with a large circulation than a stalled ox with a small one." And until Raymond had entered upon the scene the morning field had been shared almost exclusively by *The Herald* and *The Tribune.* Yet there was a compensating side to the entrance of Raymond into the publishing side of the craft. It gave Greeley another editor to quarrel with. Parton, in his highly eulogistic "Life of Horace Greeley," has this to say of the start of *The Times:*

"The success of *The Times* was signal and immediate, for three reasons: 1, it was conducted with tact, industry and prudence; 2, it was not *The Herald;* 3, it was not *The Tribune.* Before *The Times* appeared, *The Tribune* and *Herald* shared the cream of the daily paper business between them; but there was a large class who disliked *The Tribune's* principles and *The Herald's* want of principle. The majority of people take a daily paper solely to ascertain what is going on in the world. They are averse to profligacy and time-serving, and yet are offended at the independent avowal of ideas in advance of their own. And though Horace Greeley is not the least conservative of men, yet, from his practice of giving every new thought and every new man a hearing in the columns of his paper, unthinking persons received the impression that he was an advocate of every new idea, and a champion of every new man. They thought *The Tribune* was an unsafe, disorganizing paper. 'An excellent paper,' said they, 'and honest, but then it's so full of isms!' *The Times* stepped in with a complaisant bow, and won over twenty thousand of the ism-hating class in a single year, and yet without reducing the circulation of either of its elder rivals.   Where those twenty thousand subscribers came from is one of the mysteries of journalism."

We must allow for Parton's partisanship.

The chief reforms proposed in the resolutions offered by Raymond sought to take from the Aldermen their power to sit as Judges and to appoint policemen.   It was also proposed to abolish the Board of Assistant Aldermen.   In its stead a Board of Councilmen was proposed consisting of sixty members—three times the number of Assistant Aldermen.   And appropriations could be initiated only by the popular branch of the Common Council.

The proposed changes in government met with almost universal approval.   The political leaders, seeing the drift of things, were loudest in their praise of the Raymond resolutions. Every political group in the city passed resolutions indorsing the recommendations of the City Reform Party, and urged, as had been resolved at the meeting, that the State Legislature embody them in a referendum.   This the Legislature did, and in June of 1853 the proposals of the reformers were ratified by the overwhelming vote of 36,000 to 3,000.

Before these changes could be effected in the city government it was necessary that a majority pledged to the program of the reformers be elected to the Common Council.   With this in mind they nominated Democrats and Whigs who had shown independence within their party ranks and who were untainted by any talk of scandal.

Only the more reckless members of The Forty Thieves sought reëlection.   Tweed was cautious.   He did not believe in courting disaster.   Anyway, he could make a graceful exit, as he would take his seat in Congress that year.   And he had another explanation to offer to friends.   His business cares were increasing.   He had recently joined in partnership with his father and his brother Richard in the chairmaking business. They had a large and growing trade which called for direction that neither of them could give. But Bill—as his family always called him—never failed at anything. They had faith in him. And they looked to him to expand the chair industry far beyond their own limited capacity. Both pleaded with Bill to retire from politics at the end of his term in Congress. The father argued that they were in the way of making big profits, and further, he could see no reason why a decent man would seek election to office nowadays. When he was young it was a mark of honor to hold public place. Now the good had to share the censure of the bad. Politics had grown into a dirty business, at least in the city. Everybody was talking of the corruption in public life. It was worth a man's reputation to hold office. Tweed knew his father. He let him talk on. He admitted, and this pleased the elder, that they could make greater profits out of the two factories by devoting all their energies to them, and he promised to divide his time between the brush factory and the chairmaking establishment. But—and this Tweed did not utter aloud—he knew from experience that a faithless servant of the people had greater opportunities for gain than the average successful business man. He had proven it. Tweed left his father in a happy frame of mind.

Tweed warned some of his cronies in the Board not to run for reëlection that fall. He saw the reform wave approaching. So did the leaders of the two major parties, who made their plans accordingly. They fully realized that no possible amount of knavery at the polls could be effective. The people, by a vote of twelve to one, had revealed their sentiments in the June referendum. And there was no astonishment when the election returns showed that a majority of the nominees of the City Reform Party had been elected to the Common Council by decisive pluralities. The people shouted hosannas. The politicians held their peace. They knew the game. They played it every day in the year. Later on they would show the reformers a trick or two. They had already paid off a few scores. The city advertising had been taken from the newspapers which had questioned the integrity of The Forty Thieves. But this did not mean less taken from the pockets of the taxpayers. For every dollar of advertising denied the advocates of the reformers, three dollars were given to what Greeley, in telling of *The Tribune's* loss, called the *Satanic Press.*

The politicians showed the people some of their tricks before the new Common Council, controlled by men elected on the non-partisan City Reform ticket, had been in session four months. Needed changes that had been promised were not made. The attacks were leveled chiefly at the lawmakers. Greeley, although an absurd politician, was a most astute analyst of political phenomena. And thus he appraised the failure of the Council to realize the hopes of the reform elements:

"Much of the blame no doubt lies with the Common Council, and grows out of the power of those representing the great political parties in the two Boards to league together and sell out to each other the interests of the city as partisan or personal considerations may decide."

The politicians had again outwitted the people. They were all back feeding at the same old trough.

Tweed, who was now devoting most of his time to the chair and brush industries—the factories were close together on Pearl Street—seldom let a week pass without visiting the City Hall. He was always there when the Common Council was sitting if he was not in Washington attending to his Congressional duties. Tweed did not like the atmosphere of the National Capitol. A first term Congressman was merely tolerated. Every one was extremely polite, but this formalism grated on the soul of the gregarious Gothamite. He missed the friendly greetings of the lobbyists who haunted the City Hall. He missed particularly the most courageous of them all, Jake Sharp, who had paid dearly for his Broadway street car franchise, which the courts invalidated. But Sharp did not let up in his endeavors to obtain the franchise, fighting against what seemed insurmountable odds—the vast millions of the Merchant Prince and his friends, and the power that went with these riches; the opposition of holders of other street car franchises, who preferred the old stage coaches on Broadway to a competing line of horse cars. Sharp could afford to go on with the battle. He had grown rich as a dealer in timber and a builder of docks. He had invested wisely in real estate that rose steadily in value. And with his own funds he fought old A. T. Stewart and his group. Year in and year out the war of wits and wealth continued. The scene shifted to Albany when the power to grant franchises was taken from the local authorities and reverted to the State Legislature. But each year that he lived Stewart outmatched Jake Sharp. And when the Merchant Prince had amassed $30,000,000 he died. He would have left at least half a million more if he had not fought Jake Sharp's attempt to put street cars on Broadway. He never paid out any moneys in the crude shape of bribes. He was the city's great Merchant Prince, and had to sustain the quasi-royal reputation. He spent his hundreds of thousands in paying the expenses of men having influence with legislatures, for legal disbursements and other items that were wholly within the law. A fat fee to a wise lawyer is never split with a corrupt legislator. But even the grave did not prove a barrier to the extortionate demands on Stewart's purse. Ghouls, in the dead of night, stole his body from its vault in the graveyard of St. Mark's-in-the-Bouwerie and held the remains three years until a ransom of $20,000 was paid. With the death of Stewart the soul of the opposition to Jake Sharp's project died. Sharp had no foe, worthy of the name, to challenge him. He now schemed to have the power to grant franchises re-delegated to the municipal authorities. In this he had the support of most of the city's representatives in the State Legislature. He kept well in the background and the restoration was effected. There could not be any logical reason for opposition to the measure.

Once the Aldermen were again empowered to grant franchises a group of influential financiers from Philadelphia came in search of the prize that Sharp had been struggling to obtain for more than a generation. Opposing both petitioners were local traction companies whose earnings would be adversely affected by a rival's street cars on Broadway. But Sharp lavished money on the Aldermen without stint. They weltered in a veritable flood of gold. The greater splendor won. And in his long-delayed hour of triumph Sharp could not forget Sturtevant, poor old Oscar Sturtevant, with his gentle, patrician features, who had defied Justice Campbell's injunction when Sharp first sought the grant. Too bad Sturtevant had such a proud heart. To have let such a little thing as fifteen days' imprisonment wear down his spirit. But Sharp was destined to have a larger understanding of the disgrace that had sent Sturtevant to an untimely grave. Now the unsuccessful corruptionists raised the same cry of bribery and corruption that attended the granting of the first Broadway franchise. This time proofs were adduced of Sharp's guilt, and of the culpability of the Aldermen. All were indicted. Three of the Aldermen confessed and turned State's evidence. Several others fled to Canada to escape Sing Sing. Sharp was tried and convicted. He was sentenced to four and one-half years' imprisonment. His counsel appealed from the judgment of the lower court and had it reversed. Sharp, who had spent four months behind prison bars, was released on $40,000 bail. The veteran briber could now understand the great grief that had been Sturtevant's, whose death was directly attributable to Sharp's corruption. For Sharp himself fell a victim to it, dying five months after his conviction and sentence had been set aside.

CHAPTER VIII

THE year Tweed took his seat in Congress he was thirty
years old. In the summer of that year a precocious, adven-
turous youth who had been baptized Jason, arrived in New
York with a mousetrap under his arm. And like the Thes-
salian prince whose name he bore, this lad, just turned seventeen, was in search of the golden fleece. He hoped that the
mousetrap, which he invented, would point the way to the
consecrated grove. Save that he was successful in his quest,
there is no other parallel in the two Jasons. The modern
Jason, who was to play a great part in Tweed's life, was not
of heroic size. He was small, thin, frail and hollow-chested.
His face was peaked and of the color of old parchment. He
had a little dry cough that awakened pity. Yet pity he seldom
sought, and if he ever showed any to a foe, it has escaped the
record. His physical frailty was compensated by an indomitable will, a nervous energy which defied fatigue and an unscrupulous disregard of all conventions—save one. At this
early age he had already displayed the untrustworthiness that
was to be the dominant note of his life. At the age of fifteen
he worked as a clerk in a country store, whose proprietor also
did a small real estate business. The boy learned that his
employer was offering $2,000 for a desirable piece of property
for which the owner was demanding $2,500. It was worth far
more. While the negotiations were on, Jason induced his
father, who owned a small farm eleven miles away, to buy the
land. Within a short time thereafter this parcel was sold for
$4,000. This betrayal of trust cost the scheming clerk his
job. It also ended a ripening affection that had sprung up
between him and the storekeeper's daughter. But in the eyes
of this abnormal youth the handsome profit that accrued from
the deal outweighed the loss of a young girl's love and exile

95

from his boyhood scenes. The young rustic was born in the Catskills, in the little village of Roxbury. Here, too, was John Burroughs born, and here the naturalist sleeps his last, long sleep. It seems strange that the small village which produced a John Burroughs should also produce a Jason Gould, or Jay Gould, as he began calling himself about the time he came to the Metropolis with a mousetrap under his arm.

The Metropolis dazzled the country youth. He laid his mousetrap on the seat of a horse car on which he was riding while he went out on the driver's platform to see more of the sights of the town. While the car was in motion a fellow-passenger jumped off the rear platform. Gould, suspicious of all men, at once thought of his mousetrap. It was gone. He looked after the passenger who had leaped unceremoniously from the rear platform. He had Jay Gould's invention under his arm. Gould now made an unceremonious leap, and after a sharp sprint, overtook the thief, who was glad to surrender the package containing the mousetrap and make his escape. Gould sold his invention and took his departure from the city. It was not until six years later that he returned to New York to make it his home. Here he continued his plundering and betraying, only on a larger and unprecedented scale. He was an unscrupulous fellow, of whom but one good word has been said. It is said that he was faithful to his wife. We are all familiar with that phrase. We have heard it said of the most corrupt scoundrels in public life. We will cease to hear it when a Constitutional Amendment is adopted decreeing that only the epicene may hold office or positions of quasi-public trust. Let us give Gould the benefit of the doubt, a doubt raised by his constant companionship and partnership with a man who used the flesh of women as one of his forms of bribery, a doubt raised by his frequent presence in the house of a beautiful and notorious harlot which was the rendezvous of Tweed and his cronies.

Gould had made his own way in the world from the age of fourteen. Late in life, when a phase of his piratical operations in Wall Street was under investigation by a committee of the United States Senate, Gould thus described his early struggles:

"My father owned a small farm then and kept a dairy of twenty cows. I was the only boy in the family, so I had to attend to the cows in the morning and assist my sisters in milking them. I used to take them out in the morning and go for them at night. I did not like farming in that way, so I went to my father and told him I wanted to go to school. He said I was too young, but finally gave me permission, and I started off and showed myself at school. [This was at Hobart, a village eleven miles from Gould's home.] I had learned to write, and as I wrote a pretty good hand, a storekeeper in the village gave me the job to write up his books at night, and in that way I supported myself through school.

"I was about fourteen when I left home, and I spent about a year at this school; then I got into a country store and made myself useful sweeping it out in the morning and learning the business during the day. My duties employed me from six in the morning until ten o'clock at night. In the meantime I had acquired a taste for mathematics and especially for surveying and engineering. I took them up after I left school. I used to get up at three o'clock and study from three until six, when I had to open the store, and I finally got a pretty good idea of that branch and concluded to start out as a surveyor. I heard of a man in Ulster County that was looking for an assistant. He was making a map of that county and I wrote to him. He engaged me at $20 a month. When I left, my father offered me money, but I concluded to burn my ships behind me and I took only enough for my fare. This man started me out to make the surveys, to see where the roads were, and to locate the residences. The map was to be useful as a record, and when I started he said to me:

" 'Now, while you go along you get trusted for your beds, what you eat, etc., and I will come afterwards and pay them.'

"I think two or three days out I had to stay overnight at a place where they charged a shilling for supper, a shilling for lodging, and sixpence for breakfast. I explained the arrangement for payment, and took my book out to enter the amount of the bill, but the man who kept the house declared with an oath that he would not have anything of the kind.

" 'You don't know this man,' said he. 'He has failed three times. You have got the money, I know you have, and I want my bill.'

"I had not a cent, and I pulled my pockets out to show him that I had not, and I said:

" 'You must trust me.'

" 'Well, I will trust you, but I won't trust him.'

"This had such an effect upon me," Gould continued, "that it seemed to me as if the world had come to an end that day. I did not know where I was to get a dinner, and I did not try till long after three o'clock, after this rebuff. I was naturally a timid boy and it had a great effect upon me. I then debated about throwing up the whole engagement, but I went out and had a good cry where nobody could see me. Then I got down and prayed and I felt better afterwards. So I made up my mind to go ahead—made up my mind to die in the last ditch. I was hungry and I decided to go into the first house I came to and get something to eat, and I did so. The woman treated me kindly, gave me some bread and milk, and when I went away I told her to enter it down. In the meantime her husband came in, and I had got about four rods away from the house when I heard him hallooing after me. With the morning's scare in my mind I thought that he was going to finish me, but he said: 'I want you to come back and make me a noon mark.' I don't know whether you know what that is."

"Yes, I know," interjected one of the investigators, "but explain to these gentlemen what it is."

"It is a line north and south, by which the farmers can regulate their clocks, the sun being due south at noon," said Gould. "I went back with my compass and made him a noon mark, and when I got through he asked me what was to pay. I said, 'Nothing.'

" 'Oh, yes,' said he. 'I want to pay you; our surveyor always charges $1.'

"The food I had eaten was one shilling and he had paid me seven shillings, the balance of the dollar. This gave me an idea, and from this time I went on and paid my expenses making noon marks for the farmers. When I had finished my survey the man who employed me failed and could not pay me, but there were two other journeymen he had employed to make the surveys and I proposed to them to go on and finish the map. They decided to do so, but they wanted their names to it alone. I said: 'Very well, I will sell out to you,' and I sold out my interest in the map for $500.

"This was the first money I ever earned. I went on and helped them finish the map, so that I sold out my interest in the perfected map. Then I went forward with this little capital and made similar surveys of Albany and Delaware Counties, and made up my mind to go alone. They yielded me very well and I soon accumulated $5,000."

While many important particulars were suppressed by Gould in his testimony before the Senate Committee, his story of his boyhood years is true in all detail. Much that he related to the Senatorial inquisitors was told for effect. But his story of crying and praying beside the roads when hunger assailed him rings true. Before he left his father's farm he attended a revival held in the Methodist Church in the little village of Roxbury. Toward the end of the week, after an impressive exhortation by the preacher, Jason advanced to the altar, confessed his sins and prayed for salvation. But young Gould found it easy to throw off the restraints of religion whenever he found it to his material advantage to do so. And like Tweed, he recognized no particular sect. Before he attended the Methodist revival he worshiped in the Dutch Reformed Church, the popular denomination of the Catskill region. Later in life, he went on Sundays to a Presbyterian house of prayer.

From the time that Gould left the little mountain farm where he was born he came in contact with only the kindliest of men. Who would not help a youth trying to make his own way? But there was hardly a man he dealt with, even the most generous to him, that he did not defraud.

To find the cause of Gould's hardness of heart we must go back to his boyhood days on the farm at Roxbury. Gould had lost his mother at the age of four. He had only a dim recollection of her. Early he was made acquainted with a stepmother. Even a mother on a stony mountain farm, where life is a ceaseless struggle, has not a great deal of time to demonstrate her affection for her children. But there is a look in a mother's eyes that caresses the heart. Her weary smile at the end of a long day's work inspires. Her harsh word in a moment of fatigue is recognized as a mask of a love sublime. But the most devoted of foster-parents may not be abrupt with another's child without being unjustly accused of cruelty. Gould knew only a foster-mother's care. As a child he did the work of a hired man. When he was strong enough—he was puny as a boy—to carry a milk pail he was up at dawn milking cows, spending the rest of the day doing other chores that would not overtax his strength, and at dusk, a dog at his heels, he would scurry panting through the surrounding woods to find the cows that had wandered from the crudely railed-in pastures, and once they were returned to the stable for the night, he would again sit on a stool and milk with the light of a dim lantern throwing spooky shadows on the floor and rough sides of the cow shed. All this would have been a labor of love had his march back to the barnlike home ended at a supper table where a beaming mother's smile awaited him. Others who have had harder lives as children have come through the poignant sufferings of childhood with tender hearts. But Gould was of different stuff. His heart turned to stone. It is not to be wondered at that when he reached the age of fourteen he should seek other scenes. A boy with fewer talents and less self-assurance would have done it. Gould had these in large store.

Gould's father, John B. Gould, for whom he cherished a lasting love, was the first white male child born in Delaware County. From him Jay inherited his inordinate capacity for work. From him also he inherited the shrewdness that knew no bounds. After he defrauded the country storekeeper he found work with John J. Snyder, who was making a map of Ulster County, which adjoins Delaware County. Snyder was an engineer and a surveyor. To young Jason there was something godlike in such a man. But when Snyder failed him— Snyder had little and Gould still less—it was not astonishing that he should fall on his knees by the roadside and pray. Gould when he sought Divine aid had a ten cent piece in his pocket. This was all the wealth he had in the world. He never parted with that ten cent piece until he took to his death bed. It was his one superstition. Gould evidently did not include Snyder in his prayer, for shortly thereafter he left him, and took with him all the notes he had made for Snyder's projected map of Ulster County, and absconded also with Snyder's odometer, an instrument used for measuring distances. This device is ordinarily attached to the wheel of a carriage. In the jargon of surveyors, when the meter is worked by hand, wheel-barrow fashion, it is ¬alled a wheel.

Gould next formed a partnership with another local civil

engineer, Peter J. Tillson, of Rosendale. A few miles away, at Saugerties, lived Peter H. Brink, who had worked with Gould for Snyder. Brink was also taken into the partnership. At Gould's first meeting with Tillson, he told of his hardships with Snyder, and tears ran down his cheeks as he volunteered that he was almost penniless. He did not tell Tillson that he had stolen Snyder's wheel, for he sold the instrument to his new-found friend.

For six months the partnership continued. Gould and Brink spent the week-ends on the Tillson farm, comparing notes, and building up the map. Tillson's father, who ran the farm, admired the industry of young Gould, who spent the entire week-ends working on his notes under the light of a camphene lamp. Kerosene had not yet been introduced.

"He was all business," said Tillson in speaking of his associate. "Why, even at meal times he was always talking map. He was a worker, and my father used to say: 'Look at Gould! Isn't he a driver?'"

Two days after Christmas, 1852, when the work was completed, Tillson and Brink purchased Gould's interest in the map. Jason, because of his minority—he lacked five months to the day of being seventeen—acted as the agent of his father in the transaction. The paper young Gould executed then in his feminine hand, read:

Dec. 27th, 1852.

Recvd of Oliver J. Tillson & Peter H. Brink Ninety Dollars & Wheel in full of all debts and demands & dues against them & the Ulster county Map.

JASON GOULD.

for JOHN B. GOULD.

The wheel was the stolen instrument Gould had sold to Tillson. Little did any of the young mapmakers dream that December day that thirty years thence, one of them would be able to deposit $1,000,000 bail for the most notorious public thief of all time.

After Gould returned to his home in Roxbury for a brief visit, the Tillsons and Brink in examining Gould's surveying notebooks found an occasional signature reading: "Jay Gould." So we know that before Jason came to New York the following year, while Tweed, who was to be his staunch ally, was rounding out his two-year Aldermanic term with The Forty Thieves, young Gould was contemplating a change of name.

In the next three years Gould continued his surveying and mapmaking in other sections of the State. He also found time to write the "History of Delaware County and Border Wars of New York, Containing a Sketch of Early Settlements of the County and a History of the Late Anti-Rent Difficulties in Delaware [County] with Other Historical and Other Miscellaneous Matter Never before Published."

The book was published in 1856, when Gould was twenty years old, and he peddled it while continuing his surveying. About this time he made the acquaintance of Zadoc Pratt, then a man nearing seventy. Pratt had been the largest tanner of his day, and a power in New York State politics. He lived at Prattsville, Greene County, a few miles east of Gould's birthplace, and had represented the Catskill district in Congress for ten years. While making surveys for Pratt, the old tanner was impressed with the youth's boundless activity. It had once been his. Before he was sixty, Pratt had had 30,000 men on his payroll. Yet with all his press of business he found time—he felt it a duty—to grapple with the problems of government. He was one of the earliest proponents of cheap postage. He advocated the establishment of the Bureau of Statistics, since developed into the Department of the Interior, and took a prominent part in the first survey of the Pacific Railroad line. The proposition made to Gould was that he go into partnership with the old man and develop a new tannery—Pratt, nearly a decade before, had closed his extensive plant at Prattsville. The site chosen was in Pennsylvania, and Pratt named it after his protégé—Gouldsboro.

Gould threw his tireless energy into the new enterprise, going into the forest with the men who were to clear the ground. Gould felled the first tree and stripped it of its bark. A blacksmith shop was the first structure erected, and in this Gould slept and ate until the tannery was ready for operation.

Old Zadoc Pratt had put $120,000 into the Gouldsboro tannery. With Pratt's reputation as a tanner, the business was good from the start. In a year it had grown into the largest tannery in the country. Gould made an occasional visit to New York, the principal market for the tanned hides, became acquainted with the big leather dealers in "the Swamp"—Beekman's old swamp, northeast of which the first of Tweed's American primogenitors settled a century or so before. Among the purchasers of leather from the Pratt and Gould tannery was Charles M. Leupp, one of the wealthiest merchants in the city, who lived in what was regarded as the most splendid dwelling house in New York. His home, on the corner of Madison Avenue and Twenty-fifth Street, reflected the culture of the owner. Gould quickly wormed his way into the confidence of Leupp. This was not difficult. For Leupp too had been a poor youth. His industry won him a partnership in the leather business of Gideon Lee and Company and the daughter of the head of the firm. Leupp when Gould met him was an official of the Tradesmen's Bank, and a director of the Erie Railroad. He had a fondness for the frail, low-voiced youth, and sometimes lunched with him, and talked to him of the great future for the railroads. Gould saw it.

Gould now set out systematically to defraud Pratt, and unknown to the old tanner, started a private bank at Stroudsburg. Gould was now a banker. This could not remain a secret long, and when Pratt heard of it, he paid one of his infrequent visits to the Pennsylvania tannery and began an examination of the books of the concern. Gould, like Tweed, was a bookkeeper. But Tweed, unlike Gould, never robbed his private employers.

Pratt, who had wondered for months why he was not obtaining more income from the tannery at Gouldsboro, now began to suspect that his youthful partner had been defrauding him. Gould protested his innocence. Pratt insisted on going through the books. But he might as well have tried to decipher the hieroglyphics in the Book of the Dead. Those books were kept so that no one but Gould could make head or tail of them. In his low voice, his dark yellow face distorted in mock grief,

Gould pathetically insisted that Pratt was doing him a grave injustice. Pratt said that the books were improperly kept and threatened to close the tannery at once.

Gould protested his innocence, and declared that all he had taken out of the business beyond his share, which was dollar for dollar what Pratt had drawn, were his expenses and the disbursements incidental to carrying on the enterprise.

"Buy or sell!" said Pratt, peremptorily, who was so strait-laced that he could not continue in business with one of whom he entertained even the slightest suspicion. And Gould had more than half-convinced him that there had been no dishonesty.

Gould offered to buy Pratt's half-interest in the tannery for $60,000, saying that he might be able to raise the money among friends in New York.

This was acceptable to the veteran tanner. Gould went to New York and interested Leupp in the proposal, and the leather merchant agreed to let Gould draw on him for the money, in consideration of giving him a half-share in the business. Exit Pratt, another victim of Gould's ingratitude.

Gould continued keeping the books after forming his partnership with Leupp. He merely robbed Pratt. But his latest benefactor was to be treated worse. Gould, as partner of Leupp, engaged in various speculations in Leupp's name, without the knowledge of Leupp. He invested in a rival tannery. He was out to corner the market in hides. He continued drawing on Leupp for more funds until the New York merchant began to suspect that all was not well. Like Pratt, Leupp went over the books of the tannery, and when he learned the extent to which Gould had involved him financially was too overcome to protest. He returned home. The disastrous panic of 1857 had just swept the country. Bankruptcies and failures were the order of the day. Leupp, who was despondent over the general business depression, returned to New York, believing that Gould had ruined him. The treachery of his partner preyed on his mind, and on going to his home one evening, he took a last look at the fine canvases on the walls, the richly bound books on the mahogany shelves, and ended it all with a bullet.

The tragic death of Leupp stirred the town. He was one of the wealthiest of its citizens and his home, which cost $150,000 to build, was one of the most splendid pieces of architecture in the city. Years later the ghost of Leupp was to rise up and plague the man who drove him to his death.

Gould made his first big killing during the panic of 1857 and gratified the ambition Leupp had inspired—that of being a railroad owner. Railroad values went tumbling. The first mortgage bonds of a small road, sixty-two miles long, known as the Rutland and Washington Railroad, were selling for ten cents on the dollar. Gould bought all the bonds. Most of the money had been Leupp's and Pratt's. He also acquired a control of the common stock. Gould took entire charge of the road. He was elected its president, and also served as its secretary and treasurer and superintendent. Gould had celebrated his majority in May of the same year. A president of a railroad at twenty-one, with a background as banker, tanner, surveyor, country store clerk, and farm boy! One cannot question Gould's genius. His railroad venture made him a rich man.

After Leupp's suicide Gould was accused of setting out to defraud the heirs of his former partner. They were young women. That meant nothing to Gould. He wanted complete control of the tannery, and he began negotiations with that in view. Leupp's daughters were only too willing to wash their hands of a business that had brought on their father's death. After a long delay, deliberately created by Gould, the heirs were offered $60,000, the sum Leupp had given Gould to buy out Pratt. No consideration was given by Gould for the moneys he had drawn from Leupp as his partner, nor for any of the intangible assets of the property. Relatives of the heirs suggested that they refuse this offer, but the women wanted to forget Gould and his works with all possible speed. Gould proposed $10,000 cash, and the balance to be paid in five annual installments of a like sum. When an examination of the papers which Gould had drawn up and asked the young women to sign disclosed that Gould had made no provision for the payment of interest on the balance of $50,000, legal advisers informed the heirs that they were dealing with an unscrupulous swindler. The young women now turned for advice to David W. Lee, an old man, a relation by marriage of their father, and his one-time partner. Lee advised action. He was convinced that a man of Gould's heartlessness would attempt to deprive the girls of their share of the property, and that under the circumstances there was but one course to take—to take possession of the tannery and hold it until the courts determined their respective rights. One of the daughters of Leupp empowered him to act as their agent, Lee took the first train to Scranton, Pennsylvania. There the old man hired fifteen men, and then hurried on to Gouldsboro, where he barricaded the office and posted some of his little band outside. Others he placed at various points around the tannery. Some were armed.

Gould was in New York when these preparations for holding the tannery were being completed, and not until he returned to Gouldsboro did he learn of Lee's successful coup. While the move astonished Gould, he was not quite unprepared for it. Realizing that some time he might need aid, he had bestowed occasional largesse on some of the workers in the tannery, men that he instinctively recognized as leaders among their fellows.

Gouldsboro was then a village of three hundred inhabitants, most of them employees at the tannery. It boasted a small hotel where whiskey made in illicit mountain stills was the staple refreshment. Gould called the leaders of the men around him, painted a pitiful picture of a deserted village if Lee and his cutthroats from Scranton—as Gould called them—were to have their way. Gould played host to these men, telling them as they ate and drank, that he was the sole owner of the tannery, that Lee was seeking to rob him on a trumped-up claim. The simple backwoodsmen, as the whiskey began to take effect, advocated storming the tannery. Gould smiled grimly. Here was the thought that had been coursing through his mind from the moment he learned of Lee's action. Gould agreed that the tannery must be taken, but he wanted to consult with all his old employees before he took any decisive step. Let Gould say when that was to be and they would be on hand to the last man, and their friends and neighbors as well. It was now early in the forenoon. Gould thought a moment and then replied that he would meet the men at the hotel the following morning. Gould's drink-filled tools went on their way.

Nor did Gould remain idle. It was not his nature to do so. He moved among the villagers, and inspired all with a hatred of the men in possession of the tannery. Scranton cutthroats every one of them, save their leader! And he was a shrewd schemer from New York!

Had Gould been leading an army in hostile territory he could not have been more cautious. He employed scouts. One of them brought back word that Lee had a musket loaded for Gould. The next morning all the males of the village, and many from nearby farms, came to the hotel. *The New York Herald* correspondent estimated that between 180 and 250 men answered Gould's call. Most of them were armed with muskets, rifles, and other weapons. Many of them carried axes. When the men had been treated generously to whiskey, Gould mounted an upturned empty box, while his army of tanners, lumberjacks, and farmers gathered on the grounds in front of the hotel. Some of those in the crowd towered above Gould, despite the additional height given him by his rude rostrum. It was a brief address the little man made. He told them that he wanted to save the village by regaining possession of the tannery.

"Friends," said Gould in ending his speech, "use no unnecessary violence but be sure and get the tannery."

If murder were done, Gould could not be held accountable. He had warned the men not to use unnecessary violence. But he also told them to "be sure and get the tannery."

On marched Gould's little army tanneryward. Gould was with them, directing their movement. But he was far from leading them. His five feet six inches of timidity trailed in the rear, completely covered by half-drunken bravos.

Presently Gould's supporters charged the tannery. There was a crash of splintering wood as axes cut through the barricaded doors. Fast as they could shoot and reload the armed members of Gould's mob fired through the openings. Then they rushed into the building and hurled Lee's men from windows. When the uneven battle was over Gould was again in possession of the tannery. Many of Lee's defenders were injured, four of them from gunshots. One was shot through the breast.

Lee now invoked the law. Gould answered with counter-suits. The litigation was protracted and proved expensive to Gould. But he remained in possession of the tannery, which died as Leupp had died—a victim of Gould's greed.

It was not until the close of 1859 that Gould established himself in New York. He was then twenty-three years of age. He hung out his shingle on the edge of the old "Swamp" district, at 39 Spruce Street, one hundred yards or so from the birthplace of Tweed. Less than a decade was to pass before these two Titans, Tweed and Gould, were to meet, and contemporaneously set new high marks for villainy in their respective fields, Gould in the realm of finance, and Tweed in the sphere of public life.

CHAPTER IX

T<small>WEED</small>'s career in Congress was colorless. It was not his field. At the beginning of his second and last year he decided that he would not be a candidate to succeed himself. Tweed, who had now determined on a political career, and whose advice was sought in all the party councils, after taking counsel with older heads, decided that it was a bad year for a candidate in a debatable district. A nomination for local office on either the Whig or Democratic ticket almost anywhere in the North was of questionable value in the year 1854. The ranks of both parties were once more being thinned by the Native American Party, which was assuming national proportions. The South alone was comparatively free from the racial and religious bigotry fostered by the Native Americans.

Tweed, then thirty-one years old, watched in wonder the preliminary plays of the rival political leaders in the early part of the year 1854. He had made a personal canvass of his district and found that friends, men whose liberal views he would have sworn by, had joined the Native Americans with the zeal of early Christian martyrs. Tweed was invited to cast his lot with the "Know-Nothings," as the Native Americans were popularly denominated because of their uniform response to inquiries concerning the organization. Tweed declined. He did not regard any nomination that year as worthy of acceptance.

There was another drain upon the Whigs and Democrats in New York City. The City Reform Party, which had swept the city the previous year on a non-partisan platform, was making all preparations for the fall campaign, intending to put a complete ticket in the field. And this group was composed of men who ordinarily voted the Democratic and Whig tickets.

Tammany was further weakened by defections of the anti-slavery element who were acting independently as Free Soilers,

109

and who before many months were over, were to coalesce with the Whigs in forming the Republican Party. Still another element of discord weakened the ranks of the local Democrats, dividing them into two factions, of almost equal strength. One group styled itself the Softshells, abbreviated to Softs. The opposition was known as Hardshells or Hards. Both were openly antagonistic to the Know-Nothings, as Tammany's chief strength now resided in citizens of foreign birth.

The leader of the Softs was Fernando Wood. His followers, high and low, always addressed him as Fernandy. It pleased him, for he was a man of great wealth who called himself one of the people. He had the face of an Apollo. He was five feet eleven inches high, slender, and had deep blue eyes that always smiled, and a wealth of dark brown hair. His voice was low and soft in conversation, but on the rostrum it was deep and carrying. Four years before he had been the Tammany nominee for Mayor, losing by a small margin. He had financed his own campaign. Tweed, who had canvassed for Wood in 1850, had cultivated a violent dislike for Fernandy. Yet for four years Tweed had followed every movement of Fernando Wood as an astronomer follows the progress of a new star in the heavens. Wood was a luminary of lunar magnitude. Tweed disliked him for his hypocrisy. Wood was one of the numerous Whig and Democrat politicians who had clandestinely assumed the obligations of the Know-Nothings, safe in assurance that their membership would never be disclosed to any loyal member of the organization. Wood was one of the inner circle of the Know-Nothings. And now, on the eve of the nominating conventions, Wood was openly seeking the Tammany nomination for Mayor. His enemies within the organization now made public what only the Know-Nothings had known. Wood met this statement of fact with a perjured disclaimer. No viler type had Boito in mind when he penned this article of the Iagoan creed: "I believe that everything in him is a lie—the tear, the kiss, the smile, sacrifice, and honor."

Despite his given name, there was no Latin strain in Wood. He was born in Philadelphia, June 14, 1812. A mere recital of the date would not suit the purpose of Wood. For the benefit of the Native Americans he indulged in the periphrasis of prejudice, speaking always of his natal day as the day when Madison's cabinet decided to declare war against England. Twisting the lion's tail has always been the popular pastime of the American politician. Wood was of Quaker stock, the first of the family having emigrated from Wales in 1650. And thus he accounts, in an inspired biography, for his given name:

"Henry, and Isaac, and Zachariah, and Benjamin, had been the simple prenomina of his ancestors. But his mother had been reading the *Three Spaniards,* one of those blood and thunder, chain-clanking, subterranean galleried mysterious novels, brought into vogue by Horace Walpole's 'Castle of Otranto,' and Mrs. Anne Radcliffe's ditto (*sic*) of Udolpho. Now one Fernando was the hero of this famous book, a notable fellow, no doubt, at any rate much admired by Mrs. Wood, who, for such admiration's sake bestowed his name upon her son."

His father was a cigarmaker, and moved to New York shortly after Fernando's birth. At the age of eight the boy attended the private school of James Shea, teacher of mathematics in the grammar school of Columbia College—it had not yet attained the dignity of an university. At the age of thirteen Fernando found employment as a clerk in a broker's office. With his first week's salary in his pocket he determined to leave home. Before he reached his majority he had learned his father's trade. At the age of twenty he had his own cigar and tobacco shop on Pearl Street. Three years later he failed in business. He clerked for another year and in 1836 opened a groggery. In a year or so he was rich through bilking sailors and longshoremen after they became helplessly drunk from his crude, home-made whiskey. His grog shop—after he entered politics he always referred to it as a grocery store—was on the corner of Rector and Washington Streets, a block from the waterfront.

Wood uttered a half-truth in calling the shop a grocery. But the whole truth demanded more. Even groggery would have been inadequate. It was a groggery-grocery. There were many of its kind in the poorer parts of the town. And they were quaint, these places, as the following contemporary picture discloses:

"On either hand piles of cabbages, potatoes, squashes, eggplants, tomatoes, turnips, eggs, dried apples, chestnuts and beans rise like miniature mountains round you. At the left hand as you enter is a row of little boxes, containing anthracite and charcoal, nails, plug tobacco, &c. &c. which are dealt out in any quantity, from a bushel or a dollar to a cent's-worth. On a shelf nearby is a pile of fire-wood, seven sticks for sixpence, or a cent apiece, and kindling-wood three sticks for two cents. Along the walls are ranged upright casks containing lamp-oil, molasses, rum, whisky, brandy, and all sorts of cordials (carefully manufactured in the back room, where a kettle and furnace, with all the necessary instruments of spiritual devilment are provided for the purpose). The cross-beams that support the ceiling are thickly hung with hams, tongues, sausages, strings of onions, and other light and airy articles, and at every step you tumble over a butter-firkin or a meal-bin. Across one end of the room runs a 'long, low, black' counter, armed at either end with bottles of poisoned fire-water, doled out at three cents a glass to the loafers and bloated women who frequent the place—while the shelves behind are filled with an uncatalogueable jumble of candles, allspice, crackers, sugar and tea, pickles, ginger, mustard, and other kitchen necessaries. In the opposite corner is a shorter counter filled with three-cent pies, mince, apple, pumpkin and custard—all kept smoking hot— where you can get a cup of coffee with plenty of milk and sugar, for the same price, and buy a hat-full of cigars 'Americans with Spanish wrappers' for a penny."

With the moneys made honestly and otherwise in his grog shop, Wood, at the end of two years, purchased three sailing ships which engaged in the coastwise trade. Later he added five more to his fleet. In 1840 Wood was elected to Congress. He was then twenty-eight years old, and a rich man. When gold was discovered in California one of the first ships laden with Forty-niners that sailed from New York for San Francisco was the bark *John W. Cator*, which flew the house flag of Wood. A goodly part of his fortune was made in real estate transactions, and in many of these the city lost heavily, and Wood profited commensurately. Wealthy as all these ventures made him, he was made wealthier still by the lotteries which his brother Benjamin nominally owned, the same Benjamin who "often spouted [pawned] a pair of shoes to obtain fifty cents with which to operate in policies, and finally, when he became a policy dealer himself and the backer, made a sum sufficient to buy a few illegal lottery privileges down South, and out of it clears annually a few hundred thousand dollars, ruining thousands of poor but virtuous families."

Throughout his business career he was noted for his sharp practices, and had the reputation of being a swindler. He was. Money was ever a temptation to him. He cheated a business partner in a business deal in 1848 and was indicted for this, but a friendly district attorney delayed the indictment a day, and Wood escaped prosecution by pleading the statute of limitations. The presentment was twenty-four hours late. In 1849, at the age of thirty-seven, Wood retired from active business and entered a profession. Or to be precise, he created a profession, the science of politics.

When Wood retired from commercial pursuits he made no secret of his pretensions. He would be Mayor of New York, then Governor of the State and finally President of the United States.

The leaders of the Democrats—they were seldom called Tammanyites in New York at this early day, the popular appellation being Loco-Focos—had planned to nominate John J. Cisco, a Wall Street banker, who later was Assistant Treasurer of the United States. But Wood had bribed a majority of the delegates to the convention and he was nominated by a majority of seven, Cisco receiving twenty-two votes to the twenty-nine cast for Wood. Philip Hone, then in his seventieth year, has left us this impression of what the nomination of Wood meant to men who looked upon politics as something other than a means of personal enrichment:

"The Loco-Focos have nominated Fernando Wood for Mayor. There was a time when it was thought of some consequence that the incumbent of this office should be at least an honest man. Fernando Wood! Let the books of the Mechanics' Bank tell his story. There is no amount of degradation too great for the party who expects to 'rule the roost,' and probably will. Fernando Wood, instead of occupying the mayor's seat, ought to be on the rolls of the State Prison. But our blessed universal suffrage will raise a flame with this Wood to drive away Whigism, Conservatism, and good, honest Democracy as we formerly knew it. Fernando Wood, Mayor!!'"

Hone on the day following the election of 1850 was able to note the defeat of Wood. But there was no praise of the nominee of Hone's party who defeated Wood. Just the bare statement of fact: "Ambrose C. Kingsland is elected Mayor." Kingsland was not a man to praise.

There was no Hone to observe the Machiavellian manipulations of Wood for the Mayoralty nomination in 1854. He had made his last entry in his informative diary on the last day of April in 1851, and four days later the flag at the City Hall was half-masted to honor the memory of one of the most brilliant occupants of the Mayor's office.

But Tweed, who saw with a vision unknown to Hone, was there, watching every move made by the wily Wood. As the summer of 1854 waned, it was apparent that Tammany would continue divided, and that each faction would nominate its own choice for Mayor. The Native Americans would also put a ticket in the field. The City Reformers were trying to effect a working agreement with the Whigs. A fusion would give the Whig Reform ticket the lead. Wood had two objectives: to prevent the projected amalgamation of the reformers and the Whigs, and to effect a coalition of the Tammany factions. To unite his own party he spent liberally of his wealth. And in his work of forestalling the union of the Whigs and the reformers he was equally generous. In his work of destruction he was successful. Part of the battle was won. But he failed to bring the "Hardshells" and "Softshells" together. His own faction, as had been expected, nominated him for Mayor.

But the next move of Wood astonished not only Tweed, but the entire town. It was generally understood that the Hardshells would nominate Augustus Schell for Mayor. Schell was one of the ablest lawyers in the town, and a bitter partisan foe of Wood. When the Hardshells met to nominate their choice they found that Wood had outwitted them. He had packed the meeting with his paid henchmen who nominated their employer. The real Hardshells then nominated Schell. Now there were two Hardshell Mayoralty nominees.

The friends of Wood told him that he had alienated many votes by his theft of the dubious Hardshell nomination. But Wood believed otherwise.

Wood had been secretly conspiring for the Know-Nothing nomination. His hired men in this organization reminded the rank and file that Wood had been a member of the Executive Council of the party and could be trusted to live up to the principles of the faction. But the Know-Nothings, confident of success, and guided by men to whom Wood was anathema, nominated James W. Barker, an auctioneer, and a neighbor of Tweed. The Whigs named John J. Herrick, a commission merchant. The City Reform Party headed their ticket with Wilson G. Hunt, a wholesale dealer in cloths.

Here were five candidates in the race for Mayor. Two of them were Tammany men, Wood and Schell. The latter was entitled to the party label, an empty honor under the circumstance. For with two Tammany men in the field the organization's vote would be split and neither man could win. Those in control of the Wigwam did not like Wood. Realizing that Schell could not be elected, they set out to defeat Wood. This might be accomplished by throwing Schell's strength to another candidate. The anti-Wood Democrats could not side with their traditional enemies, the Whigs, who were then on their last legs as an organization. To line up behind the Know-Nothings would alienate their Catholic and foreign-born supporters. This process of elimination more than narrowed their choice. They had none. They must support the nominee of the City Reformers. Accordingly Schell, who was not ambitious for office, declined the nomination. In making this decision public, Schell urged his followers in Tammany Hall and others who supported his candidacy, to cast their votes for Hunt on Election Day.

This move had not been anticipated by Wood. But he was not lacking in resource. Wood had organized whisper squads on a scale unprecedented. These indispensable adjuncts of politicians and political organizations are far more effective than is generally known. The members of these whisper squads are recruited from every walk of life. Long before women were given the privilege of suffrage they were acquainted with the practical side of politics through their activities in these political auxiliaries.

The principal task of a member of a whisper squad is to spread the propaganda of prejudice. He also acts as a spy, and reports back to his chief any information that may be valuable in the campaign.

The success of a whispering campaign—many campaigns have been won in this way—depends more on the secrecy with which it is waged than on any other element.

Wood sent his squads into every section of the town. In Know-Nothing centers they reminded their hearers that Wood had taken the oath of a member of the order. For it was more than a political organization. To the Roman Catholics and the foreign-born the whisperers denied that Wood had ever been a member of the Know-Nothings, saying that the charge was an invention of Wood's enemies. The Whigs were told that here they had an excellent opportunity to destroy Tammany by electing a man to office who had fought Tammany within its own ranks and was bent on the destruction of the organization. The foes of Wood in Tammany were asked to believe that Schell was a secret enemy of the Wigwam and had sold out to the City Reformers. These last were urged to vote for Wood as a man of such great wealth that he could not be swerved from the path of civic righteousness by any financial inducement.

This was the less reprehensible side of the task of these slime-strewers of politics. They also spread any and all sorts of rumors that were retailed to them or suggested themselves to their fertile minds. This candidate kept several mistresses. That one had stolen church funds. Another was a common gambler. That fellow was a steady drinker and frequently beat his wife. And so on.

The motto of the whisper squad is: "Throw plenty of slime: some of it will stick." The tragedy is that some of the slime does stick.

Another important duty of the whisper squad is to meet the attacks of the opposition. Here they are left almost entirely to their own ingenuity.

Wood was not making much headway with the Know-Nothings. But he had made converts in their ranks. These were recruited from the anti-prohibition element of the order, as the Wets and Drys were having their first real battle in New York State that year. Horatio Seymour, a Democrat, who was serving his first term as Governor, had vetoed the Maine Prohibition Law that the New York Legislature, controlled by the Whigs, had passed. This made prohibition the dominant issue in the State election of 1854. The Whigs had nominated State Senator Myron H. Clark, of Canandaigua, for Governor. Clark had more pronounced views as a Dry than a Whig. Clark would appeal to the rural vote, then, as now, on the side of the Drys. But they could not win without the vote of the wet Whigs in the cities. To hold these votes they named Henry J. Raymond, editor and publisher of *The Times* for Lieutenant Governor. The nomination of Raymond proved a bitter pill for Horace Greeley. Greeley, ever since his election to a ninety-day term in Congress six years before, had been hungry for office, and a persistent seeker for honors at the hands of his party. Until Raymond's entrance in the field of New York journalism, *The Tribune* had been the organ of the party in the city as well as the nation. But the liberal views of Raymond on the prohibition question had cost Greeley the support of thousands of local Whigs and other wets outside the party. Greeley had no choice, unless he wished to throw himself outside the party fold, save to support the ticket. To Clark's candidacy Greeley gave whole-hearted loyalty.

"Mr. Clark," said Greeley, in *The Tribune* the day after the nominations, "has been an early, constant, and zealous cham-

pion of the Maine Law. It had not a more determined supporter in the late Senate."

In speaking of Raymond, Greeley, at the outset, was fair
enough. Greeley referred to Raymond's two terms in the Assembly—the second year he had been chosen Speaker of the
lower branch of the State Legislature—as "a legislative experience which will prove valuable in the chair of the Senate."
[The Lieutenant Governor presides over the Senate save when
it sits as the Committee of the Whole.] But Greeley made a
covert appeal to the Drys—and they far outnumbered the Wets
among the Whigs—to vote against the editor of *The Times.*
This appeal was subtly couched so that the charge of party
treason could not be lodged against him.

"It will be necessary to have it generally known that he [Ray-
mond] was not the author of the Anti-Maine Law articles which
have from time to time appeared in *The Times,* or that his views
have materially changed for the better since that journal com-
mended Governor Seymour's veto message as commanding the
approval of all sober men to insure his election by an immense
majority."

Greeley was an uncompromising advocate of forcible—the
word is his—restraint of the use of all intoxicating drinks.
Poison he labeled them, even three-and-one-half-percent beer.

Before the fall campaign was half over, the foes of Wood
were conceding his election. This in spite of the publication of
his corruption in commercial life and his proved duplicity. His
whisper squads were achieving successes, as the bulletins from
the battlefields put it. They had scored triumphs among the
churchmen. Wood, because of his own start in life, had the
saloonkeepers with him to the last man. The gambling element and the rest of the underworld supported him. Financial
support was given him by the prostitutes and female abortionists of the town, including the notorious Madame Restell, who
played no favorites, but contributed to all campaign funds.
She did this long before Jay Gould made bi-partisan contributions part of his faith and practice as a robber of railroads
and general financial despoiler. Wood, through his grog shop

allies, had all the thugs of the town. Rynders was with him— Isaiah Rynders, "that notorious bandit" as he had long been known, and John Morrissey, one of the most picturesque figures of New York's underworld, who was to rise in the new world of politics that Wood was creating. Morrissey was a noted prize-fighter of his day, his victory over John C. Heenan, known to the devotees of the squared circle as Yankee Heenan, giving him the title of Champion of America. Morrissey was born in Ireland. His parents settled in Troy, New York, and when young John was in his teens he became a bartender. This was in Troy. Cash registers were unknown then, and it was not uncommon for a beer slinger at the end of two or three years' apprenticeship to become his own master. Morrissey's saloon became the resort of notorious characters, "gamblers, thieves, and dissolute persons of the lowest grade." It was finally closed by the authorities.

On his arrival in New York in the Forties, Morrissey was penniless. His clothes were in tatters. But his oxlike physique and his engaging smile had not followed his money across the bar of countless saloons. He drifted to the Battery and found work as an emigrant runner, the name by which an employee of cheap hotels and boarding houses catering to those seeking a new home in America was known. This calling was one grade less low than that of a sneak thief. He was in turn a policy dealer, burglar, gambler, and most of the time a politician.

During the election following Morrissey's arrival in New York he was commissioned to recruit a gang to protect the ballot boxes where the politicians did not want the Plug-Uglies to tamper with them. Morrissey did his work so well that his services were always in great demand on the day when every American voter is a sovereign. But he did not always protect the ballot boxes.

Morrissey's days of poverty had passed before he joined forces with Wood. He was then the owner of a profitable gambling house, and had a large personal following in sporting circles. He was given a wide berth, especially when he lapsed from his long stretches of sobriety. In May of the preceding year he and a friend had been on a spree. After a breakfast which consisted largely of champagne, they entered the barroom of the Girard House on Chambers Street and West Broadway. Morrissey suddenly decided the eminently proper and fitting thing to do was to have the barroom for the exclusive use of himself and his drunken companion. So Morrissey began to clean out the place. He seized a water pitcher and hurled it at the bartender. A waiter, who did not know Morrissey, made an attempt to restrain the wine-crazed politician. Morrissey drew a revolver. The waiter fled. Morrissey fired blindly at him. The bullet crashed through a window and made a hole in the top hat of a business man walking to his office. The waiter returned with two policemen.

"There he is!" exclaimed the waiter.

Morrissey, in his fashionable full beard, did not look the dangerous assailant the waiter had painted.

"Which?" asked one of the policemen.

Morrissey now whipped out an ugly-looking dirk exclaiming: "I'll rip open the belly of the first one who comes near me!"

The policemen took his word for it. They departed and returned with reënforcements. But this time Morrissey had regained a little of his senses, and with his companion made a peaceful surrender.

Morrissey was one of the lieutenants of Wood who advised him at the beginning of the campaign that he must denounce the Know-Nothings if he expected to win. Wood was of the same opinion. Accordingly Wood appeared before a notary public and made an affidavit couched in such fashion that a first reading, save to a keen mind, gave the impression that Wood had never been a member of the order. This was printed as a campaign document and distributed at the ferries, railroad stations, on the streets, and at homes. *The Times* in an editorial on the morning of Election Day thus commented on Wood and his "disclaimer":

"Fernando Wood, the regular nominee of the Soft Democrats, is known and felt to be utterly unfit for the place. His integrity as a business man has been very seriously impeached by the publication of legal testimony, the truth of which does not seem to be controverted and which is conclusive against his fitness for any place of trust and responsibility. He has published a card, and it is said, made an affidavit, denouncing the Know-Nothings, and denying in the most explicit terms that he has any connection with the order. And yet it is known to thousands of our citizens that he has been a member of the order and has acted as one of its Executive Committee. The fact that he has since then resigned and that, in a technical sense, his assertions may be true, does not in the least relieve him from the odium of *intending* to deceive. No such man ought to be trusted in any office and it would be a disgrace to the City to elect him Mayor. If those who are convinced of this were united in their opposition to him his defeat would be beyond all doubt. Unfortunately this is not the case."

The apprehensions of the Whig organ were proved only too true before the day was over. While he polled but one in every three votes cast, Wood, due to his strategy, was elected Mayor. The total vote was 59,644. Of this Wood received 19,993. Barker, the Know-Nothing candidate, was a close second with 18,553. The City Reform candidate, Hunt, was third with 15,386. The Whigs cast only 5,712 votes for Herrick. Yet nearly double that number, or 11,127, voted for Clark, the Whig nominee for Governor. Most of the remaining Whig votes were cast for the Know-Nothing candidate. The City Reform candidate was their second choice. Wood also ran nearly 4,000 votes behind Governor Seymour, whom the Democrats had renominated. And most of the Democrats who would vote for Wood, supported Barker and Hunt. Close as was the vote in the municipal election, it was still closer in the State, Clark being elected to the Governorship by 309, the vote for Governor being: Clark, 156,804; Seymour, 156,495. Raymond was elected Lieutenant Governor, running considerably ahead of his ticket.

Tweed was learning.

CHAPTER X

To understand Tweed one must know Wood. For Tweed studied Wood, analyzing minutely every move he made. Until January 1, 1855, when Wood was inaugurated Mayor in New York's City Hall, an edifice justly appraised by F. Hopkinson Smith as one of the three most exquisite gems of architecture in the United States, Tweed's study heretofore was, perforce, restricted. But thenceforward, all of Wood's actions were matters of public record or known to the politicians who surrounded him. And no one had more of the inside gossip than Tweed, who spent such time as he could away from his business, haunting the corridors of the City Hall, or Delmonico's, or some other haunt of the bon ton of the day, swapping what he had gathered with other foes of Wood who foregathered in the evenings in the Wigwam, then a stately Colonial pile facing the eastern side of City Hall Park.

Wood knew that a majority of the braves in Tammany were awaiting the opportunity to scalp him. But that could not come about until his two-year term was nearing its end. Meantime he must build up a personal machine. He was too seasoned in politics not to know that the best of one-man organizations, without the label of a major political party, was at best of questionable worth in a campaign. But Wood was preparing for all eventualities. If he did win official recognition at the hands of the local Democrats, he would still need his own independent following, without which no great progress could be made. He knew that to obtain higher honors he must have the support of the delegates from New York. That entailed undivided control of Tammany. And that meant, in turn, the uniting of the Hardshells and the Softs, and dominating both. But that could wait. He would first beguile the citizenry into believing in him. Successful there, the rest would be easier.

The first official act of Mayor Wood was a bid for popular favor. This was his inaugural message which was read before the Common Council at its first sitting in 1855. This document set a new fashion. Therein Mayor Wood informs the world that he is a man of honor, a foe of corruption, a friend of labor and of industry, and a protector of the poor. From it we learn that one in ten of the city's population of nearly three quarters of a million is "in want of the necessaries of life." This shocking picture of poverty is not overdrawn. It was true not only in 1855, but for years before, and for many years thereafter. Several factors entered the creation of this deplorable condition, not the least of which was the unprecedented immigration that began in the Forties.

Wood was no mean student of government. His message is one of the finest of the early arguments for municipal home rule. The city was suffering not only from social conditions beyond the control of the lawmakers, but handicapped on its civic side by a hodge-podge charter that legislative tinkering had made worse. Wood fairly laid many of the evils of the local government to the charter-patching by the State Legislature. Here he was on popular ground. One of the causes of the low vote for his Whig opponent for Mayor was the growing resentment against interference by rural legislators—Whigs of course—in the city's local affairs. The charter had been granted to the city in 1830. In the quarter of a century that had elapsed, it had been so amended that little of its original intent and purpose remained. Authority was divided. Nine of the departments of the city government were elected by the people, and were responsible to no one but themselves and the Common Council—which was always on the market. Thus the city elected a Mayor and nine little Mayors. This diffusion of power made corruption easier. This document of Wood was sound, and it is the city's loss that the man who wrote it was not honest. Knowing Wood as we now do, his first inaugural message has special interest. His bravura pretensions to honesty, his pious denunciation of the corrupt Common Council in language almost identical with that used by Gerard when the City Reform Party was formed less than two years before, his references to his honor—all these make us smile cynically. Wood's address to the Common Council is here in part reproduced:

"The present is not an auspicious time to commence a new administration; it is beyond the ability of any man, exercising the duties of this office under the city charter, to give this people that government which appears to be so generally expected, and which is certainly so much required.

"However we may differ as to the cause, there can be no doubt of a pervading dissatisfaction with the municipal affairs of this city. That this feeling exists, and that there are sufficient grounds for it, all must admit; whether it arises from defects in the fundamental laws, or from improper local legislation, or from maladministration upon the part of those intrusted with the executive duties, are questions upon which there is diversity of opinion; in my judgment, all of these are the causes.

"The amended charter of 1830 was preferable to the present system. Admitting that it required modification, the subsequent amendments have but increased the difficulties.

"The Constitution of the United States is as applicable to the present greatness of the Republic as it was to the Federal Union at the time of its adoption. Had amendments been made to it at the instance of every party or statesman who deemed it insufficient, we should have fallen to the same condition as a nation that this city has as a corporation.

"Amendments to the charter of 1830 have, one after another, been adopted at Albany, until now we are administering the government by portions of *six different charters, which create nine executive departments, having undefined, doubtful, and conflicting powers,* with heads elected by the people, *each assuming to be sovereign, and independent of the others, of the Mayor, or of any other authority;* and beyond the reach of any, except that of impeachment by the Common Council, which never has been, and probably never will be, exercised.

"This irresponsibility has been productive of carelessness in expenditure, and negligence in the execution of the ordinances.

"Thus, in the attempts to remedy defects by foreign aid, which could have been accomplished at home, we have fastened upon ourselves a complicated, many-headed, ill-shaped and uncontrollable monster, which has not, in my opinion, developed its worst characteristics.

"So far as my duties are defined, I feel some embarrassment. Even coördinate powers with the several executive departments are denied to me in some quarters; and the fact that my predecessors, under the new charters, have not attempted their exercise, is re-lied upon as sustaining this position.

"Without desiring to question the wisdom of those who have preceded me in this office, I must be permitted to construe my powers and duties as I understand them. Restricted as the prerogatives of the Mayor have been by almost every legislative act appertaining to the government of this city, for several years, still there is sufficient left to instill more energy into the administration than now exists, and to hold at least a supervisory check over the whole city government.

"It is true, that though ostensibly head of the Police Department, he is not so practically, in the essential element of authority—that of controlling the retention or removal of his own subordinates. The Chief of Police holds his place independent of the Mayor, that officer having been appointed during 'good behavior,' by the late Mayor and Board of Commissioners, under the law of 1853, which they construed to give that authority. He can not, *solus,* appoint or remove the humblest subordinate in the service, nor make the rules and regulations for its governance. Of these requisites of power, so necessary to make an efficient police corps, he is by law deprived.

"We have suffered more from legislative assumptions, or misconduct of subordinates in authority, than from the tyranny or corruption of a chief ruler.

"Concentration, with ample power, insures efficiency, because it creates one high responsible authority. Decentralization is subversive of all good executive government.

"This want of concentration has been the prime cause of the immense load of taxation which we now bear.

"Surely we are admonished that if this rate of taxation be continued, more of it should be devoted to the relief of the poor, whose industry bears most of its burdens, and who are now ringing into our ears their cries of distress. Labor was never so depressed as now. Employment is almost entirely cut off, and if procured, its remuneration is totally inadequate, owing to the high price of articles of subsistence. The prices of labor and of food bear no relative equality.

"In ordinary times of general prosperity capital possesses advantages over labor.

"Capital can always protect itself, and it is only at periods of inflation, when capital is directed to speculation in the products of labor, that the operative is appreciated, and his industry rewarded by competent compensation.

"But now, when capital either timidly retreats, through fear, to the bank-vaults, or is diverted to the oppression, for gain, of those who employ labor, his condition is sad enough. Does it not behoove us, not only individually, but in our corporate capacity, to throw ourselves boldly forward to his relief?

"This is the time to remember the poor!

"Do we not owe industry everything? It is its products that has built up this great city.

"Do not let us be ungrateful as well as inhuman. Do not let it be said that labor, which produces everything, gets nothing, and dies of hunger in our midst, whilst capital, which produces nothing, gets everything, and pampers in luxury and plenty.

"It is our duty to take and administer this government under the charters and laws as we find them, until a change is effected for the better. Valuable improvements can now be made, notwithstanding these objections to the system. All the evils of which the people complain are not chargeable to wrong legislation. If the Common Council will be more cautious in the passage of ordinances, especially those involving disbursements of money, holding fast to the purse-strings as against the harpies, who for many years have hovered around its chambers, and if the executive bureaus will coöperate with me in the rigid enforcement of the laws, and particularly in restraining expense, and exacting a faithful performance of every contract, we may do much towards removing the present discontent.

"Most assuredly the people pay enough for the better administration of their public affairs; and it has never appeared to me that they were unreasonable in their requirements.

"They ask public order; the suppression of crime and vice; clean streets; the removal of nuisances and abolition of abuses; a restriction of taxation to the absolute wants of an economically administered government, and a prompt execution of the laws and ordinances. Let us endeavor to meet their expectations.

"For myself, I desire to announce here, upon the threshold, that, as I understand and comprehend my duties and prerogatives, they leave me no alternative, without dishonor, but to assume a general control over the whole City Government, so far as protecting its municipal interests may demand it. I shall not hesitate to exercise even doubtful powers, when the honor or the interests of the public is abused.

"The public good will be sufficient warrant to insure my action. Under this law I shall proceed, not doubting your concurrence and the support of the people, for whom the responsibility is assumed."

This cry for relief from interference from the State law-makers, while meeting with the hearty approval of the people and the press, was intended only as a gesture. Wood did not want the responsibility. True, it would have made him the head and font of corruption. But he would have had to share the loot with the nine little Mayors. And he was content with his present opportunities. He was a fox, not a hog. Even an honest man, thoroughly trained in the duties of administering a city, an experience Wood lacked, would have been awed by the prospect. Let us read a description of the nether side of the town, a picture none the less faithful because it was inspired by Wood:

"On the first day of January, 1855, Mayor Wood took his first official survey of the city he had been called to govern. He found the public moneys shamefully wasted, broken contracts paid for, ordinances violated for bribes or favoritism. He found the streets of this great metropolis ill-paved, broken by carts and omnibuses into ruts and perilous gullies, obstructed by boxes and signboards, impassable by reason of thronging vehicles, and filled with filth and garbage, which was left where it had been thrown, to rot and send out its pestiferous fumes, breeding fever and cholera, and a host of diseases all over the city. He found hacks, carts, and omnibuses choking the thoroughfares, their Jehu drivers dashing through the crowd furiously, reckless of life; women and children were knocked down and trampled on, and the ruffians drove on uncaught; hackmen overcharged and were insolent to their passengers; baggage-smashers haunted the docks, tearing one's baggage about, stealing it sometimes, and demanding from timid women and stranger men unnumbered fees for doing mischief, or for doing nothing; emigrant runners, half-bulldog and half-leech, burst in crowds upon the decks of arriving ships, carried off the poor foreign people, fleeced them, and set them adrift upon the town; rowdyism seemed to rule the city; it was at the risk of your life that you walked the streets late at night; the club, the knife, the slung-shot, and revolver were in constant activity; the Sunday low dram-shops polluted the Sabbath air, disturbed its sacred stillness, and in the afternoon and night sent forth their crowds of wretches infuriate with bad liquor, to howl out blasphemies, to fight, or to lie prone, swine-like, on the sidewalks and in the gutters. Prostitution, grown bold by impunity, polluted the public highway, brazenly insolent to modesty and common decency; and idle policemen, undistinguished from other citizens, lounged about, gaped, gossipped, drank, and smoked, inactively useless upon street corners and in porter-houses."

Wood had not been in office many weeks before he succeeded in persuading the good people that much in the way of reform would be achieved during his administration. Gerard, the head of the City Reform Party, for a time was gulled into believing that Wood had turned over a new leaf, and that whatever his transgressions of the past, he was now resolved to be honest, and to rule the city in a manner that would redound to his credit. He was rich and politically ambitious. So why doubt his future honesty?

Wood made his first big stroke as a reformer through the establishment of a Complaint-Book. This innovation was accorded deserved praise. Through the newspapers Wood informed the people that any one with a grievance, whether against a public officer or private citizen, would be welcomed at the Mayor's office. The Mayor personally received many of the complainants, listened to their recitals, and where possible, remedied the wrongs. Neighborhood quarrels, domestic differences, controversies over wages between servant girls—some of them children of eight and nine years of age—and their mistresses, even these were spread upon the leaves of the Mayor's Complaint-Book. No complaint was too trivial to receive attention. Some were so colorful that they found their way into the columns of the daily press. One such, minus the names of the accused and accuser, concerned a tailor and a policeman. The policeman would not pay his bill. The Mayor summoned him to the City Hall and learned that sickness had let poverty into the officer's household. Wood paid the bill.

There was one complaint common to rich and poor alike. This was the usurpation of the streets by roaming pigs who daily made their rounds in search of choice morsels in garbage cans and in the gutters. But these were not so offensive as the cattle, which wandered from their pastures into the crowded thoroughfares, running amuck and injuring pedestrians, sometimes fatally. Broadway and other principal thoroughfares at times assumed the aspect of country roads when drovers led their cattle through the streets. So numerous were these complaints that Mayor Wood, in a message to the Common Council, prayed for relief, saying:

"The practice of driving cattle through the streets of the city is another evil calling for prompt action. It is an abuse which our citizens have submitted to too long. In my opinion, the Common Council will deserve the severest censure, if, like its predecessors, it timidly skulks from its duty in ridding us of this dangerous nuisance. Not only is the health of the whole population jeoparded by the unwholesome odors arising from the collection of these animals, but it not infrequently occurs that life, limb and property are destroyed by it."

The Common Council listened attentively and promptly forgot.

Churchmen complained against drinking on Sunday. The owners of the drinking shops, some 2,300, had been with Wood in the last campaign almost to a man. The same complainants called the Mayor's attention to the gambling dens and houses of prostitution. Wood, who had assumed active command of the police department, closed the houses of harlotry, the gaming places, and proved also that the saloons could be kept closed on the day of rest and worship. Wood was hailed by the righteous side of the community as a grossly-maligned man.

The State Legislature, with more of its wanton meddling, increased the popularity of Wood when its Whig leaders caused a bill to be introduced that would deprive the Mayor of actual charge of the police department. He had effected some police reforms, compelling all to wear uniforms. The whole city was aroused against this latest usurpation of the rural legislators.

Politics were forgotten and one of the largest mass meetings the city had known was held as a protest against the proposed measure. On the platform were Horace Greeley, William B. Astor, James Lenox, James W. Gerard, Peter Cooper, Cornelius Vanderbilt, James W. Barker, William M. Evarts, George Griswold, and others prominent in the life of the city. Resolutions embodying the well-founded objections to the pending measure were adopted and forwarded to the Legislature. The bill, in the slang of the Solons, was killed. But the Legislature was not done. It was determined to make a popular hero of Wood before it adjourned *sine die*. And it did.

It will be recalled that the Whig State ticket, headed by the leader of the Drys, Myron H. Clark, had been elected the preceding November. Clark's majority over his Democratic opponent, Seymour, was 309. This hair-breadth escape was viewed by the Drys as a triumph, or, to use a catch-phrase of politics, a mandate from the people. Accordingly the Legislature passed, as had been done in the previous session, a Dry Law, or as it was popularly known, the Maine Law. And as soon as the measure reached the Executive Chamber it was signed by Governor Clark. The Drys fondly imagined that it would close the saloons, end poverty and put a stop to crime. This is not imagery. It is taken from the sober title of the law. What happened in New York after the dry Governor affixed his signature to the engrossed bill is the one amusing chapter in the long story of prohibition.

CHAPTER XI

NEW YORK was at first alarmed by the enactment of the prohibitory liquor law. The cautious laid up supplies against the dry day. Those who boasted not cellars threatened to flee the State before July 4, when the new statute, entitled "An Act for the Prevention of Intemperance, Pauperism, and Crime," was to go into effect. The Fourth of July had been chosen because it marked, in the language of the Drys, a new birth of freedom—freedom from the Demon Rum. But when the robins began building their nests, Mayor Wood issued a series of proclamations addressed to the citizens, the police, and the drinking places. So seriously were these effusions phrased, that the people at the first reading saw nothing save the intent: to nullify the Dry Law. And they applauded. But when they noted the manner in which the nullification was to be accomplished, the town shook with Bacchanalian mirth.

The modest author of the jest was A. Oakey Hall, a pale-faced young man not many years out of college, at times a journalist, lawyer, writer of verse, politician, playwright, and clubman. At this time he was a Whig and the District Attorney of New York, yet he found time to write editorials for *The Times*, to attend public dinners almost nightly where he delivered side-splitting speeches, to visit the political clubs where he met on terms of equality the butler who opened the door at a home where he was always welcome. But above all, he was a man of fashion. Just then it was the mode to part one's name in the middle. He did it. When he was appointed an Assistant District Attorney, he was Abraham Oakey Hall. In 1853 he was Abraham O. Hall. The next year he changed it to A. Oakey Hall. He was of English ancestry, of Southern birth, and gentle upbringing. He wore all the political labels of his time. He was a Know-Nothing, a Whig, a Republican, a Democrat. He believed in a popular form of government with a ruling class composed of the wealthy and the intellectual. He followed the Whigs into the Republican Party. He would have remained there but that he shared the opinion, prevalent in his circle, that the Grand Old Party had brought disgrace upon itself in nominating Lincoln. How could a gentleman support this uncouth fellow from the backwoods? It was fashionable to reject Lincoln. The Elegant Oakey had no choice. Tweed made amends by making him Mayor. He was one of the Tweed Ring. After sharing spoils with Tweed he swapped epigrams with Wilde. At a breakfast in London, when the thieves began to expatriate themselves, Hall, on hearing that there were to be no speeches, flashed this: "Eloquence is not a bird of early flight." Wilde responded with something about a Diet of Worms. Hall was eccentric. Sometimes he signed himself: *A. Okey Hall.* This has erroneously been attributed to his eccentricity. It should be ascribed to his reverence for the orthographical. He was named after John Okey, one of the Regicides of Charles the First. Okey, after the Restoration, fled to Holland. Here he was arrested, returned to London, tried, and executed. Hall was proud of his middle name, which his father had misspelled. In letters to intimates he signed himself: *Okey.*

Hall was not inspired by love for Fernando Wood in pointing to the path of Dry Law nullification. The Elegant Oakey was then a Whig. He looked upon the Dry Law as a blot upon his party's shield. He had been consulted by his party's legislative leaders and advised against the measure. Asked for his advice as to the constitutionality of the measure he warned against anything being embodied in the bill that conflicted with any Federal law or treaty. He was informed that that would be taken care of.

Wood, when he first heard Hall's suggestion, dreaded a snare. He did not want to offend the religious element who were loudly demanding that he enforce the Dry Law when it became operative on July 4. Nor did he want to offend the Wets, his chief source of strength. Hall reassured him that he was laying no trap. Wood could consult his Corporation Counsel. He would bear out all that Hall had said. Accordingly Wood issued his first proclamation. In this he emphasized how the Dry Law had been fairly placed upon the Statutes by the chosen representatives of the people, and after unburdening himself of a score or more of platitudes, he said:

"It is not contended that minorities have not grievances, and that their grievances must remain unredressed. Their rights are fully protected. The same fundamental law that binds minorities to submit, points out clearly the road to relief against an illegal or improper exercise of authority upon the part of the majority. Even whenever fanaticism rules the hour and covers the country with its baneful influence, to the exclusion of reason and justice, public opinion will soon correct the error, and restore the calm sense of mature conservative judgment. What if the law-maker proves recreant, and betrays the constituent he was chosen to represent? The wrong inflicted is not irremediable, though it may be a proper chastisement for a negligent or corrupt use of the franchise. Time repairs all the errors of legislation. Its evils and wrongs, however great, invariably recoil before public opinion and the decisions of the courts. Redress and relief can thus always be obtained. The legal tribunals and the ballot-box are never approached in vain for the maintenance of a good, or the overthrow of a bad cause. These are the only constitutional resorts—all others are treason or rebellion."

A little further on in the proclamation Wood announces his course of action. He will enforce the law—a statute he hastens to disclaim—and will require a compliance in others. Thus he addresses the people:

"It is my duty to exact obedience, and yours to obey. The officer of the law is not accountable for the making of the law; he is bound to execute it, pursuant to his oath of office, though the responsibility of the people, as the source of all political power, can not be so easily denied. As Mayor, I have endeavored to fulfill this duty. Though sometimes painful, yet it has been performed diligently and impartially. I hope to continue without relaxation. The act relating to the prohibition of the liquor traffic and consumption is now a law, holding the same position as any other law, and, until decided invalid by the courts, or amended or repealed by the Legislature, should command the same obedience. So far as its execution depends upon me, I have no discretion but to exercise all my power to enforce it. It is unnecessary for me to express an opinion in regard to legislation of this character, or of this law; for whatever that opinion may be, I can not, without dishonor, shrink from the faithful discharge of the trust confided, whatever shall be the personal consequences to myself. I now call upon the friends of law and order to aid in the performance of this obligation, and in sustaining the laws—a principle upon which rests the corner-stone of all our national prosperity and greatness."

The Drys applauded these expressions of righteous republicanism. Wood was a Wet. But what Dry could have gone further? There was some doubt voiced as to the validity of the law. But the Drys fell back for consolation on the last line but two of Wood's inaugural message: "I shall not hesitate to exercise even doubtful powers when the interests of the public is (*sic!*) abused." Wood had proven himself a man of daring. He would not let the Wets intimidate his course of action. So the Drys remained serene, even when the Elegant Oakey gave out an opinion, as District Attorney, that the law was of no effect. The Mayor had publicly asked for this advice which, however, was not binding upon him. And the Whig District Attorney's opinion was concurred in by the Democratic Corporation Counsel. Wood now sings a new song about exercising doubtful powers. "To act contrary to their direction, until it is superseded by absolute judicial declaration, would be an illegal assumption, for doubtful powers are thus made certain."

This was only one of the many disappointments Wood, with Hall's aid, had written into his second proclamation "to the citizens of New York" dated April 27, 1855. This document, issued three days before the expiration of existing licenses—oldtimers will recall that there was "prominently displayed" (such was the language of the Excise Law) in all saloons, hotels, etc.—a state liquor license, which was dated from May 1 to April 30. It cost $1,200 a year to display one of these prints in a New York saloon window in pre-Volstead days. The

saloon-keeper of 1855 drank many a toast to the Elegant
Oakey when he read that part of Mayor Wood's second proclamation wherein the District Attorney is cited as authority for
the free sale of beers, wines, whiskeys, and other intoxicating
liquors after May 1, and until July 4. Let us reproduce this
prelude to the jest that was yet to come:

"My inquiry to Mr. Hall was confined to what would be the
law governing the sale of liquor in this city after the expiration
of existing licenses (May 1) until July 4, when the penalties of
prohibition will go into effect, and as to the laws governing Sunday selling during the same period. He replied that the old
license system is superseded by the new, with its own appropriate
penalties; that the old penalties were not only specific to the old
system, but are inapplicable to the new system, as well because
penalties can not be extended by implication, as because the new
system had its own specific penalties. That by an oversight of
the Legislature the new penalties are superseded until that part of
the act creating them becomes operative. That from May 1, when
existing licenses expire, until July 4, no obstacle exists to the
free sale of liquor in this city, and that it can be sold the same
as any other commodity. And that for Sunday selling there is
no penalty save the old civil penalty of two dollars and fifty cents
for a whole day's traffic, and which is to be prosecuted and collected in a civil action by the Corporation Attorney."

The free sale of liquors, even on a Sunday, and the only
penalty for the Sabbath-breaking a fine of two dollars and
fifty cents to be collected after a civil suit is prosecuted in the
courts at the cost of many times the amount of the fine! But
this was not complete nullification. This was to be wrought
through the legalistic interpretation of the clause in Section
1 heretofore mentioned. After setting forth the sweeping prohibition of the act, there was added this qualification: "This
section shall not apply to liquor, the right to sell which in this
State is given by any law or treaty of the United States." The
Mayor only slightingly referred to this in his proclamation of
April 27, which, after descanting on the evils of drink—most of
the document is given over to this—ended with this outburst
of cant:

"Let me urge, therefore, upon all to show that the citizens of New York have within their own breasts a higher law, which governs their appetites without penal punishments, and that having tasted the sweets of quiet Sabbath; of one day's rest and repose from the toils, strifes, and wickedness of the weekly contests incident to city life, we will not again relax into what is little better than bestial indulgence on a day devoted, throughout the Christian world, to the worship of the 'only true and ever-living God.'"

Toward the end of June the jest was complete when Wood issued instructions to the police for their guidance in enforcing, or rather nullifying, the prohibition statute. These orders to the police were voluminous and verbose. They were so phrased that even the officer who wanted to enforce the law would have been intimidated into inactivity as is manifest from the following:

"You will not be authorized to seize any foreign liquors, or in arresting for the sale of the same, except upon warrant issued by a competent magistrate upon testimony other than your own. Whether liquors exhibited in your presence, either for sale or otherwise, are intoxicating liquors . . . or of foreign manufacture or not, you must judge with great circumspection, and be careful to avoid seizing any thus exempt.

"An error in this regard may lay you liable to severe personal responsibility, inasmuch as you are hereby expressly enjoined to seize no such liquors.

". . . You will therefore be careful that when an arrest or seizure is to be made on view—that is, merely as the result of your own observation—that it must be such a violation as the eye itself can fully disclose, and can not embrace offenses, where the whole of the offense does not fall under your own eye; as thus, a sale of liquor in your presence not in any of the excepted places, or by one of the licensed persons, and not dutiable, is an absolute violation of the law, calling for arrest of the person, seizure of the liquor, and complaint to the magistrate. But keeping with intent to sell or give away, is not an offense fully within the scope of the eye; the keeping is, but the intent is a matter of which the eye alone is not, and can not be a sufficient judge. You can not see the violation of this clause, for an intent can not be seen; it is only to be made out from many circumstances which are to prove it to the judgment, and not to the sight."

And so as to make it still more clear that he did not want the police to make any arrests or seizures on their own initiative, Wood further instructed the officers charged with enforcing the prohibition:

"These violations . . . do not . . . compel you to arrest or seize without complaints."

And to add to the humor of it all, just above the Mayor's signature appears this last line:

"I shall hold you to severe accountability, and trust that while the law is faithfully executed, sustained, and carried out on the one hand, no oppressive acts on the other will be perpetrated against the rights of the citizen, in the performance of the duties which are thus devolved upon you."

The Court of Appeals rang down the curtain on Playwright Hall's first comedy.

CHAPTER XII

By the time Wood had been Mayor six or seven months, he had lost the respect of the church element that he had won earlier in the year. But Wood was not worrying. He had some men, high in Tammany and equally high in the public esteem, supporting him. One of them, like Kipling's Hibernian, was of infinite resource and sagacity. This was Samuel Jones Tilden. He was two years younger than Wood, nine years older than Tweed, and had blue eyes like both of these politicians. But unlike them, he was country-bred. He was born in New Lebanon, New York, February 9, 1814. His father was a farmer. He was of Puritan stock on both sides. The first Tilden arrived in America on the ship *Ann* in 1623. His name was Thomas. He hailed from Tenterden, England, where his brother was Mayor. One of Tilden's collateral ancestors was Colonel Daniel Tilden who raised his own company of soldiers a year before the Revolution was an actuality. The Colonel was a friend of Jefferson, and aided in founding the Democratic Party. On his mother's side, Tilden traced his descent to William Jones, Lieutenant Governor of the Colony of New Haven.

Tilden entered Yale in 1833. He was tall and spare, and as a youth, of frail health. He studied too hard at New Haven, and his strength failed him before the end of his freshman year. He returned home to recuperate. Long walks and horseback rides soon restored him to health. And thereafter, no matter how engrossed he might be in the cares of law or State, Tilden never let a day pass without a walk or ride in the open air. He did not return to Yale, but went to New York, where he completed his studies at New York University. He then read law in the office of his father's friend, Judge John W. Edmonds. Tilden had little to start with save his well-

ordered mind. No one could wish for more. He did not.
Money meant little to him. Yet it rolled in on him in golden
waves. Not a dollar of it was dishonestly obtained. When
his reputation was made he was besieged by persons begging
to be his clients. Most of them were rich. Some of these he
turned away. But never a poor man with a worthy case.
We met him previously in these pages when he was at the
editorial desk of the *Morning News*. He was then thirty years
old, and had been pleading cases for three years. When
leaders of Tammany Hall suggested that the paper be started,
Tilden furnished most of the capital for the new political daily.
Every cent he contributed came from his practice at the bar.
In the previous year, 1843, he was appointed by the Common
Council as Counsel to Corporation—as the Corporation Counsel was then called. Although he had only two years' experience as a lawyer behind him at the time, he had eminent
members of his profession indorse him for the place. Among
them were David Dudley Field and James J. Roosevelt, who in
their recommendation to the Council said: "Mr. Tilden's services and qualifications are such that in our opinion his appointment would give the highest satisfaction to the Democatic
Party, the legal profession, and the public generally."

Tilden lived up to the expectations of his sanguine friends,
for in the year that he held the office he obtained one hundred
and twenty-three judgments against violators of city ordinances.
Associated with him in the management of the *Morning News*
was John L. O'Sullivan, a brilliant writer, who served as American Consul in Lisbon under President Buchanan. Tilden did
not round out a full year with the partisan organ, surrendering
the editorship to O'Sullivan. Although Tilden contributed
the larger share of the capital of the journal, he and O'Sullivan
jointly owned the paper, and when Tilden retired, he presented
the astonished and grateful O'Sullivan with his interest. But
the paper lacked the financial support needed to make it a success, and did not long survive Tilden's withdrawal from its
management. On September 8, 1846, the *Morning News* gave
up the ghost, and its sudden end was thus recorded by the
business manager of the journal:

"DEAR TILDEN,—The long agony is over—the *Morning News* is dead—dead; no time to say more.

"Truly yours,

"CLEMENT GUION."

The year following his abandonment of journalism Tilden was nominated for the Assembly, elected, and also chosen as a delegate to the Constitutional Convention, which began its labors after the Legislature of 1846 adjourned. In the fall of the year he campaigned actively for Silas Wright, who was seeking reëlection as Governor. The election meant everything to Wright. If he won, his nomination for the Presidency was assured. But he went down to defeat, and returned to his farm in St. Lawrence County where he died nine months after. A broken heart was the diagnosis of the politicians.

In 1848, Tilden, who from boyhood had an acquaintance with Martin Van Buren, President of the United States from 1837 to 1841, with the ex-President's son, John Van Buren, revised a manuscript prepared by the elder Van Buren. This document was published in the spring of the year as an address from the Democratic members of the State Legislature. John Bigelow, in speaking of this paper said: "This address deserves to be regarded as the corner-stone of the Free-Soil Party, as distinguished from the party of unconditional abolition."

Van Buren, who had suffered defeat for reëlection as the Democratic candidate in 1840, was nominated by the Free-Soilers for President largely on the strength of the address he had prepared, and which his son and Tilden—President Van Buren always called him Sammy—edited. The result was the election of the Whig nominees, Zachary Taylor and Millard Fillmore. Whatever joy this gave Tilden at the moment, was more than offset by the bitter grief in the years to come when Tweed and other enemies within his own party charged him with the defeat of General Lewis Cass, their standard bearer of 1848. Without New York's electoral votes Cass and Taylor were tied with 127 ballots each. But the Whig majority in the Empire State gave Taylor a majority of thirty-six.

Tilden after the end of the 1848 campaign refrained from

participating in active politics until he was financially independent. He had reached that state in 1855. There would be an election in November for State Attorney General. Tilden was an aspirant for the nomination. He was a member of the Softshells, who were zealously opposing the extension of slavery into the free Territories. With the aid of Wood, Tilden was nominated by this faction. His election was regarded by seasoned campaigners as certain. He was favorably known throughout the State, and was sure to command the independent voters who would be attracted by his personality and reputation. The Prohibitionists, under whose banner the Whigs—this was to be the last year of the Whigs as Whigs—gathered, were prepared to indorse Tilden's candidacy if he approved their principles. This he not only declined to do, but denounced the Maine Law they had enacted as revolutionary, and the entire spirit of the Prohibition movement as opposed to the proper concept of government. In a letter dealing with the subject he said:

"It is not strange that the authors of an act which aims at controlling the tastes and habits of three and one-half millions of people [the then population of New York State], in a matter which each individual must regard as peculiarly, if not exclusively, personal to himself—which aims at working, by a legislative fiat, an instantaneous revolution in the traditional customs of large classes, in a particular in respect to which all men are apt to be most tenacious—should deem it necessary to invoke the aid of a novel and extraordinary legal machinery. Intent on such an object, they naturally saw what it required, rather than what the Constitution allows."

And then he thus discussed the broader principle involved:

"Such legislation springs from a misconception of the proper sphere of government. It is no part of the duty of the State to coerce the individual man except so far as his conduct may affect others—not remotely and consequentially—but by violating rights which legislation can recognize and undertake to protect. The opposite principle leaves no room for individual reason and conscience, trusts nothing to self-culture, and substitutes the wisdom of the Senate and Assembly for the plan of moral government ordained by Providence. The whole progress of society consists in learning how to attain, by the independent action or voluntary association of individuals, those objects which are at first attempted only through the agency of government, and in lessening the sphere of legislation, and enlarging that of the individual reason and conscience."

What a contrast between the backing and filling of the wily Wood and the outspoken Tilden! There was no straddling there—no carrying of liquor on one shoulder and water on the other. His stand on Prohibition cost him many thousands of votes, most of which were made up by the wet support gained from other candidates.

This would have been sufficient in a single campaign for even the most courageous office-seeker. Yet Tilden was to sacrifice more for principle. The Know-Nothings, who had acquired a martyr since Wood took office, and had, consequently, added thousands of recruits to the rolls, made a more tempting offer to Tilden. The Prohibitionists had asked him to approve their principles. The Know-Nothings made no such demand. They agreed to pledge him their support—which would insure his election beyond question—if he would merely remain silent on their aims and purposes.

Tilden's advisers, almost without exception, urged him not to alienate this powerful group. Most of the Know-Nothings were Wets, and they would logically be with him, but he could not expect their votes if he should dare to attack their twin deities of racial and religious intolerance. In the preceding February there had been a cowardly shooting. The victim was a popular pugilist named William Pool. Prizefighting then was a sport and not an industry. So Pool, like other fistic champions, had to earn a living. He had begun life as a butcher, and still kept his stall in Washington Market. He also ran a saloon at Broadway and Howard Street, known to many merchants and professional men, who headed for it when a dull half-hour was theirs. In the evening it was a rendezvous of the Know-Nothings. Pool was prominent in the order. He would have fought one who accused him of being intolerant.

But like most others in the order Pool and his friends believed that they were defending the land from foreign domination, and that there was need of it.

The quarrel which led to the shooting had its origin in causes remote from the religious and racial strife of the day. This much is certain. The trouble started in a dispute between John Morrissey and Pool. In time their friends, two-fisted fellows all, as ready for a scrap as a spree, lined up behind their respective champions. Of course the Know-Nothings to a man supported Pool. Yet Morrissey, Irish-born, and a professed Roman Catholic, in his quarrel with Pool, had as his chief allies men of Protestant stock—James Van Pelt, C. Linn, James Turner, and Lewis Baker. The last-named was a policeman and knew Morrissey from the days when he was an emigrant runner. They were warm friends, and Baker revered the fighter. The two factions met at Wallack's Theater during the first half of February, but were separated before blood was shed.

On the night of February 24, Bill Pool left his saloon and walked up Broadway on his way to his home in Greenwich Village. He stopped in for a pint of his favorite champagne at Stanwix Hall. Pool, like many rum-sellers, never drank at his own bar. Morrissey and several companions, who had been making the rounds of neighborhood saloons, entered as Pool was sipping his second glass. Pool's enemies were well-liquored. A wordy row ensued which ended when the proprietor summoned the police.

A little later Lew Baker, the policeman, California Jim Turner, and "Pargene" McLaughlin entered Stanwix Hall. Pool was still drinking. He was comparatively sober. Baker, Turner, and McLaughlin were drunk. McLaughlin, the last to enter the saloon, turned the key in the door as he closed it. Pool paid no attention to them until McLaughlin, striding toward him, greeted him with:

"What are you looking at, you black-muzzled——?"

But the ancestral taunt did not provoke Pool into action. A few days before, on Broadway, when McLaughlin, again drunk, challenged Pool to fight, the latter, who could have felled "Pargene" with a blow, taunted his challenger by contemptuously tapping his nose with his forefinger as he said:

"Go along about your business. You ain't worth taking any notice of."

McLaughlin, who was then alone, went on about his business. This time he had two bullies with him. So he again challenged Pool, spitting in the prizefighter's face each time Pool declined the challenge. The spitting ceased. Then Pool, still retaining his self-control, counted out on the bar one hundred dollars in gold, and wagered it that he could whip any one of the three in fair fight.

Turner instantly threw off his cloak, saying:

"Draw your weapon!"

Turner now drew his revolver, heavy and murderous, swung it round his head, and using the hollow of his left arm as a rest, fired pointblank at Pool.

Pool was unarmed.

Turner, in the crude code duello of the barroom, had played the game fair. But in bringing his revolver into firing position he buried the muzzle in the flesh of his own arm, through which the bullet ploughed an ugly furrow. Pool was unhurt.

Groaning with pain, Turner felt his knees giving way. As he fell crouching to the floor he raised his revolver and fired a second time at Pool. The heavy slug tore a gaping wound in Pool's leg.

For a moment Pool managed to retain his feet, and in his agony staggered, involuntarily, toward Baker. Pool crumpled to the floor at the policeman's feet. Baker now drew his revolver. Pool pleaded for his life. He was answered with two shots, both of which entered his chest. Pool no longer pleaded for his life.

The three ruffians departed.

But Bill Pool was not dead. He was carried to his home when he recovered consciousness and lived for eight days. Had Pool died without regaining his senses, his murder would have been forgotten in a fortnight. But as he felt the end coming he muttered:

"I die a true American."

These words translated the rum-seller and bruiser into a martyr. And when his coffin, covered with an American flag, was borne down Broadway to the ferry, six thousand members of the Know-Nothing order, many of them in semi-military regalia, trod to the slow music of dirges, while many thousands stood bareheaded as the funeral cortège passed. Men of unblemished reputation and conspicuous in the city's life marched beside notorious gamblers and thugs. Prominent among the latter were the members of the Empire Club, Isaiah Rynders' aggregation of political mercenaries. He had another organization now, and this too, was in line. It was called Rynders' Grenadiers. They wore gaudy uniforms to match their name. For Rynders was now prospering, and had one honest means of support: his pay as a Surveyor at the United States Custom House. And Captain Rynders—thus he acquired his title— marched at the head of his bold grenadiers.

Pool's martyrdom, luridly set forth in hundreds of thousands of pamphlets that were circulated throughout the country, and the honors paid him by the mob, were recalled to Tilden by his political advisers when he announced his intention to denounce the Know-Nothings and their doctrine. He was reminded also that he had already roused one group of fanatics to an insensate fury by his attack on the Prohibition Law. Could he not at least keep quiet? That was all that was requested of him. But Tilden spurned all the advice that ran contrary to the dictates of his conscience. Following his denunciation of them, the Know-Nothings nominated an obscure lawyer of Ithaca, named Stephen B. Cushing, to oppose Tilden.

But if Tilden had two groups of fanatics actively opposing him, he had a third group, as fanatical as the Drys and the Know-Nothings, who gave him loyal support. These were the Wets. They were divided into two camps, as were the Democrats, but unlike Tilden's party, they were one when it came to Tilden. One faction of the Wets called itself the Anti-Maine Law Party. The other was officially known as the Liquor Dealers' Party. The Hardshell Democrats named a candidate, as did the Republicans (this was the first appearance of the new party on a State ticket) who were cynically referred to in

many New York City newspapers as the **Black Republicans,**
because of their championship of the freedom of the slaves.

While the campaign was on, the political rostrum was deserted by many who thronged to the theaters where maudlin
melodramas portrayed the life and death of Bill Pool. This
was true not only in New York City, but in every city of size
throughout the North. A contemporary account of these partisan plays thus depicts the dénouement: "The hero, encircling
his limbs with the Star-Spangled Banner, departed this life to
slow music and red fire, exclaiming: 'I die a true American!'"

Tilden tried to convince himself that the people would rise
above the base emotional appeals when they went to the polling
booths on Election Day. But they did not. It is not their
usual way. Tilden was defeated, and the **Know-Nothings** elected
their candidate to the office of Attorney General. The assassination of Pool had the same effect in other States besides
New York. In Massachusetts, New Hampshire, Rhode Island,
Connecticut, and California, the order elected Governors and
controlling legislative blocs. Bill Pool's soul was marching on.

With all his ideals, Tilden had no illusions about practical
politics. Although only forty-one years of age, he had been
both student and practitioner in the ancient game for two
decades. He knew that the marionettes did not move of their
own free will and accord. He had a dim recollection of another
campaign of hate. He was a boy of twelve when the hue and
cry was raised against the Free Masons. Up in the western
part of the State, in the town of Batavia, one William Morgan,
a member of a local lodge of Masons, published a book purport-
ing to reveal the ritual of the first three degrees of Masonry.
Morgan was slain. Tilden recalled vaguely the crusade against
the Masons that followed the death of Morgan. He remembered hearing of preachers who were members of the order
being driven from their pulpits; of schoolmasters who were
known to be Masons being driven from classrooms; of boys and
girls, the children of Masons, being denied admission to schools.
He remembered that politicians denounced the order as an
enemy of the Republic. Of this last he had a distinct impression, as he was sixteen when the **Anti-Masonic Party** was

organized in the City of Brotherly Love. The following year, 1831, the Anti-Masons, in their first national convention, held in Baltimore, nominated William Wirt, of Maryland, as their candidate for President, and Amos Ellmaker, of Pennsylvania, for Vice-President.

Tilden had doubted stories he had heard of the persecution of the Masons. Now he could understand how cruel bigotry could be. He, a leader of the bar, had offered his extraordinary legal talents to the State for a pittance, at a heavy financial loss to himself. All he had sought was the honor of serving the people of the State. And his offer was rejected by the bigots who elected a mediocrity of their own.

This experience with the Know-Nothings withered a part of Tilden's heart.

There was one Softshell who found a cause for secret joy in the defeat of Tilden. This was Fernando Wood. Tilden's election would have made him a rival for the Democratic nomination for the Presidency. And Wood was now unconcealedly seeking this honor. He was Mayor a little more than ten months, yet a pretentious biography of him was on sale in the bookshops. Of course there was no reference in the book to the corruption of the Mayor, who was making money fast on contracts and through sales of appointive offices. Wood saw to that when he hired Donald MacLeod, novelist, and author of a Life of Sir Walter Scott, to write the "Biography of Honorable Fernando Wood, Mayor of the City of New York." But throughout the volume we see the hand of the politician, not the writer, as witness:

"The characteristics and principles of the Mayor, and the determined action which has been guided by him, have not been without their reward. . . . It is a mistake to judge of a man's popularity by what the noisy classes say; the deep heart of the people is still, impressions remain on it, judgment is not guided by partisan feeling, observation is unprejudiced, and therefore quiet and close. And such men and women have given their admiration and respect to Mr. Wood.

"All classes, political, social, religious, moral, contribute to swell this host of his admirers. Municipal and other officers have come or sent from every part of the Union to ask the secret of his government and to imitate it, and his immense executive ability has been generally recognized.

"Nay, even in Europe he is spoken of. Various Continental papers have contained eulogistic articles on the man who has done so much for New York. A distinguished American artist, just returned from Rome, says, that Fernando Wood is become a household word in the mouths of the citizens of this country now living in the Eternal City. Ex-President Van Buren, in his late journey through the wild mountain region of Wales, was asked in a little wayside inn, by the landlord, particulars of the appearance and manner and peculiarities of the man whom they had learned to venerate.

"From the murmured or outspoken praises of his fellow-citizens, from the compliments of municipal authorities throughout the Union, and the commendations of the press from Maine to California, Mr. Wood's popularity may be reckoned as not inferior to that of any man in the country. All the way from far Iowa came a proposal to nominate him for the Presidency."

And then appeared the proposal to nominate the most popular man in the United States for the Presidency. It was in the form of a letter from a man in Davenport, Iowa. The reply of Wood followed. And Wood replied as all seekers for the Presidency do, with a shy disclaimer that he had any other thought in the world "than to discharge the duties of my present office in such a manner as to deserve and receive the applause of my fellow citizens." What a familiar ring there is to this phrase!

Unlike Tweed, Wood never revealed his political creed. But his biographer unconsciously made good the deficiency:

"It is the fortieth maxim of Adjutant and Ensign Morgan O'Doherty, that, 'you may always ascertain whether you are in a city or a village by finding out whether the inhabitants do or do not care for, or speak about, ANY THING, three days after it has happened.' In cities they don't."

It is as safe a rule to follow as any other that has been developed, intentionally or otherwise, for politicians. Many of them, who have never heard of Morgan O'Doherty, know his fortieth maxim and make it the guide for their faith and practice in public affairs.

CHAPTER XIII

In the spring following his defeat for State Attorney General, Tilden joined the faction in Tammany that sought the overthrow of the Mayor. Tweed, now School Commissioner—there was little more in the office than a title, but he kept his hand in the game—was one of the second string leaders of the Anti-Wood Democrats. Elijah F. Purdy, called the jovial old warhorse of Tammany, was the directing genius of the forces bent on the destruction of Wood.

Tweed owed no small part of his rise in politics to Purdy. The latter, a wealthy banker, first met Tweed when he was an Alderman. Purdy was involved in numerous briberies of the Common Council and other city officials. But always, of course, as the giver of the bribe—not the receiver. To accept a bribe would be coarse. To give one—well, that was done. Mr. Purdy was the quintessence of respectability. He was old-fashioned also, and prided himself on it. He wore stocks and daintily frilled shirts of the finest linen. When he bought a drink he spoke of purchasing a libation. The word grog shop to him was offensive. He could not call it a saloon, as he associated that word with society and art. But it must be called something. So Purdy compromised on refectory.

Sometimes Mr. Purdy was compelled to associate with persons much beneath his station. When he set out in 1852 to steal—it was tantamount to that—a franchise from the city for the Third Avenue Railroad Company, one of Purdy's associates was a livery stable keeper named Thomas Murphy. It was then that Tweed and Purdy began their long-standing friendship. Now Murphy, when put under oath, admitted that he contributed some two thousand or twenty-one hundred dollars to the corruption fund, frankly avowing: "The idea in my mind when I contributed the money was that it was to be

149

paid to the Common Council to get the grant through." And in the same affidavit, made while Tweed was serving his first year as a member of The Forty Thieves, Murphy said that he and the other twelve applicants for the grant had been asked a second time for the money "at a saloon in Broadway, near Fourth Street." Immediately south of Fourth Street lies Great Jones Street. This explanation is necessary that those unacquainted with the Metropolis may understand what follows.

Mr. Purdy, under oath, while admitting that he had contributed money along with other applicants to a fund "for procuring the grant," denied that he knew how the sum raised was expended, and being president of the Empire City Bank, he described the second meeting place of the bribers as "a refectory in Broadway, above Great Jones Street."

Refectories have vanished from the land. The saloons survive.

Another prominent Anti-Wood leader was Peter Barr Sweeny, a lawyer of no mean ability, and a politician of great cunning. Sweeny was born on Park Row. He knew the city and its people as few men of his time, save Tweed. He was tall, heavy set, smooth-shaven, with piercing dark brown eyes, that gleamed like orbs of polished hematite beneath bushy, black eyebrows. His hair was black, and his complexion of extreme swarthiness. Sweeny was scholarly in his habits, and inherently loathed the crowd.

That he remained in politics was due to Richard B. Connolly, who had been a silent power in Tammany for nearly twenty years. Back in the Thirties, Connolly was drafted to keep the Irish vote intact for Tammany. He did not always succeed. Yet when he failed the fault was not his. He was born in Ireland, and had the advantages of early cultural surroundings that Sweeny lacked. Sweeny's father kept a saloon on Park Row. The father of Connolly was a schoolmaster, a scholar, and wrote verse. Connolly was a bank clerk. But this was beginning to be a side-line with Connolly now, as he spent most of his time in organizing the Irish vote to prevent the renomination of Wood. This was a large order, for Wood had appointed to city jobs hundreds of Connolly's co-nationals, and they were at it day and night shouting the praises of Mayor Wood. To hear them, one would think Wood was just biding his time to lead a military expedition to free Ireland.

Connolly had been a lieutenant of Mayor Wood back in 1839, and with him, one of the organizers of the Tammany Young Men's General Committee. Connolly had been the secretary of this sham reform movement, and Wood its chairman. There was little of the practical side of politics that Connolly did not know. But as he began early in the spring of 1856 to move among the various Irish groups—they were divided among themselves into rival organizations such as Connaughtmen, and Kerrymen, and what not—he invariably found that Wood's missionaries had been there ahead of him. Connolly was welcome everywhere. And anything he said met with hearty approval so long as it did not reflect on the wily Wood.

"Wood is a friend of no one but himself!" exclaimed Connolly at one of these meetings. "He now poses as the champion of the Catholics and the foreign-born when the world knows that he was a leader of the Know-Nothings, and so far as we know, he may still be a member of that secret un-American aggregation. Wood is loyal only to Wood. Believe nothing he says. Wood is a fox."

And thereafter Wood was known among those who disliked him as The Fox.

Connolly, who heretofore was able to say early in the year whether he could swing the vote of those of Irish extraction, began to think that perhaps his hold on his people was going. If Sweeny did not have that aloof manner! If he would only learn to shake hands! Connolly was a genial, hail-fellow-well-met sort, always gay, always smiling, and with a pair of laughing blue eyes that inspired confidence. Sweeny had brains but he lacked a heart. Connolly must give him one.

And for a whole evening Connolly slapped Sweeny on the back until it was sore, shook him by the hand until his fingers ached, and made him smile and smile and smile until the muscles around the corners of his mouth twitched.

"Now," said Connolly, "if you'll only do that when you go

out among the lads you'll be a grand success. You can talk, but unless you smile, even when you're condemning your bitterest opponent, it will not have all the effect it should have."

And Sweeny went among the Irish and talked down Wood. And scores of others did likewise.

Leaders of other immigrant groups were also sent out by Tammany to work among their peoples. These met with the same experiences that Connolly encountered. This was particularly true among the Germans, who were loyal almost to a man to Wood for devising a way of keeping open their beer gardens when threatened with the padlock. And they, like the Irish, had been beguiled into believing that Wood was their best friend.

There was a fair-sized colony of English and Scotch immigrants in the Chelsea district. They too, for the most part, were with Wood.

Old line Americans in Tammany played on the fears of their friends and acquaintances, saying that Wood had the foreign-born solidly behind him, and that was something to think over. But the Tammanyites of this group, while not allied with the Know-Nothing movement, answered that Tilden had taken the part of the foreign-born and Tilden was opposed to Wood.

Wood had the advantage over his enemies in Tammany in being well supplied with campaign funds. He assessed every city employee whose tenure of office was dependent upon his pleasure. Policemen—Wood was head of the Department—were forced to give from $25 up. Many of them did not have it. They obtained it, nevertheless. One policeman refused to pay this tribute. Wood kept him on continuous duty for twenty-four hours at a stretch.

The owners of grog shops contributed liberally to Wood's war chest, as did the keepers of gambling dens and bawdy houses. Thus he was enabled to add to the huge campaign force that was on the city payroll, and which was out working with all the energy at its command, for continuance of its jobs depended upon the reëlection of Wood.

While his enemies were at work seeking to undermine him, Wood, as Mayor, occupied a strategic position. By virtue of his office he was the nominal leader of his party in the city. There was a Presidential campaign impending. He pleaded almost daily the need of uniting the Hardshells and the Softshells, stressing that the National campaign might be determined by the vote in New York City. This last counted heavily in his favor. The newly-born Republican Party, composed of the vast majority of the Whigs and other elements opposed to slavery, was feared. But the real nightmare to the Democrats in the city was the strength of the Know-Nothings. They had increased in numbers. This was known. But to what extent they had grown was as secret as their ritual.

The campaign against Wood continued among the real leaders in Tammany. Sweeny, as secretary of the Tammany General Committee, in a published attack on the Mayor on the eve of the meeting of the city convention when a Mayoralty candidate would be chosen, charged that the primary system, at which delegates to conventions were chosen, had been degenerating for years and that now it was so corrupt "as to be a mere machine in the hands of unprincipled men, by which they foist themselves upon the nominees of a party for office in defiance of public sentiment." Wood was specifically accused of stuffing the ballot boxes at the party primary, and of detailing policemen, known for their unswerving loyalty to Wood, to protect the ballot box stuffers and to intimidate his opponents. Wood, however, was renominated. But his choice was far from unanimous. There were eighty-two delegates at the convention. Twenty-six voted against him. Of the remainder, a majority were office-holders under the Mayor.

With the renomination of Wood, his appeals for an united Democracy were heeded by all but a few. Factionalism must be forgotten in a Presidential campaign. Wood next effected an amalgamation of the Hards and Softs. He had himself renominated for Mayor, but his personal enemies in the organization named James S. Libby to oppose him. The Republicans nominated Anthony J. Bleecker, and the Know-Nothings again placed Isaac O. Barker, who lost to Wood by 1,440 votes two years previously, at the head of their city ticket. The City Reformers also named a slate. They placed at its head a notorious corruptionist, James R. Whiting, who had been concerned with bribing legislatures for forty years or more. But he had been doing it so quietly that the leaders of the reformers, who were thoroughly conversant with the record, imagined that the people would have forgotten the Senate Investigating Committee of 1833 which revealed Whiting as the chief lobbyist in obtaining a charter for a group of thieves masquerading as bankers. All that could be said of Bleecker and Barker was that they were honest men.

There had been efforts made to get the Know-Nothings, the Republicans, the City Reformers, and the disaffected Tammanyites who nominated Libby to unite and support a man of capacity, ability, and unquestioned integrity. It was patent to all that such a coalition would spell certain defeat for Wood. While the preëlection fight against Wood was at its height, his corruption was made an issue. There was no disputing his villainy and venality. What was not a matter of record, was common gossip. His frauds were shouted from the housetops. His sharp practices and actual swindling in business were again spread before the people.

A few weeks before election, things had reached a pass where it was feared by the adherents of Wood that the attacks on his personal character might throw the election to Barker, the Know-Nothing. There was little chance for any of the others. Wood was desperate. But he had not lost his ingenious mind. He remembered that through his tools he controlled the assessing of real and personal property. He remembered also that merchants, some of them of high reputation in the community, sold supplies to the various city departments. Nor did he forget that banks which received the deposits of the city at a ridiculously low rate of interest profited highly on the funds of the municipality.

So Wood drew up a testimonial in which he described himself as a man of unquestionable reputation, of spotless character, of rare executive ability, and the best Mayor New York ever had. His administration was lauded as the most glorious in the history of the town. This modest document ended with a fervent prayer that Wood be reëlected.

A few days later this testimonial, signed by a number of the most respectable men in the community—bankers, merchants, and large property holders—was printed in the newspapers.

One of the signers of this long list of lies was the wealthiest man in New York, and the largest real estate owner. His name was William B. Astor, head of the house of Astor, and son of John Jacob Astor, the founder of the Astor millions.

A policeman—the one who had been kept on duty for twenty-four hours at a stretch when he refused to contribute to Wood's campaign fund—wondered why men of affairs, of learning, of distinction, were so blind that they could not see what he saw: wide open brothels, which paid his superiors for the right to carry on their ancient profession; gambling dens with marked cards, loaded dice, and crooked roulette wheels which also paid for protection; thieves who were immune from arrest for the same reason; heart-rending distress among the poor. What had Wood done to ameliorate the lot of the poverty-stricken? To stop thievery? To crush gambling? To put an end to this shameful sharing of the wages of shame? Prostitution could not be destroyed. But the official parasites could be removed from this festering sore of the ages. The policeman as he pounded the pavement knew why Wood made no effort to check these abuses. By their continuance Wood profited.

This whitewash of Wood with the weighty signatures of Astor and other men who gave generously to charity, graced social functions with their presence, and presided over meetings of merchant princes, immeasurably helped its author. It was a brilliant, as well as a novel political move. And Wood received no greater praise for his invention than from his scornful enemy, Big Bill Tweed.

Wood arranged for a ratification meeting at Tammany Hall at which Purdy, always referred to in the press as "the jovial old war-horse" presided. Now this was a Wood meeting. Wood was always prepared. He expected that some of the followers of Libby might be foolhardy enough to attempt a hostile demonstration.

A platform had been built especially for the occasion. Occupying chairs on the front row were Tweed, Sweeny, and Connolly. The last-named was candidate for County Clerk. Sweeny expected to get the place of Public Administrator, while Tweed was again seeking the suffrage of the old Seventh Ward. Tweed and Connolly were neighbors and fast friends. While waiting for the meeting to be called to order they talked things over and were agreed that things looked bad. While Tweed was deriving a comfortable income from the chair and brush factories owned by his family and his father-in-law, he was making much more from his activities outside the rail of the Board of Aldermen. And there was still much more to be made inside the brass-railed enclosure. But he reluctantly conceded that the Know-Nothing nominee for Alderman from the Seventh stood a better chance of being elected. And he was of the opinion that the Know-Nothings stood a good chance of winning in the city. Well, what did it matter since it meant the end of the arch-hypocrite? Was there, after all, much choice between a fanatic and a fraud? This was Connolly talking. Tweed, who despised Wood no less, said that while he would vote for Wood, it would be one of the most unpleasant acts of his life.

Their whispered conversation ceased as the jovial old war-horse strode to the front of the platform. Purdy was popular. He was of commanding figure, a banker, and of great wealth. To be addressed in terms of intimacy by such a man, warmed the hearts of even the most radical of Socialists, whose doctrines, at first taken up by the intellectuals, were now being embraced by some of the proletaires.

Purdy at once won the hearts of all by his denunciation of John C. Frémont, the Republican candidate for President, and of the Know-Nothing nominee for President, Millard Fillmore, who had brought disgrace not only on the great and glorious Empire State of which he was a citizen, but of the high and exalted office of President of the United States which he once filled. And what had the Republicans done to condemn the unholy doctrines of the Know-Nothings, or of Fillmore, their standard bearer, once, like most of them, a Whig? What had either Frémont or his supporters done to stamp out the infernal fires of racial and religious prejudice? Absolutely nothing. They were willing that the flames should spread rather than lose the election. But soon they would be as lifeless as the Whigs who are now *in articulo mortis*. This remnant of what is now the Republican Party had met in solemn convention and indorsed the candidacy of the unworthy Fillmore. But where did James Buchanan stand on—

Purdy never finished the sentence, for at the mention of the Democratic standard bearer men jumped on their chairs and cheered themselves hoarse for the next President of the United States.

When Purdy stilled the emotions of his audience he gave way to emotion himself. In a few low-toned sentences he reminded his hearers that the whole country knew that the Democrats had met the issue raised by the Know-Nothings, and his voice was tremulous as he referred to the Democratic platform of 1856 wherein Know-Nothingism was pilloried.

There was a religious silence as he read:

"That the liberal principles embodied by Jefferson in the Declaration of Independence, and sanctioned in the Constitution, which makes ours the land of liberty and the asylum of the oppressed of every nation, have ever been cardinal principles in the Democratic faith, and every attempt to abridge the privilege of becoming citizens and the owners of soil among us ought to be resisted with the same spirit which swept the Alien and Sedition laws from our statute books; and,

"Whereas, Since the foregoing declaration was uniformly adopted by our predecessors in National conventions, an adverse political and religious test has been secretly organized by a party claiming to be exclusively American, it is proper that the American Democracy should clearly define its relation thereto, and declare its determined opposition to all secret political societies, by whatever name they may be called.

"Resolved, That the foundation of this Union of States having been laid in, and its prosperity, expansion, and preëminent example in free government, built upon entire freedom in matters of religious concernment and no respect of person in regard to rank or place of birth, no party can justly be deemed National, constitutional, or in accordance with American principles, which bases its exclusive organization upon religious opinions and accidental birthplace. And hence a political crusade in the nineteenth century, and in the United States of America, against Catholic and foreign-born, is neither justified by the past history nor the future prospects of the country, nor in unison with the spirit of toleration and enlarged freedom which peculiarly distinguishes the American system of popular government."

A frenzied shout went up as he finished, and presently the hall became a Bedlam. Above the din was heard from time to time cheers for "James Buchanan the next President of the United States."

Even the blasé Tweed was moved. He remarked to Connolly while the cheering continued that this whole-souled enthusiasm was exceptional. Connolly nodded. And did Connolly—Tweed had a habit of deferring to an older man, if he respected him—still believe that the Know-Nothings had a chance of carrying the city on November 4? Certainly not on the National ticket, but Connolly still had his doubts regarding the vote for Mayor and other local candidates. And Connolly indicated a group of the most enthusiastic Buchanan shouters in the hall. These were reviving the cheers for Buchanan. They were hoarse from shouting for the next President of the United States. Their enthusiasm was infectious. Connolly smiled. This was one group of his countrymen that he had stirred up against Wood in the spring. And they had lost none of it. Tweed did not have to be told that these voters, loyal supporters of the National ticket, would vote for the devil rather than Wood. These Buchananites were from the Seventh Ward. Tweed called most of them by their first names. And he knew that they would vote for Libby, the anti-Wood Democrat. They were workingmen, large-boned, brawny men. But Tweed regretted that they had come to the meeting, for they were well liquored up. And Wood had the hall packed with his shoulder-hitters and bruisers. It was neither the time nor place, observed Tweed to himself, for any Libbyites to assert themselves.

When the shouting died, Purdy introduced Honest John Kelly. Kelly, whiskered like Tweed, a jolly, good-natured politician whose very name to those familiar with the period conjures up a picture of a cozy fireplace, of cities where even those of small means lived in their own houses, and planted gardens where towering skyscrapers, most of them atrociously ugly, now shut out the sun. Kelly had been a grate maker.

Kelly was on popular ground while he kept to the National ticket. But the moment he mentioned the name of Fernando Wood the Libbyites made known their presence. They hissed and groaned while the Woodites tried to drown them out with wild huzzas. And thus *The Times* described part of what followed:

"Mr. Kelly could not be heard for some time amid the din and confusion. The Wood men, becoming indignant at the conduct of the Libbyites, pitched into them hot and heavy, and for a time a scene of wildest clamor ensued. Blows were given and exchanged with great spirit, and not a few faces were badly disfigured. The timid fled to corners and mounted the platform in such numbers that great fear of its giving way was felt. Indeed a few planks of the structure were torn down adding to the confusion. At length victory perched on the party of the Woodites. The great body of Libbyites were kicked out of the room and down the stairs with a velocity proportionate to the expelling force behind."

Outside on the corner of Nassau and Frankfort Streets the expelled Libbyites cried out their contempt for Wood as they brushed the dust from their clothes. Then they sauntered across to the City Hall and thumbed their noses at the Mayor's office. Then they adjourned to what Purdy called a refectory where they consoled one another as they drank confusion to Wood and all his misguided followers.

Inside Tammany Hall the meeting proceeded quietly for a time. But occasionally a fearless Libbyite would voice his feelings and a moment later would find himself clearing a flight of stairs at breakneck speed.

Kelly, who possessed a large repertoire of catch-phrases, hurled one at the Libbyites that one of them resented.

"Some men are bound to rule or ruin," said Mr. Kelly.

A Libbyite at once shouted his agreement, adding:

"And that man is Fernandy Wood!"

"You lie, you——!"

The profane taunt was followed with cries of "Put him out!" and out went the offender, minus his hat and a small quantity of claret.

"Mr. Kelly continued at great length," *The Times* report goes on, "stopping every now and then to give the boys a chance to pitch into some obstreperous fellows who dared to say a word against the regular nominee."

But Kelly knew how to restore the good humor of the audience. All he need do was to make some vituperative reference to Fillmore and his running mate, Erastus Brooks.

Election Day of 1856 was one of disorder and riot throughout the country. Ballot boxes were destroyed, and voters battled with one another at the polls. Fists, feet, bricks, bludgeons, knives, and revolvers were freely used. Republicans, Democrats, and Know-Nothings all had their bruisers out in force from the hour the balloting began until the last vote had been counted. But this was not an ordinary election. For there were those who devoutly believed it the battle of that great day of God Almighty, and that every polling booth was a height of Megiddo.

In one of the tragedies of the day there was a note of the sublime. Here is the first act as tersely chronicled by a *Times* reporter:

"As Charles Jonas, a Fillmore voter in the employ of Hoppock, Mooney and Company, No. 138 Liberty Street, visited the poll of the Second District, First Ward this morning, he was asked by Wood's men to show his ticket, which he declined. They then forcibly took his ticket from him, tore it up and tendered him a Buchanan and Wood ticket, saying he must vote it or none. He again declined, when he was immediately felled by a blow, was beaten, and dragged out."

Jonas, bruised and bleeding, returned to his place of employment. L. H. Mooney, on hearing how his clerk came by his injuries, and learning that Jonas was not seriously hurt, suggested that the two of them go to the poll.

"I'll see that you cast your ballot for Fillmore," said Mooney, reaching for his cloak. And the two set out.

There was not a more pronounced anti-Know-Nothing in the city than Mooney. He had cast his ballot early against Fillmore, but he was ready to fight, and to die if need be, to protect even a Know-Nothing in his privilege to vote.

Muttered threats and scowling looks greeted Jonas and Mooney as they entered the polling place.

"I'm here," said Mooney, "to see that this clerk of mine casts his vote for the ticket of his choice."

The account of what happened thereafter follows:

"Immediately after Jonas had cast his vote, he was hit a blow in the mouth. Mr. Mooney ordered a policeman standing by to arrest the offender; the policeman wished to know of Mr. Mooney if he (Mr. Mooney) would appear against him. Mr. Mooney said he would. The policeman then disappeared and Mr. Mooney was attacked by a gang of ruffians, knocked down, kicked in the face, head, sides, etc. He finally reached the street where he was protected by some gentlemen passing by. Mr. Mooney is now at the National Hotel, suffering severely from the injuries he received."

In another polling booth in the same ward a voter—politics unrecorded—had his nose shot off. He was consoled by an onlooker who told him that his face was less ugly now. A policeman, who witnessed the shooting, finding that the wounded man was able to walk, advised him to go to a surgeon's office. At the polling booth at 32nd Street and Third Avenue, fifty Know-Nothings and an equal number of their opponents met and fought. Police clubs fell upon the rioters without discrimination. Part of the mob wrecked the ballot box of the Know-Nothings and with the fragments of wood set upon the police, one of whom was knocked unconscious by a blow on the head.

Mayor Wood and his Chief of Police were called upon by citizens to quell the disturbances. They refused to act. A Judge applied to the Sheriff for aid, furnishing him with the necessary papers to enroll deputies. The Sheriff could not find men willing to risk their lives in keeping order at the polls.

Several ruffians from the First Ward were arrested and brought before the Mayor. Their master discharged them. There is no doubt that many of the clashes at the polls would have happened no matter who was the city's chief executive. Yet Wood could have prevented much of the bloodshed. But to have done that would have cost him votes. And Wood was a politician first of all.

Rioting throughout the city was so common throughout the day and night that only the briefest bulletins could be published in the newspapers, as witness:

"While in discharge of his duty Officer Walsh was stabbed in the eye and had his face badly cut."

Where, when, or how, is not recorded.

The Times—a Republican organ, be it remembered—immortalized the only light note of the day. Even here there was a tragedy. The politics of the journal is stressed as a Democratic organ might have invented a like occurrence to give its readers a grim laugh at the expense of the Know-Nothings. And, of course, no such happening would be chronicled in a newspaper supporting the American Party. Said *The Times*:

"In Murray Street near Broadway, a female vocalist, very dirty, and tight as a brick, drew merchants from their counters by powerful application of her lungs to:
> "The Union of Lakes, and the union of lands,
>   Who shall sever?
> The union of Hearts, and the union of Hands,
>   And the flag of our Union forever!"

She sang this verse over and over, and at the end of each outburst of melody, as she staggered from one side of the pavement to the other, a motion of which she was proudly conscious, "she declared herself willing to stand still long enough to lam anything in pantaloons that would hurrah for anybody but Fillmore and Erastus Brooks."

Nobody took up her challenge.

Her singing attracted visitors to the City Hall, which stood a little more than a hundred feet away. No one who heard the singer dreamed that within five years the God of War would be invoked to answer the question in her song while a wondering world waited wistfully for his response.

The vote cast that day throughout the country swept the Democrats into office. The popular vote for President was:

Buchanan, Democrat 1,838,169
Frémont, Republican 1,341,264
Fillmore, Know-Nothing 874,534

Fillmore carried but one State—Maryland. Frémont won in Connecticut, Iowa, Maine, Massachusetts, New Hampshire, New York, Ohio, Rhode Island, Vermont, Wisconsin, Michigan. Buchanan swept Alabama, Arkansas, California, Delaware, Florida, Georgia, Illinois, Indiana, Kentucky, Louisiana, Mississippi, Missouri, New Jersey, North Carolina, Pennsylvania, South Carolina, Tennessee, Texas, Virginia.

The vote of the Electoral College was:

Buchanan 174
Frémont 114
Fillmore 8

The Congress which went in with President Buchanan stood: Senate—Democrats, 39; Republicans, 20; Know-Nothings, 5; House—Democrats, 131; Republicans, 92; Know-Nothings, 14.

The Republican sweep in the State carried John A. King into the Governor's chair. But in the city the Democrats triumphed. Wood ran more than 7,000 behind Buchanan, and some 9,000 ahead of Barker, the Know-Nothing candidate. Had it not been a Presidential year Wood would have gone down to defeat. That alone saved him. The vote for Mayor was: Wood, Democrat, 34,860; Barker, Know-Nothing, 25,209; Bleecker, Republican, 9,654; Libby, anti-Wood Democrat, 4,764; Whiting, City Reform, 3,646.

There was an editorial comment on the municipal Armageddon worthy of preservation if for no other reason, than to give a model to a tired editorial writer the morning after any city election, where a union of forces would have effected the defeat of a crook in office. All that needs to be done to bring the editorial down to the moment is the substitution of a name or two. The editorial was written by Raymond of *The Times*, who was a founder of the new Republican Party, and who was never charged with being a mugwump.

"Mr. Wood owes his re-election mainly to the folly of those who professed to be the most bitterly hostile to him. The general cry among men of all parties, including very many of his own, was, *anybody* but *Wood;*—and yet there was not one of the various parties in opposition that was ready or willing to surrender its own candidate for the sake of securing his defeat.

"If the Americans, [Know-Nothings] Republicans, and disaffected Democrats,—all of whom professed to think alike, had consented to act together upon this issue,—if they had selected as their common candidate, some well known citizen of high character and eminent fitness for the place,—they could have elected him in opposition to Wood. They preferred Wood to such a surrender of their party predilections; and in the preference thus indicated by their acts, they have been gratified. . . .

"Mayor Wood has more executive ability than any Mayor this City has had for twenty years. If he would now discard party considerations and devote himself to the welfare of the City, he could do more for himself personally as well as for the interests committed to his care, than any of his predecessors. He promised to do so last year;—his failure to redeem that promise has lost him the support of thousands of our best citizens.

"Whether he will renew the promise—and the forfeiture of it—remains to be seen."

The Buchanan vote not only elected Wood, but most of the other local Democratic candidates. One who went down to defeat was Tweed. Like Tilden in the preceding year, Tweed spurned the Know-Nothing indorsement, and denounced its doctrine of racial and religious discrimination. The result was that for the next two years the Seventh Ward was represented in the Board of Aldermen by a member of the secret political order.

CHAPTER XIV

THE second administration of Fernando Wood was the most shamelessly corrupt in the history of American municipalities up to that time. Those who knew the inside of things in his first two years in office did not believe that a viler two years could be possible. The riots at the polls on the Election Day past were not fomented by Wood, although his acts of omission were in no small measure responsible for many of them. It was revealed, however, before he was seven months in office in his second term, that he was capable of instigating a riot if it served his purpose to do so.

A repetition of the maladministration of its two years which began with January 1, 1857, would not be possible in any city in the Union to-day. It was duplicated in the Sixties and Seventies, and during the reign of Tweed, magnified many times. The conditions which made possible these horrible blots on our early history, for the most part, no longer exist. Where, in the civilized world of the twentieth century, could vice openly advertise its wares in the columns of the average daily newspaper? Where, to-day, would helpless, homeless children, be permitted to roam in the streets without any thought from those in official authority? These little ones, who slept wherever night overtook them, numbered not less than 10,000 in any given day. Some statisticians of the period placed their total at 30,000.

To find a parallel for the callous indifference of that grim generation to children of the poor, one has to go back to the days of Paganism. The abandonment of children of destitute parents had the approval of Plato. In *Heauton*, Terrence has his noble character who has given us the apothegm—"I am a man, and nothing belonging to a man is alien to me"—advise his wife to destroy their unborn child, if it be a girl, rather than expose it. For female infants were exposed at the base of a column near the Velabrum at Rome, their adopters raising them as slaves, or prostitutes, or beggars. Some were maimed and trained to be mountebanks. Boys were seldom exposed unless deformed or sickly.

Harriet Ward Beecher Stowe did not have to seek among the blacks for a Topsy. She could have found her in any one of the hundreds of little girls of six to ten years of age, who swept the crossings of the principal streets of New York. These children, in ragged dress and pinched face, broom in one hand, and the other extended, depended for their living on the chance coins bestowed on them by those whose boots were kept clean through their exertions.

Most of these homeless children had in their infancy what passed for homes. But they fled these hovels when old enough to understand. Newspapers and pamphlets of the period are filled with these tragic tales. Here is one, shorn of its more horrible passages, as told by a woman who left her "home" at the age of eleven:

"The first thing I can remember is being cold and hungry, and half naked and ragged and sent out in the rainy mornings into the streets barefooted, to sweep the crossings and beg for pennies. I have a sort of dim remembrance of suffering and misery before that —but nothing distinct. I was so young and used to plead so hard that I did a very good business, and often used to carry home half a dollar at night—which seemed to me quite a fortune. We lived in a little back cellar down in an alley in Orange Street (now Baxter), where I don't remember at this moment ever to have seen the sun enter. The floor was only loose boards, and the black mud and slime used to ooze up through the cracks all about, until it was sometimes quite slippery. The fireplace wasn't made for drawing, and there was but one little bit of a window in the whole room, and that wasn't more than half above ground: half the glass at least being broken out and its place supplied with old rags. So the room was dark enough, and generally pretty well filled with smoke. The damp used to come out on the walls, and stand there year after year, in big, gummy drops. There was a little closet in one corner of the room—a pine table against the wall, three or four wooden chairs that had been gradually broken down to stools, and a large collection of rags, shavings, straw and other rubbish in the corner opposite the closet. I remember all these details very vividly, because they constituted the home of my childhood, and I knew no other place of shelter in the world where I could set my foot. Whether I remember it with pleasure or hatred you may judge for yourselves.

"At any rate, in this one cellar my father and mother, my two brothers and sisters and myself all lived together—ate, slept, cooked washed and ironed, did everything in this one dank and noisome hole. My family was mostly kind to me and to each other. They never beat me when I had been unlucky in my day's work: but oftener when I came home crying bitterly, with my little frozen fingers almost empty, and dragging my old broom wearily over my shoulder, my mother's face has beamed with an expression of genuine sympathy and affection—I know it must have been, for it was so different from all I have seen since. Both my father and mother drank whisky whenever they could get a chance, and I early imbibed a passionate fondness for it.

"When I got older they wanted me to leave off street-sweeping and take to thieving. But I had not been on the crossing four or five years for nothing, and I had formed designs of a different character."

These designs she carried out.

These children generally abandoned their homes in the summer. Then they could walk a mile or two to the outskirts of the then city and return with bouquets of wild flowers for my lady's corsage. They hawked newspapers, oranges, apples, candy, shoe laces, sponges, colored lithographs, and other small wares that required little capital. Some sang and played instruments in the streets. Among the boys, next to selling papers, the favorite occupation was blacking boots. They—boys and girls both—slept in tenement hallways, under porches, in empty houses, in stables, in cellars, in covered wagons that were left in the street overnight, among bales of merchandise on the wharves and piers, in brief, anywhere and everywhere their childish ingenuity regarded as a place safe from the prying eyes of adults. Two of these boys slept one whole winter through in the iron tube of the Harlem Bridge.

Another found solitary shelter in a burned-out safe in the ruins of a fire in a Wall Street office building.

But there was a brighter side in the lives of these tender unfortunates. This was night, when the plutocrats sat in judgment on a performance in the Old Bowery Theater with its classic Greek façade. Some of the older boys attended the fights. Some of these were between humans, others between game cocks. In addition to the cock pits, there were several rat pits in Water Street and on other riverfront thoroughfares where rodents were readily obtainable. Here wagers were made on the number of rats a fox terrier could kill in an hour. A rat pit was usually flanked on either side by two or more sailor's dance halls where the chief attractions were half-naked women and drink. A gamin with a passable voice was usually welcome in these places, and at the end of his concert gathered up coppers and coins from the floor. He gambled. His favorite game was policy. His hard-earned pennies thus swelled the incomes of Mayor Wood and his brother Benjamin.

He loved freedom. He was the first to find shelter for a slave who decided to abandon his Southern master before the return trip home.

There was never a good-sized riot in which these street arabs did not participate. It did not matter on which side he fought so long as he was permitted to fight.

It was not until 1853 that any systematic attempt was made to relieve the lot of these miserable children. In that year the Reverend Charles Loring Brace with a bare handful of co-workers, organized the Children's Aid Society. "The public . . . immediately came forward with its subscriptions—the first large gift (fifty dollars) being from the wife of the principal property holder in the city, Mrs. William B. Astor." The quotation is from Brace's story of the founding of the society. The wealth of the Astors in 1853 is not readily ascertainable. In 1845 John Jacob Astor was worth $25,000,000, and his son, William B., had more than $5,000,000 to his credit. That more than fifty dollars was not donated by the Astors, who have never been unresponsive to worthy causes, indicates that Brace was regarded as a well-meaning sort of chap with a mad Utopian idea. For does not the Bible tell us that "ye have the poor always with you"?

Before the end of the year 1857 the people learned that poverty was not peculiar to the youth of New York, for in August a financial panic seized the country. Followed a suspension of every bank in the city. A like fate befell the financial institutions throughout New England and other parts of the country. Old commercial firms, industries of long standing, railroads—all went down before the storm. This panic intensified the poverty that had been widespread in the large cities'for nearly a decade. The suffering was keenest in the seacoast towns where there had been an unhealthy settling of the vast majority of the hundreds of thousands of immigrants that began to come to these shores in the late Forties.

The panic of 1857 temporarily focussed attention on the abnormal accretions to the population in these centers. In one ward alone north of New York's City Hall, ten thousand hungry were fed in one day. This was the Sixth Ward. In the Seventh Ward, Tweed headed the list of donors with $500, and set an example which other politicians followed. No one lacked fuel in his district that winter, or any other winter thereafter. Henceforward Tweed made charity an auxiliary of his crimes.

Undernourished bodies alone would not have made possible Wood's second administration. There must be famished minds. And not only the poverty-stricken were thus afflicted, but in time almost the entire population fell victims. The body politic is like the human body. Let one part be infected and the entire system suffers. Newspapers, the principal food of the mind of the mass, were in the hands of rank partisans, many of whom were corrupt. A dispassioned account of even the most casual ephemeral occurrence, in which the elements of race, religion, or politics entered, was almost unheard of. These journals were almost wholly organs of political parties or of groups with some special interest to serve. In an earlier day editors who differed with one another, or with men in public life, not infrequently had their final inning on the field of honor. But the sword and pistol had long since given way to the pen and pencil—at least among the editors. Occasionally a victim of editorial censure who had no paper of his own in which to respond, purchased a cowhide and lay in wait for his victim in some prominent street.

The Saturday following the local election of 1850, James Gordon Bennett, founder and editor of *The Herald*, was cowhided in Broadway by the defeated Democratic candidate for District Attorney. Allowing for the manners of the time, there was no justification for this attack. Even Philip Hone, who detested Bennett, referring to him as an ill-looking, squinting man, a degrader of public morals, a scandalmonger, and profane, and who believed that Bennett sold the columns of his paper to the highest bidder, made this comment on the incident:

"I should be well pleased to hear of this fellow being punished in this way, and once a week for the remainder of his life, so that new wounds might be inflicted before the old ones were healed, or until he left off lying; but I fear the editorial miscreant in this case will be more benefited than injured by this attack. The public sympathy will be on Bennett's side; the provocation was not sufficient, the motive was a bad one, and the character of the assailant not much better than that of the defendant."

A few years before this incident Bennett was fined $100 for publishing a libel on Mordecai M. Noah, then a Judge of the Court of Sessions. Mordecai was not above publishing a libel himself. Horace Greeley, who pleaded the cause of freeing the slaves in and out of season, looked upon the Negroes as unworthy of association with white men. Greeley's views on this were known to all. Yet Noah, then editor of the *Union*, published in his journal a baseless story accusing Greeley of having violated "the usages of society" in breakfasting with two colored men at a boarding house in Barclay Street. Greeley paid no attention to the canard until it had received wide circulation through the columns of other rivals of *The Tribune*. Greeley replied in an editorial which won for him the commendation of Noah's co-religionists. The sum of Greeley's response is found in its closing paragraph:

"We have never associated with blacks; never eaten with them; and yet it is quite probable that if we had seen two cleanly, decent colored persons sitting down at a second table in another room just as we were finishing our breakfast, we might have gone away without thinking or caring about the matter. We choose our own company in all things, and that of our own race, but cherish little of that spirit which for eighteen centuries has held the kindred of M. M. Noah accursed of God and man, outlawed and outcast, and unfit to be the associates of Christians, Mussulmen, or even self-respecting Pagans. Where there are thousands who would not eat with a Negro, there are (or lately were) tens of thousands who would not eat with a Jew. We leave to such renegades as the Judge of Israel the stirring up of prejudices and the prating of 'usages of society,' which over half the world make him an abhorrence, as they not long since would have done here; we treat all men according to what they are and not whence they spring. That he is a knave, we think much to his discredit; that he is a Jew nothing, however unfortunate it may be for that luckless people."

Greeley, until he became mad with the thirst for political preferment, was the most influential journalist of his day. His pen knew no guide save his conscience. He was the champion of lost causes long before he founded *The Tribune*. When he edited the *New Yorker* he wrote feelingly on "Relief of the Poor." He was a slave of the emotional side of his intellect. His columns were open to all the new isms, some of which he embraced with the same alacrity that he discarded them. He was an ardent advocate of woman suffrage. Overnight he changed and declared that woman's place was in the home. He defended Secession. In the next breath he denounced States Rights. He urged a vigorous prosecution of the Civil War. On the eve of the fall of Vicksburg and the immortal battle at Gettysburg he pleaded for an acknowledgment of the success of Southern arms. He pictured Jefferson Davis as a traitor. Yet when the leader of the Lost Cause was put in chains at the close of the war, Greeley risked everything he had in the world to undo this wrong. And he nearly lost all, for the circulation of *The Tribune* dwindled almost to nothing within a few days after Greeley signed the bond on which Jeff

Davis was released. The Bloody Shirt was being waved early. Suffering always made a strong appeal to him. The dire distress of the poor in the hard times of 1836 prepared the way for Greeley's conversion to Socialism. One could be a zealous Whig or Democrat then and still advocate Communism—as the word was used nearly a century ago. Greeley proved it, for while openly professing the materially economic theories of Fourier, he edited the leading Whig organ of the country.

Greeley was twenty-five years of age when he was placed in charge of the relief of the Sixth Ward during that winter of unprecedented suffering. Hundreds died from hunger. Many were found frozen stiff when relief parties arrived too late at their fuelless homes. Workingmen, after begging from shop to shop for weeks in search of employment, swallowed their pride and went from door to door to beg bread for their children. Greeley himself had made the rounds of shops for work. He knew how sad the smile and the shake of the head of a helpless foreman could make one. He too had known poverty. He was scarcely ten years of age when his father, to escape imprisonment for debt, had to flee their rocky New Hampshire farm in Amherst. Greeley never forgot the day when the Sheriff knocked at the door of their farm house in the dead of winter, and informed the lad's weeping mother that he was there to seize everything. In the meantime Greeley's father had found work as a "hired man" on a retired merchant's country place in Westhaven, Vermont. Here the Greeleys were reunited. They lodged in the gate-keeper's house.

His total disregard for dress—for which he was notorious—was acquired in these early days. Most of the year he wore only a tow shirt, a pair of trousers made from his father's cast-off garments, the cloth for which Mrs. Greeley spun and weaved, and dyed crudely with the bark of the butternut tree. A straw hat, generally dilapidated, covered his shock of pale, tow-colored hair. His younger brother and his sisters fared no better. In the cold, bleak winters of the Vermont hills, there was added to this raiment a jacket, a muffler, and a pair of shoes and stockings. In summer he wore shoes only on Sunday when attending church.

Greeley left the paternal roof at the age of fourteen. He had been the brightest pupil in the village school, a typical, one-room shack, such as still persists in rural districts where the "ungraded" school is the vogue. He left home with a definite purpose—to be apprenticed to a printer at East Poultneyville, Vermont. Greeley got the job.

Out of the scanty sum left after he paid the tavern-keeper where he boarded, Greeley set aside a little each week to help out at home. He was not quite twenty when he landed in New York on Friday, August 20, 1831. He wore trousers that did not reach his bare ankles—he scorned socks—a round jacket of coarse linen, which like his nether garments, was too small for him, and an overhanging straw hat. He had ten dollars and seventy-five cents in his pocket. Beyond this small sum and the clothes he wore, all he had in the world was an extra suit of clothes, a change of linen, and a half dozen handkerchiefs. These he carried in a knotted square of cotton fastened to the end of a stick slung over his right shoulder. He had neither friend nor acquaintance in the entire city. He tried several taverns before he found one to suit his modest purse. This was kept by an Irishman named M'Golrick, on West Street, near Washington Market. Sailormen while waiting for a ship sometimes stopped there. M'Golrick served good food and drink. Greeley was a teetotaler. For two days Greeley tramped from one printing shop to another. In some, because of his youthful appearance, he was accused of being a runaway apprentice.

On Sunday Greeley attended services at a Universalist Church. That afternoon, when he had about determined to return to Vermont, half-convinced that he could not find work, and fearful of what might happen if he found himself penniless in the city, a compatriot of M'Golrick, a shoemaker, decided Greeley's fate. This cobbler, who lived in a boarding house where several printers lodged, told Greeley that he had over-heard one of the printers say that hands were wanted in West's printing house at 85 Chatham Street. He was put to work at a case, and remained at West's until November when he found work in the composing room of *The Evening Post*. Although a first-class compositor, he was fired from this job because of his peculiar dress. This intensified his natural antipathy for snobbery.

Following the hard times of 1836, Greeley began to cast about for a remedy. He then had his own printing plant as well as a paper. So he could write what he pleased. He did. Accordingly there appeared a series of articles in the *New Yorker* in 1839-40 under the title "What Shall Be Done for the Laborer?" They attracted considerable attention, and were widely commented on. Albert Brisbane, the son of rich parents, who a short time before had completed his education abroad, with the usual residence in Paris, journeyed from his home in Batavia, New York, to make the acquaintance of the writer. The two became fast friends. Brisbane converted Greeley to Charles Fourier's concept of Socialism.

In his "Recollections of a Busy Life" Greeley says: "The propagation in this country of Fourier's ideas of Industrial Association was wholly pioneered by Mr. A. Brisbane, who presented them in a series of articles in *The Tribune*, beginning in 1841, and running through two or three years."

Greeley founded the paper with which his name is forever associated on April 10, 1841. The advent of *The Tribune* was heralded in *The Log Cabin* a week before. The announcement, which bore the caption, "New York Tribune," read:

"On Saturday, the tenth day of April instant, the Subscriber will publish the first number of a New Morning Journal of Politics, Literature and General Intelligence.

"The Tribune, as its name imparts, will labor to advance the interest of the People, and to promote their Moral, Social and Political well-being. The immoral and degrading Police Reports, Advertisements and other matter which have been allowed to disgrace the columns of our leading Penny Papers, will be carefully excluded from this, and no exertion spared to render it worthy of the hearty approval of the virtuous and refined, and a welcome visitant at the family fireside.

"Earnestly believing that the political revolution which has called William Henry Harrison to the Chief Magistracy of the Nation was a triumph of Right Reason and Public Good over Error and Sinister Ambition, the Tribune will give to the New Administration a frank and cordial, but manly and independent support, judging it always by its acts, and commending those only so far as they shall seem calculated to subserve the great end of all government—the welfare of the People.

"The Tribune will be published every morning on a fair royal sheet—(size of the Log-Cabin and Evening Signal)—and transmitted to its city subscribers at the low price of one cent per copy. Mail subscribers, $4 per annum. It will contain the news by the morning's Southern Mail, which is contained in no other Penny Paper. Subscriptions are respectfully solicited by

"HORACE GREELEY, 30 Ann Street."

The newspapers which Greeley ranted against were incredibly vile. Even the most vicious of sex-appealing tabloids of our own day are pure compared with the advertising columns of these journals. Bawdy houses advertised by street and number. When prostitutes moved from one house to another notice of the fact was printed in the "Personal" columns of some of the dailies and weeklies. Advertisements of charlatans, medical quacks, debauchers, thieves, and sharpsters, were also published at so much per line. Contraceptionists brazenly advertised their services. The most notorious of these was professionally known as Madame Restell.

In the year 1857, this woman was worth easily a half million dollars. How many times that sum she had earned in her unholy work can only be conjectured. With her money she controlled the courts, and the police. George Matsell, for many years Superintendent of Police, was on her payroll. She was known the length and breadth of the land. Correspondents of out-of-town newspapers in their weekly news-letters were never at a loss to fill out a column. There was always something to be said about Madame Restell. Pamphlets were written about her. On the cover of one of these, a contemporary wood-cut artist pictured her as a bat-like creature of the night, with distended maw, in the act of devouring a new-born infant.

Some of these unwanted infants were born alive. If the mother did not want to take the baby with her, Madame Restell and her kind would agree to dispose of it for a price. They had their own private agencies through which they would sell the little ones to those seeking to adopt a child. Many of them advertised for foster-parents in the "Personal" columns while their vile cards appeared in the "Medical" columns. This evil reached its peak in the late Sixties. In one issue of *The Herald*—Bennett's paper was the worst offender—immediately after the close of the Civil War six infants were offered for adoption. In the medical columns of the same number "ladies in trouble are guaranteed immediate relief" if they would call on Dr. Grindle. The doctor had a card in the "Personal" column reading:

"A beautiful female infant, four weeks old, American parentage, for adoption. Call on Dr. Grindle, No. 120 West Twenty-sixth Street. See medical card in this paper."

Madame Restell was never known to advertise infants for adoption under her own name. Her card in the "Medical" columns was enough. Then, too, she was a pioneer advertiser. Children pointed out her house of horrors. Citizens, rich and poor, wrote to the authorities asking them to take action against her. These protests were ignored. Ministers of the Gospel in their sermons called upon the authorities to drive her from the city. Bishop Hughes thundered anathema at her from the pulpit of old St. Patrick's Cathedral in Mott Street. But what were their voices against her money?

Madame Restell resented these pulpitarian outbursts as wanton attacks upon her and her profession. She took her calling seriously, as witness the opening line of her advertisement in the daily press:

"A certain cure for married ladies, with or without medicine, by Madame Restell, Professor of Midwifery."

She was wealthy, as we know. She was no mere charlatan. Of that she was convinced. No mere doctor: she was a Professor.

This unusual woman was born in Painswick, Gloucester-shire, England, in 1812. Her maiden name was Ann Trow. At the age of fifteen, while a servant in a family in her native country, she met and married a journeyman tailor named Henry Somers. Somers was a widower with one child, a daughter. Four years after they were married, the couple and Somers' child, emigrated to this country, arriving in New York the same summer that Horace Greeley first saw the city. They had not been in the city long before Somers fell victim to one of the periodical visitations of yellow fever.

Her brother Joseph Trow, who came to this country shortly after his sister and her family left England, was clerking in a pharmacy when Somers died. He contributed to her support and that of her child for a few months. But thereafter his help was not needed, as she made a good living as a seamstress. This continued until 1835, when she married Charles Lohman, a compositor on *The Herald*.

Lohman always had his eye on the main chance. His brother-in-law was a pharmacist. His wife was handsome. She had dark eyes, raven black hair, and a deep olive skin. Some thought she had Gypsy blood in her veins. Her love of gay colors heightened this impression. She had a soft but commanding voice. The result of Lohman's cogitations was his wife's entrance into the carnal field which she was to dominate. Her brother made the pills. Her husband wrote the advertisements, and within a year she had a midwife on her staff.

The name Restell was not acquired during a sojourn in Paris as some of the contemporary accounts have it. Firstly, she never visited Paris. Secondly, her mother's maiden name was Restell.

Soon her establishment at 146 Greenwich Street had hollows worn in its brownstone steps by her callers. She took in any one who had the price, but most of her patients, or those responsible for their condition, were well-to-do. And her wealth grew with her infamy. The people called her Madame Killer.

In the winter of 1864 the public clamor against her assumed threatening proportions. The Superintendent of Police detailed four of his men to protect Madame's establishment. This was only to be expected. She was his patroness. Ostensibly these policemen were stationed at the place to intimidate all who visited Madame's by asking their names. Mayor Havemeyer had ordered the officers posted in front of the house at the instance of the artful Matsell.

This official act followed the issuance of a warrant by Mayor Havemeyer on February 5, 1846, on the complaint of Mary Applegate, of Philadelphia, who had not yet arrived at her eighteenth year. Miss Applegate had been a patient of Madame Restell, and when she demanded her child, she was informed that a woman had adopted the infant, and all further information was denied her. The distracted mother won the sympathy of Havemeyer, one of the few honest executives of the period. But Madame Restell had aided, in her own peculiar way, several politicians, and had contributed to the campaign funds of many. These gifts to the war chests of aspirants for office were always made unostentatiously. She sent out presents to her friends in office at Christmas time—always in the shape of new gold pieces. When Tweed ruled Tammany Hall he warned the treasurer not to take a cent of Madame Restell's money.

Madame Restell cared little for warrants or courts. For years her money thwarted all efforts to drive her out of business. Citizens of distinction had endeavored to suppress her. Clergymen had demanded her expulsion from the city from their pulpits. And all had been in vain.

From the birth of the Republic, until the close of the period we are dealing with, it was not uncommon for people, or a part of them, when they did not like a law, or felt aggrieved at the manner in which it was being administered, to take matters into their own hands. It will be recalled that in the case of the Forrest-Macready riot, the mob was summoned to the Astor Place Opera House through the medium of broadsides posted throughout the town.

The people, or a part of them, decided that this was the

only way to restore Mary Applegate's child to her, and at the same time, rid the city of Madame Restell.

Persons going to their places of worship on the morning of Sunday, February 22, 1846, stopped to read large broadsides headed:

"ANTI-RESTELL MEETING"

In peaceable language the notices called upon citizens to assemble at the foot of Cortlandt Street at noon for the purpose of appointing a committee to wait upon Madame Restell and request her to leave the city.

Madame Restell's place on Greenwich Street was two blocks from the scene selected for the mass meeting.

By noon the following day a crowd began to gather, not at the foot of Cortlandt Street but in front of Madame Restell's. The reason for this change was due to the presence of fifty policemen at the place named in the broadsides. Superintendent Matsell quickly remedied this, and dispatched his men to Madame Restell's house where they found the mob demanding Mary Applegate's child and uttering many blood-curdling threats against Madame Killer.

The mob parted to let the police reach the entrance of the house. The officers immediately took up their position on the doorsteps and faced the crowd, their locust sticks held menacingly in their right hands.

There was an ominous muttering among the citizens, but at the command of one of their number, all marched peacefully down to the foot of Cortlandt Street. Here an empty hogshead was loaned by a ship chandler, and on this a spokesman climbed. He advised against violence. This pacific proposal was booed. Some of the mob were for overpowering the police and seizing Madame Restell, and riding her on a rail to the ferry across the street from where they were meeting. The speaker again warned against violent measures and asked that a committee be appointed, not to wait upon Madame Restell, but on the Mayor.

At this the mob shouting "Traitor!" abandoned the speaker to his hogshead and returned to Madame Restell's.

Here the crowd, which had increased in numbers, resumed their threats, and cries of "Give Mary Applegate her child!" All afternoon the mob remained in front of the house, milling to and fro. The noisiest of the lot were a number of ragged boys. At any moment the citizens could have rushed the police and overpowered them. But the sex of the object of their wrath prevented them. Madame Restell continued in business, unmolested, for another year.

In the summer of 1848 she was indicted for manslaughter. She had killed an unborn child and its mother, a young girl of sixteen named Maria Bodine, of Walden, New York. The public now demanded that justice be meted out to Madame Restell. The trial lasted eighteen days and proved a *cause célèbre*. A verdict of guilty was returned by the jury. The case proved expensive for Madame, who spent $100,000 in counsel fees, suborning witnesses, and in largesse to court officials and others. The public expected that she would receive a long term in Sing Sing. Instead, she escaped with the light sentence of a year in the County Penitentiary.

But Madame, thanks to her bountiful purse, was not placed in a cell. The principal keeper on Blackwell's Island, Jacob Acker, surrendered his quarters to her. She was permitted to receive her husband and her friends at any hour of the day or night. For these special privileges the prisoner parted with another fortune. All these facts were brought out by an Aldermanic investigating committee, all save what was given to Acker in return for the favors shown Madame Restell.

While in prison Madame purchased a large house at 162 Chambers Street, and had it converted into a hospital. Here she moved on completing her sentence.

At the beginning of Mayor Wood's first administration Madame Restell's stepchild, then a young woman of thirty, was married. This was one of the happiest days in Madame's life. She knew she was accursed of Hera and never could have children of her own. But on this wedding day she prayed, and wept as she prayed, for she loved this daughter of her first husband with all the affection of a mother. And in her prayer she pleaded that her hopes of a lifetime be realized. She wanted heirs, believing that her gory gold could be purified by the hands of children. She had but one name for her stepchild. It was *Daughter*. And Somers' child called this red-handed woman by the most holy of human names. Madame presented the bride—the only thing she really loved—with a dowry of $50,000, and paid the expenses of a honeymoon in Europe.

Madame had one undying hate. This was directed against all clergymen. She looked upon them as the cause of her imprisonment. And she had an unquenchable ambition. She wanted a position in Society—society with a capital S! Others, whose callings she regarded as not a whit better than her own, had bought their way into it. Why not she? She had money and was willing to spend it. Through her husband, the one-time compositor, now competing in friendly rivalry with his wife under the name of Dr. A. M. Mauriceau, she induced the publishers of the city directory to place after her name—"Female Physician and Professor of Midwifery." This was a start.

At the outset of Wood's second administration Madame commenced to lay her plans for meeting the Astors and the Belmonts on terms of social equality. She must have a house on the Avenue. That was a prime essential. And in gratifying this ambition she saw a means of revenging herself on one of her enemies—Bishop, now Archbishop, Hughes.

In the late Fifties the Archbishop and other leaders of his church planned the new St. Patrick's Cathedral on Fifth Avenue. Superintendent Walling, who succeeded Matsell as the uniformed head of New York's police, thus relates how Madame sought to even up scores with the prelate: "When the site of the new cathedral was bought, and the Archbishop designed to build the Episcopal residence at Fifty-second Street and Fifth Avenue, Madame Restell stepped in, and after running the property up to a price beyond its value, bought it."

The land faced the site of the Roman Catholic Orphan Asylum, which occupied the block immediately to the north of, and on the same side of the Avenue as, the Cathedral. On this parcel of ground Madame erected one of the most showy mansions in the city. It took two years to build. It had a frontage of forty-one feet on the Avenue, and was of brownstone, trimmed with Parian marble. An elaborately carved entrance opened on a wide and curving staircase of mahogany. At the head of the stairs stood two life-sized marble busts of Washington and Franklin, each surmounted by a silken Stars and Stripes. Madame's stable, which adjoined on the side street, harmonized with her mansion. Even the stalls were of mahogany. They were trimmed with silver. Her carriages, and the trappings of her thoroughbreds, were mounted with the same precious metal.

There was a side entrance to this building—part of it was fitted up as a hospital for Madame's wealthier patients, although she still continued her Chambers Street establishment. This was used by those who came to consult Madame professionally.

This palace, as the daily press generally referred to it, was occupied for the first time in 1864. Madame celebrated the event with a reception and ball. She was attired in a Paris creation of silver brocade, and on her black tresses, slightly streaked with gray—she was fifty-three years old then—was a crown of diamonds. The same precious stones glittered in her bracelets and on her fingers. A dog-collar of brilliants adorned her neck. Clusters of blue-white gems dragged heavily on the lobes of her ears.

A contemporary account of this event tells us that while dancing was going on in several spacious rooms, in others card-playing was indulged in. Wealthy merchants, brokers, railroad executives, lawyers, physicians, and "even a few magistrates and legislators"—the names charitably omitted by the chronicler—accepted Madame's invitations to her housewarming.

"Servants, wearing black garments and white neckties, were busy carrying refreshments around. Many persons, preferring the pleasure of eating to those of playing or dancing, were seated in another room at a table loaded with meats and delicacies. Next to this, another room, elegantly furnished, was crowded with young and old men, indulging in smoking. Boxes of cigars were piled up on elegant étagères. Many a smoker, besides the cigar he was smoking, filled his pockets with that luxury. Some of these rooms were lined with fine brocatelle, imported from France, Italy, China and Japan, the latter conspicuous for their fantastical drawing and patterns; others with Persian and Indian cloths; and the several pieces of furniture were of unexceptionable taste. Some were inlaid with gold, bronze or china; some were made up of rosewood, artistically carved. Gems of art and curiosities of every description were displayed upon étagères; and through the house, made bright as day by hundreds of gaslights, one walked on soft, smooth carpets of the best manufactures of Europe. They alone were worth a fortune."

While the merriment was on downstairs, in rooms on the upper floors some of Madame's patients were dancing with Death.

The day after this strange soirée, Madame, dressed in flaring colors, and glittering with diamonds, took her daily drive in Central Park. People stopped as the gorgeous turnout passed. Madame smiled. She was very happy that morning, for her daughter—her stepchild—had written that she and her husband and their child were coming to live with her. That little girl was six years old. And she called Madame—Gran'ma. All grandmothers are respectable.

When Tweed ruled the town Madame Restell offered a handsome sum to any of her circle who could induce this lion of politics to attend one of her dances. Harry W. Genet, grandson of Citizen Genêt, and known because of his lavish entertainments—often given on borrowed money—as Prince Hal, carried Madame's invitation to The Boss. Tweed stared for a moment at Genet, and without a word, turned on his heel and left the room to Senator Genet.

When a single word from Tweed would have closed this human abattoir, an appeal was made to him to put an end to Madame's career. But Madame knew too much. Tweed did not want to bring down her wrath upon his friends. While Tweed was in prison, Anthony Comstock, then beginning his crusade of purification, obtained evidence against the old tigress. She was then sixty-seven years old. After her arrest she was bailed out. Her trial was set for ten o'clock in the morning of April 1,

Madame, however, did not appear in court at the fixed hour. She had defied courts all her life. Why change now? The word spread that Madame had played an April Fool joke on the court by fleeing to Europe. She had not fled to Europe. She was still in her Fifth Avenue Palace, as the newspaper headlines had it next day, lying in a bathtub, her head above the water which ran crystal clear through the overflow outlet. She seemed to have two mouths, for her wrinkled neck was parted in a ghastly grin. But her right hand, which hung over the side of the tub, still clenched the knife.

The hand was crimsoned, as it had been for nearly half a century.

Hera was avenged.

The year 1857, which witnessed the beginning of Madame Restell's mad dream for social recognition, also marked the beginning of Tweed's real rise to power. Tweed, although defeated the year before by a Know-Nothing for Alderman, had not suffered the slightest loss of prestige among his friends in Tammany, especially among the older men, the real leaders of the organization, who saw in Tweed a capacity for leadership that no one else possessed.

An act passed by the Republican-controlled legislature in the spring of the year, and signed by New York's first Republican Governor, furnished the Democratic leader with the machinery through which he obtained a firm foundation in politics. This was the reform measure creating the bi-partisan Board of Supervisors. And in this same act, designed by its sponsors to prevent corruption, the first Tweed Ring had its origin. By the provisions of this law, the Board was to consist of six Democrats and six Republicans, to be chosen at the general election. The Republicans, with the holy zeal of a new-born party, believed that their half of the Board could successfully check any evil plans of the Democrats. For the Republicans were convinced that no good could be expected from a party that produced a Fernando Wood.

This measure, *per se*, was iniquitous, as it meant that the nominees of the Democratic and Republican conventions—six of one and half a dozen of the other—must be voted for by the people, willy nilly. This reform measure destroyed the old check on corrupt majorities by making impossible a choice by the voters between two sets of candidates. The people must vote for the nominees of hand-picked caucuses when it came to choosing the men who would audit county expenditures, appoint inspectors of elections, and perform other highly important functions.

The primary purpose of the Republicans in making the Board of Supervisors bi-partisan was to prevent the appointment of corrupt election boards throughout the city as had been the vogue, the Democrats, when they were in power, appointing members of their party who were not too squeamish when it came to stuffing ballot boxes, or if need be, destroying them, just as their opponents did when they held the reins of government. But by giving the two major parties equal representation on the Board, this no longer would be possible. There was a perfect system of checks. And, of course, this also would apply to the spending of the taxpayers' money. The reasoning was sound.

Tweed was elected to this Board of Supervisors. Another Democratic member was the eminently respectable Elijah F. Purdy, bank president and briber, but one who never took any corrupt money himself.

Like a new broom, the new bi-partisan Board of Supervisors swept clean the first year. No act of corruption is traceable to it during this twelve-month period when all eyes were focussed upon it.

The Republicans also put through another bill to correct an evil that they encountered at the preceding election. This was to take the police out of the hands of the city authorities and vest the appointing power and complete control of the force in the State authorities. This was done through the same ingenious bill that had roused the opposition of the entire city, Whigs and Reformers, and Democrats alike, in the first administration of Mayor Wood. There was no outcry from the good citizens of the town when this measure was reintroduced in the legislative session of 1857. On the contrary, there was widespread approval of the proposal. That it violated the principle of home rule was conceded. But what was this when it meant the end of the continuance of the control of these guardians of the peace by the iniquitous Wood? And all knew that in the last election Wood had given furloughs to many policemen whom he knew to be loyal, that they might electioneer for him, while those on duty at the polls made possible the theft of many thousands of ballots. The Republicans charged that, in the old cities of New York and Brooklyn in the election of 1856, at least 10,000 fraudulent votes were credited to the Democratic candidates. That undoubtedly was true. It was likewise true that there were many votes wrongfully counted for Republican candidates in bailiwicks that had seldom gone Democratic.

But there was more than the offenses committed by the police at the polls charged against them. Their open alliance with the underworld was urged as an additional reason why the Metropolitan Police Bill, as the measure was entitled, should be enacted into law. The act, which was signed by Governor King, created a new police district out of the counties of New York, Kings (which embraces Brooklyn), Richmond and Westchester. The Bronx was then part of the last-named county. This sub-division constitutes the present City of New York, plus, of course, what is now known as Westchester County. The control of the new police department was vested in a board of five commissioners, with the mayors of Brooklyn and New York members ex-officio.

When Governor King appointed the Board, James W. Ney, one of its members, later United States Senator from Nevada, announced that the entire Municipal Police, as the New York City force was officially known, would be taken over bodily.

Wood appealed to the Municipal Police not to recognize the State officials, saying that the act creating them was unconstitutional. Wood knew that the contrary was true. A ballot was taken and 800 of the 1,100 policemen voted to remain loyal to Mayor Wood. These 800 were Democrats.

The 300 policemen who voted to recognize the duly constituted State Board of Police Commissioners were, for the most part, Republicans. They formed the nucleus of the Metropoli-

tan force in New York City. The State Board immediately
went through the formality of trying the 800 who remained
loyal to Wood for insubordination and appointing a like number of Republicans in their places. Wood did likewise with the
300 who joined the Metropolitans and added a like number of
Democrats to the old Municipal force.

The city now possessed two police forces, of equal strength,
and each regarding the other as a body of outlaws.

Wood gave a semblance of legal authority to his defiant attitude by appealing to the courts to sustain his contentions
that the act creating the Metropolitan Police District was
invalid.

Citizens watched this unique situation, knowing that it was
only a question of time when these two police forces would clash
in serious combat, as an intense feeling of pronounced bitter-
ness prevailed.

The anticipated clash occurred on June 16.

A few days before the Street Commissioner had died. His
Deputy claimed the right to succeed him. But he had no
money, so Wood would not recognize him. And as he was
not a Republican, the Governor ignored him. The Governor
erroneously assumed the power of appointment in such a con-
tingency, and named Daniel D. Conover, a partisan. The
Democratic Mayor named Charles Devlin, who paid Wood
$50,000 cash for the honor. His politics did not matter.
Wood never made an appointment to an office where the possi-
bilities of illicit gain were present, without demanding a price
in advance.

Conover, with the Governor's appointment in his pocket,
called at the City Hall. Wood, wholly within his legal rights,
ordered his illegal Municipal Police to eject Conover. They
did it. And many of Wood's hangers-on aided the police. But
Conover did not go to the City Hall alone. He had a dozen
or more friends accompany him. These, too, were set upon.
They fought back, but they were quickly overwhelmed.

Conover then went to a Republican judge, Recorder James
M. Smith, and swore out a warrant for the arrest of the Mayor,
accusing him of assault and with inciting a riot. The warrant,

accusing the Mayor of the latter crime was given to Captain Walling, of the Metropolitan Police, to serve. He was one of the 300 who deserted Wood.

Walling went to the City Hall. He had to make his way through a mob who were attracted by the unusual spectacle of 500 policemen—the outlaw Municipals—drawn up around the building. Inside were garrisoned a reserve force of 300 to 400 more.

Walling was permitted to enter the Hall, and eventually was allowed to enter the Mayor's room. Wood knew the reason for the visit.

"Well, sir, what do you want of me?" asked the Mayor, his hands resting on the end of a Colonial desk that separated him from the police.

"I have here a warrant for your arrest," replied Walling, exhibiting the court order.

"You are not an officer. I dismissed you from the force."

"I am an officer. I am a member of the Metropolitan Police."

"I do not recognize the legality of the service or the existence of the Metropolitan police. I will not submit to arrest, or go with you, or concede that you are an officer."

"I shall have to take you forcibly if you resist."

"I will not be taken!" exclaimed Wood, glaring at Walling. "You may consider that answer resistance, if you please."

"No," smiled Walling, as he started around the desk to where Wood stood, "No, sir, that is not resistance—only refusal."

"Go way!" commanded the Mayor, striking a bell on the desk.

Wood was prepared for all eventualities, for no sooner was the bell struck than three doors leading into the room suddenly opened and from each poured a half-dozen Municipal Police, who seized Walling and thrust him unceremoniously into the corridor.

Walling returned to Recorder Smith with news of what had happened. The Judge immediately issued an order directing the Sheriff of the County to arrest the Mayor.

By the time that Walling reached the Sheriff's office, all sorts of rumors concerning how he had fared at the City Hall at the hands of Wood's Municipal Police had reached the headquarters of the State Board of Police Commissioners. One report was that Walling had been badly mauled and was kept a prisoner by Mayor Wood.

A force of Metropolitan Police, numbering fifty, under command of Captain Jacob Seabring, at double-quick time, hastened to Walling's rescue.

This little handful of duly constituted guardians of the peace, their batons drawn, swung bravely into City Hall Park, while thousands of citizens from safe vantages on Broadway and Park Row, breathlessly awaited the outcome.

They did not have long to wait, for no sooner had the Metropolitans reached the front steps of the City Hall than they were set upon by the eight to nine hundred Municipal policemen with whom Wood had surrounded himself in anticipation of such a visit.

From all sides the Municipals swept down on the puny force. For three or four minutes the battle raged. Although outnumbered some sixteen to one, the Metropolitans asked no quarter but returned blow for blow until their more numerous foe had driven those still able to keep on their feet from the field, while several of their comrades lay groaning or unconscious on the ground. Twelve of the Metropolitans were severely injured.

After the battle, Captain Walling accompanied by Sheriff Westervelt and the latter's counsel, called at the City Hall.

Again the Mayor refused to submit to arrest, shouting:

"I will never let you arrest me!"

Three men, although the law was on their side, were no match against one with eight to nine hundred at his call.

An hour or so later, the Seventh Regiment, in command of General Sandford, of the State militia, was marching down Broadway, colors flying and band playing. The regiment was on its way to Boston to aid in celebrating the anniversary of the Battle of Bunker Hill.

The members of the State Board of Police Commissioners appealed to General Sandford for aid in arresting the Mayor.

The regiment, which had halted while the parley was on between its commander and representatives of the State, resumed its march. This time there was no gay music. Only the ominous dull tread of marching men.

As the Seventh reached Warren Street it swung into City Hall Park and was halted when the head of the column came abreast of the windows of Mayor Wood's office.

Wood now submitted to arrest, and the Seventh proceeded on its way to the Hub.

But this did not end the intense feeling, not only among the two rival police forces, but among the citizens, who were taking sides, and it was deemed advisable to keep nine regiments under arms.

Both the State and city authorities realized that a truce must be declared pending the decision of the courts on the questions raised by Wood as to the validity of the Metropolitan Police Act, to avoid other sanguinary encounters, in which the troops could participate. Accordingly it was agreed that the Metropolitans, and Wood's outlaw police, were to patrol the streets jointly, and must exchange salutes when they met.

This lasted until July 1, when the Court of Appeals decided against Wood. And later the Metropolitans who were injured in the battle with the Municipals in front of the City Hall obtained judgments against Wood totaling $13,000. This was the only punishment—if punishment it can be called—meted out to the Mayor for these riotous disturbances.

The decision of the court threw eleven hundred men out of work. There was no employment to be had by thousands of clerks, mechanics, and laborers who had been vainly seeking employment for months. So there was little hope for these.

But a few of these former policemen found work on July 4.

On that day rioters, for the first time in the history of the country, threw up barricades in the streets.

This riot had its genesis in the previous election, when thugs from Tweed's ward, the Seventh, had some differences at the polls with a group of a similar type from the Sixth Ward.

The Sixth Ward gang was known as the Dead Rabbits. Tweed's constituents were known as the Bowery Boys.

Both factions went out on the Night Before the Fourth—it was celebrated with firewater then, as the day following was observed with fireworks.

The Fourth of July fell on Saturday in 1857. About one o'clock in the morning a gang of Dead Rabbits, numbering less than a score, decided to pay its respects to the Bowery Boys, who made their headquarters in a saloon at No. 40 Bowery. As the Dead Rabbits turned into the Bowery at an easy march they were shouting: "Down with the Bowery Boys!"

Just ahead of them were two members of the new State police. Instantly their battle-cry gave way to: "Down with the Metropolitan Police!" and "Down with the Black Republicans!" Simultaneously they quickened their pace, and presently broke into a run.

One of the policemen, named Lord, was standing in front of the coffee house of Henry McCluskey. The place, fortunately for the Metropolitan, catered to the all-night trade.

Into the coffee house plunged Lord, and the proprietor, at the frantic appeal of the policeman, locked the door.

The other policeman was in front of the headquarters of the Bowery Boys. His name was Florentine.

To the Bowery Boys a Metropolitan was as much an object of hatred as a Dead Rabbit. All gangsters despised the new force, for they were adherents of Wood. But when Florentine rushed into the saloon, exclaiming: "For God's sake lock the door or I'm a dead man!" he found sanctuary in the haunt of his foes. And when the Bowery Boys learned, as they did the moment the bolt had been turned in the lock, that he was being pursued by their traditional enemies, they resolved to protect him with their lives if need be. There were only five or six of them, but they were determined to make up in valor what they lacked in numbers.

In a moment the havens of the two policemen were stormed by the Dead Rabbits, who had divided themselves into forces of equal strength. While they hurled paving stones at the saloon and at the coffee house, their cries of "Down with the Metropolitans!" and "Down with the Black Republicans!" brought them many recruits.

The Bowery Boys who had never turned their backs on a fight shattered a tradition as they saw the size of the mob without. They realized that their safety lay in flight. This they effected by turning out all the gas-jets and escaping through a rear door. The Metropolitan, discarding his tunic and hat, to avoid being recognized, went with them.

The proprietor of the coffee house, and the policeman who took refuge there, and his three or four customers, also fled the fury of the Dead Rabbits through a rear door.

The Dead Rabbits, on discovering that they had been outwitted, continued their bombardment until they had wrecked the saloon and the coffee house.

The town awoke at sunrise to the usual firing of cannon and the explosions of firecrackers. It was a day of general rejoicing save among the Bowery Boys, who talked of nothing but the early morning rout of five or six of their number by the Dead Rabbits. That they were greatly outnumbered was forgotten. All they remembered was the galling fact that the Dead Rabbits had put them to flight.

Early in the afternoon of the Fourth the Bowery Boys went among their auxiliaries in the Seventh Ward and recruited their strength to a little more than three hundred. Some carried stout cudgels. Others had knives. Some were armed with pistols. Those armed with pistols were men who, up to three days before, had been members of the outlaw Municipal Police.

At a point a few blocks east of their wrecked headquarters the Bowery Boys held a council of war. After they had exchanged views they began to round up the trucks, drays, and wagons that were parked in the streets in the immediate neighborhood over the holiday. The owners of these vehicles, in leaving them in the public thoroughfares, violated a city ordinance. But the Bowery Boys vindicated the majesty of the law, and dragged their prizes through East Broadway to Chatham Street, thence north to the Bowery, and reaching Bayard Street, they halted.

Ordinarily these three hundred men—they were little more than boys most of them, for few of them had reached their twenty-fifth year—would have been shouting or singing as they

marched through the streets. Some small boys who ran beside this little army shouted occasionally to one another, or
called out to some older companion, who, because of his size,
was permitted to march with the men. There was quite a
number of these youths. Most of them were in rags. One
of them carried a pick-ax on his shoulder. He executed a weird
dance from time to time. This was because the cobblestones
burned his bare feet.

Just above the corner where the Bowery Boys halted—a few
doors to the north—was their wrecked headquarters. And two
doors nearer them were the shattered doors and windows of the
coffee house.

The irregular rectangle of streets of which the notorious Five
Points was the center, and on whose eastern boundary line they
stood, was the Sixth Ward, the Bloody Sixth Ward, the
hitherto undisputed territory of the Dead Rabbits.

The Bowery Boys now held a second council of war on the
very ground on which the Dead Rabbits had triumphed some
twelve hours earlier, long before the day had dawned. It was
now two o'clock. There was no mistaking the day. From all
quarters came the incessant rat-tat-tat of exploding Chinese
firecrackers. Now and then a more venturesome celebrant of
the eighty-first anniversary of Independence Day discharged
a firearm.

The result of the second council was the dispatching of a
half-dozen squads of the Bowery Boys to the tenement houses.
When they rejoined the main force, which had not stirred,
they were weighted down with mattresses, trunks, and kitchen
tables.

Now the whole force swung east into Bayard Street behind
the wagons, trucks, and drays, which they took the precaution
to shove before them, like moving breastworks. Immediately
behind these marched men holding the mattresses before them.
Next marched those who carried tables and trunks. These too
were held before the bearers in shield-fashion. Bringing up the
rear were about twenty former members of the Municipal Police
and the youth with the pick-ax. The rest of the force, some

two hundred or so, remained where Bayard Street crosses the Bowery.

The newspapers and other records of the day are silent on the identity of the leader who made these dispositions. There is no hint as to his name, or what he looked like. That he had knowledge of the warfare in the streets of Paris we know. And there is ample evidence that his commands were obeyed. Beyond these deductions nothing is known of this enigma.

When the van of his forces reached the first street that runs at right angles to Bayard Street, paralleling the Bowery, they halted. This is Elizabeth Street. It begins at Bayard Street. A block further west is Mott Street. A block beyond this is Baxter Street. Here Bayard Street ends blindly. Elizabeth Street is the first thoroughfare to cross Bayard Street after it leaves at the Bowery. Mott Street, south of Bayard, makes a crooked turn for a short stretch until it meets the Bowery. To-day, this irregular little patch of New York bounded by the Bowery, Bayard, and Mott Streets, constitutes Chinatown.

The moment the Bowery Boys reached Elizabeth Street they turned the trucks and drays and wagons over on their sides. The mattresses were propped up against the vehicles and lashed fast with ropes. The tables and trunks were used to reënforce the barricade. A livery stable on Bayard Street, near Elizabeth, supplied a few more vehicles to strengthen the fortification. The youth with the pick-ax proceeded to loosen the cobblestones.

When the building of the barricade commenced, some of the Bowery Boys who had remained on the corner of Bayard and the Bowery, detached themselves into squads to search the wooden rookeries on either side of the street between the Bowery and Elizabeth Street. They did not want to be sniped at from the rear.

Word that the Bowery Boys had invaded the domain of the Dead Rabbits and had thrown up a barricade quickly spread through the district.

Flushed with their victory of the early morning, the Dead Rabbits rallied to their forces, until they equaled, numerically at least, the invaders. Within half an hour after the first barricade had been erected, a second had been constructed at Bayard and Mulberry Streets. The latter thoroughfare led straight into the heart of the Sixth Ward, just as Bayard Street commanded a direct approach into Tweed's bailiwick.

The barricades could not have been erected at more strategic points. And as much mystery shrouds the tactician of the Dead Rabbits as does the leader of their enemies.

The Dead Rabbits were not permitted to build their barricade in peace. When the Bowery Boys saw the Dead Rabbits trundle the first wagon up Mulberry Street, they fired at them. No one fell, and the Dead Rabbits, returning the fire, went on with the work before them.

After a minute or two of firing, fifty or more of the Bowery Boys charged the enemy. But they learned that they were in hostile territory before they advanced a hundred feet, for occupants of the houses in the No-Man's Land between Elizabeth and Mulberry Streets showered flat-irons, candlesticks, bottles, and heavy dishes on their heads. The Bowery Boys beat a precipitate retreat. Two of the Boweryites fell. Their comrades picked them up as they ran and carried them back to the shelter of the barricade. One was shot clean through the body. The bullet had pierced his heart. This was the youth who had started the work of ripping up the paving stones with a pick-ax. The other escaped with a slight wound in the fleshy part of the thigh. Those who were not armed with pistols—these were keeping up a rapid fire on the barricade of the Dead Rabbits— scrutinized his features. No one knew him. There was nothing in his pockets to disclose his identity. It was useless to look for the marks of the makers of his rags. Two of the Boweryites lifted the slain youth tenderly and carried him into a hallway of a tenement house immediately in the rear of their barricade.

The two gangs fought for the next half-hour without any further serious casualties. During the first hour and a half no one save those in the immediate neighborhood knew of the Battle of Bayard Street. The shooting could be heard for blocks around, in fact, as far south as the City Hall. The shots were distinctly heard a few hundred yards to the north-west where, on White Street, the Sixth Ward Police had their headquarters. But they, like all else who did not witness the riot, believed the irregular fusillade was part of the customary noisy celebration of the Fourth.

Before the battle was on an hour the first report that a riot was in progress was brought to the commander of the Sixth Ward Police.

"The Dead Rabbits are fighting down at the Five Points!" exclaimed the excited citizen.

To the Five Points, some several streets south of the barricades, went twenty-five policemen. But they found no rioters there and returned to their station house. In the next hour the police went out at least half a dozen times.

The reason why the police could not see the barricades was that each time they went out they turned down Center Street from which Bayard Street cannot be seen, and the shots of the rioters on their left were balanced by the shots and popping of firecrackers on all sides.

At four o'clock the police were informed of the location of the street battle. At this hour the Dead Rabbits had six dead behind their barricades. Forty or fifty of their number were wounded. These, too, were fighting. A dozen or so of the Bowery Boys were wounded, but none mortally. Their marksmanship was by far the more effective. This was due partly to the greater number of former members of the Municipal Police who fought on their side. But they were confronted by an auxiliary of the Dead Rabbits which they could not fight back. This was the little army of housewives who rained flat-irons, candlesticks, bottles, and crockery on the invaders' heads. All the Dead Rabbits had to fight from overhead was the scorching sun.

When the police started from their headquarters in White Street at four o'clock, they marched double quick to the scene of the riot. As they swung south on Baxter Street, after leaving Bayard, some scouts of the Dead Rabbits called out the warning: "Here come the Metropolitans!"

The Dead Rabbits for a moment were panicky. But at the

sight of the police—enemies of their Mayor and patron—one of the Dead Rabbits shouted:

"Three cheers for Fernando Wood!"

Another cried:

"Down with the Metropolitans!"

And with these and other battle-cries—another favorite was "Down with the Black Republicans!"—a hundred of the Dead Rabbits were ordered to charge the advancing police. That left about twice that number to defend the barricade.

There were only twenty-five policemen. The Dead Rabbits outnumbered them four to one. And they were as well armed.

As the police, who had their clubs drawn, neared Bayard Street, the Black Rabbits, firing their pistols, rushed fearlessly at their new foe.

The police returned the fire.

Two Dead Rabbits fell, and one policeman. All three were dead.

The police, who were also attacked from the windows of the houses, after their first and only volley, turned tail and fled, leaving their dead on the ground. The Dead Rabbits without stopping to reload their pistols, pursued them as they fled to their station house, tearing the policemen's hats from their heads, and after unfastening the police shields, pinned them on their own breasts and returned in triumph to their barricade.

The Dead Rabbits now felt invincible. A few minutes before they had routed the police, and they now planned to rout the Bowery Boys. That would mean taking the barricade at the other end of the street. This they were confident of doing.

Presently the Dead Rabbits rushed from their shelter, runing full tilt toward the enemy, who held their fire until the Dead Rabbits reached the edge of the barricade. Then the Boweryites fired a deadly volley which was accompanied by showers of paving stones hurled over the top of the fortification. The Dead Rabbits beat as precipitate a retreat as had the Sixth Ward Police a few minutes before. Several of their number, who were wounded by the fire, lay groaning in agony where they fell.

When news of the complete rout of the policemen and the

death of one of their number reached Police Headquarters, none of the Commissioners was available, it being a holiday. But within an hour Simeon Draper, President of the Board, was found.

By this time the entire city knew that street fighting, such as the city had never before witnessed, was going on somewhere near the Five Points. And as the story spread the riot was magnified into an insurrection. Children were called in from the streets and doors and windows bolted. Thousands believed that the rioters from the downtown wards were preparing to march into the fashionable sections and sack the houses. Consternation seized all. Even Draper was affected. He caused a telegraphic dispatch to be sent to Boston ordering home the Seventh Regiment, which was still at the Massachusetts capital. Three regiments in town were ordered out.

While preparations were being made to quell the riot, one of the most singular events in the history of street fighting occurred.

A policeman, in the uniform of the hated Metropolitans, with a club in his hand, walked down the Bowery and saluted the armed lookout of the Bowery Boys at the entrance to their barricade. He was promptly covered with their pistols.

"Don't shoot!" he exclaimed. "I come as a friend. I want to lead you."

His name was Peter Anderson.

There was no questioning his sincerity. The armed Boweryites advanced toward him. Several of their fellows joined them.

Anderson explained, while a dozen pistols were pointed at his head, that he was a friend of H. H. Hitchcock, the policeman who had been slain by the Dead Rabbits.

He was taken to the barricade. He was one to four hundred, for the Bowery Boys had increased their forces since the fighting began. He could not have played traitor even if he desired, save at the cost of his life. He observed several stands of pistols.

A few minutes after Anderson joined them, the Bowery Boys widened the narrow apertures at either end of the barricade, and through these openings, with Anderson at their head, waving his policeman's club in lieu of a sword, poured three hundred Boweryites, yelling like Indians, as they stormed the barricade of the Dead Rabbits.

The Dead Rabbits, more frightened than the Sixth Ward police an hour before, deserted the barricade, leaving it in the possession of Anderson and his followers.

But the Dead Rabbits rallied after running several blocks, and loading their pistols, returned to the barricade, which they took after a short engagement. The Bowery Boys made only a half-hearted resistance, for their force was not sufficiently strong to hold two barricades against a mob nearly as large as their own.

Until seven o'clock the two gangs fought each other from the protection of the barricades. Then the rioting ended suddenly—for the day. The militia, some 3,000 strong, was approaching. Word of the coming of the soldiers reached the fighters several minutes before the guardsmen arrived on the scene.

Ten were killed in New York's first battle of the barricades. More than a hundred were wounded.

The next afternoon the Dead Rabbits carried the warfare into Tweed's ward, but were quickly driven out. Another riot, in which little blood was spilled, occurred the same evening, but the mob dispersed when they saw the militia marching toward them. And again, in the latter half of the month, there were two days of rioting in the upper East Side wards. But these were the usual commonplace clashes between rival gangsters which did not rise to the dignity of barricade fighting. The time was not ripe.

Tweed was busy preparing for the coming municipal campaign. He was certain of being chosen a member of the bipartisan Board of Supervisors. He was not concerned about his own election. He was more concerned with the defeat of Wood, who was not only a menace to his friends in Tammany, but to himself. Purdy was out opposing Wood. So was Tilden. Wood's continuance in office would destroy all semblances of an organization and make it a one-man machine. This must not be permitted. Wood was influential with the mass. He had catered to it. And all concerned in his overthrow understood that something extraordinary must be done to dislodge him. Wood had control of the nominating machinery of Tammany, and his renomination was assured. Outside of the organization Wood had enemies equally powerful—all property owners, big and small, who had seen their tax bills double under his maladministration.

This fight on Wood was led by Purdy and Tilden, openly at first, but covertly after the organization renominated him for Mayor. One may knife a partisan, but one must do it in the dark.

While Tweed was engaged in this fight to destroy Wood, he was furthering his own ambition to build up himself. Wood had committed a grievous blunder in not surrounding himself with men in high place who owed their election to office to him. Tweed saw this tactical error. He profited by it. So Tweed set out to make himself powerful by placing his friends in office. He had Peter B. Sweeny, thenceforward his tool, nominated for District Attorney. George G. Barnard was named for Recorder. Barnard was then in his early thirties, a tall, commanding figure, with long, wavy, jet-black hair and mustache, large, lustrous eyes of piercing brown, a pale-olive complexion, and the features of an aristocrat. He carried himself like a soldier, and dressed like a fop. Wood cherished the illusion that Barnard was his man.

Barnard and Sweeny were elected. This gave Tweed control of the county prosecutor's office and of a Judge with the power of trying a capital case. And his Judge would sit on the bench for four years. And if he did Tweed's bidding, Barnard knew he could look forward to greater honors at his patron's hands as his term neared its end. If they played fair with Tweed, all three could be rich. Sometimes men under similar circumstances rose to the dignity of their positions and forgot the man who made them. This happened occasionally, as Tweed well knew. But he felt he could rely on these. He had obtained their nominations without charging them a cent. Sweeny and Barnard knew that Tweed could have sold

these nominations for a small fortune. Tweed banked on their
gratitude.

As the returns came in election night showing the triumph of
Barnard and Sweeny, Tweed's joy was almost complete, for
earlier reports indicated the defeat of Wood for Mayor. Wood
ran on the regular Democratic ticket. Tweed, until the final
count was in, doubted that Wood could be defeated. Wood
campaigned under circumstances that would have spelled overwhelming defeat to any other man. Less than a month before
election proofs of his corruption were presented in the Supreme Court. It was shown that he and his brother Ben,
through a contract awarded by Wood, stood to profit more
than $40,000 on the sale of glass ballot boxes. Brother Wood
had purchased 4,000 of these contrivances for less than $20,-
000. And Mayor Wood contracted to purchase them for the
city for $60,000. The sales of countless offices by Wood, his
incitement of the police riot in front of City Hall, his swindling
of the city by the purchase of land at extravagant prices and
in other ways—all these things were charged against him.

At the ratification meeting in Tammany Hall, which Tweed
did not attend, Wood answered his critics. This he did in
resolutions praising himself, and informing the voters that he
was not the only man who had been attacked and vilified by
the enemies of the people. He instanced the cases of Thomas
Jefferson, Andrew Jackson, and Daniel Webster. These
statesmen, said Wood through his spokesmen, had been hounded
to their graves by harpies. This had ever been the fate of
honest, self-sacrificing public servants.

But this time Wood could not persuade the chief of the
house of Astor to head a list of prominent citizens to certify
to his honesty. These wealthy whitewashers were shamed or
frightened into silence by the united opposition of every
decent element in the town to the Mayor. There was but one
candidate in the field against Wood, Daniel F. Tiemann, a member of Tammany Hall. Republicans, and Independents, in and
out of Tammany, and even the Know-Nothings, indorsed the
candidacy of Tiemann. While Tweed cast his vote for Wood—
he must remain regular if he was to get anywhere in his organ-

ization—he had the Bowery Boys out on Election Day doing effective work at the polls for Tiemann, who was a member with him in The Forty Thieves.

The Dead Rabbits—such of them as were uninjured in the street fighting of the Fourth of July and the following day— were out for Wood. Both sides, as usual, hired gangs to bruise and repeat for their respective candidates. Tiemann won by a little more than 2,500 votes, the official count giving him 43,216 and Wood 40,889.

Tweed, in analyzing the campaign conducted by Wood, noted that a new feature which Wood had introduced into election-eering had not been properly played by its ingenious creator. Wood had devised the scheme of turning out new voters on the eve of election. To Judges who were friendly to him, he sent a large number of newly-arrived immigrants. Each bore a card signed by one of his lieutenants reading: "Please naturalize the bearer." Some 4,000 citizens were made by this process—all, be it said, legally. The nominal court fees were paid by Wood. This, plus promises of jobs, was all that these 4,000 votes cost him. He could have obtained 10,000 as readily. That he did not do so was an error and cost him the election.

Wood, although defeated for reëlection, was far from de-stroyed, as Tilden, Purdy, Tweed, and others planned. The indorsement of Tiemann by the Know-Nothings alienated a vast majority of Catholics and the foreign-born from Wood's enemies in Tammany. This was evidenced at the meeting of the Democratic General Committee in the Wigwam on Decem-ber 8, 1857, after the defeat of Wood at the polls.

This was an important meeting. The General Committee, whose members were chosen at what passed for a party pri-mary, controlled Tammany. Wood had controlled this com-mittee prior to his defeat for reëlection. Did he control it still? This was the question all eagerly asked. For the enemies of Wood had promises from supporters of Wood, which, if kept, would wipe out his majority in the com-mittee.

United States Marshal Rynders, gang leader and thug, was chairman of the General Committee, and as such, presided at the meeting. He was avowedly anti-Wood. He had an opportunity to display his sentiments when the question came up of deciding who were the properly accredited members from the Ninth Ward—the only district where there was a contest. An active partisan of Wood had been duly chosen by the voters of the Ninth Ward. An anti-Woodite, with little color to his claim, asserted his right to sit in the General Committee. Wood's follower should have been seated. But the General Committee—Wood was soon to be an ex-Mayor, and what is more friendless in politics than an "ex"?—voted by a majority of six to seat the anti-Woodite. Rynders, in putting the motion, let his voice assume a sneering tone when he mentioned the name of the Wood supporter in presenting the majority report recommending the seating of the anti-Woodite.

While the General Committee was in session a young man named Cornelius Wood—no relation to the Mayor—was sitting in a chair in the barroom at peace with all the world. He was very quiet. He could hear snatches of the deliberations in the General Committee room by not making any noise. He had only a curious interest in the proceedings, and had come to have a drink at the bar which was open to the general public.

A gangster known as The Cockroach, and two companions, came into the barroom looking for Stump Ferris, who ran the saloon and hotel known as the Essex House at Essex and Grand Streets. Stump was an anti-Woodite and a leader in the Thirteenth Ward. The Cockroach had been drinking heavily. He did not know Stump. But earlier in the evening Stump had been pointed out to him. In his present state any one resembling Stump was Stump to The Cockroach.

Young Cornelius Wood had the misfortune of looking like Ferris. And it was the youth's further ill-luck that The Cockroach had not been kept in the penitentiary until he had served out his term, instead of being paroled so that he might help the Mayor in his fight for reëlection.

The Cockroach and his pair of bruisers walked over to where the youth who looked like Stump Ferris sat and pitched into him. When the assailed showed fight, The Cockroach and one of his friends each fired a shot at him. One of them lodged in his left shoulder.

There were several policemen on duty at the Wigwam. But for some time they had been in the basement taking a quiet drink from time to time to relieve the monotony. Hearing the shots they rushed upstairs. Seeing the wounded man staggering toward the bar, the policemen, who did not know what they were doing, imagined he had fired the shot, and before they could be apprised of their mistake, had knocked him to the floor, their clubs laying open the unfortunate's skull in three places.

This act of violence, which temporarily halted the proceedings of the General Committee, did not add to Wood's popularity in that body. It was the last act of violence by adherents of Wood before this most corrupt Mayor retired from office at the hour of noon, January 1, 1858.

CHAPTER XV

On January 1, 1858, an inventory of Tweed's political vest pocket assets would reveal a Judge—Recorder Barnard; a county prosecutor—District Attorney Sweeny; a county clerk—Tweed's old friend and neighbor from the Seventh Ward, Richard B. Connolly. A few minor office-holders were indebted to Tweed, but not 'as these three were. And we must not forget that Tweed was a member of the powerful bi-partisan Board of Supervisors, which he was soon to dominate. Nor must we omit Mayor Tiemann, who occasionally made a gesture in keeping with his position as a wealthy dealer in paints.

Tiemann, elected as a fusion, or reform, candidate, gave nearly all the good jobs at his disposal to Tammany leaders, and Tweed obtained not a few of these for friends and others. Where there were any peculiar perquisites attached to the office, Tweed obtained his share. And in grafting, as in politics, he learned much from Wood. When Wood appointed men to office, he not only exacted a price for the place in advance, but insisted on receiving a generous part of the graft as it came to his appointees.

About this time Tweed began to pay less attention to the making of chairs and brushes, and to devote more of his time to politics. His services as a lobbyist in the Common Council—of which he was not a member—were always in demand, as he had justly earned a reputation for making good on almost any mission he undertook. Tweed was growing rich—out of politics.

Tweed celebrated his thirty-fifth birthday on April 3, 1858, with a dinner at the old Westchester House, Bowery and Broome Street. This was a great jollification meeting.

Every one ate heartily. No one enjoyed the food more than Tweed. There were many courses. One was soft shell crabs. These delicacies, which are not to be found in New York waters until midsummer, were gathered for the occasion in a Virginian bay. Tweed had several helpings of crabs. In fact he ate little else. Rare wines were served with every course. Lawgivers, lawmakers, and lawbreakers toasted one another, and all toasted Tweed. Tweed raised his glass to every toast. It was always a glass of champagne. Those who sat next to Tweed observed that he scarcely sipped the wine when he placed the glass to his lips. Yet each time he made a pretense of swallowing. But there was still a little wine in the glass when the dinner was over. A stranger entering the banquet hall when the talk was loud and the laughter louder, seeing Tweed's ruddy countenance, and hearing his talk and laughter, which were in keeping with the rest, would have assumed that he, too, was in his cups.

Ten days after this dinner, there was held, in this same hotel, a meeting of the members of the Tammany Society. It was a meeting a little out of the ordinary. The Tammany Society during its first hundred years or so, exercised almost as much power—sometimes more—than the purely political side of the organization. On more occasions than one the Tammany Society, through its Council of Sachems, had decided which of two warring factions was the regular organization of the county. Men living in all parts of the country, who never cast a vote in New York, were members of the Society. On this day there were men from the West in attendance at the meeting. They had been summoned by urgent appeal to aid in preventing former Mayor Wood from capturing the Tammany Society, and in turn, possibly, the entire organization. Wood planned to do this by electing his own Council of Sachems. But in this he was outwitted, and the anti-Wood ticket, headed by Isaac V. Fowler, a leader of society, a lawyer, and Postmaster of the city, was elected. Fowler at this time was generally regarded as an honest man. He was at heart a thief. But he was no whit worse than his brother, John Walker Fowler, who, as clerk to Surrogate

Tucker, fled with more than $30,000 of the moneys entrusted to him by this court of widows and orphans.

With the election of Fowler as Grand Sachem, Wood's power in the organization was at an end. Wood saw that it was useless to continue to fight from within, so he started a rival Democratic organization which took its name from Mozart Hall, where the Wood faction first met. Wood announced that the Mozart Hall Democracy was the only true Democratic party in the city. Many thousands believed him. Wood's whisper squads went among the foreign-born citizens and spread the word that Tammany Hall had fallen into the hands of the Know-Nothings. How was Tiemann elected? Tiemann was a member in good standing in Tammany, and an unrelenting enemy of Wood. Wasn't Tiemann elected by the Know-Nothing vote? Did not this bunch of bigots support him to the last man? Who was running Tammany now? Fowler, the aristocrat, and the Know-Nothings. The Know-Nothings and the aristocrats had no use for Wood because he hated them and wanted them out of Tammany Hall. And that was why they cast Wood out of the organization. And this fantastic fable was dinned into the ears of the immigrant population, both Catholic and Protestant.

But Connolly and Sweeny, and Schell, and others who knew the Irish and the German voters, for these comprised the bulk of the new stock, laughed at Wood's attempt to build up an independent organization on these base appeals. But Tweed, who had been through one campaign where he had been defeated by the Know-Nothings, knew how unreasoning a man can be when his religious or racial prejudices are whipped into a frenzy of fanaticism. Wood, driven from the Democratic Party, was looked upon as a political *Pantalone* by all, save Tweed. Nothing must be left undone, cautioned Tweed, to checkmate every move Wood made. Wood was spending a fortune in building up his mushroom organization, hiring halls where meetings were held, club rooms where his followers could foregather, and distributing largesse among the various gang leaders. It would not be possible to unite the Republicans and Know-Nothings behind Tiemann again, for long before his term ended, these allies would know how Tiemann had betrayed them into the hands of their common enemy. Thus, argued Tweed, persistently. At length his advice was heeded and a search for an available candidate began.

In September of Tiemann's first year as Mayor, the people of Staten Island—then not a part of New York City—staged a most unusual riot. The mob included some of the wealthiest citizens of the old towns of the Island. Some wore masks. A goodly number wore no disguise.

This riot was the outgrowth of the refusal by the authorities to heed the numerous petitions asking for the removal of the Quarantine buildings. The riot was incited by the Board of Health of Castleton. Two days before the riot the Board adopted resolutions ending with this advice to the people of the entire Island:

"The Board recommends the citizens of the county to protect themselves by abating the abominable nuisance without delay."

These inflammatory resolutions were printed and posted at once throughout the Island. The following evening more than a thousand men assembled at Fort Hill, one of the forts erected by the Hessians during the Revolution. Many were armed with muskets and shotguns. A speaker asked the assemblage if it would follow the advice of the Board of Health. A few minutes later the mob, in columns of four, marched to the Quarantine buildings. There were several physicians in the mob.

On reaching Quarantine, which was surrounded by high walls enclosing the hospitals and numerous outbuildings, the mob discovered that Dr. Thompson, the Health Officer, had armed a large number of stevedores with muskets with orders to protect the buildings at all hazards. These guards were quickly disarmed. The walls were then battered down and the mob swarmed onto the grounds, invaded the hospitals, and removed the sick to nearby private homes. The doctors, nurses, and attendants were then driven from the buildings. Next the torch was applied to the yellow fever and smallpox hospitals, the Health Officer's residence, and upwards of a dozen other structures.

The local police could not cope with the mob, which remained at the scene of the conflagration to see that their incendiarism was successful. A boat was dispatched to New York for help, but before the mob returned to their homes for breakfast the following morning little was left of the Quarantine buildings outside of a mass of smoldering ruins.

The month following the firing of Quarantine, New York was reminded in a serio-comic manner of the wholesale robbery of the treasury during the Wood administration. Robert W. Lowber, a Wall Street broker, one of the many through whom Wood added to his ill-gotten riches, brought suit against the city for $228,000. This action was predicated on a purchase made by the city, through a corrupt alliance of Mayor Wood and the Common Council, of a parcel of land worth $60,000. Lowber had only a third interest in the lot. In spite of this, $196,000 was duly agreed upon as the price to be paid. When Wood left office the city authorities refused to pay this extortionate sum—nearly three and one-half times the value of the real estate, and $176,000 more than the $20,000 equity Lowber had in the property.

Technically and legally, Lowber was in the right, and the city, in refusing to complete the bargain, was legally and technically in the wrong. The city lost its case. Lowber, tiring of the specious pleas made when he demanded the $196,000 plus interest, costs of the trial, and damages, bringing the total to $228,000, placed the judgment for this sum in the hands of the Sheriff.

The Sheriff had but one choice: to seize property of the city that would realize the amount of the judgment at public auction and sell it. Whereupon he posted a notice announcing a Sheriff's sale of the City Hall! And to be knocked down at the same time, the vendee buying not only the city's seat of government, but every bit of equipment within its graceful walls, from the Mayor's chair up and down. The purchaser would hold title, and could do with the property as he saw fit.

A well-defined rumor was current that former Mayor Wood intended to bid in the City Hall, dispossess Mayor Tiemann, convert the Mayor's office into a headquarters for his Mozart

Hall Democracy, and with a grand gesture announce that all
the other departments of the city government using the building were at liberty to continue therein during their pleasure.

Beads of perspiration rolled down the worried face of Mayor
Tiemann as the Sheriff announced the terms and purposes of
the sale. Tiemann was rich. He, too, intended to bid in the
City Hall, and hold it until the city could reimburse him. But
the unscrupulous Wood had far more money and could outbid
him. To be dispossessed from his office by Wood! And what a
disgrace that would be! The ridicule! It would be unendur-
able.

The City Hall was knocked down to Tiemann for the nominal
sum of $50,000. Wood after all, did not compete with him.
No one did. And for a short time the title to the property
was vested in Tiemann until the municipality repurchased it
at the price the Mayor had paid.

While Wood and his henchmen absented themselves from the
sale of the City Hall that October day, they were everywhere
else, particularly on primary day when the Democrats elected
their delegates to the various nominating conventions. Wood
had put his own candidates—they bore the tag of the Mozart
Hall Democracy—in the field, and in some districts where they
knew the vote was against their chief, the gangsters of Wood
assaulted the election officials and destroyed ballot boxes. His
Dead Rabbits were out with their pistols, and like parapher-
nalia. Two of them were shot.

The Democratic primary returns showed a defeat of the
Wood candidates in nearly every Ward. But Tweed knew the
extremes to which it had been necessary to go to defeat the
Mozart Hall candidates. Wood had been underrated as a foe.
Wood was powerful. More than that: he was a menace. And
Tammany, to win back from Wood the large numbers of citizens
of Irish birth or descent, gave to representatives of this race
a generous share of the places to be filled at the general election. This was done largely at the suggestion of Tweed.

After the party primaries had been held, a fusion was effected, as in 1857, of the Republicans, Know-Nothings, and

independents. This combination elected two-thirds of the Councilmen, sixteen out of twenty-four.

And -Tweed and all Tammany were glad that this was not the election of 1859 when they would have a Mayoralty contest on their hands. No one any longer doubted the seriousness of the situation. And to three men Tammany looked for salvation: Tweed, Purdy, and its new Grand Sachem, Postmaster Fowler.

CHAPTER XVI

THE campaign to destroy Wood and his Mozart Hall
Democracy directly led to the formation of the first Ring with
which the name of Tweed is associated.

"The very definition of a 'Ring' is that it encircles enough influential men in the organization of each party to control the
action of both party machines; men who in public push to extremes
the abstract ideas of their respective parties, while they secretly
join their hands in schemes for personal power and profit."

This masterly description of a Ring was written by one who
had occasion to watch the growth of the successive Tweed
Rings, and understood them as no other man on the outside
of these corrupt bi-partisan combinations—Tilden.

This Ring was formed in the Fall of 1859 within the Board
of Supervisors, which was composed of an equal number of
Democrats and Republicans. Corruption in such a body, in
the opinion of the Republican lawmakers who created it, would
be impossible. A week before, the Board met to appoint the
inspectors for the general election. Tweed and other Democratic members of the Board met at the home of John R.
Briggs, one of their number. Just as they were seated a carriage drove up and out stepped Postmaster Fowler in his
inseparable top hat.

Fowler after bowing gracefully to the six—Purdy was among
them—drew their host apart, apologizing for doing so, and
held a whispered conversation with him. Fowler then departed.
Briggs informed Tweed and the other four Supervisors that
Fowler had raised $2,500 to bribe Peter P. Voorhis, a Repub-
lican member of the Board, to remain away from the next meeting when the appointment of election officials would be made.

212

Fowler gave the money to Briggs who turned it over to Voorhis, who lived up to his end of the bargain. Voorhis was a coal dealer.

Tweed oversaw the preparation of the list from which the 609 election inspectors were made. Of these 609, nearly 550 were Democrats. Gamblers, saloon-keepers, and gangsters were among those appointed by Tweed to protect the sanctity of the ballot. These inspectors were, by virtue of their position, able to permit the stuffing of the ballot boxes, and to make fraudulent tallies, and false returns of the count. Their capacity for evil was almost limitless. They could—and often did—defeat the will of the voters.

Tweed defended this action as eminently proper and in keeping with the common practice of partisans. Under oath and telling some of the things he knew, he was pressed to admit that the bribing of Voorhis with its attendant appointment of crooked election inspectors were improper. Tweed rejoined:

"Oh, no! I don't think men are governed in these matters by the ideas of what should be [in civil life] between man and man. I have never known a party man who wouldn't take advantage of such a circumstance."

And no one challenged Tweed's frank statement.

Of the entire 609 election inspectors appointed by Tweed, not one could be counted as a Wood man. Yet in the face of this, Wood had himself nominated for Mayor by his Mozart Hall Democracy. Tammany named one of the outstanding citizens of the day, William F. Havemeyer, banker and philanthropist, and twice before elected to this office.

The Republicans nominated George Opdyke, a wealthy importer, and founder of the banking house of George Opdyke and Sons. He was indorsed by the Know-Nothings, and the independents, who were strongly organized under the label of the People's Party. With Wood and Havemeyer dividing the normally Democratic majority, the odds were heavily in Opdyke's favor.

At the Tammany ratification meeting the orator of the evening was James T. Brady, one of the leading lawyers of the town, who made a speech characterizing the recent raid on Harper's Ferry as "the most important event which had happened in our day in America." He expressed astonishment that Henry Ward Beecher in his sermon the previous Sunday had uttered no word in reprehension of this riot, treason, and murder. "I am sorry for old Brown," said Brady. "I do not think there was any necessity for the haste which marked the trial, not that there was ever any chance for his acquittal, but I believe that it would best please the honest democracy were the old man to be pardoned, and sent back to shame the men who used him, lacking courage themselves."

Then Brady wanted it observed that the first note of sympathy for John Brown's life had been heard at a Democratic meeting. The speaker then ridiculed the Abolitionists and reformers in general in the following verse:

> "I thank my God the sun and moon
> Are both stuck up so high
> That no presumptuous hand can stretch
> And pluck them from the sky.
> If they were not, I do believe
> That some reforming ass
> Would recommend to take them down
> And light the world with gas."

Brady then denounced William H. Seward for adding to political parlance "the terrible phrase," *the irrepressible conflict.* He warned against the consequences of the continuance of this agitation for slavery, saying:

"The irrepressible conflict, which we hear of, if it ever comes, will result in the extermination of the black race. The black race must go down."

The audience was with Brady to a man. All that Brady said on slavery was outmatched at the meetings Wood addressed. Wood had no sympathy for old Brown. The sooner they hanged him and all Abolitionists, the better he'd like it.

Brady and every other speaker lauded their candidate for Mayor. And Havemeyer was worthy of all the good that could be said of him. For no Mayor since Philip Hone excelled him, and the latter only in his art as an observer and recorder of life.

Of Opdyke, as a citizen, nothing but praise could be uttered —then. But perhaps he may be pardoned for turning white with fear before a hostile mob, even if Tweed were by his side to protect him.

Yet both Opdyke and Havemeyer came in behind Wood on Election Day. Wood's old alliance with the saloon-keepers and the underworld stood him in good stead. But these votes alone would not have availed him were it not for the response of the foreign-born to his caterings to their bigotry. He carried the Irish districts solidly. And every extreme Southern sympathizer in the city cast his ballot for Wood. Thousands of votes were stolen from Wood and Opdyke and credited to Havemeyer, yet in spite of all these frauds—Wood in times past had profited by similar thefts at the polls—the official count stood:

Wood	29,940
Havemeyer	26,913
Opdyke	21,417

Before the end of 1859 the name of Tweed ceased to be identified with chairmaking. Tweed's father, now a man of sixty-nine, had not been connected actively with the craft for several years. That old pain in the heart, which had laid him up when Tweed was a small boy, had come back. He now seldom left his room, and when he did, he leaned heavily on his white-haired wife. For four years the old couple had made their home with Tweed.

Tweed kept from his father knowledge of the passing of the chairmaking industry. It would have broken the old man's heart if he were to know one-half the truth. The business had been going from bad to worse for more than a year. Yet every week Tweed rendered a fictitious account of the business as he handed his father "his share of the profits." Tweed was wealthy, even though he was not taking in anything from the old family business. Nor was he any longer drawing any income from the brush factory, for that had been sold months before with the passing of his father-in-law. This, of course, Tweed's father knew. There was nothing shameful in that. But there was in filing a petition in bankruptcy. For that was what Tweed had done as head of the firm of Richard Tweed and Sons, Chairmakers. Tweed could have paid the creditors of the firm and never missed it. He was worth at least $50,000 when the firm failed.

Wood began his third term as Mayor on January 1, 1860. That same day Tweed embarked on his first year as a politician untrammeled with business cares. Thenceforward he devoted every hour of the day and night to the new science which Wood had instituted. And before the year was ended there was conferred on him the title of Boss. Tweed liked the word to such an extent that in time even his intimates ceased addressing him as Bill. Even behind his back he was referred to as The Boss when his friends and supporters spoke of him. No one— save scriveners of the opposition press—spoke of him any longer as Bill Tweed, or Big Bill Tweed.

The title of Boss was not bestowed on Tweed as a symbol of affection, but as a reward of merit. Tammany's great problem was to remove the label of bigotry that Wood had affixed to the organization. This must be accomplished before an attempt could be successfully made to win back the Irish vote which had, until Wood started his Mozart Hall Democracy, been Tammany's undisputed asset for several years.

In the year 1860 the population of New York City numbered 813,669. If there had been nine less inhabitants in the Metropolis, the emigrants from Ireland alone would have been exactly one-quarter of the people, as there were 203,740 natives of the Emerald Isle residing on Manhattan Island. The next largest group of foreign-born consisted of the Germans, who totaled 119,984. The English came next with 27,082, the Scotch followed with 9,208, the French numbered 8,074, and the Italians, 1,474. There were only 383,345 native-born whites, less than half the number of the city's inhabitants. Negroes and peoples from countries other than those enumerated made up the remainder.

Wood's success was due more to the dense ignorance of both

the foreign and native stocks than to any other factor. More than one in every seven adults in the city were unable to read or write any language. They were divided: native-born, 26,163; foreign-born, 95,715.

It was through the discovery of the dishonesty of Postmaster Fowler that Tweed became known as Boss. Tweed, of course, had no hand in Fowler's undoing. That was due entirely to the vigilance of auditors of the Federal Government. This was May 10, 1860. Fowler had stolen $155,000 of the Post Office receipts. The warrant for Fowler's arrest was given to Isaiah Rynders, then serving his last year as United States Marshal. Rynders knew what it was to be arrested himself. And he knew how it felt to be freed. But Fowler could not escape as he had, once he was arrested. The proofs against him were overwhelming.

Rynders went to Fowler's hotel. Fowler was in his suite— the Postmaster's. He spent $25,000 annually in living and entertaining at the hostelry. Rynders knew Fowler was in, and instead of calling on him immediately on reaching the house, he went into the bar and ordered a drink. He had several. And with each drink he announced that he had come to arrest Fowler as an embezzler of Government funds. Eventually he went to Fowler's apartment. But the society favorite had departed. He was *en route* to Mexico where he was safe from extradition.

This left the office of Grand Sachem of Tammany vacant. Several names were suggested. All save one were native-born and Protestant. The exception was James Conner, a Roman Catholic, and popular with his people. Tweed was his sponsor. And through Conner's election as Grand Sachem Tweed removed the label of bigotry that Wood had placed on Tammany, and thus paved the way for the return of the Catholics and the foreign-born who had been beguiled by Wood—the one-time member of the inner circle of the Know-Nothings—into believing him to be their saviour.

Eight days after Fowler fled to Mexico, Tweed's father died. In *The Herald* of May 19 appeared in the obituary column:

"Tweed—In this city on Friday Morning, May 18, of disease of the heart, Richard Tweed, in the 70th year of his age. The friends of the family, of his sons Richard Jr., and William M., and grandson, Charles Rodgers, are respectively invited to attend his funeral from his late residence, 237 East Broadway, on Monday afternoon at two o'clock, without further notice."

In the same issue the lead story tells of the nomination of Lincoln at Chicago the preceding day. Throughout the paper Lincoln's first name is spelled Abram. This error or slight is repeated for many days. From a sketch of the nominee published in *The Herald* of May 19, we quote:

"Mr. Lincoln was comparatively unknown to the people of this section of the Union until during the past Winter when he made a tour of the Middle and New England States, delivering stump speeches at twenty-five cents per capita admission. He delivered a speech in the Cooper Union Institute which he evidently carefully prepared for the newspapers, but on the night of the lecture he interspersed it with radical Republican sentiments as treasonable as Seward's 'irrepressible conflict' doctrine. He realized $200 from this lecture. He next visited Connecticut and stumped that State for the Republicans. The fact that he charged an admission for his lectures—a thing unknown before in our political history—was the subject of comment among leading Republicans, and in several instances, received the rebuke which such political showmanship deserved."

A few days later Bennett penned these appraisals—in charity let us characterize them as snobbish—of Lincoln:

"A rough-spun, disputatious village politician, who is known as 'Honest Abe' Lincoln—honest because he has the reputation of being as truculent as he promises, and like John Brown, means what he says. Seward was a refined Republican whom his party could not force beyond his own judgment. Lincoln is exactly the same type as the traitor who was hung at Charleston—an Abolitionist of the reddest dye, liable to be led to extreme lengths by other men. Without education or refinement, he will be the plaything of his party, whirled along in the vortex of passion if he should gain control of the government. The comparison between

Seward and this illiterate Western boor is odious—it is as Hyperion to a satyr."

Bennett was not a philosopher, and a democrat only in name. Ralph Waldo Emerson, some three years later, saw Lincoln somewhat as Bennett did. Emerson dubbed Lincoln a clown, of narrow horizon, undignified, disputatious, but honest meaning, and faithful to the public interest. This is the philosopher's appraisal of Lincoln:

"You cannot refine Mr. Lincoln's taste, extend his horizon, or clear his judgment; he will not walk dignifiedly through the traditional part of the President of America, but will pop out his head at each railroad station and make a little speech, and get into an argument with Squire A. and Judge B. He will write letters to Horace Greeley, and any editor or reporter or saucy party committee that writes to him, and cheapen himself.

"But this we must be ready for, and let the clown appear, and hug ourselves that we are well off, if we have got good nature, honest meaning, and fidelity to public interest, with bad manners,— instead of an elegant roué and malignant self-seeker."

Yet Emerson hailed the election of Lincoln in '61 as an act sublime—a pronunciation of the masses of America against Slavery. We all have our little weaknesses. Emerson did not like to see a man wearing a top hat who was not born with one on his head. This was not the fault of Emerson. It was the fault of Boston.

Lincoln's vote in New York City was very light. Out of a total of 85,922, he received 33,311.

The vote for Lincoln would have been larger—by at least one ballot—if he had been popular in the drawing room of the Astorocracy, as New York's society was referred to by the scoffers. His very name made the ladies reach for their smelling salts. To the Elegant Oakey Hall, Lincoln was more of an abomination than to Bennett. The Elegant One felt that it was personal disgrace to remain in a party which nominated Lincoln. So he publicly renounced the principles of the Republican Party and its new leader and turned Democrat. Tweed embraced him and made the society favorite his lieutenant. A Lincoln for a Tweed! The Elegant Oakey was an esthete. Also a materialist. For Tweed had much to give. Hall did not have to wait long, for Tweed had him nominated and elected District Attorney.

Tweed, that autumn, gave the Elegant Oakey an example of how he rewarded those who were faithful to him. Recorder Barnard's term was expiring. Tweed could always count on Barnard's word. If one of Tweed's strong-arm men ran afoul of the law and he was tried before Barnard, Tweed's intercession was equivalent to a dismissal of the case. Tweed intended to elevate Barnard to the Supreme Court Bench. United States Marshal of the Southern District of New York, Isaiah Rynders, and a few other prominent members of Tammany, had their own selection for the Supreme Court, and, before the judicial convention met, Rynders and his group had a majority of the delegates.

Barnard, since Tweed so willed it, was nominated. In this case Tweed achieved his end through an appearance of successful floor work. This method consists of circulating in the gaze of all, among the opposing delegates at the convention before the vote is taken and persuading them to change their minds. Tweed, however, had won over these delegates, in his own fashion, long before the convention met. Tweed was a master of convention practice.

Tweed presided at conventions where he had any doubt as to the outcome. There were but few of these. When he found the delegates beyond his control, he would arbitrarily announce that his candidate had been nominated and declare the convention adjourned. Rynders, after one of these decisions, thrust a pistol against Tweed's breast. Tweed turned his piercing blue eyes on Rynders and stared at him until the weapon was lowered. Elijah Purdy, patronizer of refectories, promised Tweed that he would preside at a nominating convention for a minor judicial office where he was interested in seeing a friend nominated. Here again Rynders was leading the opposition. Tweed suspected that the respectable Purdy would not keep his word when he was likely to face a riot, as he and Tweed had agreed that Rynders' candidate must not be given the nomination.

"So I went to the convention that night," said Tweed in relating the story afterward, "and behold! no Purdy came. 'Come on,' said I, 'I'll preside.' And I took the chair, and it wasn't very comfortable either. I saw, as the roll call proceeded, that Doyle [Rynders' candidate], had a majority of the delegates. Said I to the secretary: 'Have a motion made to dispense with the calling of the roll!' It was done."

Following his custom as in such emergencies, Tweed had another motion made to nominate the organization candidate by a *viva voce* vote. This was done. Tweed in the storm of "Noes" which followed the announcement of his decision, declared the convention adjourned. A riot ensued. Tweed was driven into a corner by Rynders and his delegates. Rynders threatened Tweed. Whereupon The Boss smilingly responded: "I'm not afraid of a whole ward of your fighting villains."

This adventure added immeasurably to Tweed's political reputation.

The war clouds were gathering fast when Barnard took his seat on the Supreme Court Bench. And New York had become the Richmond of the North. On January 5, the *Star of the West,* a merchantman, put out secretly from the port with men and arms for the relief of Major Anderson at Fort Sumter. South Carolina had seceded from the Union two weeks before. Dr. Alexander Jones, a Virginian, telegraphed South of the departure of the vessel, and its destination. The result was that when the ship sailed into Charleston Harbor with the American flag flying she was fired on from Morris Island where the Palmetto flag flaunted in the breeze. For several minutes shot fairly rained around the Stars and Stripes, one shot striking the ship in the port side as she was swinging around to head for the open sea.

The return of the *Star of the West* to New York, without having accomplished her mission, was a cause of almost universal jubilation in the city. This sentiment was not the feeling of the mass alone. The sympathy for the South was shared by bankers, merchants, and business men generally. The trade with the South was extensive. Many of the prominent citizens of the town were united to aristocratic Southern families by marriage. There was a general commingling of interests. Many who voted for Lincoln were opposed to freeing the slaves, or interfering with the Southern States regardless of what they did. Even Greeley at this time had not embraced the doctrine of Abolition and defended Secession as a States Right. He did not believe in a Union of States pinned together with bayonets, and sought to persuade the North that Secession would only add to the prosperity of the North. When Mississippi, Alabama, Florida, Georgia, and Louisiana in the first three weeks of the year had followed the example of South Carolina, Greeley wrote:

"The Secession movement is bringing business and prosperity to the North which will daily increase until the South shall be no account whatever except as a cotton field."

Wood was bound to the South by strong bonds. He and his brother Ben, now a Member of Congress, were owners of lotteries with charters from Southern States. They were honest in their pro-slavery views. They openly advocated the cause of the South in their organ, *The News*. The staff of this daily was composed of Southern sympathizers as rabid in their prejudices as the most pronounced Abolitionist. Southern journalists never visited New York without paying a call at the office of *The News*.

Two days after the *Star of the West* sailed South on its mission of failure Wood startled the country with a formal proposal to the municipal legislature that the City of New York secede from the Union and institute her own independent government. That he had conceived this daring move after a consultation with representatives of the slave-holding States was manifest by the assurance he gave the Common Council that New York would "have the whole and united support of the Southern States," should she withdraw from the Union. And while disclaiming a readiness "to recommend the violence implied in these views," Wood in the next sentence said:

"In stating this argument of freedom, 'peaceably if we can, forcibly if we must,' let me be not misunderstood."

So that Wood may not be misunderstood, we quote the pertinent parts of his *argument of freedom*:

" . . . It would seem that a dissolution of the Federal Union is inevitable. Having been formed originally upon a basis of general and mutual protection, but separate local independence—each State reserving the entire and absolute control of its own domestic affairs, it is evidently impossible to keep them together longer than they deem themselves fairly treated by each other, or longer than the interests, honor and fraternity of the people of the several States are satisfied. Being a government created by opinion, its continuance is dependent upon the sentiment which formed it. It cannot be preserved by coercion or held together by force. A resort to this last dreadful alternative would of itself not only destroy the government but the lives and property of the people.

"If these forebodings shall be realized, and a separation of the States shall occur, momentous considerations will be presented to the corporate authorities of this city. We must provide for the new relations which will necessarily grow out of the new condition of public affairs.

"It will not only be necessary for us to settle the relations which we shall hold to the other cities and States, but to establish, if we can, new ones with a portion of our own State. Being the child of the Union—having drawn our sustenance from its bosom and arisen to our present power and strength through the vigor of our Mother—when deprived of her maternal advantages, we must rely upon our own resources and assume a position predicated upon the new phase which public affairs will present, and upon the inherent strength which our geographical, commercial, political and financial pre-eminence imparts to us.

"With our aggrieved brethren of the slave States we have friendly relations and a common sympathy. We have not participated in the warfare upon their constitutional rights or their domestic institutions. . . . The City of New York has unfalteringly preserved the integrity of its principles in adherence to the compromises of all the States. We have respected the local interests of every section, at no time oppressing, but all the while aiding in the development of the whole country. Our ships have penetrated to every clime, and so have New York capital, energy and enterprise found their way to every State, and indeed to almost every county and town of the American Union. If we have derived sustenance from the Union, so have we in turn disseminated blessings for the common benefit of all. Therefore New York has a right to expect and should endeavor to preserve a continuance of uninterrupted intercourse with every section.

"It is, however, now folly to disguise the fact that judging from the past, New York may have more cause for apprehension from the aggressive legislation of our own State than from external dangers. We have already largely suffered from this cause. For the past five years our interests and corporate rights have been repeatedly trampled upon. Being an integral portion of the State, it has been assumed, and in fact, tacitly admitted on our part, by non-resistance, that all political and governmental power over us rested in the State Legislature, even the common right of taxing ourselves for our own government has been yielded, and we are now not permitted to do so without this authority.

"The enormous expense of the government of this city, its insufficiency for the correction of abuses and securing of economy, and a state of administration throughout bordering on anarchy and utter confusion, all irresistibly impel me to the serious inquiry whether the legislature has power and authority to effect these mischievous changes in the organization of our municipal affairs. I would be recreant to my duties as a citizen if I forbore protesting against what I am convinced has been a series of usurpations on the part of the State Legislature as detrimental to our city as unwarranted by every consideration of common justice. The legislature could only enlarge the powers of the corporation for the better government of the city and the comfort, prosperity and good will of the people, but was not permitted to annul, limit or abridge that municipal independence which New York has enjoyed for a period long anterior to the Revolutionary struggle.

"On the change in the political relations which ensued at the successful termination of the memorable war for independence, it must be conceded that the regulation of commerce passed in the hands of Congress, and the city became for general political purposes, a portion of the State, but without in the least surrendering that municipal self-government which had been granted in the amplest terms that language could employ. These prerogatives and immunities were to remain inviolable forever, and in all the local concerns of the city, in her domestic policy, in the management and enjoyment of her franchises, and in the regulation of internal order she was to be entirely independent.

" . . . It has been the settled policy of all civilized countries to encourage the growth and stability of their commerce by giving to the cities which are its seats municipal charters of such character as to secure their dignity and respect in the eyes of the world. Governments, the most despotic, have tolerated there, if in no other place, liberty, in order to foster trade. The municipal rights of Soudan and the seaports of England; of Hamburg and the free cities of Germany, have always been regarded as inviolable. The same sanctions were intended to apply to the civic privileges of New York.

" . . . The Legislature in which the present partisan majority has the power, has become the instrument by which we are plundered to enrich their speculators, lobby agents, and Abolitionists. Laws are passed through their malign influence, by which, under the forms of legal enactment, our burdens have been increased, our substance eaten out, and our municipal liberties destroyed. . . .

"How we shall rid ourselves of this odious and oppressive connection is not for me to determine. It is certain that a dissolution cannot be peacefully accomplished, except by the consent of the Legislature itself. . . .

"Much, no doubt, can be said in favor of the justice and policy of a separation. It may be said that secession or revolution in any of the United States would be a subversion of all Federal authority, and, so far as the central government is concerned, the resolving of the community into its original elements—that, if the part of the States form new combinations and governments, other States may do the same. California and her sisters of the Pacific will no doubt set up an independent Republic and husband their own rich mineral resources. The Western States, equally rich in cereals and other agricultural products will probably do the same. Then, it may be said, why should not New York City, instead of supporting by her contributions in revenue two-thirds the expenses of the United States, become also equally independent? As a free city, with but a nominal duty on imports, her local governments could be supported without taxation upon her people. Thus we could live free from taxes and have cheap goods nearly duty free. In this she would have the whole and united support of the Southern States, and of all the States to whose interests and rights under the constitution she has always been true.

"It is well for individuals and communities to look every danger squarely in the face, and meet it calmly and bravely. As dreadful as the severing of the bonds that have hitherto united the States has been in contemplation, it is now an inevitable fact. We have now to meet it, whatever the consequences may be. If the Union is broken up, the government is dissolved, and it behooves every distinct community as well as individual to take care of themselves.

"When disunion has become a fixed and certain fact why may not New York disrupt the bonds which bind her to a venal and corrupt master—to a people and a party that have plundered her revenues, attempted to ruin her commerce, taken away the power of self-government, and destroyed the union of which she was the proud Empire City?"

This amazing proposal made Wood the lion of the town. Wood now believed that his Mozart Hall Democracy was invincible. Tammany would have to capitulate to him. And this thought was shared by many of the leaders in the organization which had outlawed Wood. From all parts of the North, Wood received letters of praise from leading Democrats. Tweed and a number of the Tammany leaders were worried over Wood's rise in popular esteem. Some, especially the Union stalwarts, were for attacking Wood as a traitor. Tweed, politically wise, counseled silence. Election Day was many months off and much could happen in that time. Give him plenty of rope and he would hang himself. All were for the hanging as they accepted Tweed's advice.

The spirit of repression was growing. The North, which had listened with respect to the Abolitionists, now began to treat them as enemies of peace. Even Boston felt the swing of the pendulum. *The Herald*, on January 17, 1861, observes on the editorial page:

"What are we coming to? Henry Ward Beecher is egged at New Haven and sworn at in Philadelphia; Wendell Phillips cannot speak unprotected in Boston; H. Ford Douglas, agent of the Massachusetts Anti-Slavery Society is hooted out of Lancaster, Mass.; and Susan B. Anthony is mobbed at Rochester, and can't for any consideration obtain a hall in Albany."

This was the negative expression of the Southern sympathizers. United States Marshal Rynders—Buchanan was still President and maintaining the *status quo*—called a meeting at which resolutions were adopted praising the Secession movement as being "in support of the Constitution and Liberty."

One of the fire-eaters at the Rynders meeting was Congressman James Kerrigan, a soldier of fortune, who had fought with Walker at Nicaragua, engaged in a pistol duel on the Bowery, and was forcibly restrained from throttling Wood at a Democratic State Convention.

About the time of the Rynders meeting *The Herald* and *The Tribune* published a story that Kerrigan had raised an army of 5,000 to aid the South in the event of war and that one of their objectives would be the seizure of the forts in the harbor —an easy undertaking for 5,000 determined and well-armed men. One of Kerrigan's friends sent a telegram to Governor Pickett of South Carolina assuring him of his support. This alarmed the Unionists who persuaded the Government to impanel a grand jury to investigate. But Kerrigan's army existed only in the imagination of its putative commander.

Wood was lending more than words to the cause of the South. On January 22, three days after Georgia joined the seceding States, the Metropolitan Police seized a shipment of arms destined for Savannah.

Telegrams of protest came from the leading citizens of Georgia. Wood responded that he had no control of the Metropolitan Police, adding if he had, he would summarily punish them for this unwarranted and unjustifiable outrage. No one in the city more regretted the seizure of these arms, for they were bought for their Southern consignee by an employee of Mayor Wood's office.

A few days afterward, on January 29, Tweed, at a meeting of the Board of Supervisors, called up a bill of Edmund Jones and Company. This was a printing house favored by Wood, and Tweed had reason to believe that Wood, and his brother Ben, were profiting from the excessive charges made by the printers for stationery and other supplies delivered to the city.

"I move," said Tweed, "that this bill be referred back to the committee on Printing and Stationery with power to send for persons and papers. Why, there isn't any proof that any of the items charged on the bill have even been delivered."

As a result of Tweed's motion the printer was sent for, and thus began the corrupt relations between Jones and Tweed.

CHAPTER XVII

On February 18, 1861, the Mozart Hall Democracy and Tammany were agreed on one thing—that their members should keep off Broadway and several other streets the following afternoon. Lincoln was coming to visit the city. Tweed's Bowery Boys, and Wood's Dead Rabbits, and all other gangsters, were directed to avoid the line of march. Orders not to fly the Stars and Stripes were given to merchants and others. While the Democrats were determined on making the reception of Lincoln as cheerless as possible, they did not want any bloodshed. There was reason for fearing trouble. Early the preceding month Captain Walling and another New York detective were sent on a secret mission to Baltimore. They were to aid in preventing the culmination of a plot to assassinate Lincoln in that city before he was inaugurated. The object of the detectives' mission was known to Tweed and every one else in an important position in the city. All feared that, if the hot-heads of gangdom were near any particularly demonstrative Lincolnites when the President-elect was passing through the streets, trouble, and possibly fatal rioting, might ensue.

On the morning of his arrival the newspapers told of Lincoln's reception in the upper part of New York State.

"The crowds at Little Falls, Fonda, and Schenectady were immense in numbers, and very enthusiastic in spirit," read a special from *The Herald's* correspondent on the Lincoln train. "At all the stops impertinent individuals addressed Mr. Lincoln in a very familiar manner and offered to back him against the world. He very good-naturedly submitted to the rough courtesies of the crowd, and his remark that he had the advantage of the crowd as to looks, elicited cheers and laughter."

229

Lincoln arrived in New York at 2:55 in the afternoon. Distant guns from the forts in the harbor boomed a welcome. The President-elect, as he left the old Hudson River Railroad depot at Thirtieth Street and Ninth Avenue, stepped into an open barouche which had been used by the Prince of Wales some months before on his visit to the city. Mrs. Lincoln and other members of the family rode in another carriage. There were thirty carriages in line. A platoon of mounted police led the way. Their progress was slow. It took them more than an hour to cover the three miles or so to Lincoln's hotel.

The plaza in front of the Astor House was thronged with men. There were few women. Some five hundred policemen, their faces tense, held the crowd in place. Hemmed in by the multitude was a Broadway stage coach. It was drawn up against the curb. On a seat on top of the coach sat a man with a large head and long hair. He was a poet. His name was Walt Whitman.

Eighteen years later, poor and partly paralyzed, the poet described the scene to a group of friends in a small hall in Fourteenth Street. They had paid to hear him. Whitman's description is preserved in *The Tribune* (Semi-Weekly edition) of April 18, 1879:

"I shall not easily forget the first time I ever saw Abraham Lincoln. It must have been about the 18th or 19th of February, 1861. It was rather a pleasant afternoon in New York City, as he arrived here from the West to remain a few hours and then to pass on to Washington, to prepare for the inauguration. I saw him on Broadway, near the site of the present post office. He came down, I think, from Canal Street, to stop at the Astor House. The broad spaces, streets and sidewalks in the neighborhood and for some distance, were crowded with solid masses of people—many thousands.

"The omnibuses and other vehicles had all been turned off, leaving an unusual hush in that busy part of the city. Presently two or three shabby hack barouches made their way with some difficulty through the crowd and drew up at the Astor House entrance. A tall figure slipped out of the center of these barouches, paused leisurely on the sidewalk, looked up at the dark granite walls and looming architecture of the grand old hotel—then, after a relieving stretch of arms and legs, turned round for over a minute to scan slowly and good humoredly the appearance of the vast and silent crowds.

"There were no speeches—no compliments—no welcome,—so far as I could hear, not a word said.

"Still much anxiety was concealed in that quiet. Cautious persons had feared some marked insult or indignity to the President-elect—for he possessed no personal popularity at all in New York City, and very little political. But it was evidently tacitly agreed that the new political supporters of Mr. Lincoln present would entirely abstain from any demonstration on their side, if the immense majority, who were anything but supporters, would abstain on their side also. The result was a sulky, unbroken silence, such as certainly never before characterized so great a New York crowd. Almost in the same neighborhood I distinctly remembered seeing Lafayette, on his visit to America in 1825. I had also personally seen and heard how Andrew Jackson, Clay, Webster, Hungarian Kossuth, Filibuster Walker, the Prince of Wales on his visit, and other citizens, native and foreign, had been welcomed there, at various times—all that indescribable human roar and magnetism, unlike any other sound in the universe, the glad, exulting thunder-shouts of countless unloosed throats of men! But on this occasion, not a voice, not a sound!

"From the top of an omnibus (drawn up on one side, close by, and blocked by the curbstones and crowds), I had, I say, a capital view of it all, and especially of Mr. Lincoln—his look and gait, his perfect composure and coolness—his unusual and uncouth height, his dress of complete black, stovepipe hat pushed back on the head; his dark brown complexion, seamed and wrinkled, yet canny-looking face, his black bushy head of hair, disproportionately long neck, and his hands held behind as he stood observing the people. He looked with curiosity upon that immense sea of faces, and the sea of faces returned the look with similar curiosity. In both there was a dash of comedy, almost farce, such as Shakespeare puts in his blackest tragedies. The crowd that hemmed around consisted, I should think, of thirty or forty thousand men, and not a single one his personal friend—while I have no doubt (so frenzied were the ferments of the time) many an assassin's knife and pistol lurked in hip or breast pocket there, ready, soon as break and riot came.

"But no break or riot came. The tall figure gave another relieving stretch or two of arms and legs; then with moderate pace, and accompanied by a few unknown looking persons, ascended the portico steps of the Astor House, disappeared through its broad entrance—and then the dumb show ended.

"I saw Abraham Lincoln often during the four years following that date. He changed rapidly and much during the Presidency—but this scene and him in it are indelibly stamped upon my recollection. As I sat on the top of my omnibus, and had a good view of him, the thought, dim, and inchoate then, has since come out clear enough, that four sorts of genius—four mighty and primal hands, will be needed to the complete limning of this man's future portrait—the eyes and brains and finger-touch of Plutarch and Aeschylus and Michael Angelo, assisted by Rabelais."

When Lincoln entered the Astor House there was a little cheering. This acclaim came from some Republicans—including the policemen on duty inside—who were in the hotel to welcome him. Mrs. Lincoln shared in the unpopularity of the President-elect. Instead of several hundred women attending the reception at the Astor to Mrs. Lincoln, a bare hundred or so appeared. The name of a Mrs. Belmont was published in the newspapers as one of the ladies who had paid her respects to Mrs. Lincoln. There was only one Mrs. Belmont. Her husband, August Belmont, the American representative of the House of Rothschild, was prominent in the national councils of the Democratic Party and intensely pro-Southern. Moreover, the Belmonts were of the social elect. The day following the newspaper accounts of the reception to Mrs. Lincoln, Society was informed through the press that Mrs. Belmont was not presented to Mrs. Lincoln. Whereupon Society breathed easier.

The Lincolns simply didn't belong. The whole town said so! Look at what happened at the Irving Place Opera House the night following their arrival in New York. *Un Ballo in Maschera* was being sung. In the cast were Mmes. Colson, Hinkley, Phillips, and Mm. Brugnoli, Ferri, Coletti, and Deubreul. Signor Muzio, the conductor, introduced a *grand gallop* for the occasion, and Signor Ronzani directed the *ballet divertissement*. All New York was there. And yet Lincoln left at the end of the second act! *Mais pourquoi?* Oh, he would rather talk politics with other horrible politicians at the hotel than to listen to Verdi's divine music! What a fellow! All that Bennett had ever said about him was only too true! But what can one expect in a Republic? Impossible creatures in public office—even in the Presidency! France rid herself of all this degrading tomfoolery. It was time America followed her example. No wonder the Elegant Oakey preferred Tweed!

Bennett, who did not side with Lincoln until the beginning of the latter half of the war, greeted the President-elect the morning after his arrival with a sneering "village politician." In the same editorial we read:

"The President-elect arrived here yesterday and received a formal reception at the hands of the city government and thirteen hundred Republican policemen. The masses of the people did not turn out on this occasion. There was a faint cheer as Mr. Lincoln entered his carriage at the railway station, but none of the spontaneous enthusiasm for which our people are noted, and the assemblage in Broadway was not much more than upon ordinary occasions. In and around the Park and the Astor House, however, the crowd was very large. It was quite evident that the people of the Metropolis, viewing the election of Mr. Lincoln in the light of a great public calamity, one which bears more especially upon their material interests and hitherto kindly relations with the South, had resolved to give expression to their feelings by denying themselves the satisfaction of their natural curiosity."

Bennett threw open his columns to any sort of abuse or ridicule directed at Lincoln. In a column close to *The Herald's* select list of bawdy houses, a patent medicine quack advertised:

"PRESIDENT LINCOLN! PRESIDENT LINCOLN! PRESIDENT LINCOLN! DID YOU SEE HIM? DID YOU SEE HIM? DID YOU SEE HIM? DID YOU SEE HIS WHISKERS? DID YOU SEE HIS WHISKERS? DID YOU SEE HIS WHISKERS? RAISED IN SIX WEEKS BY THE USE OF BELLINGHAM'S ONGUENT!" Et cetera. Et cetera.

This was the first time Lincoln was called President in a New York paper. He left the unfriendly Metropolis on February 21. Eleven days later he registered in Heaven an oath to preserve, protect and defend the Union. A little more than a month and Fort Sumter had been bombarded and captured by the Southerners. The day after he issued a proclamation calling for 75,000 men.

CHAPTER XVIII

THE morning following the issuance of Lincoln's proclamation there was little trace of the anti-war spirit noticeable in the town. Yet it was there. For the time being supporters of the Administration and War Democrats had it their own way. One of the latter was William D. Kennedy, who had recently succeeded James Conner as Grand Sachem of Tammany Hall. Kennedy, in his capacity as head of the Tammany Society, raised a regiment of volunteers composed exclusively of Tammanyites. Tweed, then thirty-eight years old, and with a physique and voice that were alike commanding, declined a commission under his friend Kennedy. Tweed had a battle on at home. He was maneuvering, and successfully, to bring about his own election as chairman of the New York County Democratic Central Committee, the purely political side of Tammany. Kennedy proceeded with his recruiting without Tweed, and in June, Tammany's Grand Sachem, in the uniform of a Colonel, marched the Tammany regiment, known as the Forty-second New York Infantry, for the front. The Forty-second New York made a distinguished record, participating in thirty-six battles, losing 420 by deaths and wounds, and 298 missing. Colonel Kennedy never took part in an engagement, as he died within a week after the regiment arrived in Washington. The command was then taken over by a regular army man.

One of the followers of Mayor Wood turned traitor to his chief at the very outbreak of hostilities and went to the front with the battery of volunteer artillery—the New York Eighth Militia. He was well known in the Fourteenth Ward. His name was James Lynch. He owned a foundry. His intimates called him Jimmy. Before the end of the year everybody in town knew Jimmy Lynch.

The brunt of the coming campaign fell upon Tweed. Mayor Wood offered to make peace with Tammany on condition that the organization support him for Mayor. Tweed compromised with Wood by sharing with the Mozart Hall Democracy the nominees for the State Legislature and some of the minor local offices. But on the city and county-wide tickets Tweed insisted on fighting it out with Wood as Wood was unwilling to forego his ambition to run for Mayor again. Tweed was determined that Wood should be destroyed, even if it meant the sacrifice of every man on the regular Democratic city and county tickets, including himself, for Tweed was a candidate for Sheriff.

The Republicans, supported by the People's Party—the Know-Nothings had ceased to exist as a political party—put a candidate in the field against Tweed, and a group of independents who had cut adrift from the People's Party, nominated a third choice for Sheriff. The Mozart Hall Democracy nominated Lynch.

Lynch, who had enlisted the first day of the war—all enlistments at the outbreak of hostilities were for three months—had been discharged on July 20, on the eve of the first Battle of Bull Run. He returned to the management of his foundry.

It was not a creditable return. Lynch never talked about it. But others did. General McDowell, in his report of the battle says:

"On the eve of the battle the 4th Pennsylvania Regiment of Volunteers and the battery of volunteer artillery of the New York Eighth Militia whose term of service expired insisted on their discharge. I wrote to the regiment expressing a request for them to remain a short time and the Honorable Secretary of War who was at the time on the ground tried to induce the battery to remain at least five days. But in vain. They insisted on their discharge that night. It was granted, and the next morning, when the army moved forward into the battle, these troops moved to the rear to the sound of the enemy's cannon."

Lynch was one of the spokesmen of the men of the Eighth New York who insisted on their discharge. One of the finest

pieces of campaign verse penned was written around this incident and sung by Irishmen to an old Fenian tune at Tweed's
meetings. The song began by reciting the bravery of
Meagher's Zouaves, and other Irish units at the battle. Then
occurred this verse:

> "And where was Jimmy Lynch?
>   Says the Shan Van Voght.
> He surely did not flinch?
>   Says the Shan Van Voght.
> Did he hear the bugle sound?
>   Did he see the balls rebound?
> Where was he on the ground?
>   Says the Shan Van Voght."

Then the Shan Van Voght wailed that Jimmy was not there,
and told how he took his leave. And the song ended with.

> "And now he runs for place!
>   Says the Shan Van Voght.
> How can he have the face?
>   Says the Shan Van Voght.
> He's politically damned,
> And Fernando has his hand,
> Oh—to blazes with the band!
>   Says the Shan Van Voght!"

The Republicans elected Opdyke to the Mayoralty—the
same Opdyke who was defeated two years before by Wood.
Lynch, however, was elected Sheriff, his vote being almost
double that of Tweed's. Yet Tweed could look on this defeat as his greatest victory, as it was the beginning of the
end of Wood's career in politics.

Wood ran third. Yet he came within a few hundred votes
of winning. Tammany nominated to oppose him the rich merchant, C. Godfrey Gunther. His record was as unassailable
as Opdyke's. The vote was the closest in any three-cornered
contest in the history of the city. The final returns showed:
Opdyke, 25,380; Gunther, 24,767; Wood, 24,167. To the
Republicans and the War Democrats the balloting was far

from pleasing. Wood and Gunther were anti-war, although grand gestures were made by some of their campaigners and their organizations to win the suffrage of supporters of the Union.

The usual violence occurred at the polls. But Opdyke's supporters were no more backward than the others. Two brothers, James and Thomas Martin, looking after Opdyke's interests at the polling place, at Tenth Avenue and Twenty-seventh Street, were attacked by one of Wood's gangs. The assault ended when Thomas Martin shot one of the Woodites dead.

Wood really defeated himself. The anti-war spirit of the town elected his candidate for Sheriff. But those opposed to the war were not corruptionists. Indisputable proofs of dishonesty were published. More than $250,000 of the city funds were stolen by Wood—who went unpunished. In one case alone it was shown that Wood had awarded a five-year street cleaning contract for $279,000 a year when another bidder offered to do the work for $84,000 less. The Mayor's brother, Ben, had a quarter interest in the contract. It was shown that Wood had sold nominations on his Mozart Hall ticket. Two lawyers paid him $5,000 each for the dubious honor of running for the Supreme Court on the Wood ticket.

Tweed's defeat cost him every cent he had in the world. He had more than $100,000 when the campaign started. Tweed gave all he had, and several dollars more that he raised among those who had been the beneficiaries of his peculiar talents, to his various Ward managers. Some of it was spent, but most of it stuck in the pockets of those he depended upon to distribute it where it would do the most good.

Not until he had made another fortune did Tweed reveal that he had been bankrupted by his contest with Lynch. For there is but one thing more fatal to a man in politics than losing his money; it is having it known. The office of Sheriff of New York County was worth all that Tweed spent, as there was close to $100,000 to be obtained honestly in fees. Tweed would have readily doubled that sum.

Tweed had just been elected Chairman of the Democratic Central Committee of New York County. This was a high sounding title and nothing more. It was equivalent to the present-day Chairman of the New York County Democratic Committee. And equally as far removed from the leadership of Tammany Hall. The Grand Sachem then was everything. Tweed felt sure of him. But why fret? Tweed was still Supervisor. That job was to be his until the last. He had systematized the collection of corruption money by the Supervisors. Thus Tweed explained how it was done:

"Pretty nearly every person who had business with the Board of Supervisors, or furnished the county with supplies, had a friend on the Board of Supervisors, and generally with some one member of the Ring. And through that one member they [those who sold supplies to the county] were talked to, and the result was that their bills were sent in and passed, and the percentages were paid on the bills, sometimes to one man, sometimes to another."

It was, an old device. But it remained for Tweed to convert it into a system. One of Tweed's partisans in the Board of Supervisors was Smith Ely, Jr., a leather merchant. He did not need any of the loot that Tweed and the other Supervisors shared. Ely wanted to be Mayor. He did everything conceivable to attain the honor. When he visited Europe he wrote travel letters to the politically powerful Fenian weeklies which then flourished in New York. He catered to every group and faction. He was financially honest. He never did anything publicly that could not be described as respectable.

Tweed would not be long in recouping the $100,000 he had lost in the campaign. About half of it he had made in the last two years. His friends in the Common Council and in other branches of the local government could be relied on in his activities as a lobbyist. The Elegant Oakey was District Attorney. Barnard was on the Supreme Court Bench. And more than all this, Tweed was The Boss. The Chairman of the local Central Committee had never amounted to anything politically before. Tweed was going to shatter another tradition.

CHAPTER XIX

Opdyke soon learned that a man could be elected Mayor and be little more than a figurehead. The Common Council, by a bare majority, could override his veto on any corrupt measure it passed. And many corrupt bills were sent to the Mayor. Some were so skillfully disguised that they became law with his signature. Others, palpably dishonest, he vetoed.

One of these has always been credited to Tweed, and while he was not a member of the Council, his word was law in the municipal legislature. There is every reason to believe that the idea was Tweed's. It was in keeping with a practice that he put to the most extensive use afterwards.

This particular measure was passed a few days before Christmas, 1862. It provided for the payment of $200 to each of the newspaper reporters assigned to cover the City Hall and the higher courts. This plain bribery was designed primarily to keep the reporters from making ungenerous comments on the proceedings of the Courts and the Common Council. Both needed charity. Opdyke promptly disapproved the bill. It was repassed over his veto at the meeting of December 29.

Opdyke's administration, were it not for the tragic occurrence of July, 1863, would be colorless. A war Mayor, he could do little of moment to aid the war. Such enlistments as were made in the city—and the city did not fail to give its due share of men, in spite of the defeatist attitude of many of its leaders—were made without the aid of the trappings of propaganda. In the November election the city vote insured the election of Horatio Seymour as Governor of the State. Seymour was an Anti-War Democrat. He and Tweed were close political friends, several of The Boss's immediate followers finding place under Seymour when he assumed the direction of the State government on January 1, 1863.

Tweed, penniless in the fall of 1861, was a rich man again in the spring of 1863. In addition to the wealth that rolled in to him from beneficiaries of a corrupt ring of office-holders— and he also levied tribute on some of the men in public place —he was rapidly becoming a war millionaire. When Harlem Hall was sold to be turned into a church, its equipment was disposed of at public auction. Tweed, who was on the Committee on Armories in the Board of Supervisors, purchased three hundred benches at the rate of five dollars each, a total of $1,500. The cashier of the Home Insurance Company was there to bid in some of them. Tweed told him he would let him have them at the price he paid, as the insurance man wanted only seventeen. Tweed turned the remaining benches over to the furniture house of Ingersoll and Company, owned by a friend of his father—both had been chairmakers together. These benches, which cost five dollars each, were later sold to the county for its armories at six hundred dollars each. The total bill, $169,800, was paid by New York's taxpayers, making a net return to Tweed and his associates of $168,300, plus the $85.00 he received for the seventeen benches he sold at cost.

But they were all—all who could—making money out of the war. In the first eighteen months a list of one hundred and fifty New Yorkers who had made from $150,000 to $1,500,000 in this manner was compiled. "These shoddy aristocrats," wrote Bennett in an editorial, "have added about 200 brilliant new equipages to the ring at the Park and will soon figure at the watering places. Jay Cooke, the banker, cleared $300,-000 by the conversion of government bonds alone."

Bennett, who was not as yet won over to the war, was constantly denying the canard that Greeley was repeating whenever he was at a loss for something else to hurl at the editor of *The Herald.* "For the fiftieth time," wrote Bennett in the spring of '63, "*The Tribune* asserts that at the time of the fall of Fort Sumter we had a secession flag in this office ready to be unfurled when a mob (led by attachés of *The Tribune*) intimidated us and prevented it. We again and again pronounced this to be a falsehood, but *The Tribune* sticks to it, knowing it to be false. Now we have the very best authority, and we are ready to prove it, that at the crisis in question, Greeley had a secession flag hung up in his editorial sanctum. Will he dare to deny this? He was then, as he has been ever since, in favor of letting the South go according to the principles of the Declaration of Independence."

A few days later—some three weeks prior to the Draft Riots—Bennett wrote that *The Independent* was authority for the announcement that spiritualists had been in communication with the ghost of Stonewall Jackson, and that the great hero and warrior-evangelist of the South had become a strong anti-slavery man since he departed this earthly sphere. Bennett also informed his readers (many thousands of whom took it for Gospel truth) that he had it from the same source that Greeley and Henry Ward Beecher "will be Union men within five years after they are hanged in 1865 by the Democratic administration." Here were two good reasons why the Republicans should be defeated. But they were not new, as the hanging of Beecher and Greeley was proposed in and out of the Houses of Congress. There were places in New York where it would not be safe for either of them to venture alone—or together. *The Independent* was then being run by Beecher and his friend—then—Theodore Tilton. These three—Tilton, Beecher, and Greeley—frequently foregathered at this time at Tilton's home in Brooklyn, which was a rendezvous for the leading exponents of woman suffrage, free love, and other fads of the day. At these gatherings extreme Republicans and Southern sympathizers met on common ground. The misrepresentations and violence of the editorial sanctum and the rostrum were forgotten in this sanctuary.

There was a strong pro-South sentiment among the prominent men of the city which became intensified as the war approached the end of the second year. Numerous meetings of protest were held by the Democrats. The most important of these was held on February 5, 1863, at Delmonico's. Samuel F. B. Morse, the inventor of the telegraph, presided. Before adjourning, the Society for the Diffusion of Political Knowledge was formed. The Republicans looked upon this body as the most menacing of the Copperhead aggregations because of the eminence of the men associated with it. Tilden was one of its directors and founders, and his speech at Delmonico's was interpreted by *The Evening Post* as the beginning of a revolutionary intrigue to rid the country of Lincoln. There is no question that Lincoln was losing the respect of Greeley and many other powerful Republicans in the East, particularly in New York. These men were regarding Lincoln as a blunderer —a failure.

Tilden replied to *The Evening Post* and inferentially said that men had talked of revolution to him. And directly he said that he had warned against any violent measures. This letter of Tilden's, which save for an innocuous paragraph was omitted from his authorized biography by Theodore P. Cook when Tilden was a candidate for the Presidency, was circulated throughout the country in pamphlet form by the Society for the Diffusion of Political Knowledge. No more savage assault was made on Lincoln and his policies than by Tilden in this letter. It was not the savagery of a man with a cudgel, but of a man of arms whose rapier was part of his right hand. After denying the revolutionary aspect placed on his speech by *The Evening Post*, Tilden describes the course of the Ship of State as "The voyage of a ship with a false compass; particular deviations are discovered after they have been committed, but they recur in indefinite series, because their source remains prolific as at first."

Then Tilden, a master of the art of achieving effect by understatement, describes Lincoln as "a man whose whole knowledge and experience of statesmanship was derived from one term in Congress, a long service in the county conventions at Sangamon, a career at *nisi prius* in the interior of Illinois, and some acquaintance with the lobby at Springfield."

Lincoln, lobbyist, inferior court practitioner, county politician, and a one-term Congressman, was not capable, wrote Tilden, of dealing with "the greatest questions and most complicated forces of modern history." He saw the magnitude of the problem, but was blind to the greatness of the man.

In the pamphlet in which Tilden's letter to *The Evening Post* was printed, and in the numerous other publications of the society, the objects of the organization were set forth in phrases that inflamed the mass who were incapable of the subtleties of the language.

"To disseminate a knowledge of the principles of American Constitutional liberty; to inculcate correct views of the Constitution of the United States, and of the powers and rights preserved to the States and the people; and generally to promote a sound political education of the public mind to the end that usurpations may be prevented, that arbitrary and unconstitutional measures may be checked, that the Constitution may be preserved, that the Union may be restored, and that the blessings of free institutions and public order may be kept by ourselves and transmitted to our posterity."

The suspension of the writ of *habeas corpus* was denounced by Tilden and his associates as the passing of the liberty of the American people. This was done by quoting the pessimistic dialogue between Lord Shelburne and Henry Laurens, President of the Continental Congress sixty-three years before, and recorded in Laurens' journal.

The Draft Act, passed in March, was equally objectionable to the Anti-War Democrats.

Governor Seymour, who was in sympathy with the South, went further than any man, in or out of office, in his speech at the Academy of Music. This was a week before the Draft Riots began. Vallandigham did not approach the violence of Seymour's speech of July 4, 1863. In these riots "more than a thousand" civilians, policemen, and soldiers were slain in the streets of New York. This indefinite estimate is official. Seymour used the phrase in a message to the Legislature. Sometimes Seymour was given to understatement. The minimum number may well have been 2,000. No estimate has ever been made of the wounded.

This long-drawn-out riot might have developed into an insurrection but for the arrival of ten thousand veterans who were withdrawn from the Army of the Potomac to put down the disturbances. Bennett, who gave belated approval to the

SAMUEL JONES TILDEN

THE BATTLE FOR THE UNION STEAM WORKS ARSENAL

(From an engraving in The New York Historical Society Collection.)

draft two days before the drawing began, invariably referred
to the Draft Riots during the four days of terror as a popular
uprising. Sometimes he described it as "a formidable movement of the people." It was a revolt of the people against
themselves. They had leaders, men in high place, who directed
them. These leaders were never brought to justice. This
attack upon democracy was ended with muskets and cannon.
When it was all over, the unprecedented tragedy was tacitly
declared a closed incident by the local, State, and National
Governments. Lincoln knew the leaders. Prominent Democrats, associates of the men who inspired and directed the
Draft Riots, disclosed enough to bring out the facts in a judicial investigation. All this was submitted to the President.
For days Lincoln debated what course he should pursue. In
his "Personal Recollections of Abraham Lincoln," James R.
Gilmore, who always had entry to the White House, when he
asked the President why he did not act in this case, was answered in Lincoln's "peculiar, half-bantering manner":

"Well, you see if I had said no, I should have admitted that
I dare not enforce the laws, and consequently have no business
to be President of the United States. If I had said yes,
and appointed the judge, I should—as he would have done his
duty—have simply touched a match to a barrel of gunpowder.
You have heard of sitting on a volcano. We are sitting upon
two. One is blazing already, and the other will blaze away
the moment we scrape a little loose dirt from the top of
the crater. Better let the dirt alone—at least for the present.
One rebellion at a time is about as much as we can conveniently
handle."

New York was only one of many volcanoes. There were
more than two. Other craters were in the West. Lincoln knew
where they were. And how to keep them quiet.

At this Academy of Music meeting Seymour compared
Lincoln to Charles I. He was beheaded. What an analogy!
Lincoln was denounced as a tyrant, and for not "heeding
our prayers" to compromise with the South. The exiling into
the Confederacy of Vallandigham by the impetuous General
Burnside—a tyrannical act which gave Lincoln pain—was ar-

raigned. Tweed, and the Elegant Oakey and others who sat on the platform, led in the thunders of applause when Seymour mocked the defense of the Draft Act and the suspension of the writ of *habeas corpus.* Both of these war-time measures were regarded as unconstitutional by the Anti-War Democrats.

"Remember this!" exclaimed Seymour in an apostrophe to Lincoln and all Republicans. "Remember this: that the bloody, treasonable, and revolutionary doctrine of public necessity can be proclaimed by a mob as well as by a government."

And again addressing himself to the Republicans—there were not many within sound of his voice save the policemen on duty—Seymour asked:

"Can you tell when ambition, love of plunder, or thirst for power, will induce bad and dangerous men to proclaim this very principle of public necessity as a reason why they should trample beneath their feet all the laws of our land?"

This speech of the Governor was too fiery for any paper in town with the exception of the *Daily News,* which printed it in its entirety.

Five years later, when Seymour was nominated for President, David G. Croly, who was selected by Seymour to write his biography, distorts what was said on this occasion into: "Governor Seymour . . . made an appeal to the Republican leaders, imploring them to refrain from all unjust and illegal violence against their political opponents. At the same time he invoked his own political friends at all times to render obedience to those in authority and to submit to their laws, where they had the right to make them, whether such laws were agreeable or not."

In this same biography the dispatch of New York regiments in June, when Lee was preparing to invade Pennsylvania by way of Maryland, is spoken of as having been "sent to support the flag of the country." In his Fourth of July speech in 1863 no such language was used. Then the troops were sent "to the aid of a sister State." The language is Seymour's. There was no talk of country then.

Seymour opposed the draft from the very beginning. He and other Democratic leaders charged that it was a device of the Republicans to kill off the Democrats, to make the State safe for Republicanism. This may be true, as partisanship stops at nothing. Color was lent to the accusation when it transpired that the State had been asked for more than her proportionate share by some 14,000 men, and it was likewise shown by a Federal investigating commission that most of this excess was levied on the densely populated strongholds of the Democrats. It has yet to be demonstrated that angels aid in the conduct of wars.

The draft had been in progress in New England for days before it was due to begin in New York. Seymour knew all this. Yet he left the city with less than eight hundred troops, many of them men fresh from hospitals, to man the forts on the harbor and to protect the entire city. And two days before the draft began in the Metropolis, Seymour left the State to spend a vacation at Long Branch, New Jersey, then the fashionable watering place on the Atlantic Coast. And he also sent his Adjutant General, John T. Sprague, to Washington, in a last-minute attempt to induce Lincoln to suspend the draft in New York. James B. Fry, Provost Marshal General of the United States during the war, after commenting caustically on the absence of adequate militia from the city, and the departure of the Governor and the Adjutant General of the State, observes:

"Fortunately the invaders of Pennsylvania were beaten back. The campaign of Gettysburg ended in our favor, and part of the Army of the Potomac became available for a campaign in New York."

Justified as was the draft, there was an unjust clause in the Act which hit only the poor. This provision enabled any man with $300 to avoid service. This was class legislation of the most indefensible sort. Lincoln, who saw everything, overlooked this.

CHAPTER XX

THE draft began on Saturday morning, July 11, in the Enrolment Office at the corner of Forty-sixth Street and Third Avenue. This was the only office in the city ready on that day. Crowds surrounded the building all day. There was a squad of veterans present in charge of a corporal. These were members of the Invalid Corps—all wounded men. Of the eight hundred troops available for service in the city, five hundred of them were members of this regiment of disabled soldiers. A dozen policemen under command of a sergeant were also on duty. But there were no disorders. When the lottery wheel, from which the names were drawn, ceased turning at six o'clock, the curious departed in peace.

On Sunday there was much secret activity throughout the city. Men met in halls, in the backrooms of saloons, in homes— anywhere that chance dictated or fancy suggested. Most of these were clerks and workingmen. There were others, well-dressed, who mingled with them and talked to them. These men did not stay long in any one group.

On Monday morning thousands of men did not report at their offices, stores, shops and factories. They were elsewhere. Some were at points a mile north of the Enrolment Office. Others took up positions a mile south of the place where the draft went on so peaceably on Saturday. These men took up their positions on Second and Third Avenues. Their orders were to stop the horse cars running on these two thoroughfares at nine o'clock and to direct the drivers to stop work when they returned to the car barns. The instructions were carried out effectively fully a half-hour before the appointed time. The men giving these orders were armed with cudgels and iron bars. Some of them had revolvers concealed. But they did not have to resort to force.

248

While these two lines of street cars were being stopped, gangs of other workmen, armed with axes, were at work on all sides of the Enrolment Office, cutting down telegraph poles. A little before nine o'clock Police Headquarters had information of what was going on in Second and Third Avenues. There were eleven hundred policemen in the city. These, with the five hundred soldiers in the Invalid Corps, the three hundred in the forts and at the Brooklyn Navy Yard, were the only defenses for the city. Nineteen hundred men against untold thousands! The only precaution taken against a possible riot was the detailing of a sergeant and fifteen policemen to guard the Arsenal at Seventh Avenue and Thirty-fifth Street. This had been done on Saturday. J. A. Kennedy, Superintendent of Police, had done this instinctively. In the meantime this force had been supplemented by a handful of the Invalid Corps. Sharply at nine o'clock the following order was telegraphed to all police stations in New York and Brooklyn:

"Call in your reserves. Platoon and hold them at the station houses subject to further orders."

At this hour the workers, who had cut down the telegraph poles, had assembled in front of the Enrolment Office. The crowd of Saturday was now a mob—as yet, however, peaceable. On the outskirts of the mob were twenty-five members of the *Black Joke* Fire Engine Company. They were also known as Number 33. Tweed as a boy had admired "33" and had the numerals intaglioed on the leather of his suspenders. But now "33" was a good three miles from the headquarters of the original company. The *Black Joke* was stationed at Fifty-eighth Street and Broadway. One of their number had been drafted on Saturday. Others of their number also lived in the same district.

Police from two neighboring precincts, to the number of sixty, now appeared on the scene. The mob parted to let them enter the building where the drawing was soon to resume. The lottery wheel was in a store on the ground floor. The three upper stories were occupied by poor families.

For an hour and a half the police had no difficulty with the mob. On the minute of half-past ten a pistol was discharged in the air. This was the agreed signal. Instantly a volley of paving stones crashed through the windows of the Enrolment Office. The members of the *Black Joke*, who by this time were on the inside ring of the mob, rushed through the cordon of police. Their first objective was to destroy the lottery wheel. But by the time they entered the building the Government officials in charge of the draft had escaped, together with the wheel. They had fled through a rear window. The mob now turned their attention to the police and drove off the sixty guardians. Fists and sticks alone were the weapons used on both sides.

The guard of the Invalid Corps were late. They had not as yet arrived on the scene. A few minutes after the mob had driven off the police and the draft officers they saw the Invalids marching up the Avenue, their muskets at right shoulder arms. These men, all suffering from wounds received on the Southern battlefields, were delayed because the mob had stopped the horse cars two hours earlier. Their work was made as light as possible for them. They walked only when it was necessary. Many of them limped as they marched. Half of the mob marched down to meet the crippled soldiers. At Forty-second Street the two forces met. The civilians outnumbered the military twenty to one. As they came in contact the mob showered stones on the soldiery. The officer in command ordered a volley of blank cartridges to be fired by half his force. One rank loaded with ball. A half dozen of the mob fell, three of them killed outright.

In a moment the mob swallowed up the fifty crippled soldiers. Their weapons were now in the hands of the rioters. All save three of the Invalids were permitted to flee after being beaten. Two were pounded to death with the stocks of their own muskets. A third ran toward the East River. The soldier took refuge on a ledge of rocks at the top of the cliff. A section of the mob pursued him to his haven and hurled him to his death on the rocky beach below. To make certain that the dead Invalid had not escaped them, huge bowlders that took two strong men to lift, were cast by the dozen on his corpse.

There is something more hellish than war.

When the rout of the Invalids began, that part of the mob which had remained at the Enrolment Office drove the women and children in the tenements on the upper floors from their miserable homes. These poor people were not allowed time to take such extra clothes as they possessed. Once the building was emptied the mob put a torch to it. In a few minutes the structure and three adjoining houses were in flames. Across the street three other four-story tenements were fired. Firemen who answered the alarm were driven off. Among the engines which responded was that of the *Black Joke* Company.

Mobs had sprung up in various parts of the upper portion of the city simultaneous with the attack on the Third Avenue Enrolment Office. Rioting in the downtown sections did not begin until the afternoon. There was a reason for this delay in the lower wards. Here were the factories and workshops and shipyards. And the morning was spent by the mobs in calling at these places to draw off the workingmen who had not as yet joined. Nearly all quit work, and many remained in their homes during the rest of the week. If the sole object of these mobs, or their leaders, was to stop the draft, they had succeeded within forty-five minutes of the first outbreak, for at 11:15 A.M., the draft offices throughout the city, under orders from the Government, had closed.

If there were any doubts in the minds of the police as to the rioters, or part of them, being directed, they were dissipated before the noon hour ended, for at one o'clock all but two of the main telegraph wires leading into Police Headquarters had been cut. The mob knew nothing of these wires, which were tapped, and connections reëstablished with the various precinct houses.

Many of these mobs carried banners reading: "No Draft!" Not a few marched behind the Stars and Stripes, keeping the flag aloft while they battled with the police and with soldiers sworn to uphold it.

In the first two or three hours of rioting the mobs routed most of the bodies of police or soldiers they encountered.

A little after noon a mob, bent on sacking and burning the home of Mayor Opdyke, on Fifth Avenue near Fifteenth Street,

was induced to leave without accomplishing its purpose by
Tweed's tool, Supreme Court Justice Barnard. Where muskets
and police and soldiers failed, a word from one of the Boss's
friends triumphed.

About this same hour, the rioting populace began to arm
itself with the most modern equipment. These weapons were
new. They were taken from the many gunsmiths' shops which
had grown up in all sections of the city since the beginning
of the war. Fortunately for the police, and soldiers, these
well-armed men were so distributed among the many mobs
that the chief weapons the authorities had to contend with
were old-fashioned pistols that had to be reloaded after each
firing, clubs, and pick-axes. These last were a prolific provider
of the principal ammunition of the mobs—paving stones.

The mobs not only sacked the shops of gunsmiths, but they
descended upon saloons whenever thirst overtook them. One
half-drunken mob raided the stables of a line of horse cars
and commandeered the slow-going steeds. This troop of cavalry
disbanded after executing weird maneuvers in the vicinity of
Union Square for an hour. The sun was scorching hot, and
the heat, together with more rum, forced the only troop of
cavalry the rioters boasted to abandon their mounts.

Fear gripped the town. The streets were deserted save for
the rioters, the police, and the soldiers. Mayor Opdyke summoned the Common Council to meet in extraordinary session.
Tweed had tried to induce a number of those he controlled to
attend the meeting. Less than half a dozen Aldermen responded. It was obvious that a quorum could not be obtained
that day. Considerable apprehension was felt for the safety
of the Mayor—a Republican, a Black Republican, and an
Abolitionist. Mobs howled outside his window. They attempted no harm. There were too many police garrisoned inside the City Hall. At the suggestion of Tweed and other
Democrats the Mayor moved his office to the St. Nicholas
Hotel, on Broadway, corner of Spring Street. A strong guard
was thrown around the hotel.

Early in the afternoon the mobs had what amounted to complete control of the town. The streets were given over to them

and to the police and soldiers. Central Office, as Police Headquarters was officially known, was growing anxious over its
own safety. At three o'clock calls for men from various precincts to garrison the Central Office met with such telegraphic
responses as this from the 18th precinct:

"One of our officers just in says that not one of us can get
to the Central Office, in uniform, alive. They will try in
citizens' dress."

By four o'clock every person of means who did not have to
remain in the city was leaving town. Every passenger vessel
in the harbor, no matter whither bound, was crowded. The
railroads had ceased running at noon, as the tracks were torn
up in the upper parts of the city. Conveyances of every
description were pressed into service for the exodus of those
able to depart from the scenes of riot. By nightfall there was
not a rig of any sort, save those owned by the city or still
locked up in private stables, to be had in the entire town.

At the beginning of the afternoon the comparatively few
soldiers were drawn from the forts to protect the several
arsenals throughout the city. Converted warehouses manufacturing muskets and munitions of war, and factories trans-
formed into gun shops, went by this name. Small detachments
of these newly-arrived forces were sent to aid the police. The
approaches to the Navy Yard were defended by the guns of
four steam gunboats, a corvette, and a receiving ship. The
iron-clad *Passaic* and the steam gunboat *Fuchsia* took
up positions at the mouths of the Hudson and East Rivers.
Their guns protected the financial district as well as Governor's Island, which had been denuded of its garrison. A
battery of artillery was stationed outside the Sub-Treasury.

The hardest fighting of the day was in Second Avenue below
Twenty-third Street. On the corner of Twenty-second Street
and Second Avenue was the Union Steam Works building, since
the war given over to the making of rifles. It was a huge
structure, so large that its top floor was used as a drill room
for recruits. There were more than four thousand finished
carbines and rifle muskets in the building, and a large amount
of ammunition. This was known to the mob which stormed

the building after some sixty policemen had entered it to prevent the rioters from seizing the weapons.

The police entered the building a little before one o'clock. By two o'clock there was a mob of several thousand, many of them armed with muskets, besieging the arsenal. Police were sent to the rescue of the sixty inside the building, who were now literally prisoners. Several times the police tried to break through the mob to get to their comrades inside the building. Each time, after stubborn fighting, they were beaten back.

Several hundred members of this mob were in various stages of intoxication. There were women in this mob too, and they were shouting "Burn the cops!" There were many boys among the rioters—homeless little fellows who were having the adventure of their lives. For some of them it was to be their last.

At two o'clock the police from the other precincts who were sent to succor the beleaguered sixty were routed. No shots were fired by either side. The police used their clubs. Now several attempts were made to fire the building. But the shell was of brick and soon the mob found that it must enter the building, whose interior was of pine, and saturated with oil from a long period of gunmaking. At three o'clock the mob rushed the main entrance. They broke down the door. They fell back when the police, who stood on the stairs inside, met them with revolver fire. The leader of the attacking party fell dead on the doorstep. None of his followers passed the body, for many of them fell in a heap behind him. They were dragged away by their friends.

Now the men in the mob began to mutter threateningly, while the women shrieked: "Burn the cops!" But to do that meant passing the gaping doorway which was guarded by the revolvers and carbines of unseen policemen. The leaders shouted down the women with "Let's capture the arsenal and kill the cops!" There were four thousand stands of rifles and carbines inside. They were needed.

Fifteen minutes after the mob made its first unsuccessful attempt to get into the building, it made a second attempt. This time it rushed madly through the open doorway led by men with revolvers and muskets who shot blindly straight ahead as they charged through the opening. But no policemen answered their shots. The mob then searched every floor, but not a policeman was anywhere. They had made their escape through a manhole after shedding their tell-tale tunics, and made their way across backyard fences to the police station at Twenty-second Street and Third Avenue, a block away.

With no police to kill, the mob moved among the oil-soaked floors jostling one another as they ripped open boxes containing carbines and rifles. Many of them rushed out with arms filled with these weapons. Others remained to break open closets in search of loot. The mob inside the arsenal numbered at least one thousand. Hundreds of these went to the drill floor with their newly acquired rifles and carbines and began drilling. One of their leaders had closed the door behind them to prevent their being disturbed.

Meanwhile one of the drunken members of the mob touched a match to a pile of oil-soaked rags on the street floor. Instantly there was a scramble for safety as those within realized that the building was on fire. By this time a company of Zouaves followed by a compact body of police, which had been fighting its way slowly up the avenue, reached the arsenal. The mob charged them. The Zouaves fired with ball into the brown of them. When the volley was fired the entire building was a roaring furnace. The mob knew that many of its number, including women and boys, were trapped in the roaring furnace they had stormed not many minutes before. Most of them were on the drill floor. The thought of their terrible death and the gayly garbed Zouaves who had just fired into them caused them to flee. As they fled the entire inside of the building fell a blazing mass. No one ever knew, save the police, as to the probable number of rioters who were burned to death, for when the ruins were being cleared, no civilian, save the excavators, was permitted within the police lines. But many barrels of charred human bones were taken from among the burned timbers.

While the fighting around the arsenal was at its height another mob, numbering 3,000, had attacked the Colored Orphan

Asylum, which occupied the entire block on Fifth Avenue, from Forty-third to Forty-fourth Streets. For by this time mobs, all over town, were beginning to turn their wrath on Negroes, regarding them as the primary cause of the War. There were two hundred and twenty-five pickaninnies under the age of twelve in the building. These were led from the building before the mob arrived. The mob set fire to the Asylum in several places, fighting back the firemen until the flames had done their work.

At the same hour a mob set fire to the Enrolment Office at 1190 Broadway, and the flames spread until the entire row of buildings between Twenty-eighth and Twenty-ninth Streets was destroyed. Here, as in numerous other instances of a like nature, there was considerable looting.

When dark fell on the city, low-hanging clouds cast back a lurid glare from the burning buildings on the town. Some forty fires had been kindled by the mobs. Most of these were now blazing.

Over on Clarkson Street, near Hudson, a mob danced around a small bonfire. Barely within reach of the flames were the feet of a Negro, who was hanging from a tree. This fire was kept burning long after the Negro's body had ceased to writhe. Police who attempted to cut down the body had their weapons taken from them and were told to return to their station. They had no choice save to obey.

During the day the rioters talked of burning down *The Tribune* building. Twice during the evening the same mob was prevented from carrying out these threats. The mob was led by a game-legged barber who predicted he would be shaving Jeff Davis in New York before long.

All during the early part of the night the street fighting and killing and incendiarism continued. At ten o'clock at night a mob drove the police from their station house in East Twenty-second Street, a block from the burned arsenal. The building was then fired and the mob remained in the glow of its flames until its destruction was assured.

Half an hour before midnight a drenching rain, which had been threatening all evening, deluged the sweltering, terror-stricken city. It cooled the atmosphere and the fighting ardor of the mobs. There was not a shot fired or blow struck after the rain fell. The police of the Greenwich Street Station were asked if the Negro's body was still hanging from the tree on Clarkson Street. "Yes," came back the telegraphed reply. Back went the order: "Take it down forthwith." At 12:25 Tuesday morning the commander of the precinct telegraphed the Central Office that there was one mob still out, rain or no rain, and that it refused to let the police near the tree.

The Negro's body was still swinging from the tree when the birds began their morning song in its branches.

Tweed was up with the birds. So were the mobs.

CHAPTER XXI

THE occasion for Tweed's early rising the second day of the riots was the expected arrival of Governor Seymour, who had been telegraphed early the preceding day at his retreat at the New Jersey watering place. Seymour should have arrived the evening before. But for reasons best known to himself he delayed starting for the Metropolis until after he had breakfasted Tuesday morning.

Tweed, with the Elegant Oakey Hall, Richard O'Gorman—called by his enemies the greediest man in Tammany Hall, and one of the city's most brilliant orators—and others whose faces were familiar to the mobs met Seymour as he stepped off the ferry boat.

Seymour's face was ashen gray. The horror of it was apparent before he reached the city, as a heavy pall of smoke had settled over the roofs of the houses. A scorching sun beat pitilessly through the haze of smoke and fog. Long before the Governor arrived the mobs had resumed their work of destruction, fighting, burning and looting. Before the city had breakfasted they had set fire to many houses, including the homes of two government officials who were connected with the draft.

As the Governor and his escort were driven up Broadway to Mayor Opdyke's temporary office at the St. Nicholas Hotel, they passed several mobs. Hats were raised and cheers given, first for the Governor, then for Tweed, then for the Elegant Oakey, and their companions. Tweed sat beside the Governor in the first of the two carriages. Sheriff Jimmy Lynch joined the conference at the St. Nicholas. The morning reports of the commanders of the various police precincts were called for. These would show the known number of slain in each Ward in the city.

258

These reports, recounting the details of police work of the previous day, had been sent to Police Headquarters as usual. They had been destroyed at Headquarters, and the police captains did not make any further morning reports until the riots were suppressed. The Governor learned that citizens, many of them veterans of the war, were volunteering to aid the police. There had been but a handful of Zouaves available for street fighting on Monday. But now there were five hundred—all of the Tenth New York. There were many howitzers —those snubby cannon that tear wide breaches in masses of closely packed humanity with more effectiveness than any other weapon known. No deadlier weapon could have been devised for street fighting.

Seymour had heard enough. Now the party adjourned to the City Hall. A mob of many thousands had gathered there, as word went forth that the Governor would address them. From the top of the broad stretch of marble steps, the Governor made the most astonishing speech one in authority ever delivered to a mob with blood on its hands. On one side of the Governor stood Tweed and the Elegant Oakey. They were smiling. On the other was the Mayor, his face a ghastly white. He was observed to tremble. In his person he symbolized the fear that possessed the town.

"I come," said the Governor, "not only for the purpose of maintaining law, but also from a kind regard for the interests and the welfare of those who, under the influence of excitement and a feeling of supposed wrong, were in danger not only of inflicting serious blows to the good order of society, but to their own interests. I beg of you to listen to me as your friend, for I am your friend, and the friend of your families."

This is Seymour's expurgated version of what he said on the score of friendship. He said more. He said he came to give the mob a test of his friendship. He also said, and this he admits, that he had ever been opposed to the draft. The Governor ended by saying that he had warned Washington the previous Saturday to suspend the Act. He had.

The mob cheered him and was permitted to depart in peace

to continue its work of destruction. This was the only period of truce during the four days of rioting.

While the Governor was speaking, barricades were being erected on the east and west sides of the town.

That afternoon, the Governor, accompanied by Tweed, Hall, and Sheriff Lynch, journeyed through the town. The mobs were fighting and defeating soldiers as well as police, and applying the torch to the homes of the wealthy. These and Negroes were the objects of special hatred. The rich they regarded as being immune to the draft, and they were, or at least such of them as cared to escape it by putting up $300 or finding a substitute. Before he started on his tour of inspection—its extent or any details of it are not known to us—the Governor issued a proclamation on a level with his speech from the steps of the City Hall in which he promised that "the right of every citizen to make such an appeal [to the courts against the Draft Act] will be maintained and the decision of the courts must be respected by rulers and people alike."

The phrase *the decision of the courts must be respected by rulers* was deliberate. Seymour knew that an hour earlier, one of Tweed's corrupt judges, John H. McCunn, of the City Court, had discharged a prisoner conscripted on Saturday, holding that the Draft Act was unconstitutional, void and inoperative. This demagogic decision was published in the newspapers of that afternoon.

Mobs of homeless boys, acting independently of their elders, were roaming the streets armed with stones, stout sticks, and matches. Several mobs of these children, whom society had neglected, were now proving how much cheaper it would have been to have succored them. The police of the Twenty-ninth Precinct, which embraced the fashionable residential section east of Madison Square Park, were routed twice during the morning by a mob of these small boys. As early as 10:45 A.M. the police from this precinct, whose headquarters were on Twenty-fourth Street, a few doors from the park, telegraphed the Central Office:

"We want assistance immediately, as boys are setting fire to private dwellings and robbing them."

Another mob of small boys entered a tenement house occupied by Negroes. As the urchins yelling "Kill the Niggers!" rushed for the house, all inside escaped by rear windows—all save a little pickaninny of two years. This child was in a front room on the third floor. One of the boys threw the child out the window. Its dead body lay on the street for hours.

In Crosby and Mercer Streets, and other "red light" sections, the mobs invaded the bawdy houses. The woman members of the mobs stripped the courtesans of their silken lingerie and gaudy finery after rifling their bureaus. By Tuesday night every house of prostitution in the city was emptied of its inmates.

On First Avenue a mob had erected barricades at Twelfth, Thirteenth, and Fourteenth Streets. There was ugly fighting here all day, the mob forcing their attackers to retreat after each charge. These were baby barricades, like those of Paris. On the west side of the town, on Ninth Avenue, the mobs erected a barricade that set a record for size. It was nearly a mile long. It extended from Twenty-fourth to Forty-first Street. This barricade was constructed of telegraph poles, boxes, barrels, drays, barouches, and every other conceivable sort of vehicle, all firmly bound together by wires that had been stripped from the poles after they had been felled.

There were thousands—how many has never been estimated—camped behind this barricade throughout the day. New musket rifles and carbines could be seen above the barricade. These rioters possessed a cannon which they trundled defiantly up and down in front of the rude breastworks. A downtown mob possessed four cannon. These they secreted under a pile of debris in the Centre Market, at Broome and Centre Streets. How these cannon came into possession of the rioters is a mystery, since, while the authorities report their recovery, no, military report tells of the capture of any of their guns by the mobs.

The severest fighting of the day occurred on Second Avenue, south of Thirty-fourth Street. Here, shortly before noon, about two hundred policemen, one company of the Twelfth Regiment and two from the Eleventh New York, had a hand-to-hand fight with a mob of 2,000. The troops, all veterans of the Civil War, were led by Colonel H. F. O'Brien, Commander of the Eleventh Regiment. He was on horseback. O'Brien lived only two blocks away. Many in the mob knew him. The military had two howitzers with them. These were turned on the mob, and the grape and canister tore gaping holes in their ranks.

While the soldiers were fighting in the streets the police—some of whose number had been injured—charged the members of the mob, some of whom fled into the houses, where they were pursued by the police who clubbed many of them to death.

After a half-hour of this, the mob fled from the scene. The police and soldiers continued up the avenue.

In the afternoon Colonel O'Brien and his troops returned to their barracks. The Colonel had been on duty for nearly twenty-four hours. He took a carriage to drive to his home near the scene of the noon rioting. When he reached Thirty-fourth Street and Third Avenue, he dismissed his driver. He was in full uniform, a revolver in his holster, his sword clanking and his spurs jangling as he walked. As he reached Second Avenue, where he had battled a few hours before, he entered a drug store. Instantly a mob of three hundred assembled in front of the pharmacy. The druggist fearful that the mob would destroy the store if the Colonel remained, suggested that he leave.

O'Brien was without fear. As he stepped out of the drug store, sword in his right hand, and his revolver in his left, he was felled with a blow on the back of the head. In another moment he was on the sidewalk, the crowd fighting one another to kick the helpless soldier. Rostand had not written, nor Hooker translated: "By the sword of a foeman let me fall, steel in my heart, and laughter on my lips." Members of the mob then seized the unconscious officer by the legs and dragged him to a lamp-post. One of the mob, who knew that O'Brien was a devout Roman Catholic, summoned a priest from the church he attended. When the clergyman reached the Colonel's side to administer the last rites to the dying—O'Brien was of powerful physique and still breathing—several of the rioters hurled the priest aside and danced upon the unfortunate soldier's body. But this did not kill him. The lips, red, torn, distorted, moved as if in defiance. Perhaps, in the delirium of death, O'Brien was back on the battlefield, leading an invincible host! Next a rope was slipped around O'Brien's neck and in another minute he was swinging from the lamp-post. What happened thereafter is told by a *Herald* reporter who witnessed the final scenes of this pitiable tragedy:

"After a few minutes the body was taken down, he being still alive, and thrown, like so much rubbish, into the street. The body lay in the middle of the street, within a few yards of the corner of Thirty-fourth Street. Nature shudders at the appalling scenes which here took place. The body was mutilated in such a manner that it was utterly impossible to recognize it. The head was nearly one mass of gore, and the clothes saturated with blood. A crowd of some three hundred persons surrounded the prostrate figure. These men looked upon the terrible sight with the greatest coolness, and some even smiled at the gory object. Our reporter walked leisurely among the crowd which surrounded the body, and gazed upon the extended mass of flesh which was once the corpulent form of Colonel H. F. O'Brien. Notwithstanding the fearful process which the soldier had gone through, he was yet breathing. The eyes were closed, but there was a very apparent twitching of the eyelids, while the lips were now and again convulsed, as if in the most intense agony. After lying for about an hour in this position, several of the crowd took hold of the body by the legs and dragged it from one side of the street to the other. This operation was gone through with several times, when the crowd again left the body lying in its original position.

"Had Colonel O'Brien been a man of weak constitution, he would certainly have ceased to exist long before this time. He was, however, a man of great natural strength, and this fact probably kept him breathing longer than would any common person. The crowd remarked this, and watched his every slightest movement with the most intense anxiety. Now and then the head would be raised from the ground, while an application of a foot from one of the crowd would dash the already mangled mass again to the earth. This conduct was carried on for some time; and when our reporter left the body was still lying in the street, the last spark of existence evidently having taken its flight."

At night the priest who had been hurled from Colonel O'Brien's side when he attempted to give him the consolation of religion, was permitted to take the mutilated corpse to the morgue in a hand cart. The mob would not allow the use of even a dray. "A hand cart is good enough for the Irish ——."

Before night fell on the second day of the riots many buildings including a government store on Greenwich Street, and the Weehawken ferry house at the foot of West Forty-second Street, had been burned down. This last was the work of the rioters entrenched behind the mile of barricades on Ninth Avenue. This same mob had ripped up the railroad tracks in their rear on Eleventh Avenue—the tracks now used solely by freight trains of the New York Central. It was not until toward nightfall that these barricades were taken. Strong forces of military, supported by police, took them after heavy losses had been suffered by the defenders of the street fortifications. The cannon the rioters had was recaptured by the troops. It had not been fired, for the mob lacked suitable ammunition.

The night saw many Negroes dangling from trees and lamp-posts. One colored youth who had been hanged from a lamp-post at Twenty-eighth Street and Seventh Avenue had the flesh cut from his body. Again, as on Monday night, the city glowed luridly from fires all over the town. Most of Tuesday's blazes were started in the wooden shacks occupied by Negroes.

On Wednesday the rioting spread to various parts of the Metropolitan area. In Brooklyn the mobs set fire to the grain elevators at the Atlantic Docks. A banner was stretched across one of the principal streets by this same mob. It read: "No $300 arrangements with us." This had its counterpart in rude placards carried by a New York mob reading: "The poor man's blood for the rich man's money." The belief was prevalent that the unjustifiable clause in the Draft Act was designed solely to force the poor to do all the fighting. Whatever its design, it had the effect of rousing a class-consciousness that added to the horrors of the riots.

Early in the morning the police made one of the comparatively few arrests of the rioters. The prisoner was one of Fernando Wood's henchmen, and a Deputy Sheriff under Wood's man Lynch. He was addressing a crowd near St. John's Park. "Rise and protect yourselves against this Draft Act!" exhorted Evans.

When Judge Betts, of the Federal District Court, ascended the bench that same morning, a clerk whispered to him, and then His Honor announced that a mob had threatened to destroy the United States Courts Building, and adjourned the sitting.

Wednesday afternoon the Common Council, or enough of it to make a quorum, met in the City Hall, adopted resolutions denouncing the draft, and appropriated $2,500,000 as a fund on which any poor man could draw $300 to place him on all fours with those able to raise this sum to avoid conscription.

The most sanguinary battle between the troops and the rioters took place Wednesday evening when three companies of regular troops, Duryee's Fifth Zouaves, commanded by Colonel Cleveland Winslow, came in contact with a mob of 3,000 at Nineteenth Street and First Avenue. Two howitzers, in command of Colonel E. Jardine brought up the rear. This mob was the best armed that any of the forces of law and order had encountered. The rioters opened fire with a volley from revolvers and rifles. Hundreds of women in the rear of the mob shouted encouragement to the men. The troops replied with bullet and grape and canister. But the deadly fire of the howitzers failed to budge the mob. For twenty minutes the desperate fighting continued. By this time every tenth man in the United States troops was dead or lying helpless from wounds. A captain, a lieutenant, and several non-commissioned officers, were among the slain. The soldiers, no longer able to hold their own, fled down Nineteenth Street. Colonel Jardine and a soldier, both wounded, escaped into a house where they were sheltered and their injuries treated—without the knowledge of the mob—for two days.

Thursday forenoon witnessed the arrival of five New York regiments from the Army of the Potomac. These had been ordered to the city the night before as Mayor Opdyke was informed in this telegram from the Secretary of War:

"Five regiments are under orders to return to New York. The retreat of Lee now becomes a rout, with his army broken, and much heavier loss of killed and wounded than was supposed. This will relieve a large force for the restoration of order in New York."

These seasoned troops, with those already in the city, under command of Brigadier General Harvey Brown, U.S.A., did effective work during the day. They were aided by a detachment of sailors and marines who were under Lieutenant-Commander R. W. Meade, U.S.N. By midnight Thursday the city was restored to normal quiet.

On Friday morning there were thirteen regiments of regulars—one was a Michigan regiment, the Twenty-sixth—in the city. These remained until the draft was resumed a month later. The newspapers of the first morning when New York again went about her accustomed ways, published a second proclamation by Governor Seymour. It had been issued the night before, July 16. Yet it bore the date of his first proclamation of two days before—July 14! In this belated pronouncement the Governor declared the city in a state of insurrection and warned all that who, "after the publication of this proclamation," resisted the efforts to quell the disturbances, would render themselves "liable to the penalties prescribed by law."

So this stupendous tragedy ended with a sorry jest.

CHAPTER XXII

WITH the end of the Draft Riots, Tweed turned to the plans for the fall campaign. He was not pleased with the outlook. Gunther, the wealthy fur dealer, who campaigned against Opdyke in the last Mayoralty campaign, was not pliable enough to suit Tweed. Gunther was powerful with the anti-war Democrats. He was outspokenly pro-Southern. And Gunther announced that he would run as an independent if Tweed did not nominate him. Tweed decided to risk everything and nominate Francis I. A. Boole for Mayor. Boole was a friend of The Boss, and corrupt. Gunther was nominated by a group of independents while the Republicans named Orison Blunt. Opdyke had had his fill of politics. The Republicans had had their fill of Opdyke, whose lack of decision during the Draft Riots was still calling censure down upon him. Gunther carried the city by a majority that topped Boole, his nearest rival, by nearly 7,000. There were only 19,383 votes cast for Blunt, an ardent pro-war Republican, and a supporter of Lincoln, who did not have too many advocates among his partisans in New York.

Blunt, in his campaign, might have quoted Lincoln's immortal address at Gettysburg if Greeley or some other editor had seen anything in it besides a perfunctory utterance of a President of the United States. Lincoln had delivered his dedicatory address two weeks before the Mayoralty election. Every newspaper in the city—and elsewhere so far as we know—made not a mention of it in their lead on the morning of November 20. The speech was thus introduced in *The Tribune:* "The President then delivered the following dedicatory address." No correspondent thought of telling how he looked or acted or spoke. The few simple words of Lincoln, after Everett's classic oration, were unworthy of comment!

Another speech Lincoln made at Gettysburg which is now forgotten, was treated as of greater importance by Greeley's correspondent on the famous battlefield. This speech was made the night before the one the world now knows by heart. Lincoln had finished supper when he was serenaded by "the excellent band of the New York artillery" and "after repeated calls, Mr. Lincoln at length presented himself when he was loudly cheered." And here is the forgotten speech over which New Yorkers chuckled as they read it:

"I appear before you fellow citizens merely to thank you for this compliment. The inference is a very fair one that you would hear me for a little while at least were I to commence to make a speech. I do not appear before you for the purpose of doing so, and for several substantial reasons. The most substantial of these is that I have no speech to make. (Laughter.) In my position it is somewhat important that I should not say any foolish things."

A voice: "If you can help it."

Mr. Lincoln: "It very often happens that the only way to help it is to say nothing at all. (Laughter.) Believing that is my present condition this evening, I must beg of you to excuse me from addressing you further."

And then *The Tribune's* correspondent observed: "The President retired amid cheers."

This speech was human interest! News! This was Emerson's clown making the public laugh! Let rulers be solemn or silent. What had Lincoln ever said that Orison Blunt or any other Republican in the December municipal election of 1863 could find worthy of quoting?

Blunt's defeat was foreshadowed. Opdyke did not care what happened in the local election. For in the first week of November—a month before Gunther was elected—His Honor the Mayor welcomed Admiral Lessoffsky, commander of the Russian squadron, that came with decks cleared for action in case guns could render service to Lincoln and his ideals. Opdyke and other New Yorkers slept a little more soundly after the Russian squadron's arrival. Gothamites had been going to bed fearful lest they be awakened by the thunders of British warships engaged with the forts in the harbor. Some of them visioned Lee again undertaking a march through Pennsylvania, for his army had not retreated in the rout that Secretary of War Stanton had described in his telegram to Mayor Opdyke during the Draft Riots of three months back. The country was apprehensive of a conflict with England. French troops had conquered Mexico and had crowned Maximilian, the Austrian Archduke, Emperor of the Republic to the south of us. The advisers of Napoleon III were as much feared as the cabinet of Victoria. But Lessoffsky made New York forget its fears.

A despotism that enslaved whites sends aid to a democracy that fought to free blacks!

Mayor Opdyke presided at the municipal banquet that welcomed the officers of the Czar's squadron, who, in their speeches, made no reference to England's victory over their forces in the Crimea.

Tweed forgot the defeat of Boole to prepare for the next campaign. And for the first time since he abandoned his chairmaking, he was making money in a manner that had the color of honesty. He was now a lawyer, having been admitted to the practice of law, including the privilege of trying cases in the Supreme Court and the Court of Appeals, shortly before election through the kindness of his protégé, Judge Barnard. It was an easy matter then, and for many years thereafter, for even an ignorant ward politician to be made a lawyer in the privacy of the chambers of a friendly judge. And Tweed was being appointed a receiver and referee by the courts—some of the judges refused to recognize this made-while-you-wait type of lawyer in dispensing these eagerly sought after appointments.

The year the Russian squadron arrived in New York, Tweed opened an office at 95 Duane Street. On the glazed glass door, in letters of gold, there was set forth: "William M. Tweed, Attorney-at-Law." Clients who called at Tweed's office came to consult The Boss on matters that did not call for his legal opinions. No one is known to have retained him to appear in court. Yet the fees paid him were tremendous. More than $100,000 was paid him by the Erie Railroad for "legal services."

When Gunther took office in 1864, Tweed organized two new enterprises. One was a company to engage in the quarrying and sale of marble. Tweed and his friends paid $3,080 for the quarry, which was located in the town of Sheffield, Massachusetts, and before the end of 1865 Tweed and other members of the Board of Supervisors audited the extortionate bills, totaling $420,000, for rough marble for the new County Court House.

Tweed's other business undertaking was his entrance into the printing business. When he had the Board of Supervisors question a printing and stationery bill of Edmund Jones in 1861, and had the printer summoned before the Board, Tweed had only the thought of making a profitable contact. But Tweed was an inventive genius. Jones, through his printing concern, had only been swindling the city. That was old. Why not extend the swindle to include corporations of a quasi-public character? These civic adjuncts could do as the city did when robbed—make the taxpayer pay. Accordingly Tweed bought a controlling interest in the New York Printing Company, and forced the railroads and ferry companies dependent on the city for small or large favors, to give his company the contracts for printing their tickets and timetables. Insurance companies and banks and every other user of plain or printed stationery were called upon to follow suit. They did. And all paid extravagant prices to Tweed's printing house. But none of these institutions paid the mad, mad prices that the city paid. In December of 1865 Mayor Gunther disapproved a bill of the New York Printing Company as a steal. The Board of Supervisors immediately repassed it over his veto by a vote of seven to one. Tweed by this time controlled the bi-partisan Board—there were six Republicans on it to keep the six Democrats honest!—to such an extent that when an outrageous piece of jobbery was being put through, he could always induce the two or three Republicans who declined to vote with him, to refrain from voting rather than have themselves recorded in the opposition. The value of this lay in Tweed's friends being able to say: "Why, there was only one vote cast against the measure!" This was an argument bound to appeal to a democracy.

In the year that Gunther took office there came to New York a man who was to play a large part in Tweed's life. This was James Fisk, Jr., who in a few short years was to earn the title of Prince of Erie. The Boss and the Prince were not to meet for another three years. Jay Gould was to introduce them. Gould and Tweed had formed an acquaintance for mutual profit a short time before. Gould and Tweed had been brought together by another corruptionist, Hugh Hastings, one of the many venal journalists of the time. Hastings was editor of *The New York Commercial-Advertiser.*

Fisk was the youngest of the three. He was but twenty-nine years of age when he came to New York. A more picturesque figure never entered Wall Street. He was born in Burlington, Vermont. His father was a peddler who traveled from village to village in a covered wagon. Beneath the arched canvas was a miniature department store, containing everything from a paper of pins to a suit of Sunday clothes.

Under the tutelage of this shrewd Yankee father Fisk had his first training. But he tired of peddling in the Green Mountains, and set out to see the world. His first job was as a waiter in a tavern. He then became a barker in a circus. Then he returned to his father and was admitted to partnership.

Fisk's experience as a showman taught him that the people like color, sparkle, and dash. He proposed to his father that they adapt the methods of the circus to peddling. His father instantly shook his head. Fisk elaborated on his idea. It was simple: abandon the old covered wagon and its heavy horse, and buy several wagons, each of them new and many paneled, the panels gaudily painted with colorful scenes. Each wagon instead of being pulled by one work horse, to be drawn by four spirited steeds, with richly mounted trappings, the collars of the harness topped with jangling silver bells. Again the father shook his head, and declared it would never go, at least in the Green Mountains. The upshot of it was that

Fisk bought out his father, and demonstrated that his idea was not only practicable, but profitable. Whenever Fisk, or any of his drivers, approached a village the rule was to snap the whips over the horses' heads, give them the reins, and drive into the community with all speed the steeds could make. Another fixed rule was: one price only. He prospered.

Fisk attracted the attention of the head of the great department store of Jordan, Marsh and Company, of Boston. He was cutting into their trade. He was made a member of the firm. Then he opened his own dry goods establishment. Fisk's profits from Jordan Marsh amounted to more than $100,000. He lost a little of this in his new venture, as he bought cotton when it was high, and prices were beginning to tumble. So he sold out and struck for New York, and of all places—Wall Street. He was quickly wiped out. He returned to Boston, borrowed some money, and returned to the Metropolis. But he had something more than money this time. He had a letter of introduction to Daniel Drew, whose name is perpetuated in the Drew Theological Seminary at Madison, New Jersey. In all things save one, Drew was a man of God. The exception was his business, for all Drew possessed he earned in shady gambles in Wall Street, particularly in the stocks of steamship and railroad lines. His specialty was Erie. This too was the pet hobby of Commodore Vanderbilt. And when Fisk entered New York in 1864, these two notorious speculators, Vanderbilt and Drew, were on the eve of their famous battle for control of the Erie Railroad. Gould was now a pupil of Vanderbilt, as Fisk was of Drew.

During the two years of Mayor Gunther's term, Tweed knew nothing of the existence of Gould or Fisk, and cared less. He avoided Wall Street and all in it, as he looked upon the Street as his natural enemy. It was not so long ago that nominations were made in the counting houses of bankers. Tweed wanted a monopoly of naming candidates, at least in his own party. And he wanted a voice in the other.

Tweed was determined to have Boole run again for Mayor as the city campaign of 1865 approached. There were many protests among Tweed's own friends against Boole. His cor-

JAY GOULD

JAMES FISK, JR.

ruption was generally known. Tweed brushed all these protests aside. He knew that Boole could be relied upon. In the first year of Gunther's administration Boole, who had jurisdiction over the cleaning of streets—Tweed was Deputy Street Commissioner—awarded the street cleaning contract to a friend of Tweed who received $800,000 for the job, when the low bidder had offered to do the work for exactly $500,000 less!

Boole was nominated as Tweed had planned. But there was such an outcry raised when some of the corrupt deals of which Boole was guilty were disclosed that Tweed had him resign, and named John T. Hoffman in his stead. Hoffman had been Recorder and made a good record as a judge. Gunther sought reëlection as an independent. The Republicans, hoping to capitalize the martyrdom of Lincoln, put up Marshall O. Roberts, millionaire, patron of arts (his gallery of paintings was appraised at $500,000), and more important than all from a politician's view, the owner of the *Star of the West*, the ship that was fired on by the South Carolinians when she attempted to aid the beleaguered Major Anderson at Fort Sumter before the outbreak of hostilities. Here was reflected glory. There were enough returned soldiers to insure the election of any man they supported. Roberts appealed for their support.

Horace Greeley and other Republicans, tiring of the so-called leaders of their party, and their subserviency to Tweed and his lieutenants in Tammany, cast about for a worthy citizen to lead a second independent ticket. Gunther was unclean to Republicans of the type of Greeley. So was he to many Democrats who had violently opposed Lincoln and his policies while Lincoln lived. And so John Hecker was nominated on the Citizens', or Reform, ticket.

Hecker was the largest miller of the town. His flour mill at the foot of Cherry Hill was one of the pride industries of the Metropolis. He had a chain of bakeries scattered all over the lower part of the town. He was noted for his philanthropy. The managers of his bake-shops gave a loaf of bread to any beggar who came to the door. Hecker was a sincere Chistian and a citizen who felt he was indebted to the community. He was always ready to serve it. A dozen years back he had served in the Common Council. He was active in church work, and edited *The Churchman.* He was a member of the Board of Education. He wrote "The Scientific Basis of Education." He started out to be a printer. He worked for Harper and Brothers before he began the career of baker and miller. He did not possess a dollar that he had not earned honestly.

Neither the Republicans nor Tammany relished the entrance of Hecker into the race. A friend of Tweed in the Board of Supervisors, Smith Ely, Jr., was dispatched to persuade Hecker that he was making a mistake to run. Hecker heard him through. Then he replied:

"Mr. Ely, you form your opinions in the ordinary way of a business man and a politician."

And knowing that he was regarded by the politicians as a religious fanatic, Hecker quickly added:

"But I receive my impressions directly from on High!"

Smith Ely, Jr., left Hecker convinced that the miller was mildly mad.

There were some eighty odd thousand votes cast for Mayor. Of these Hecker received 10,465. Hoffman led with 32,487. Roberts ran second with 31,416. Mayor Gunther came in last with 6,681.

The reason for this low vote—the smallest a Mayoralty candidate ever received in the history of the city—was Gunther's veto of a resolution of the Common Council looking to the illumination of public buildings, to honor "the recent victories on land and sea."

Let us quote one sentence from Gunther's veto message to show the temper of the city at the time—for Gunther's act was cordially approved by the citizenry:

"I yield to no man in my attachment to 'the Union as it was and the Constitution as it is,' but as the President demands of the Southern people to abandon the rights which the Constitution confers, I do not see how those who have always held that the Federal Government has nothing to do with the domestic institutions of the States, can be expected to rejoice over *victories, which, whatever they may be, surely are not Union victories.*"

Lincoln was unpopular in New York till the hour of his martyrdom. When he ran for reëlection he lost the Metropolis to McClellan by more than 37,000. Until the surrender of Lee's starved troops at Appomattox, the majority of New Yorkers looked upon Lincoln as a hopeless blunderer. His assassination five days later tore the veil of prejudice from their eyes. Emerson's clown and Bennett's boor gave way to the Man of the People.

CHAPTER XXIII

TWEED had all the evidences of wealth with the close of the war. Four years before he was stone-broke after his unsuccessful shrievalty campaign. Now he was a millionaire. A large amount of Tweed's ill-gotten wealth came from the bounties appropriated by the city for substitutes of drafted men. Says *The Herald:* "The bounty ring was of the most elaborate description, a ring in which Supervisors, recruiting officers, doctors, bounty brokers, and policemen were interested, and in the profits of which they shared." General L. C. Baker, in his "History of the United States Secret Service," published in 1867, in telling of his unsuccessful efforts to break up the bounty ring in New York, refers to the "high social and official position of many of the suspected parties" and of the refusal of the New York police to render him assistance when called upon.

Tweed became known as a liberal contributor to charity immediately following the laying down of arms. He had never the reputation of being tight-fisted. A politician cannot be niggardly and successful. But now he had developed the habits of a spendthrift. At luncheon or dinner in any of the eating places near the City Hall—his favorite places were the Astor House and Delmonico's—Tweed always paid the check, no matter who was in the party, or who suggested it. It was an age of display. Men were as fond of diamonds as women. Tweed wore a blue-white gem in his shirt front the size of a small cherry. The cartoonists played with it. It was left to a millionaire politician of our own generation to answer such envious critics fittingly: "Them as has 'em, wears 'em."

There were many sad reminders of the war—the disabled veterans who were dependent on the charity of passersby. These youths, with legs and arms shot away, or otherwise too badly maimed for work, stood on the prominent corners of

276

Broadway, at the entrance to ferry houses, piers and railroad terminals. Most of them wore their old blue uniform and the forage cap with its patent leather peak. Occasionally, one would see a Zouave in his faded multicolored dress, more like the garish garb of a comic opera chorister than a soldier. Many of them turned organ grinders. Others sold shoe laces from wooden trays. Tacked to the little tray of one who stood outside the Astor House was a card informing the passersby that its wearer had been at Gettysburg. It is said of Tweed that he never passed one of these veterans without dropping a crumpled bill unostentatiously into the wooden tray as he helped himself to a pair of shoe laces.

Hoffman took office the first of January, 1866, and gave the city one of its most popular administrations. Little else can be said of it. Toward the end of his first six months, Hoffman's popularity had extended beyond the confines of the city, and he was his party's nominee for Governor in the fall of the year. The Republicans renominated Governor Reuben T. Fenton, who defeated him. In the same year, Tammany, or rather Tweed, elected Hoffman Grand Sachem of the society. Tweed had longing eyes on the headship of Tammany ever since his election as Chairman of the local Central Committee in 1861. No one had ever held both places simultaneously, but Tweed intended to shatter this tradition, as he had many others. He must, however, prepare the rank and file of the organization for such a radical move.

Hoffman's first year was signalized by the issuance of bonds to build the Brooklyn Bridge. But for Tweed these bonds, aggregating $1,500,000, would not have been issued—at least in 1866. The Common Council refused to give its approval, demanding $65,000 for authorizing the Comptroller to issue the securities. Unless the Aldermen could be whipped into line by The Boss, who alone could sway them, the backers of the project would have to submit to extortion. Tweed was appealed to to save the situation. Tweed was The Boss, but he was not unreasonable. He sympathized with his visitors— and with the attitude of the Aldermen, for he had been an Alderman himself. So the $65,000 was given to Tweed, and he paid it to the boys at the City Hall. Tweed fared almost as well as the Common Council. He was given a block of stock of the Brooklyn Bridge Company, having par value of approximately $40,000, and later made a director of the corporation.

There was another matter that went before the Common Council in 1866 which added to the wealth of some of the Aldermen. And Tweed got more out of it than any one—a hearty laugh on Peter B. Sweeny, who paid $60,000 for the amusement of The Boss. Sweeny wanted to be Chamberlain. But again the Common Council would have to give its consent to the appointment, which was made by the Mayor. Sweeny was acceptable to Hoffman. Tweed did not care for Sweeny. But Sweeny, like Connolly, was indispensable, because of his hold on his people. The Boss did not dare oppose Sweeny, who was thus described by Tweed:

"Sweeny is a hard, over-bearing, revengeful man. He wants his way. He treasures up his wrath. He has considerable ability of a kind."

And of the relations between Tweed and Sweeny, The Boss said:

"We were so opposite and unalike that we never got along very well."

The Common Council held up Sweeny's appointment until he paid the "strikers" $60,000 for its approval.

This was a small price to pay for the post of Chamberlain where one of the perquisites of the office was the interest from deposits of municipal funds. The Chamberlain selected the depositories, and in earlier days, when there were no rigid banking laws, some of the banks selected by the Chamberlain were known as skeleton banks. These institutions "failed" so that their organizers might rob the depositors. The returns to a scrupulously honest man would be at least $250,000 in the late Sixties. What could a dishonest Chamberlain make in addition to this by demanding bonuses from banks in which the city's money was deposited at two per cent per annum? Sweeny had long ago lost most of his conscience.

Tweed, who was now forty-three years of age, had a family

which was fast growing up. His wife urged this as a reason for moving from the section where the Tweeds, for three generations, had lived. There was another reason. Cherry Hill, once the home of the country's first citizens, and the rest of the East Side were being invaded by the newly arrived immigrants, and the old families were going farther uptown. After the death of Tweed's father in 1860, the Tweeds changed their address to 197 Henry Street. This was a modest house of red brick, but their new home of stylish brownstone, with an English basement, was on the fringe of the world of fashion, 41 West Thirty-sixth Street. Tweed's family now had their own carriages, and spent the week-ends at nearby watering places.

The Boss seldom accompanied them, as he was beginning to lead a life that removed him more and more from his family. Sometimes he would be seen dining in one of the flashier type of oyster saloons, far removed from his usual haunts. His companion in these out-of-the-way haunts was a little blonde, who did not reach to his shoulders, and many years his junior. There was gossip.

Three years before Tweed met his charmer, he had joined the Americus Club. Contrary to the assumption which prevailed even in Tweed's day, The Boss had no hand in organizing this society, which is forever identified with his name. It was formed by ten young men of the Seventh Ward in 1857. Some of its founders were volunteer firemen, and the name of Tweed's old fire engine company, popularly known as *Big Six* or *Americus*, appealed to their fancy. Tweed, as we know, had given *Big Six* its name, and its emblem—the tiger. "Ed" Marriner, foreman of Engine Company Number 12, was President of the Americus Club when Tweed became a member.

The club in the beginning was only a name for a group of congenial spirits which pooled its resources to hire a small boat every Saturday in the warm weather to take them to Greenwich, Connecticut, where they spent the night and part of the following day. These charter members of the Americus Club tented out on the beach. Fish were always running in Long Island Sound from early spring until late in the fall, and clams could be had for the raking, or the still more primitive fashion of treading, that is, walking in shallow water and scooping them up with the bare foot. These were cooked over fires on the shore.

Tweed had changed all this by 1866. These simple outings were a thing of the past. In another year the Americus Club had a pretentious home at Greenwich, directly on the Sound, and a dock to which Tweed's yacht was often moored. The initiation fee was made one thousand dollars. A tiger's head, in gold, relieved by blue enamel, a copy of the emblem of Tweed's old organization of red shirts, denoted membership in the Americus Club. The Boss and his immediate friends wore tigers' heads whose eyes were set with rubies. These cost two thousand dollars each. It has been erroneously assumed that Nast's frequent picturing of these pretentious badges in his cartoons of Tweed and the Tweed Ring led to the adoption of the tiger as the emblem of Tammany Hall. Nast never drew a tiger's head in connection with Tweed or Tammany until the end of 1869. More than three years prior to this famous Nast cartoon the Tammany delegates to the Democratic State Convention which nominated Hoffman for Governor, were distinguished by the tigers' heads which adorned their badges. Tweed, as Chairman of the Democratic Central Committee of New York County, led the delegation. It was not, however, until after Nast's cartoons that the tiger was associated with Tammany by the outside world.

When Tweed learned that his little affair with the blonde was causing talk, he thought of Greenwich. So he built his inamorata a retreat a short distance from his Americus Club. This passed as the home of his coachman. For Tweed knew that there was one convention that he could not flout without bringing down upon him the wrath of many who would wink at public plundering. And so circumspect was he in his amour that it was kept a secret in Cos Cob and in nearby Greenwich as is instanced by the following contemporary newspaper paragraph:

"Tweed gave to the Methodist Society, of Greenwich, Connecticut, money which they used to beautify the edifice they worshiped in."

Had these Methodists lived in New York Tweed would have built a new church for them. While he gave, and gave generously to charity régardless of sect, he believed that charity, especially in politics, begins at home. And when he gave, whatever Tweed's wishes may have been, it was not long before his good deeds were being proclaimed from the housetops by his followers.

On the authority of *The Herald* we have it that Tweed offered a Roman Catholic priest half a million dollars to build a charitable institution on the site of Tweed's birthplace. This was more in the nature of a grand gesture, as the house at No. 1 Cherry Street was destined for demolition to make way for the Brooklyn Bridge.

Shortly after the election of Hoffman as Mayor, Tweed, with Sweeny, Connolly, the Elegant Oakey, and two or three others, made a practice of lunching almost daily at the City Hall. These noon-day meetings at the City Hall were wholly political. The Mayor was present. Loot was never discussed in Hoffman's presence.

In the Congressional elections of Hoffman's first year as Mayor, John Morrissey, sometime champion of the fistic ring, and who had also abandoned his career of thug and thief, was elected to the House of Representatives from Tweed's old district. Morrissey was now respectable. He operated two gambling houses, one in the city and another in Saratoga. Horace Greeley also ran for Congress. He was a candidate in the Fourth Congressional district. The editor lost, receiving only 3,717 votes out of a total of 17,720. Greeley's defeat astonished the city. Two years before a War Democrat carried the district by nearly 6,000 majority. There had been no change in sentiment in the district. Greeley was the loudest supporter of the war in the country, once he warmed up to it. The election of Morrissey only stressed the defeat of Greeley. We could understand Greeley's defeat had the election taken place a year later, for it was in May of 1867 that he and fifteen others signed the $100,000 bail bond on which Jefferson Davis was released after two years' imprisonment. This act of the ever humane and always erratic Greeley seriously affected for a time the circulation of the journal in which he had buried his heart. The sale of Greeley's "American Conflict" almost ceased, thousands of subscribers declining to accept the work. But to leave the leader of the Southern cause without reproducing the last words of his history *The Rise and Fall of the Confederate Government* would be an injustice to the memory of this whole-souled sportsman: "The Union, *esto perpetua.*"

On July 4, of Hoffman's second year as Mayor, the cornerstone of the present Tammany Hall was laid. There had been talk for years of moving the headquarters of the organization from its site opposite the City Hall, which the old *Sun* was to take over. All were agreed that the Hall should be where it would be most convenient for "fifty years to come." No one dreamed then that old New York would grow at such a pace that within half that time Fourteenth Street would be farther removed from the center of population than the City Hall was in 1867, when there were approximately 900,000 on the Island of Manhattan.

That same summer plans were made at the luncheons at the City Hall for the coming campaign. Hoffman, of course, was to be renominated. The political destinies of others were decided, including Connolly. He like Sweeny, the year before, selected the most important place in the city government outside of the Mayoralty—the office of Comptroller.

"He [Connolly] was a powerful man in his ward and district," said Tweed. "We could not get along without him, and annexed him for the vote he controlled."

Tweed, with every one else who knew the amiable and artful Connolly intimately, was friendly to him, and admired his political sagacity, masked most of the time by a delightful and feigned insouciance. His ready wit was made to appear all the more sparkling because of his extremely sober dress. He always affected a suit of black broadcloth.

There was one other decision made at the City Hall luncheon

conferences more important than all the rest. This involved the Democratic nomination for State Senator from the Fourth District. Tweed cast himself for this rôle. There were two reasons which determined The Boss to go to the Legislature. The immediate and lesser motive was to be where the city obtained the annual privilege of imposing taxes. In the tax levy measure were omnibused all appropriations for the maintenance of government for the fiscal year. For the New York County Board of Supervisors alone, of all the Boards in the State, did not have the power to tax. The size of the levy and appropriation defined the extent to which public improvements could be made, the number of city employees, and their remuneration. It very frequently happened that, in order to get the city tax levy bill through the State Legislature, those most interested in its enactment had to bribe the "strikers" at the State Capitol. The Boss wanted to be on the scene where this was being done. The controlling factor was Tweed's ambition to dominate the State as he did the City. This he aimed to do by electing Hoffman to the Governorship. It would not be an easy matter. Politicians are chary in naming a man a second time for the same office after he had made an unsuccessful race. Then there was powerful opposition developing within the party to the growing power of The Boss. Men of influence who thought in terms of national politics were lending their support to this movement. They feared a scandal. Tilden was always credited with being at the head of the anti-Tweed faction. Tilden was at this time the recognized leader of the party in the State, and Chairman of the Democratic State Central Committee, as Tweed was of the local organization. Tweed and Tilden cordially disliked each other and from different motives. Tweed always regarded Tilden as his foe. He did not conceal this belief, or the hatred it inspired. Invariably when these two leaders came face to face in the private councils of the party, the effect was like setting a match to a fuse. Tilden was the match. Tweed sputtered. There were times when Tweed vented his wrath on Tilden in public places. Tweed had command of a fluent vocabulary of profanity. Tilden ignored these outbursts.

Tweed believed that he could successfully meet any move of Tilden if he could spend a session in Albany, where, during each sitting of the Legislature, every county leader of moment is to be seen. And the representatives in the Legislature, even to the least appealing of the first-term members, are all men of influence in their districts. This is always especially true of the men from the rural districts. Among the leaders of the farming sections Tilden was most powerful.

Tweed had no more doubt of his own election than he had of the majority of the candidates on the local ticket, from Mayor down. He had improved on the rough methods of Wood, who relied exclusively on strong-arm tactics at the polls. Tweed did not abandon the use of thugs and repeaters. He concentrated their activities in wards where he did not have the Republican leader on his payroll—or on the city's. It did not matter which, as Tweed obtained his money, directly or indirectly, from the taxpayers. And in neither case was the Tweed Republican expected to perform any labor—save on primary or Election Day or at a convention caucus. In many of these wards Tweed was as powerful in the Republican organization as he was in the Democratic. He dictated the nominations, paying for the privilege and gladly.

While the campaign was on a singular thing happened. Sweeny announced that he surrendered all his rights as Chamberlain to the interest on city moneys on deposit with the banks. This amounted to at least $100,000 a year. This is the only act of a member of the Tweed Ring where public funds, honestly or dishonestly obtainable, were not taken. Sweeny's motive for the unique act is not known. Whether it was done of his own volition, or at the request of The Boss, so that the praise showered upon Sweeny would redound to the credit of the Tweed Ring, is likewise unknown. Bennett, who on occasions attacked the Ring—never severely while it was in power—delivered an extravagant and fantastic panegyric in *The Herald* on the unholy thief, likening him to the Gracchi, to Regulus, and to other patriots of ancient Rome who made supreme sacrifices for their country. Sweeny could well afford to pay this price for the pleasure of seeing how it would look to be pictured as an honest man. He stole that much every month. For at this time the Ring was looting the city to the extent of fifteen dollars for every eighty-five dollars it actually owed on bills rendered, and the Ring's percentage and stealings were to increase many fold. Sweeny's share was ten per cent of all the loot!

Tweed worked day and night in this municipal election. As head of the Street Department—although his title was Deputy Commissioner, he generally saw to it that some respectable figurehead subservient to him was appointed over him—he was head of a small army of laborers and mechanics, who were on the city payroll and in the employ of private contractors. His department enjoyed jurisdiction over the opening of streets, their paving, grading, and regulating, the construction and maintenance of all public thoroughfares, the building and repairing of docks and piers, the custody of public buildings, and the lighting of all highways, piers, and docks. The many who were engaged on these various works were urged to enlist all their friends in the coming canvass. They required no second urging. Every other department of the city and county government did likewise.

The exertion put into the campaign was reflected in the vote. Fernando Wood, whose constant overtures to Tweed for peace had been spurned, thought to bedevil the election by running for Mayor backed by his Mozart Hall Democracy. But Tweed was now master, and all that Wood polled was 22,930. This, however, was in excess of the vote for William A. Darling, the Republican nominee, who received 18,465. The rest of the 104,325 votes cast for Mayor, or 63,030, were credited to Hoffman. Wood named a candidate to oppose Tweed for State Senator. His name was Bagley. The official returns gave the Mozart Hall nominee nine votes! Tweed received 15,446, some 9,600 more than his nearest competitor.

The vote in the city and State gave the Democrats control, for the first time in years, of the lower branch of the Legislature. They elected seventy-six Assemblymen, a majority of twenty-four over the Republicans, who, however, managed to retain control of the Senate.

This unexpected overturn in the Assembly precipitated the first fight in the open between Tilden and Tweed. This was over the control of the Assembly. Tweed forced the issue. It was an audacious move. Tweed won.

CHAPTER XXIV

This victory over Tilden made Tweed the most influential figure in the State government next to the Governor. The dream of The Boss of State domination was being realized faster than he had anticipated. This power came to Tweed through the Speaker of the Assembly. In this officer who is chosen at an open session of the Assembly, resides more control over the making of laws than in the Governor. The Speaker appoints the committees to which all measures are referred. Through these bodies he exercises mastery over every bill from the moment it is introduced. No proposal can be voted upon until it is reported out by the committee to which it was referred.

Tilden sought to elect as Speaker John L. Flagg, member of Assembly from Rensselaer County, and Mayor of Troy. Flagg had ability. Tweed's candidate for Speaker was Walter Hitchman, a municipal department clerk—a political hack from the upper East Side of New York. Tweed had a bloc of twenty Assemblymen to start with when the Democratic caucus was held. He needed nineteen more in order to make Hitchman the unanimous choice of the seventy-six Democrats, as a majority vote binds a minority in a party caucus. He got them, and a few more to spare. Some were from the rural sections, where Tilden had his greatest following.

During the legislative session of 1868 no one went to the office of the Speaker of the Assembly in the old brown stone Capitol to advance or defeat some pending piece of legislation. Instead petitioners went to the regal suite in the Delevan House of Boss Tweed—School Commissioner of the City of New York, Assistant Street Commissioner of the City of New York, President of the Board of Supervisors of the County of New York,

Senator of the State of New York, and Chairman of the Democratic Central Committee of New York County. And before the year was over he was to add another title to this list— Grand Sachem of Tammany Hall. Tweed was the only one to head the twin organizations which constitute Tammany Hall.

The suite of The Boss on the second floor of the Albany hotel consisted of seven spacious rooms. Six were fitted up with sideboards glittering with cut glass and decanters of whiskey, brandy, Holland gin, and other exotic distillations. The seventh was the sleeping chamber of The Boss. Steel engravings hung on the walls, and from brackets near each window were suspended brass cages housing golden songsters. Potted plants and vases of cut flowers added other splashes of restful color to the rooms. Tweed was partial to flowers and canaries. Gleaming porcelain cuspidors, decorated with sprays of roses, were scattered around on the carpeted floors.

Attendants stood outside the doors of these rooms to see that none entered who did not have business with The Boss or one of his retinue. The two end rooms were reserved for Tweed. Admittance to the first of these, Tweed's reception room, which boasted a square grand piano, could be obtained by the average caller only after passing the guards at the inner doors. There was an outside guard on this reception room. He admitted only those known to him to be welcome at any time by The Boss, such as Connolly, Sweeny, the Elegant Oakey, and Hoffman. The Mayor seldom visited Albany during 1868, but the others came on summons. Sweeny and Hall scanned every measure introduced in either house to prevent the enactment of innocent-appearing bills containing valuable grants of public property or a delegation of power for which the price had not been paid.

The return to Albany of many rural legislators is determined by their ability to obtain appropriations for needed improvements at home, such as construction or repairs of bridges and dredging of waterways. All had to see The Boss before their measures passed the Assembly, or were provided for in the annual appropriation bill. Each and every one of these measures was approved by Tweed, who was ingratiating in his reception of the men from the farming districts. No one was taxed—the euphemism is Tweed's—a dollar for these measures. Tweed, with his hearty handclasp and his beaming smile and cheery manner, made all these lawmakers feel that they had found a real friend in The Boss. It mattered not what their politics was—all were received with the same cordiality and reminded that he kept open house for his friends. Thus Tweed helped to pave the way for the nomination of Mayor Hoffman for Governor in the coming fall.

While The Boss was working up sentiment for his candidate for Governor, the Common Council in New York passed an ordinance "opening, regulating, and improving the avenues or boulevards north of Central Park." Tweed, in company with many public-spirited citizens sponsored this project, chief among them being Andrew H. Green, who after a lifetime unselfishly devoted to the city was to be shot down by a jealousy-maddened Negro who had mistaken him for the principal in a sordid intrigue with a mulatto wench. Green and his sort had vision of the city's rapid growth and planned accordingly. Tweed, as the actual head of the Street Department would award the contracts for this extensive program.

Therein lay his chief interest in the project.

A delegation representing the largest taxpayers in the Metropolis induced Mayor Hoffman to veto the measure. Not to have done so would have offended them and lost him their support. The Mayor did this without consulting The Boss. Tweed was in Albany. He returned immediately to the city and called at the Mayor's office. Tweed hastened back to the State Capitol that evening. The following morning the Metropolitan dailies printed dispatches under Albany date-lines announcing that Tweed was a candidate for Governor and that there was no doubt of his ability to obtain the nomination.

Tweed made no move to undo Mayor Hoffman's veto beyond his visit to the City Hall and his announcement the same evening in Albany that he was a candidate for the Governorship in the ensuing fall election. What was said at the interview between The Boss and the Mayor was known only to them, and neither spoke of it.

The Mayor was restored to Tweed's good graces when the Common Council, after some of its members conferred with the Mayor, repassed the measure over his veto.

The trips between New York and Albany were made by The Boss in the same regal state in which he lived at the Capitol. He rode in a Wagner parlor car reserved for his exclusive use. No one else, save his personal attendants, shared it with him, except on invitation. He did not enter or leave the New York terminal of the road with the general public. The gates on the Thirtieth Street side were thrown open for his barouche. Through these same gates Lincoln made his entrance into New York in 1861 when he was en route to Washington. Tweed, while cognizant of his power, was not afflicted with delusions of grandeur. He drove in his carriage through the private entrance to and from the parlor car to avoid the hordes of job seekers on his trail.

Tweed maintained this suite of seven rooms at the Delevan House until his overthrow. Jay Gould and James Fisk, Jr., whom he had met shortly after his election as Senator, were frequent callers. So too was Hugh Hastings, the Republican editor, who brought the three together. Hastings was very helpful to Tweed. He knew all the men worth knowing in the Republican Party—all the old wheel horses in the Legislature. Tweed testified that he paid Hastings richly for his work, which consisted of lobbying for bills. For his adroitness in behalf of one measure Tweed paid Hastings $20,000 by check.

Until The Boss went to the State Capitol, the legislators who rang the bell—the strikers, and others who sought election to the Legislature for their personal profit—were a captainless band. Tweed drilled these mercenaries until they became worthy of the name of The Black Horse Cavalry. They attacked measures as well as defended them. No railroad or other corporation obtained a favor without paying for it. Even one of their own band was not immune, for in matters of legislation The Black Horse Cavalry knew no brother.

A more degraded Assembly than the one over which Tweed's Speaker presided is hard to conceive. There have been others more corrupt. But this one was without shame. One of its rural members, E. M. K. Glenn, representing the second district of Wayne County, unable to endure the unconcealed corruption beyond the third month of the session, rose to a question of personal privilege on the floor of the Assembly and charged that the Erie Railroad, through an agent of Daniel Drew, builder of churches and founder of a theological seminary, had been bribing members. Glenn himself had been offered $500. He demanded that the Speaker appoint a committee of investigation. Tweed's dummy complied with the request, and in a week or so the committee reported back to the parent body that it had examined the books of the Erie Railroad, and found that there had never been appropriated a cent for influencing the Legislature. Assemblyman Glenn at once informed the people of the State that he could no longer remain a member of the Assembly of the State of New York after it accepted the report whitewashing the Erie lobby. He resigned and went back home.

At the close of the legislative session, on July 4—a year to a day after the laying of the corner stone—the new Tammany Hall on Fourteenth Street was formally opened when August Belmont called the Democratic National Convention of 1868 to order. This was Saturday. On Monday Horatio Seymour was chosen chairman of the convention. For four days the delegates were deadlocked. On the twenty-second ballot the dark horse of the convention, the presiding officer, was nominated for President. This was Seymour who had received a complimentary vote on the third day, when nine delegates voted for him. A few complimentary votes—from Kentucky and Nebraska—were cast for Mayor Hoffman on the seventeenth, eighteenth, twentieth, and twenty-first ballots.

With Hoffman's nomination for Governor secured, a canvass made by the Democrats revealed that the Republicans would poll a vote up-State that would overcome any majority the city could roll up for Hoffman. Tweed stepped into the breach. Hoffman must be elected! He was not concerned over the national election. Seymour was Tilden's friend. Tweed at once put into practice a device invented by Wood—the naturalization of immigrants eligible for citizenship. Wood in one election added a few hundred votes to his total in this manner. But Tweed increased the number of qualified voters in these twenty days by nearly 60,000! The magnitude of these frauds can be understood when the records of the preceding twelve years showed that there had been only 70,604 naturalizations, or an average of less than 6,000 a year.

In this wholesale fraud Tweed induced his tool Judge Barnard to establish a naturalization mill in the Supreme Court. Hitherto all applications for citizenship in the State's courts were passed upon by judges of the Superior Court and the Court of Common Pleas. Tweed was always creating precedents. Not one of Barnard's associates on the Supreme Court bench would be a party to this debauchery of the ballot box. In the Superior Court, Judge McCunn alone was concerned in the fraud. Tweed could not induce a single one of the five judges of the Court of Common Pleas—although all were Democrats—to be party to this plot to steal the election.

The Congressional Committee appointed at the instance of the Union League Club on December 14, 1868, to investigate these frauds, traced more than 15,000 naturalizations to McCunn. Barnard admitted making 10,070 new citizens. The Congressmen could not find the 27,068 additional naturalization blanks which should have been on file in Barnard's court, indicating that this judge had administered the oath of allegiance to more than 37,000 applicants! A member of the Court of Common Pleas, Judge John R. Brady, testified that in his thirteen years on the bench he had never been able to naturalize an applicant for citizenship in less than "three to five minutes." And he was then speaking of the highly intelligent. Judges Barnard and McCunn seldom examined an applicant for citizenship. Batches of naturalization blanks approved by Tweed's lieutenants were placed on their desks and they scrawled their initials on the papers. Then the future citizens, in groups "averaging one hundred and forty" would have the oath administered to them.

Tweed resorted to the telegraph to carry out his plot to steal the election for Hoffman. This is the first case on record where this invention was used to aid an assault upon the ballot box. Tweed wanted to know the vote, approximate or estimated, of each town and city in the State, at the close of the polls on Election Day. With this information he would know how many fraudulent votes would have to be credited to Hoffman in the city to insure his election. Tweed obtained the up-State election returns from members of the State Committee and other local leaders who had received the following letter:

"Rooms of the Democratic State Committee,
                              "October 27, 1868.
"My Dear Sir: Please at once to communicate with some reliable person in three or four principal towns and in each city of your county, and request him (expenses duly arranged for at this end) to telegraph to William M. Tweed, Tammany Hall, at the minute of closing the polls, not waiting for the county, such person's estimate of the vote. Let the telegram be as follows: 'This town will show a Democratic gain (or loss) over last year ——— (number.)' Or this one, if sufficiently certain: 'This town will give a Republican (or Democratic) majority of ———.' There is of course, an important object to be attained by a simultaneous transmission at the hour of closing the polls, but no longer waiting. Opportunity can be taken of the usual half hour lull in telegraphic communication over lines, before actual results begin to be declared, and before the Associated Press absorb the telegraph with returns and interfere with individual messages, and give orders to watch carefully the count.
                    "Very truly yours,
                    "Samuel J. Tilden, Chairman."

Tilden did not sign the letter. Nor did he write it. The Elegant Oakey Hall testified before the Congressional Investigating Committee that he composed the missive and affixed Chairman Tilden's name to it. Hall was Secretary of the Executive Committee of the Democratic State Committee at the time, and explained he was but following the custom of his predecessors in signing the chairman's name to the document.

And Hoffman, after he took office as Governor on January 1, 1869, was succeeded in the office of Mayor of New York by the Elegant Oakey. Tweed nominated him and The Boss elected him, as he had Hoffman. A Governor, a Mayor, and the most powerful political organization in the country were Tweed's. It is not to be wondered at as he surveyed the prospect on this particular New Year's Day that he should have dreams of larger fields to conquer. New York City was his. New York State was his. Why not the United States? This was not an idle dream. By reëlecting Hoffman in 1870 he would have a formidable contender for the nomination for President, and further, Tweed knew how to manipulate conventions. He had not yet tried his hand on a national convention. Well, he would have an opportunity in 1872. Tilden's friend Seymour—there was balm in the remembrance of Grant's victory—was out of the way. The defeat of Seymour would be reflected on Tilden. And he would scotch Tilden before long. True, Hoffman was inclined to be rebellious at times, but he would handle him. And when he placed Hoffman in the White House he would move Hall into the Governor's chair at Albany. Then the State Capitol would cease to know Tweed as a representative from the Fourth Senatorial District, for The Boss would go to Washington as United States Senator from New York.

Tweed, who thought as a professional politician, was confident that while he was The Boss, Tilden would not dare to make a move to dethrone him. He reasoned, and justly so, that a practical man with Presidential aspirations will not do anything to interfere with his progress to the political Parnassus.

Tilden had been, as Greeley phrased it, a passive accomplice in the election frauds of 1868. A year after this canvass, the editor wrote this open letter to the politician:

"To SAMUEL J. TILDEN,
    "Chairman Democratic State Committee.
    "SIR: You hold a most responsible and influential position in the councils of a great party. You could make that party content itself with the polling of legal votes if you only would. . . . Mr. Tilden, you cannot escape responsibility by saying, with the guilty Macbeth,

" 'Thou canst not say I did it;
  Never shake those gory locks at me,'

for you were at least a passive accomplice in the giant frauds of
last November. Your name was used, without public protest on
your part, in circulars sowed broadcast over the State, whereof,
the manifest intent was to 'Make assurance doubly sure,' that the
frauds here perpetrated should not be overborne by the honest
vote of the rural districts. And you, not merely by silence but
by positive assumption, have covered those frauds with the mantle
of your respectability. On the principle that 'the receiver is as
bad as the thief,' you are as deeply implicated in them to-day as
though your name were Tweed, O'Brien [the Sheriff of New York
County], or Oakey Hall. . . . Now, Mr. Tilden, I call on you to
put a stop to this business. You have but to walk into the
Sheriff's, the Mayor's, and the Supervisor's offices in the City
Hall Park, and say that there must be no more of it. Say it so
that there shall be no doubt that you mean it, and we shall have
a tolerably fair election once more. Will you do it? If we Republicans are swindled again as we were swindled last fall, you and
such as you will be responsible to God and man for the outrage.

Yours,

"HORACE GREELEY.

"NEW YORK, October 29, 1869."

Tilden did not answer this letter. He was too practical to
attempt the impossible.

CHAPTER XXV

The Tweed Ring of history had its beginning on January 1, 1869. Four men comprised this unholy alliance: Tweed, Sweeny, Connolly, and Hall. Shortly after the inauguration of Hall as Mayor, the Ring ceased to hold its noon-day luncheons at the City Hall. Instead, the conferences were held at Tweed's law office on Duane Street. There was no attempt to conceal these meetings. The town knew of them, the town talked of the Ring, and of Tweed especially, and of his millions—one newspaper estimate placed his wealth at not less than $5,000,000 nor more than $10,000,000—and of his constantly growing power. Every office in the city government was controlled by Tweed. While he had lost the Assembly in the last election, he had the Governor.

All the prominent leaders in the local Democratic organization, and a number of the New York City Republican leaders, were rapidly growing rich with Tweed. The loot was seeping into the lower levels. Many made rich by the Ring were entirely devoid of background. They had become affluent overnight. They bought silk hats and diamonds. Any one could wear diamonds. But there was an art in wearing a top hat. They wore theirs on three hairs. Some of the journalistic enemies of The Boss referred to these resplendent ones as Tweed's shiny hat brigade. The Boss could not endure ridicule. So he insisted that all the shiny hatted ones, who were Democrats, must join the Americus Club. Here they would have an opportunity of observing how others, accustomed to good things, comported themselves. These they were to imitate. The Boss wanted those around him to be worthy members of the political aristocracy he had created.

The Tweed Ring was not a haphazard group. Each of

Tweed's lieutenants had a definite rôle. Sweeny, who was Chamberlain, was assigned to keep a check on the judiciary and to select the candidates for the bench. Connolly, the Comptroller, was well-grounded in finance from his years as bank clerk, and for him Tweed cast the part of the financial agent. The Elegant Oakey, because of his great knowledge of law, was the legal adviser. Tweed was the final arbiter, vetoing or approving all proposals made by his aides.

While Tweed was looting the city, he aided Jay Gould and James Fisk, Jr., to loot the stockholders of the Erie Railroad. Tweed and Sweeny were elected members of the Board of Directors of Erie, and with their aid, forced Daniel Drew and Cornelius Vanderbilt out of the picture. Vanderbilt had been Gould's patron, as Drew had been Fisk's. But this unscrupulous pair forgot their gratitude at the sight of the millions which could be stolen from the road over which Vanderbilt and Drew had battled so long.

Until the election of Sweeny and Tweed to the Erie directorate, Vanderbilt was able to get injunctions from Judge Barnard to aid him in his fight against Drew and Fisk. But then Vanderbilt could boast of the passing friendliness of Tweed. This was during the legislative session of 1868. Tweed at that time was one of Vanderbilt's agents on the floor of the Senate. After Tweed was won over by Fisk and Gould with the gift of a large block of Erie stock and a controlling voice in the executive committee, Vanderbilt fought on for a time. But he saw the futility of attempting to make headway against this combination. Fisk, who was the head of the Erie Ring, made Gould president, and himself, treasurer of the road. These two, with Tweed and Frederick Lane, counsel for the Erie and a member of the board of directors, constituted the executive committee.

Many of the meetings of the executive committee of the Erie Railroad were held at the home of the beautiful Josie Mansfield, Fisk's mistress. This retreat was purchased by Fisk early in 1868. It cost $40,000, and was on Twenty-third Street, just a few doors west of Pike's Opera House at Twenty-third Street and Eighth Avenue. This famous show house was bought in the same year by The Prince of Erie—with $820,000 stolen from the road. Fisk refitted and redecorated the Opera House at considerable expense. He renamed it the Grand Opera House, and made it a home of *opéra bouffe.* Fisk had one manager after another, quarreled with them all, as he insisted on directing the rehearsals. With Max Maratzek, who toured Europe for him to obtain the services of the noted stars of England, France, Germany, and Italy, Fisk came to blows on the stage of his opera house during a dress rehearsal.

The women members of the cast screamed as the professional and amateur impresarios pummelled one another until they were separated. Fisk moved the offices of the Erie Railroad to the second floor of his opera house, receiving $75,000 yearly rental, thus to insure him against any losses that he might sustain from the lavish performances that he presented.

Tweed was fond of Fisk's society. And Fisk liked Tweed and was proud of the friendship of The Boss. Even in the height of a campaign, Tweed would readily accept an invitation to dine at Josie Mansfield's home. Fisk made no secret of his attachment for the black-eyed Josie. Even in the canvass of 1868, when Tweed was superintending the grinding of the naturalization mills and otherwise directing the fight to make Hoffman Governor, he dined at Josie's establishment, as the following note indicates:

"187 West Street, Tuesday, October, 13, 1868.
"My dear Josie:—James McHenry, the partner of Sir Morton Peto, the largest railway builder in the world, Mr. Tweed, and Mr. Lane, will dine with us at half-past six. I want you to provide as nice a dinner as possible.
"JAMES FISK, JR."

Fisk was devoted as well as generous to Josie, who was amused by her admirer's theatrical clothes, for he affected a mulberry coat glittering with gold buttons on the double-breasted front and on the sleeves, and all bearing the monogram of the Narragansett Steamship Company, which operated a fleet of steamers between New York and Fall River, Massachusetts. A huge diamond sparkled in his black silk four-in-hand knotted carefully over his ruffled shirt. No mere mulberry coat with gold buttons sufficed when Fisk was aboard one of these ships. Then Fisk was uniformed as a United States Admiral. The only difference was the monogram on the buttons. It was this playboy side of Fisk that appealed so strongly to Tweed. He was accustomed to associating with men always on their dignity, pretended or natural, and the change amused him.

There was also a generous, an admirable side, to Fisk. He was charitable, and like Tweed, ostentatiously so. Obvious frauds, who came with hat in hand, were as quickly aided as the few who were really worthy of alms. The doors of the pretentious offices of Erie in the Grand Opera House—Fisk spent a third of a million dollars in fitting up the rooms with carved walnut and silver—were never closed to those seeking Fisk's charity.

Josie Mansfield, who was to cause Fisk's death, was at this time twenty-nine years of age. She looked younger. Her coral red lips enhanced the pearl and pink oval face. She had "a full dashing figure, yet not gross, with deep, large, almond-shaped black eyes, luxuriant purple black hair, worn in massive coils." She was soft-spoken, given to flowing dark silks and masses of Valenciennes lace. And to cap it all, she had a nose that bewitched, "neither retroussé and yet not straight." She had a demure look. To heighten this effect she wore a plain cross of gold.

Fisk was fond of parading her. But Miss Mansfield was not his only light of love. He had many who came and went with the companies that played on the boards of the Grand Opera House. But she was his favorite, and never displayed the least jealousy. She was paid to subdue this passion. It was a common sight to see Fisk on Broadway, driving a six-in-hand, taking some of his beauties for an airing. Josie was always on these outings.

Fisk made a practice of entertaining legislators and judges at midnight parties at Miss Mansfield's, a custom that had neither its Alpha nor Omega with The Prince of Erie and the Admiral of the Narragansett Fleet. A frequent visitor at the

Twenty-third Street rendezvous was Judge Barnard. Prior to Tweed's election to the Erie board of directors, Fisk's enemies could always count on an injunction from Judge Barnard, for the wars of the corrupt financiers were waged with the aid of corrupt courts as well as corrupt legislatures. But this was all changed now. Tweed had brought about the transformation. For the first year of Tweed's association with Fisk, the enemies of The Prince of Erie continued their warfare, only to find their various moves checkmated by orders issued by Judge Barnard. On one occasion August Belmont appeared in court at the opening of the daily session to ask for the appointment of a receiver for the road. But Fisk, who had learned of Belmont's intentions, had gone to Barnard's home while Tweed's judge was breakfasting, and obtained an order making Gould receiver. Barnard completed the comedy by accepting Fisk as surety that Gould would honestly and faithfully discharge his duties as agent of the court. One did not have to go to Barnard's home for judicial orders. Some were granted at the *ménage* of Miss Mansfield.

Early in 1869 Vanderbilt—now the principal foe of Fisk and Gould—decided that it was wasted time and money to continue the fight against Fisk and Gould and Tweed. Vanderbilt's principal aim in seeking control of the Erie was to prevent it from competing with his road, the New York Central, as well as to monopolize the railroad connections between New York and the West. Once Commodore Vanderbilt joined forces with Fisk and Gould. This was to obtain some needed legislation in Albany. Gould and Fisk wanted to insure their control on the board of directors of the road for some years to come. This they sought to effect by having it enacted that only one-fifth of the directors be elected annually. Commodore Vanderbilt wanted to legalize some stock dividends that had been declared on New York Central securities. Senator Tweed put both measures through and Governor Hoffman signed them.

The Erie paid heavily for these favors, judicial and legislative. In the three years that Tweed was on the road's executive committee, which approved all bribery outlays, nearly

$1,500,000 was spent in this manner. These bribes were classi-
fied under the traditional heading: "Legal Expenses." Jay
Gould had charged against him under this euphemism $586,000.
Fisk distributed bribes in excess of $193,000. Peter B. Sweeny
was allowed $150,000. To Tweed, as "Legal Expenses," was
given $105,662.86.

In Tweed's first year in Albany—prior to the Tweed Ring
with which we are now concerned—Tweed and his fellow corruptionists stole as flagrantly from the city and county as in
the years in which he, Hall, Sweeny, and Connolly flourished.
It was an open secret in political circles. It was known in
newspaper offices. Sometimes the journals of the time hinted
at the frauds—but never so as to do any real hurt to The
Boss. Tweed's old friend J. H. Ingersoll rendered a bill of
$1,063,498.27 for furniture—almost wholly fraudulent. It
was passed by the Board of Supervisors, and of course by
Hoffman, then Mayor, who also approved a bill of another
tool of The Ring, A. J. Garvey, who charged $646,516.56 for
repairs to plaster on the Court House in 1868. The furniture
was also for the Court House. These, however, were small
stealings.

There is ample evidence that these Court House thefts were
known to the New York dailies in 1868. Let us examine
Exhibit A, a cartoon by Nast during the campaign in the
fall of that year. Mayor Hoffman is depicted on a four-
fold screen behind which thieves are shown looting a strong
box labeled "City Treasury." Over one group is a signpost
reading: "Court House." Above all appears the commandment: "Thou Shalt Steal As Much As Thou Canst." It is
signed: "The Ring."

The bribes that the Metropolitan newspapers received from
the Tweed Ring in the guise of advertising largely accounts
for their silence on the stealings of The Ring. In addition to
the big dailies there were weeklies almost without number. At
one time eighty-seven periodicals were sharing in the
plunder of the city in the guise of advertising. More than a
score of these publications ceased when *The Times* began its
expose in the summer of 1871, and revived the hope of a free

press. Messages of the Mayor, printed in the news columns, were paid for by the city as advertisements. The charge was one dollar a line! Some of the evening papers were awarded a flat subsidy of $1,000 a month. During the period beginning January 1, 1869, and ending the first half of the year 1871, the Tweed Ring paid, out of the city treasury, $2,703,308.48, to the newspapers of New York City for advertising. How much more The Ring paid for the silence of the Metropolitan press is not indicated in the records. Tweed was always contributing out of his own pocket to unscrupulous journalists.

It was also necessary that The Ring, in order to carry on its schemes in the State Legislature, bribe the newspapers in Albany. Here Tweed could not draw directly upon the taxpayers of New York City, but he could tap the State treasury. This he did through the medium of the appropriation for printing the sessions laws. This, in legislative parlance is known as "State printing." Let us take a single newspaper in the State Capitol—*The Argus*. In 1868 the State paid this newspaper the sum of $5,000 for this work. *The Argus* was owned by William Cassidy, a prominent Democrat of Albany, and a warm friend of Tilden and former Governor Seymour. In the year 1869 Tweed increased this sum exactly sixteen-fold, to $80,000. This was more than doubled in 1870, when the State paid $176,000 to Cassidy's paper, and in 1871, the year of the expose of The Ring, to the record sum of $207,900 for publishing the laws enacted in that year. There was a slight slump in 1872, when Cassidy's *Argus* was given $136,400 of this honest graft, and a slight increase in 1873 to $138,850, and then there was a precipitous drop to normal thereafter.

Now we would have little concern with the money that found its way from the coffers of the State treasury into the pockets of Cassidy, but for an illuminating item of correspondence that passed from former Governor Seymour to Tilden concerning Cassidy and his attitude toward Tweed when The Boss stood defiantly with his back against the wall. The letter is dated October 8, 1871. This communication to Tilden reveals that Seymour knew of the vast wealth that had been thrown to Cassidy by Tweed, and the former Governor discusses the incident as though there was nothing improper in it. Cassidy, as the letter relates, was one of the leaders of the Democratic Party throughout the State who opposed Tilden in his fight against Tweed. After referring to this Seymour wrote:

"It is not in my heart to say an unkind word of Cassidy. In many ways he has had a hard time. His fine mind has been used by others while he was left poor. It was the strange policy of the New York Central Railroad men to give wealth to [Thurlow] Weed and others, who fought them if they did not, while Cassidy was helped to live by loans and in other ways which kept him poor. When Tweed went to Albany he turned a stream of patronage into *The Argus* office which made it strong and rich. I think Cassidy means, in the main, to stand up for the right, but it is hard for him to strike men who have lifted him into wealth and when all about him shrink back."

Low as journalism had fallen in Tweed's day, it had not reached the depths into which politicians, high and low, had sunk, for it was the redeemed press which roused the people and brought about the destruction of the Tweed Ring. There were men of unquestioned personal integrity in the craft. This too, was true of men in public life. These latter, at any time, could have effected a change, had they but moral courage to forget their political ambitions and remember the public good. They alone could readily obtain the proofs of the corruption.

John D. Townsend, Tweed's counsel when The Boss was ready to tell all, but was denied this opportunity, in his "New York in Bondage" wrote:

"With protection given them by the judiciary and the press, and with support of first class citizens, the Ring was perfectly secure until it fell to pieces from exposure to the light."

And Tweed when asked how he managed to keep public sentiment suppressed, responded:

"Well, we used money wherever we could."

Several daily and weekly publications began their short careers with the inception of the Tweed Ring. One of these had no thought of obtaining any of the city or county advertising that was being showered upon the press by The Boss. This rare exception was *The Imperialist*. It made its bow to an astonished New York on April 10, 1869. Let us reproduce the leading editorial of the initial number of *The Imperialist* in its entirety:

"Though unannounced, this journal is not unexpected. It is the open expression of opinions long held and cherished by thousands of intelligent men and women, in all parts of the country, who will hail its advent as the beginning of a new era in the political history of America.

"The platform of *The Imperialist* is revolutionary; its object is to prepare the American people for a revolution that is as desirable as it is inevitable.

"We believe Democracy to be a failure. Though theoretically plausible, in its practical workings it has been found totally inadequate to the wants of the American people.

"We believe the national faith, if left in the keeping of the populace, will be sullied by the sure repudiation of the national debt, and that an Imperial Government can alone secure and protect the rights of national creditors.

"We believe that an Imperial Government, in its paternal relation to the people, will care equally for all citizens and while guarantying security to the rights of capital will zealously protect the interests of the industrial classes.

"We believe, in short, that Democracy means lawlessness, corruption; insecurity to person and property; robbery of the public creditors and civil war, that the Empire means law, order, security, public faith, and peace.

"This creed, *The Imperialist* will advocate earnestly, fearlessly, and without compromise, thereby expressing the honest convictions, not only of those who contribute to its columns but of an intelligent and powerful constituency.

"In the discussion of political and social questions now agitating the mind of the American public, *The Imperialist* will unite the high tone and thorough culture of the standard British weekly press, with the lighter and more popular features of the best current literature of the day, and its columns will be free from low and commonplace vulgarisms that have heretofore disgraced American Journalism."

This was the first time the advocates of an American aristocracy had an organ of their own. They lost it after June 12, when the tenth number of *The Imperialist* was published. Here are the last notes of the swan song of America's only frankly outspoken imperialistic editor:

"We believe that but a small percentage of the American people can be considered fit by character or education for the unrestricted exercise of self government, and that conscious of this truth, they have already resigned the absurd theory which is advanced in their behalf."

The editorial offices of *The Imperialist* were on Mercer Street, No. 37. Mercer Street, for many years before and for some time after 1869, was notorious as the Street of the Prostitutes. The imperialists were reformed with the street.

About the time *The Imperialist* suspended publication there came to New York one of the most forceful women of her day, who added to her native talents those of a charlatan. This was Victoria Claflin Woodhull. She was just turned thirty and was maturely beautiful. She was accompanied by her sister, Tennie C. Claflin, who was even more charming, and had the bloom of a girl of sixteen. Tennie, however, was twenty-four. They had been wandering around the country for six years after Dr. Woodhull, the first of Victoria's husbands, was separated from her by the courts. Victoria was the bread-winner of the pair, practicing medicine and clairvoyancy. On arriving in New York Victoria began to preach and practice free love and woman suffrage, and proudly boasted her advocacy of both. She was the first to resort to the militant tactics which made the suffragists unpopular half a century later in England. She bobbed her hair before she descended upon a New York polling booth to demand that her vote be recorded. She was intensely philodramatic. Victoria and her sister invaded Wall Street and opened a stock brokerage office at 44 Broad Street. By the end of 1869 the sisters had amassed a fortune. Theodore Tilton was enamored of Victoria. She, who made no secret of her amours, described Tilton as her accepted lover. He amazed all his religious subscribers when he devoted an entire number of one of his *Golden Age Tracts*—usually treating of a phase of the sinful life—to a biography of his charmer. In this sketch Tilton said that Victoria's wealth at the end of 1869 amounted to $700,000 and repeated Victoria's story of having been under the care of the spirits of the Greek patriots from the day of her birth in the little Ohioan village of Homer. Demosthenes was her especial guide and visitant, and directed her to come to New York, as Tilton informs us:

"The chief among her spiritual visitants, and one who has been a majestic guardian to her from the earliest years of her remembrance, she describes as a matured man of stately figure, clad in a Greek tunic, solemn and graceful in his aspect, strong in his influence, and altogether dominant over her life. For many years, notwithstanding an almost daily visit to her vision, he withheld his name, nor would her most importunate questionings induce him to utter it. But he always promised that in due time he would reveal his identity. Meanwhile, he prophesied to her that she would rise to great distinction; that she would emerge from her poverty and live in a stately house; that she would win great wealth in a city which he pictured as crowded with ships; that she would publish and conduct a journal; and that, finally, to crown her career, she would become the ruler of her people.

"At length, after patiently waiting on this spirit guide for twenty years, one day in 1868, during a temporary sojourn in Pittsburgh, and while she was sitting at a marble table, he suddenly appeared to her, and wrote on the table, in English letters, the name 'Demosthenes.' At first the writing was indistinct, but grew to such a luster that the brightness filled the room. The apparition, familiar as it had been before, now affrighted her to trembling. The stately and commanding spirit told her to journey to New York, where she would find, at No. 17 Great Jones Street, a house in readiness for her, equipped in all things to her use and taste. She unhesitatingly obeyed, although she never before had heard of Great Jones Street, nor until that revelatory moment had entertained an intention of taking such a residence. On entering the house, it fulfilled in reality the picture which she saw of it in her vision—the self-same hall, stairways, rooms, and furniture. Entering with some bewilderment into the library, she reached out her hand by chance, and, without knowing what she

did, took up a book, which, on idly looking at its title, she saw
(to her blood-chilling astonishment) to be 'The Orations of Demosthenes.' From that time onward the Greek statesman has been,
even more palpably than in her earlier years, her prophetic monitor,
mapping out the life which she must follow, as a chart for the ship
sailing the sea. She believes him to be her familiar spirit, the
author of her public policy, and the inspirer of her published
words."

Tilton aided her to create the impression that she and her
sister were protegées of Commodore Vanderbilt, winning his
good graces by their indomitable energy. "Both with and
without Commodore Vanderbilt's help, Mrs. Woodhull has
more than once showed the pluck that has held the reins of the
stock market," wrote Tilton.

Tilton introduced the Claflin sisters into his household on
Brooklyn Heights, and presented Victoria to Henry Ward
Beecher before his rupture with his pastor and friend of many
years.

Had the spirit of Demosthenes ceased its visitations to
Victoria Woodhull after the Pittsburgh materialization, there
is every reason to believe that Beecher would have had more
time to give to his attacks on the Tweed Ring, instead of
being compelled to defend himself from the attacks on his
character by Theodore Tilton, which first saw the light of day
in *Woodhull and Claflin's Weekly*. But the old Greek appeared to Victoria again in December, 1869, and "wrote on a
scroll the memorable document now known in history as 'The
Memorial of Victoria C. Woodhull.'" The following February,
Victoria, without saying anything of Demosthenes to Susan
B. Anthony, Elizabeth Cady Stanton, and other suffragists,
presented her memorial to Congress on behalf of the Woman's
Rights Association. She was not chosen by this pioneer
suffrage organization as its spokesman because of her relations
with the Athenian orator, but because she was the most effective public speaker among the women suffragists of the day.
While sitting in the room of the Judiciary Committee of the
House of Representatives, according to Victoria, a strange
gentleman—so she described him—said: "I am reliably assured

that Mr. Beecher preaches to at least twenty of his mistresses every Sunday." After Beecher had twice slighted her, Victoria published this piece of sheer hearsay, on which has been built the oft-repeated canard that "it has been proven that Beecher preached to at least twenty mistresses every Sunday."

It was after her trip to the National Capitol that the romantic Victoria met the amorous Tilton. Her mode of living, her lectures on woman suffrage and on free love, soon made her the butt of the Metropolitan press. For a time she ignored the journalistic jibes. She was busy with *The Victoria League* which she organized in 1871, and the League nominated her as its candidate for President in 1872. In her letter accepting the nomination she wrote:

"I ought not to pass unnoticed your courteous and graceful allusion to what you deem the favoring omen of my name. It is true that a Victoria rules the great rival nation opposite to us on the other side of the Atlantic, and it might grace the amity just sealed between the two nations, and be a new security of peace, if a twin sisterhood of Victorias were to preside over the two nations. It is true, also that in its mere etymology the name signifies Victory! and the victory for the right is what we are bent on securing. It is again true, also, that to some minds there is a consonant harmony between the idea and the word, so that its euphonious utterance seems to their imaginations to be itself a genius of success. However this may be, I have sometime imagined that there is something providential and prophetic in the fact that my parents were prompted to confer on me a name which forbids the very thought of failure; and, as the great Napoleon believed the star of his destiny, you will at least excuse me, and charge it to the credulity of the woman, if I believe also in fatality of triumph as somehow inhering in my name."

Victoria was sensitive to scorn, and inordinately vain and proud. Beecher cut her sorely when he declined to preside at one of her sensational lectures. Tilton, who had a reputation throughout the country as a lecturer, acted in the famous preacher's stead. Again, in the midst of her amusing campaign for the Presidency—she took it very seriously—she was "hunted down by a set of males and females who are determined that I shall not be permitted to live even, if they can prevent it." Thus she wrote to Beecher telling him how her persecutors had caused her to be "shut out of hotel after hotel" until she found a temporary haven in the Gilsey House. In her appeal to Beecher she said:

"Now I want your assistance. I want to be sustained in my position in the Gilsey House from which I am now ordered out, and from which I do not wish to go—and all this simply because I am Victoria C. Woodhull, the advocate of Social Freedom. I have submitted to this persecution just so long as I can endure. My business, my projects, in fact everything for which I live, suffers from it, and it must cease. Will you lend me your aid in this?"

Beecher declined to assist her. Five months later she published the story that had been the gossip of the town for two years. All who frequented the Tilton home talked of it, for both Tilton and his wife told various friends their varying versions of the story involving not only the reputation of Beecher, but the honor of Mrs. Tilton.

It is doubtful if even the insidious stratagems of Beecher's clerical enemies within his church, who were offended by his heterodoxy, would have been able to maneuver the scandal into the courts—ecclesiastic, civil, and criminal—but for the publication of the unsavory story in the Claflin sisters' periodical.

While the Claflin sisters were playing the game of which Vanderbilt was a past master, Gould was plotting the most disgraceful act of his shameless career. This was the gold panic which had its disastrous climax on Black Friday. Again Gould demonstrated his capacity for the basest villainy when money was at stake. A mob of bankers and brokers sought his life, but he escaped with the aid of Fisk, who was then ignorant of the treachery of his partner. Only once was Gould treated with a modicum of his just deserts. Some eight years after Black Friday Gould played one of his traditional double-dealings on a broker named Major A. A. Selover. The Major was huge, blond, muscular, and towered almost a foot over the puny Gould. The two met outside a brokerage office at

65 Exchange Place. Selover, with very few words, slapped Gould in the face, and while the crooked financier was staggering from the effect of the humiliating blow, lifted him up and tossed him over a low iron railing surrounding an areaway and then walked on. Gould fell in a crushed heap to the bottom of the rectangular pit, which was some eight feet from the level of the sidewalk. He was not seriously injured, and was helped out of the hole by one of the speculators of the Street.

Gould began to plot the corner of the gold market of the country early in 1869, and through this, place the business interests of the country at his mercy. At first Gould worked alone. "In character he was strongly marked by his disposition for silent intrigue," says Henry Adams. "He preferred, as a rule, to operate on his own account without admitting other persons into his confidence, and he seemed never to be satisfied except when deceiving every one as to his intentions. There was a reminiscence of the spider in his nature. It is scarcely necessary to say that he had not a conception of a moral principle." But as the spring of the year was drawing to a close Gould lured Fisk into the web he was spinning.

To corner the gold supply Gould needed the aid of the United States Treasury, as success would be impossible if the government should sell gold with a liberal hand. Gould sought the aid of A. R. Corbin, Wall Street speculator, who had married a sister of President Grant. James McHenry, the English capitalist and partner of Sir Morton Peto, whom he met at Josie Mansfield's establishment in the previous October, at a dinner with Tweed and Fisk, lent a touch of plausibility to the scheme by advancing the theory that an advance in the price of gold would benefit the Western farmers in giving them a better price for their products.

With Corbin's aid, Gould now laid siege to the Grant Administration, which had come into power the previous March. Gould had two objects in view: to bribe the influential members of the Grant administration and to convert the President to the theory suggested by McHenry.

About the middle of June President Grant arrived in New York en route to Boston to attend the Peace Jubilee. The

President while in the Metropolis was a guest of his brother-in-law.

Corbin suggested to Gould that he call on the President, a proposal that met with ready compliance. On June 15 Grant went to Boston, a guest of Gould and Fisk, on one of Fisk's Fall River steamers. Fisk presided at a dinner on the boat that evening at which the President, Gould, Cyrus W. Field, who laid the first cable between this country and Europe, and other solid citizens of New York and Boston were guests. Fisk, attired in his Admiral's uniform, and the wily Gould, led the conversation into the realm of crops and gold, Gould arguing that the government should aid the upward price of gold in the fall to give the farmers better prices for their crops, thus making better business for the railroads and the country as a whole.

Gould, the guilty plotter in all these criminal proceedings, as James A. Garfield, chairman of the Congressional Committee of Investigation, and later President of the United States, described him, in his testimony before the Garfield Committee, said:

"At this supper the question came up about that state of the country, the crops, prospects ahead, and so forth. The President was a listener; the other gentlemen were discussing; some were in favor of Boutwell's selling gold, and some opposed to it. After they had all interchanged views, some one asked the President what his view was. He remarked that he thought there was a certain amount of fictitiousness about the prosperity of the country, and that the bubble might as well be tapped in one way as another. . . . His remark struck across us like a wet blanket."

Gould abandoned the President at Fall River, but not his plot to convert him. Fisk continued on to Boston, with the Presidential party, returning with it to the Metropolis, where the President, Mrs. Grant, and their daughter went to hear Des Clauzas and Irma sing Offenbach's *La Périchole*, at the Fifth Avenue Theater, of which Fisk was part owner. The President and his family were the Prince of Erie's guests. Corbin also sat in Fisk's box. So did Gould.

On or about the first or second of September Gould was satisfied that he had converted the President against governmental interference in the price of gold. Gould saw Grant on one of these days. On September 1, the President wrote to George S. Boutwell, his Secretary of the Treasury, that it would not be wise for the government to sell gold so as to force down its price while the crops were moving during the fall months. Boutwell, then at his home in Massachusetts, received the letter on September 4 and at once telegraphed the Assistant Secretary of the Treasury in Washington not to sell any gold until he had heard from him. The latter in turn telegraphed these instructions to General Butterfield, who had charge of the Sub-Treasury at New York.

On September 2 Gould began his operations in the New York Gold Exchange. On that day he bought $1,500,000 of gold for the President's brother-in-law, $1,000,000 for Butterfield, and $500,000 for General Horace Porter. Porter and Butterfield repudiated these purchases as having been made without their knowledge, but Butterfield did accept a loan of $10,000 from Gould. In two days the price went up five points. With the raise of each point, Corbin, who was admittedly in on the conspiracy, made $15,000—on paper. Gould at this time paid $25,000 on account to Corbin.

The available gold outside of the United States Treasury did not exceed $20,000,000. The government held in its vaults between $75,000,000 and $100,000,000. Soon Gould had bought more gold than was in the market, yet by the middle of September the price was two points below the level of September 4, the third day of Gould's heavy operations. Gould now sought the aid of Fisk, whose very presence in any movement was affected by his boundless enthusiasm. Fisk did not like the look of things, but Gould assured him that Corbin had Butterfield and the President "fixed all right." When he was told that the Secretary of the Treasury had been forbidden to sell gold, Fisk joined the conspiracy. To give Fisk still further assurance that he was not playing him double, Gould induced Corbin to write a letter to President Grant urging him not to let the Treasury sell any gold. Gould sent the letter by W. O.

Chapin, Fisk's most trusted employee. He delivered it to the President on September 19, in a mountain town in Pennsylvania, bearing the same name as the national Capital. The messenger had entrée to the Nation's Executive because of a letter of introduction to the President's secretary from Corbin. Fisk's man, after delivering the letter, telegraphed back to New York: "Letter delivered all right."

On the strength of this Fisk began to buy heavily. Immediately gold began to climb, and on Wednesday, September 22, it closed at 140½. That day Mrs. Corbin received a letter from her sister-in-law, Mrs. Grant, saying: "Tell Mr. Corbin that the President is much distressed by your speculations and you must close them out as quickly as you can." Gould had been a nightly visitor at the home of Corbin, who kept him informed of all he knew, and on Wednesday evening when he called at the home of the President's brother-in-law he was shown the letter from Mrs. Grant. Corbin asked Gould to settle with him as he wanted to write that night to the President that he had not a particle of interest in the gold corner. Gould replied that he was much concerned and added: "I interpret that letter to mean that the President is offended. But if I close this transaction as you suggest there may be a breakdown in the market, and will be if the government should interfere, and how can I [in that event] afford to pay you?" Gould went home and returned to Corbin's house early the following morning. He had $50,000,000 of gold standing in his name. He did not want the letter from the President's wife to become public property. "If it does I'm a ruined man," said Gould to Corbin, offering him $100,000 if he would remain in the market and take his chances. But Corbin did not dare to accept in face of the letter from his sister-in-law.

Gould in a black mood went to Wall Street "determined to betray his own associates." He gave secret orders to his brokers to sell. Fisk, in accordance with his agreement with Gould, kept faith and continued openly buying while Gould was covertly selling. Gold closed Thursday night at 144.

The next day was Friday, September 24—Black Friday. Fisk breezily entered an ante-chamber of the Gold Room—as the

Exchange was commonly called—and loudly gave orders to Albert Speyer to buy all the gold available up to 145. When that price was reached Speyer was handed a slip of paper from a messenger reading: "Put it up to 150 at once. James Fisk, Jr." Speyer obeyed. Then he went to the adjoining room where Fisk and Gould were—Fisk was still ignorant of Gould's secret selling—and the voluptuary waved his cane as he told Speyer to go back and buy all the gold he could up to 160. "But you'll be too late," added Fisk, "as I've given orders to other brokers to buy at 160."

This was half an hour before noon. The Gold Room was a frantic frenzied mob of distracted men. Speyer, who had bought $60,000,000 of gold since the opening of the market that morning, was the cock of the walk. He had now in his name for Fisk's account half, at least, of all the gold in the country, both in and out of the United States Treasury. He was making financial history. Many envied him.

A few minutes before noon, gold was selling at 160. Fisk, twirling his gold-headed cane, was happy. Then the Scotch banker, James Brown, entered the room. When the price was bid up to 162 by Fisk's brokers, who shouted they would take any part of $5,000,000 at that quotation, Brown quietly said: "Sold one million at 162." His second million was sold at 161. Then five millions at 160.

The market broke. Ten minutes later word came that the United States Sub-Treasury on orders from Washington, would sell $4,000,000 of gold on the following day. Now the break was complete. Within fifteen minutes after Brown had begun to sell at declining figures the price had fallen twenty-nine points.

Speyer was now distractedly walking around the Gold Room repeating: "Some one has threatened to shoot me. Let him shoot."

A mob, led by brokers demanding settlement, gathered in front of the brokerage house of Smith, Gould, and Martin, in Broad Street, shouting for Gould. Another mob assembled before the office of Fisk and Belden, seeking Gould's accomplice. Fisk and Gould, anticipating all this, had fled the financial district when the market broke. They found refuge in the Erie offices in Fisk's Grand Opera House. There they were guarded all day by their hired thugs.

When a mob surged through Wall Street some one remembered the suicide twelve years before of the honorable old leather merchant, Charles M. Leupp, after he found that Gould had tried to corner hides on Leupp's credit. This some one cried:

"Who killed Leupp?"

We are told that a hundred throats answered:

"Jay Gould!"

Half of Wall Street was ruined. This was the testimony adduced before the Garfield Committee. "The legitimate business of the country had been paralyzed," says James Ford Rhodes in his "History of the United States."

Gould made money in this criminal conspiracy which dishonored the country. And until the Garfield Committee completed its investigation, many unjustly believed that Grant had accepted more than the hospitality of the corrupt Fisk and Gould. Neither the President, nor any of his kin, with the exception of his sister's husband, profited in the shame of Black Friday. Fisk lost nothing, as he repudiated his millions in debts with the aid of Boss Tweed's corrupt judiciary. The Prince of Erie forgave Gould for his treachery, and they continued friends.

While Gould and Fisk were plotting the corner in gold, Tweed, with the aid of Hugh McLaughlin, the Democratic leader of Brooklyn, and others he had enlisted in his cause, agreed among themselves to depose Tilden as State Chairman. But the delegates to the State Convention voted down the proposal.

Tweed ran again for Senator in the November elections of 1869. The returns made him rub his hands with joy, as the Democrats, for the first time in twenty-four years elected majorities to both branches of the State Legislature. Not since 1845 had the Democrats carried both the Senate and Assembly. Let Hoffman be re-elected Governor next fall and nothing save death could stop The Boss from making him Presi-

dent of the United States.   Then he would advance the Elegant
Oakey to the Governorship and he himself would go to Wash-
ington as the junior Senator from the State of New York.
And at the national Capital, as at Albany and New York,
Tweed would be The Boss.

The stealings of The Ring from the city treasury now
averaged more than a million dollars a month—and there was
much whispering concerning it.   The corruption of the judiciary was a daily topic in every law office, and plans were discussed for taking justice out of the market place.   Lawyers
and laymen alike hesitated to name Tweed, fearing his power
and wealth, and the wealth and power of his allies.   The Boss
was now a director of Gould and Fisk's bank, the Tenth
National, as well as of their railroad.   He was also on the
directorates of the Harlem Gas Light Company, the Brooklyn
Bridge Company, and the Third Avenue Railway Company.
He was president of the Guardian Savings Bank.   This bank
Tweed plundered.   The thought of the combined forces of
all these corporations overawed the timid respectables, Republican and Democratic, in public and private life.   They had
their shallow excuse—how could they rouse New York when
more than half of the voters were of foreign birth, and largely
Irish and German at that?   Virtue could not reside in these.

Tweed's power could have been destroyed by an honest Republican machine.   But one did not exist.   What passed for the
New York County Republican Committee was owned, lock,
stock, and barrel, by Tweed, who had fifty-nine Republican
leaders on his payroll.   The Grand Old Party!

In this first year of the Tweed Ring one man was brave
enough to go to the people and denounce The Boss.   Standing on a street corner until a crowd assembled, he then
harangued them on the evils of their local government.   He
would generally end his speech with:

"All who are in favor of hanging Tweed, say 'Aye!'"

The ayes always had it.

This man was of military bearing, flowing, black curly
hair, and a trooper's mustache, a carefully trimmed goatee,

clothes faultlessly tailored. He had a sumptuous villa at Newport.

His name was George Francis Train, truthfully described as the most eccentric and picturesque character New York has ever known. There was a touch of genius in him. He was born in Boston, March 24, 1829. He was of old New England stock and by inheritance a profound believer in popular government. His grandfather was the Reverend George Pickering, who emancipated his slaves and declined a Methodist bishopric. Train was orphaned at four, and his grandparents looked after him. At an early age he was taken into his uncle's shipping house, and when twenty-two had $10,000 a year. He built his own fleet of ships which plied between America and Australia, and at the age of twenty-four his annual income had mounted to $95,000. Then he turned to railroads. He was a prime mover in the building of the Union Pacific Railroad, and was responsible for the organizing of the Credit Mobilier in 1864. His growing eccentricities forced him out of both these interlocking ventures before some of the huge profits of the Credit Mobilier and stock of the railroad were distributed among several influential members of Congress in return for favorable legislation. This scandal also drove from public life Schuyler Colfax, of New York City, Vice-President of the United States during Grant's first administration.

After organizing the Credit Mobilier, Train paid little attention to business, and became an enthusiastic supporter of the Irish cause, both here and in Ireland, addressing Fenians wherever he happened to be. In 1868 he was arrested in Dublin for his Fenianism. From his cell he assailed England in erratic prose and verse. Through jailers who sympathized with the cause he espoused, he had his diatribes mailed to the American supporters of the Irish movement, who published them in pamphlet form. One of these communications began: "Dear Fenian Brotherhood: Incarcerated for Ireland. Outraged for your cause. All I have done I do (*Sic!*) for love." This letter ended:

"Sic semper tyrannis!" be the Fenian cry.
"Delenda est Britannia—do or die!"

The year after he had proposed hanging Tweed, Train
landed at Marseilles where he organized the Commune of
1870. He had been lured by his friend, General Gustave Paul
Cluseret, Chief of the Paris Commune. Cluseret had many
admirers in this country, having served on the staffs of Mc-
Clellan and Fremont during the Civil War.

The adorable eccentric returned to New York as Citizen
Train, and was an independent candidate for President in 1872.
Unlike his independent rival for the Presidency—Victoria Claflin Woodhull—Train spent money on his campaign, and traveled to most of the principal cities where he made speeches. His
platform consisted of these six planks: Woman Suffrage; Re-
publicanize Europe; *Le Drapeau Rouge;* Success to Strikes;
Penal Servitude for Briber and Bribed; Inland and Ocean
Penny Postage. He distributed a copy of a pamphlet wherever he stopped. This was entitled: "The Man of Destiny."
Train had written it. Much of it was in rhyme. One long
piece of versification had the refrain:

"Wake up, people! Smash the Rings!
"Down with party! Death to Kings!"

After the Presidential campaign of 1872 Victoria Claflin
Woodhull and her sister Tennie were arrested by Anthony
Comstock for publishing in their weekly an article concerning
an obscure Wall Street broker. Comstock believed that the
scandalous piece tended to destroy the morals of the community. Train also had his own personal organ, *The Train
Ligue.* One defeated candidate for the Presidency must help
another. He issued a special number of his periodical in defense of the charming Claflins. He, too, was arrested by the
vigilant Comstock for publishing indecent literature. He was
placed in a cell in the Tombs on the tier known as Murderers'
Row. Twenty-three of his fellow inmates were either under indictment for murder or had been convicted and sentenced to
be hanged. Train formed the Murderers' Club which elected him

MRS. VICTORIA CLAFLIN WOODHULL

MRS. VICTORIA CLAFLIN WOODHULL ASSERTING HER PRIVILEGE TO VOTE

(From a sketch by A. Balling in the collection of The New York Public Library.)

president. Clark Bell, his counsel, in arguing for his release, referred to his client as "The President of the Murderers' Club, the head of Commune, the illustrious Chief and Captain of the Internationale." Citizen Train was vastly pleased.

Train grew more eccentric with the years. He organized his own congregation and advertised in the daily press. One notice read:

REV. GEORGE FRANCIS TRAIN
Bombarding 'Hell-be-Damned'
Sundays, 10:00 A.M.—8 Union Square Hall

His sermons were bizarre, and sprinkled with damns. Citizen Train always explained with a broad grin that damn was a South Sea Island expression meaning banana. One of his pulpit themes considered the habit of people in prayer closing their eyes.

"What in Hell do they do that for?" shouted the self-styled Reverend Mr. Train.

Sometimes his sermons were cut short by small riots. The police were always present to see that no heads were broken. Citizen Train called his pastorate "The Church of the Laughing Jackass."

This delightful adventurer passed the last years of his life surrounded by the birds and children in Madison Square Park. He became known to the country as the gentle philosopher of Madison Square. His hair was now white, and long and flowing and curly as ever. He had abandoned conventional dress. Sometimes he would appear in an Old Guard dress coat, but never without his Communist red sash and his green umbrella and chain of medals and Chinese coins. In his travels around the country he occasionally managed to get into a controversy with the authorities—which he enjoyed doing. Sometimes he succeeded in having himself put in jail—which he relished even more. For anything he said from a prison cell always was first page copy. In fact all that he did or said was news. He never gave up hope that something would happen to make him President of the United States. Citizen Train cherished two essentially distinctive eccentricities to the last. He would not shake hands with any one over twelve years of age lest he lose part of his psychic force. The other was the green umbrella with which he shaded his uncovered head to ward off malign influences.

He always gloried in having been the first to suggest the hanging of Boss Tweed.

CHAPTER XXVI

THE November Election of 1869, which gave the Democrats control of both branches of the State Legislature for the first time in twenty-four years, was generally believed to be the last election of the year. After Election Day, Tweed informed those who inquired as to the likelihood of a December canvass that no reason existed for holding one. Mayor Hall had been elected the preceding year to succeed Governor Hoffman. Some lawyers held the opinion that Hall was elected only to fill out the unexpired term of Hoffman, which would end at midnight, December 31, 1869. Others contended that Hall was elected for a full two years' term.

In the first week of December, The Boss demonstrated his complete domination of the local Republican machine when it permitted, unprotested, the distribution of ballot boxes on Monday afternoon, December 6, for the election of Mayor the following day. The rank and file of the Republicans were unaware of Tweed's plot to steal this election in a manner never before attempted. They were too stunned even to demand of their leaders—most of them paid servants of Tweed—that a nominating convention be held. No one made an attempt to stop this palpably illegal election by resorting to the courts for a restraining order. There were 65,565 votes cast for Hall, and 1,051 for such opposition candidates as occurred to the disorganized minority that went to the polls to register its protest.

It does not seem possible that any one would dare to order an election of such importance on a few hours' notice. The day after this mockery, *The Times* commented:

"The Mayoralty voters generally were surprised to find at the various polling places, ballot boxes for the reception of votes for

Mayor, as it had not been intimated in any quarter until late Monday afternoon that there was to be any election for Mayor. . . . It is difficult to see how an election, of which no notice was given to the people, official or otherwise, can be legal, even if it shall be declared to have been necessary."

While Tweed was having things all his own way with the Republicans, there developed within his own party, shortly after the election of Hall, a formidable opposition. This anti-Tweed faction, known as the Young Democracy, was nominally led by three men. None of them possessed the ability, capacity, and resourcefulness reflected by the insurgent movement. Tweed and his friends looked upon Tilden as the adviser of this group. Tilden always denied this charge which carried with it an implication of party treachery. There are few offenses more heinous in the eyes of partisans than a secretly directed revolt.

Tilden had nothing to do with the start of the Young Democracy. This reform organization came into being when two thieves fell out—Tweed and Sheriff James O'Brien. Tweed, it is scarcely necessary to say, made O'Brien Sheriff. The Boss explained their row by saying that O'Brien demanded payments in excess of the allowances agreed upon. O'Brien's bills against the city as Sheriff, which Tweed would not approve, eventually amounted to more than a third of a million dollars.

When O'Brien started the Young Democracy he raised a banner whose device read: "Reform!" One of the "reformers" who aided O'Brien was Prince Hal, in private life Henry W. Genet, and a member of the Senate of the State of New York by grace of The Boss. A third was the one-time pugilist and thug, now a gambler, Representative John Morrissey, whom Tweed had sent to Congress. Also in the front ranks of the reformers we find Edmund Jones, of Jones and Company, printers and stationers, who Tweed testified, parted company with him when The Boss disapproved some of the extortionate bills of the printing company. Through Jones and Company the members of The Ring and their lieutenants acquired fine

desks, paintings, robes for carriages and sleighs, in short—
to use the language of Tweed—"anything that man would
require and billed [them] to the city as stationery."

It is inconceivable that Tilden, early in the spring of 1870,
was not advising Tweed's enemies. They had grown powerful,
and had enlisted more than half of the General Committee of
Tammany Hall. This gave the Young Democracy the power
to depose Tweed. This they set out to do. Tilden's only hope
of achieving the nomination for President was through the
overthrow of Tweed, as The Boss was openly announcing that
he was for Hoffman for President and Hall for Governor.
Tilden was the only one capable of directing a fight such as
the Young Democracy was waging. Would he fail them when
he had more to gain than any one else?

The Boss, at this time—penniless in 1861—was reputed to
be worth $12,000,000. This was doubtless an exaggeration.
Tweed himself said that he was never worth more than $2,-
500,000 to $3,000,000. This is far too modest. He had some
$2,000,000 invested in real estate, and was the third largest
owner of land in the city, being outclassed only by Astor and
Stewart. One day's crookedness alone netted him approximately
$1,500,000. He was living the life of a multi-millionaire. His
tastes had outgrown the modest brownstone house on a Murray
Hill side street. He was now occupying one of the finest mansions on Fifth Avenue, No. 511, on the southeast corner of
Forty-third Street. A single night's entertainment in his regal
suite at the Delevan House at Albany cost more than his salary
for an entire year as State Senator—legislators were then paid
$300 annually. He had his steam yacht, and his barouche
and four. His younger children were attending boarding
schools. Yet no one asked him how he managed it on his beg-
garly visible means of support.

It was an open secret that for years Tweed and several of
his associates on the Board of Supervisors had made fortunes
from padded bills rendered for building, repairing, and furnishing the Court House, and for like work in armories. It
was being gossiped during all this time that the Supervisors'
Ring, headed by Tweed, was stealing hundreds of thousands

annually, and that Tweed's share of the thefts averaged twenty per cent. Subsequent disclosures revealed that in 1868 alone the corrupt Supervisors divided nearly $3,000,000 among themselves, and that The Boss received twenty-five per cent of the loot this year, or approximately three-quarters of a million dollars. This was an exceptionally good year for them, and a bad one for the taxpayers. Again, no one raised an inquiring voice.

Some of this silence was bought. There was another reform organization, and unlike the Young Democracy, it was not of recent growth, having been in existence since 1863. This was the Citizens' Association, the first non-partisan society formed to cope with municipal maladministration. Its head was Peter Cooper, the venerable philanthropist. He, and other honorable members of the Association, depended for guidance on Nathaniel Sands, a Republican, secretary of the body. Tweed made Sands a Tax Commissioner at $15,000 a year. This was the price of Sands. Three or four other officials of the Citizens' Association were bribed by The Boss in like manner.

Speaking of the spring of 1870, Tilden said: "None of The Ring ever came near me; but Mr. Nathaniel Sands often called to talk over city reform. He sometimes brought my honored and esteemed friend Mr. Peter Cooper. They were convinced that The Ring had become conservative—were not ambitious for more wealth—were on the side of the taxpayers."

This frank admission was made by Tilden following savage attacks on him by *The Times* in 1873 for his silence while The Boss was in his glory. It was embodied in a letter of some twenty thousand words, defending himself, and excoriating *The Times*. When *The Times* declined to publish it, Tilden had it printed as a pamphlet.

We have, in Tilden's explanation, an index to the general attitude toward corruption in public life in the generation that was nearing its end. ". . . My honored and esteemed friend Mr. Peter Cooper . . . [was] convinced that The Ring had become conservative—[that its members] were not ambitious for more wealth—were on the side of the taxpayers." Tilden does not fix the time when Cooper voiced the sentiments that do not accord with the accepted moral code. The context does, as Tilden speaks of his refusal to heed the pleadings of Peter Cooper, who like other misguided civic leaders, was zealously aiding Tweed in enacting a most stupendous sham, a new city charter. This charter became a law April 6. Cooper, like every one else in town, was aware of the corruption of The Ring. The old philanthropist, who had given generously and well to his city, would have suspected the traitorous officials of the reform association had they attempted to paint Tweed and his associates as maligned men. Other officers of the Citizens' Association—this is indicated in Tilden's twenty thousand words—argued that it was better to deal with Tweed and his Ring, who were surfeited with riches, than with a new and hungry horde, such as was represented in the Young Democracy. The reasoning was insidiously sound. Thus ill-advised, Cooper and other eminent men of unquestioned integrity, who were incapable of detecting the masked malevolence of innocent looking phrases in legislative acts—jokers the Solons call them—gave their approval to Tweed's charter.

This charter had the semblance of virtue. It provided a seeming home rule for the city. For a generation the city had been clamoring for a restoration of the privileges of local autonomy. In advocating this cause, the infamous Fernando Wood made people for a time forget his villainies and shout his praises. To have acceded to the demands of the people would have meant the end of The Ring. A sham—as Tilden said years later—was necessary. The charter appeared to center responsibility in the Mayor. It did—in the incumbent, the Elegant Oakey, not only during his term of office, but for three to seven years after his term expired. And for the same length of time, the hands of Hall's successors were tied, and detection of the looting of the city treasury delayed correspondingly. This iniquity was accomplished by vesting Hall with the power to appoint the heads of all city departments—including those hitherto appointed by the Governor—for periods of from four to eight years. Still greater power to steal, and to steal undetected for years, was granted The Ring by the creation of a Board of Audit. This board was to consist of the

Mayor, the Comptroller, the Commissioner of Public Works, thus conferring power on Tweed, who was appointed Commissioner of Public Works when the bill passed, with Connolly and Hall to audit all bills against the city but not the county. Another joker provided that Tweed could be removed only after being convicted on charges preferred by the Mayor and at a trial before all the six judges of the Court of Common Pleas. The absence of a single judge would have prevented Tweed's removal. In this new office to which Hall appointed Tweed, were vested all the powers of the Street Commissioner, and of the Croton or Water Department. This charter also took away most of the legislative powers of the Board of Aldermen and lodged them with Hall, Connolly and Tweed.

It was the Elegant Oakey who conceived the Board of Audit for the city, which was incorporated in the Tweed charter, and he also devised the following joker embodied in the Tax Levy of 1870: "All liabilities against the County of New York, incurred previous to the passage of this act shall be audited by the Mayor, Comptroller, and President of the Board of Supervisors." Tweed was head of the Board. So that again, in the hands of the same men, was placed the power of determining how much should be paid for charges against the county. Sweeny, while not a member of the Board of Audit, was continued as one of the four who constituted The Ring. He was made Commissioner of Public Parks. Nothing had been forgotten.

The joker in the Tax Levy was not observed—so far as the records disclose—by Tilden or any one else. Tilden fought the Tweed charter, but in an academic fashion, as he did the corrupt judiciary at the meeting of lawyers on February 1 when the Bar Association was formed. These attorneys represented the foremost legal talent of the day. All were sincere in their endeavors to rid the bench of the sordid influences of Tweed, Fisk, and Gould. No one dared to name them or their judicial tools. The most forceful passages from Tilden's speech were:

"If the bar is to be merely an institution that seeks to win causes.

and win them by back-door access to the judiciary, then it is not only degraded but corrupt. If it will do its duty to itself, if it will do its duty to the profession which it follows, and to which it is devoted, the bar can do everything else. It can have reformed constitutions, it can have a reformed judiciary, it can have the administration of justice made pure and honorable, and can restore both the judiciary and the bar, until it shall be once more as it formerly was, an honorable and elevated calling."

Tilden in opposing the Tweed charter on April 4 addressed himself to the Senate Committee on Cities, over which Senator Tweed presided as Chairman. He stressed that the charter did not make for popular or responsible government. Toward the end of his speech, mild and inoffensive, Tilden roused—as he always did—the ire of Tweed by his very presence. The statesman, meek, sought to mollify the feelings of The Boss almighty, and said:

"I come here, sir, to aid no party of men; I come here simply to contribute what I may be able, however little, to a result in which you, I, and all of us have a great interest, and you a great duty. And let me say here, that if I know my own heart, I have no feeling of unkindness to any human being. To yourself, Mr. Chairman—"

Here Tweed, who had endured Tilden as long as he could without turning upon him, interrupted angrily with:

"I am sick of the discussion of this question."

Tilden, ignoring the interruption, continued as though no rudeness had been offered him.

"—or to anybody else, I am unconscious of ever having done an unkind act or entertained an unkind feeling."

This was typical of the timorous, cringing attitude of foremost Democrats as honest financially as Tilden—prior to the overthrow of Tweed. All feared him. And when they turned on the stricken tiger, *The Times* said of them:

"They denounced when it was no longer dangerous to denounce. Their indignation concerning The Ring was most edifying—after The Ring was down."

The Tweed charter passed the Assembly before it was considered by the Senate. Tweed had little worry over its passage through the lower house, although the Black Horse Cavalry, who knew no brother in matters legislative (as Tweed had taught them) charged him sorely for their support. The measure was on the Assembly's Third Reading Calendar, on Monday night, March 28, awaiting the motion of its sponsor: "Mr. Speaker, I move its final passage."

This Monday night was one of the most important sittings in the legislative session of 1870. Tweed should be there. The leaders of the Young Democracy contrived that Tweed should not be in Albany when the Clerk of the Assembly read his charter, whose crooked clauses they knew by heart. O'Brien, Genet, and Morrissey, also planned to have The Boss preside at a meeting of the General Committee of Tammany Hall on that night and entertain a motion calling for his deposal and the election of one of their number in his stead as Chairman of the Democratic County Committee.

No mere ward politicians devised this humiliating program for Tweed to sit through. Under the rules and by-laws of Tammany, Tweed had no choice but to call the meeting as demanded by the Young Democracy, as more than half the total membership of the General Committee signed the demand. For Tweed to refuse would render him liable to removal on charges.

Sheriff O'Brien, on this Monday afternoon, a few hours before the scheduled hour of the meeting, flung public defiance in the face of Tweed by summarily removing from office Deputy Sheriff John J. Gumbleton, one of The Boss's most ardent followers.

It was a momentous day for Tweed. From early morning he sat in his law offices at 59 Duane Street receiving reports from the camp of the enemy, his alert mind intent on a means of avoiding the snares laid for him that evening. We learn from *The Evening Post* of the following day:

"Reporters called upon Tweed at his office in Duane' Street. The stairways and ante-rooms leading thereto were perfectly be-

sieged with politicians of all grades, Senators, Assemblymen, Aldermen and Assistant Aldermen, Police Justices, Coroners, and others,
all in *omnium gatherum,* were congregated to see the 'Big Indian.'
He sat in his private office, calm, collected, and cool, and received
each visitor with a smile and thanks for their kind wishes for his
success.

"Mr. Tweed told our reporter that he felt confident of success;
that the men who were now endeavoring to injure him had received
their positions from his hands, and now cowardlike, were doing
their utmost to displace him from power; but notwithstanding this,
the fight was his; he would be the winner, all reports to the contrary
notwithstanding."

Two hours before the Young Democracy started for Tammany Hall to depose Tweed they met in Irving Hall nearby,
where it was found that two other State Senators had joined
their ranks. These were Michael Norton, the "discoverer" of
Coney Island, whose name is perpetuated in the point of land
at the eastern extreme of the popular seaside resort, and
Thomas J. Creamer, who had spent part of the afternoon
"drinking lager and eating pretzels with his German constituents." Creamer was chosen chairman. This was good politics. The honor of a revolt nominally led by a man with an
Irish name was shared by a man with a German cognomen. We
must cater to the groups.

The Young Democracy was organized primarily with a view
to appealing to the huge German and Irish vote which followed Tweed blindly because of his recognized leadership in the
local fight against the Know-Nothings. Creamer's election as
chairman of the Irving Hall meeting stressed this. And the
nominal leader of the faction, O'Brien, was being hailed as the
next Mayor of New York, the argument advanced being that
it was time that a Roman Catholic of Irish blood was chosen
to rule over a city where voters of Irish birth or ancestry and of
O'Brien's faith comprised the largest group.

The meeting in Irving Hall was for the purpose of determining upon the procedure of the Young Democracy when it
foregathered in Tammany Hall. They had a majority of the
General Committee, and once inside the Wigwam, short shrift

would be made of Tweed's leadership. They had the votes. They need but agree upon the method.

The leaders of the anti-Tweed faction were marvelling at the originality and audacity of their plan when word was brought to them that policemen, in full uniform, with drawn clubs, were marching in countless platoons from all points of the compass toward Tammany Hall.

"The policemen in Fourteenth Street," *The Tribune* said, "outnumbered the civilians. The northern sidewalk was filled with them. Each stoop of Tammany Hall contained nearly 100, all ready for action. . . . Inside the Hall were 300 policemen, a number of whom were peering out of the windows. Bryant's Minstrel Hall was closed in consequence of a request of the Grand Sachem. The police outside numbered about 500, drawn up in two lines."

When members of the General Committee attempted to enter Tammany Hall, they were barred by the police. Senator Creamer, accompanied by Prince Hal and others, inquired of Inspector Walling and Chief of Police Kelso, by what right they were denying them admittance to Tammany Hall. Walling "blandly informed him it was by order of the Tammany Sachems." This information was answered with growls from the Young Democracy, and "Genet denounced Tweed, and said he had shown the white feather."

The audacity and originality of the Young Democracy was outdone by Tweed. It was all within the law. The Boss, as Grand Sachem of Tammany Hall, had advised the Republican Police Commissioner, Henry Smith, that a meeting in Tammany Hall might lead to a riot, and further, that the police, to guard against possible panic in Bryant's Minstrel Hall next door, should close the theater. This last lent a suggestion of civic virtue to Tweed's advice. Accordingly, the playhouse was closed for the evening, and more than half the police of the city, in the name of law and order, went forth to win Tweed's battle. Tweed wanted time. Money would do the rest. He had the money. Thanks to his friend "Hank" Smith he was given the respite he sought. And when O'Brien, Genet, and

Morrissey counted noses the following morning, they discovered that many of their supporters were missing.

Tweed returned to Albany the next day. A long cape overcoat draped itself gracefully over his tall and portly form like a toga. He was now forty-seven years old, and the lack of exercise was beginning to tell in the surplus flesh. In a corridor of the Capitol a knot of legislators surrounded him to offer their congratulations. Tweed's only response, as he thrust his right hand above his head, was:

"By ——, I'll show them that The Boss still lives!"

The following morning, Assemblyman Alexander Frear, of the Fifteenth New York, who fostered the charter in the lower house, moved its passage. Only seven out of one hundred and eleven votes were recorded against it.

On April 2, three days before Tilden voiced his lukewarm protest against certain provisions of the charter, Moses Taylor, H. B. Claflin, C. L. Tiffany, Arnold and Constable, Andrew Gilsey, W. and J. Sloane and Company, and other individual and corporate members of the Citizens' Association, forwarded an unqualified indorsement of the charter to Tweed. Prefacing the list of notable signatures was:

"We the undersigned citizens and property owners of the City of New York, respectfully petition your honorable body in favor of the passage of the bill entitled 'An Act to reorganize the local government of the City of New York' which passed the Assembly, March 30, 1870. We consider that this bill should receive the support of all who desire to give to New York City a symmetrical and honest local government." This was addressed "To the Honorable, the Senate of the State of New York." Tweed filed it with that body.

Mere talk and indorsements did not get the charter through the Legislature. Tweed testified that he paid more than $600,-000 for the legislation. Tilden has declared that The Boss spent more than a million dollars to get the measure through the two houses of the Legislature. It was a failing of Tweed to understate his resources and his expenditures. At times it was with the thought of saving a friend from sharing his shame.

In his testimony before the Aldermanic Investigating Committee, Tweed said that he obtained this $600,000 from Fisk, Gould, and from various tradesmen and contractors who dealt with the city and worked with The Ring. He further testified that he paid $200,000 for the bribery of five rural Republican Senators.

Several Senators were bought at $5,000 each, and some were paid "$1,000 to-day, $500 to-morrow, and $10,000 the next day." Tweed testified that he paid his lobbyist, the Republican editor, Hugh Hastings, $20,000 by check. With rare exceptions, all the lawmakers took their bribes in cash. Where payments were traced to them, their explanation, when one was made, was that they had borrowed the money from Tweed. All had forgotten to repay him.

The votes of only two of the thirty-two members of the Senate were cast against the Tweed charter. One was that of Senator Francis S. Thayer, of Troy. The other was Senator Genet's.

The charter passed the Senate the day after Tilden's appearance before Tweed's Committee on Cities. Greeley was not unaware of the evils latent in the charter. He had a mild editorial where he described it as surrendering "our city to the rule of Tweed and Sweeny for a number of ensuing years." But his party had supported the measure, the ostensible *quid pro quo* being a bargain on the part of Tweed to pass an election reform law that the Republicans professed to advocate. "We do not realize that our city should have been given over to the Tammany Ring for an indefinite future in payment for such a law," observed Greeley. "Those who have done it meant well; but they have judged ill, as time will make plain."

Oblivious alike to extravagant praise and weasel-words of blame—so far as the record discloses—was Tweed.

CHAPTER XXVII

AFTER the charter was signed, Tweed returned from Albany to find himself a hero. Nearly all the papers praised him. On his arrival in the city one of the morning papers told that "a fine full-length portrait by Thomas Hicks was yesterday hung in the Chamber of the Board of Supervisors. It was said to cost $2,500." He would not have to sit for the noted Academician that week-end. Hicks was the vogue at the time. He had done canvases of Hamilton Fish, Henry Ward Beecher, Parke Godwin of *The Evening Post*, and Edwin Booth. The tragedian was depicted in his rôle of Iago.

Judge Edward J. Shandley, who arranged most of the demonstrations that were designed to keep Tweed in good favor with the masses between elections, met The Boss at the depot and informed him of the big public meeting to be held the following night in Tweed Plaza, where East Broadway and Canal Street form a triangular open space. This was to celebrate the enactment of the charter, and at the same time, to afford his supporters an opportunity to denounce the Young Democracy. And Tweed must be there without fail.

On Saturday night the whole East Side tried to crowd into Tweed Plaza, which was strung with softly glowing Chinese lanterns of grotesque shapes and countless in number, and where cannon thundered a welcome as the torchlight processions approached the specially built rostrum, whereon Fink's Washington Band was blaring the Star Spangled Banner.

The first contingent to arrive was "The Young Men's Democratic William M. Tweed Club." One of the paraders carried an illuminated banner—the language is *The Tribune's*—on which was a good likeness of Mr. Tweed. Over his portrait were the words: "Let us muster men for law and order. It

333

will be our shield." Beneath were the following words: "Let justice strike when ingrates dare the field."

The ingrates—O'Brien, Morrissey, Genet, and the rest of the Young Democracy—were dealt with fittingly by some of the speakers. All took the cue from Judge George M. Curtis, of the Marine Court, which was: "Sustain Mr. Tweed under the present circumstances." Between speeches the band played, and hot-air balloons were released. The crowd was more intent on seeing and hearing Tweed, who was expected momentarily.

The Boss disappointed the waiting thousands. They forgave him, and cheered enthusiastically, when a letter from him was read. Part of it ran:

"The generous confidence and unwavering friendship of constituents toward a public servant is his highest praise. Duties of an urgent public character compel me to be absent; they, of course, are superior to political pleasure, or to the pleasant society of friends.

"In political contests as in military battles, the person happening to be at the head of the forces at the moment of victory obtains the primary credit, and his name becomes most conspicuous at the early bulletin. Yet there are always among his associates and soldiers those who perhaps deserve more credit. I congratulate you, fellow citizens, upon the restoration of municipal rights. I trust our victory will, by wise use of its fruits, result in raising our party above the plane of selfish aggrandizement and redound to the harmony and success of our majestic party in this Metropolis and throughout the State and Union."

Tweed, as the last line indicates, was no longer thinking merely of the City and State, but of the entire Nation. Let him reëlect Hoffman Governor and he would rule the Nation! But Tweed was not forgetting that that could not be done without the people. Throughout his letter he subordinated himself, praised his associates as deserving of more credit, and congratulated his fellow citizens on the victory. Tweed did not have to be told that "the mob is an old Narcissus; adoring itself, and praising the mob."

Immediately after the signing of the charter, the newspapers now seemed to vie with one another in seeing which could be most extravagant in its praise of The Boss. Some of the Republican journals exceeded their Democratic contemporaries. When Tweed, to get rid of two of the leaders of the Young Democracy, abolished the Board of Supervisors, *The Times* said editorially:

"Senator Tweed is in a fair way to distinguish himself as a reformer. Having gone so far as the champion of the new Election bill and charter, he seems to have no idea of turning back. Perhaps, like Macbeth, he thinks that under existing circumstances 'returning were as tedious as go o'er,' but at all events he has put the people of Manhattan Island under great obligations. His last proposition to abolish the Board of Supervisors of New York and transfer their functions to the Mayor, Recorder and new Board of Aldermen is the crowning act of all.

"It strikes a blow at one of the most corrupt Departments of a government, and one which is as useless as a fifth wheel to a coach. We trust that Senator Tweed will manifest the same energy in the advocacy of this last reform which marked his action in regard to the charter."

Tweed did, and with the passing of the Board of Supervisors, The Boss struck two of his enemies from places of power. These were John Fox and James Hayes. Other members of the Board of Supervisors who were deserving of his gratitude, were placed in departments. Tweed himself confessed that his primary purpose in abolishing the Supervisors was to get rid of Hayes and Fox.

So important a department of government as the Board of Supervisors could not have been wiped out without the real purpose of Tweed being known in the editorial sanctums. Yet there is no mention of Tweed's personal malice toward Hayes and Fox in any of the praise heaped upon Tweed for this particular act. That the Board was, as *The Times* said, as useful as a fifth wheel on a wagon, cannot be gainsaid. It was a reform, although not intended so. We can picture the chagrin of some of the staff of *The Times* as they read the undeserved eulogy of Tweed. The Boss seemed to have a powerful supporter in nearly every newspaper office. His influence in *The Times* may be traced to James B. Taylor, one of Tweed's partners in the New York Printing Company, which received the lion's share of the $7,168,212.23 appropriated by The Ring for public advertising and printing during the thirty months ending with its downfall. Taylor was one of the three directors of *The Times*.

Chafing under the restraint, more than any member of his staff, was George Jones, who, in the preceding June, became publisher of *The Times* on the death of Henry J. Raymond, its founder. Jones had been associated with Raymond from the establishment of the daily, but on the business side. In his new post as helmsman of *The Times*, he began to conceive ways of rousing the city to the menace of The Ring.

While the newspapers remained silent, Nast, in *Harper's Weekly*, kept hammering away at The Ring. Jones, with the unquenchable zeal of a true journalist, was anxious to follow the trail blazed by Nast. He was confident that once started, he would quickly outdistance the weekly, not alone because he had a daily audience, but by virtue of the greater facilities at the disposal of a newspaper for gathering and presenting news. The lootings could not go on undetected forever. Some day they would have to be published. Apart from the duty the paper owed the people, there would be greater glory than ever befell a newspaper. Jones had for managing editor Louis John Jennings, who later returned to his native heath, where he was elected to Parliament. Jennings had distinguished himself as an editorial writer under Raymond. Like Jones, he was incorruptible. How often Jones must have regretted conditions which prevented his giving the Englishman the same free hand that the Harpers gave their German-born artist! Things must change, sooner or later. There was consolation in that.

Tweed too was thinking. The annual election of the Tammany Sachems would be held on April 19. Here was another opportunity to humiliate the Young Democracy which he had routed with eight hundred policemen. The insurgents had given up, temporarily, all attempts to wrest control of Tammany from The Boss. Some two hundred and sixty-five of the Braves assembled at the Wigwam on the night of the annual election. All were loyal to the last man to Tweed. Tweed's unanimous reëlection as Grand Sachem, and that of the thirteen Sachems, headed by the Elegant Oakey and the two other members of The Ring, Peter Barr Sweeny and Richard Connolly, was assured.

Tweed must have grinned as the thought occurred to him to nominate a rival ticket headed by his old enemy Tilden. Tie him up with the defeated Young Democracy! Make him a part of this routed faction! Put on the ticket John Morrissey and Hayes and Fox, the two Supervisors who had also dared to challenge his leadership. This was done, and word was passed to twenty-three of the two hundred sixty-five to vote for this ticket which Tweed labeled the Young Democracy's.

The newspapers told of Tweed's defeat of Tilden and the Young Democracy by a vote of 242 to 23—more than ten to one! Said *The Tribune* in its head: "Triumph of Tweed. The Young Democracy Squelched." *The Times* thus exulted: "Now is the triumph of Tweed Complete."

Then The Boss forgot, for the time being, the existence of the Young Democracy, and turned his thoughts to recouping the $600,000 spent by The Ring in obtaining the crooked charter. And it would cost a large sum to put through the Tax Levy with its glaring steals. This, too, must be realized.

His first move was to assemble The Ring and form a new compact. At the beginning of the year, at the Delevan House in Albany, in the rooms, not of Tweed, but of Peter B. Sweeny, it was agreed that thirty-three and one-third per cent of the amount of all bills rendered against the city and county must be fraudulent. This meant that one dollar in every three paid out of the city treasury went to The Ring. Tweed testified that under the original agreement, he, Connolly, Sweeny, and the Elegant Oakey shared alike, each taking twenty per cent of the loot. The remaining fifth was thus divided: half of it went into a reserve fund, to be used for bribery purposes, and the residue was evenly apportioned between the two agents of The Ring, James Watson, and A. E. Woodward. The latter was a clerk in the Board of Supervisors, and had attached himself to the Board long before Tweed was a member. The story is told that Woodward at first served in the capacity of self-appointed lackey to the Board, being ready with a lighted match when he saw a Supervisor reach for a cigar, helping them on with their wraps, and performing other like services. For these labors he received nothing save tips. In time he was made a clerk with a small salary. Then Tweed took him on, using him to collect the personal levies he had imposed on those who had been paid moneys on order of the Board. Watson was one of the important functionaries in the Comptroller's office. He had charge of the records of all transactions involving the payment of moneys charged against the county. His title was County Auditor. Watson also had long been associated with Tweed and his various rings in their thievings and had grown rich on the share allotted to him. Watson and Woodward were now the bookkeepers and paymasters of The Ring, and were millionaires.

Tweed presided over a meeting in the new County Court House shortly after the passage of the charter, where it was decided that all moneys paid to contractors and merchants who worked for, or sold supplies to, the city must be evenly divided between these creditors and The Ring. This was the basic minimum. Where conditions warranted, the share of Tweed and his associates was to be as large as circumstances permitted.

An example of the growing greed of The Ring was exhibited at one of the first meetings of the Board of Audit, composed of Tweed, Connolly, and Hall. This was on May 5, 1870. On that day, in a single morning sitting, the Board authorized the payment of $6,312,500. More than $5,500,000 of this sum was fradulent, and was divided among the members of The Ring. Here nearly ninety per cent of the total sum was split up among the members of The Ring.

This entire sum was ostensibly for work on the new County Court House, and its furnishings and equipment. The total price paid by the taxpayers for this structure, and its fittings, was in excess of $12,000,000. It has been estimated that $3,000,000 would have been an outside price for the building and its equipment. The other $9,000,000 and more went into the pockets of The Ring. The Court House, which within another eighteen months was to be sung in jeering song and story throughout the civilized world as "The House that Tweed Built," is situated immediately to the north of the City Hall, in the Park.

"The aggregate of fraudulent bills, after April 5, 1870, was, in the rest of that year, about $12,250,000, and in 1871, $3,400,000," wrote Tilden in 1873. "Nearly fifteen and three-quarter millions of fraudulent bills were the booty grasped on the 5th of April, 1870 [the date of the enactment of the Tweed charter]. Fourteen, perhaps fifteen millions of it were sheer plunder."

In the spring of 1870, probably shortly after the ordering of the payment of $6,312,500 on charges against the Court House, Connolly protested against the division of spoils, saying that as Comptroller, nothing could be done without him, and demanded more.

Tweed agreed that nothing could be done without Connolly, and ordered that thenceforward The Ring's share of every dollar paid out on bills against the city and county must be sixty-six and two-thirds cents. Still later The Ring's share was raised to eighty-five per cent of the total of the face of the bill.

When the bills of the contractors and tradesmen did not come in fast enough, Tweed directed Watson and Woodward to make out vouchers to imaginary firms and individuals, and to non-existent hospitals, dispensaries, and other fanciful charitable institutions, which, under the law—if they had existed—would have been entitled to governmental aid.

The Ring shared in the loot obtained through the fictitious charitable institutions. But Tweed had some private enterprises of his own. In addition to the New York Printing Company in which Taylor of *The Times* was a partner, he also was the proprietor of The Manufacturing Stationers' Company. Through this last-named he sold blank books, paper, pens, ink, and similar supplies to the city's schools and to the various departments of the city. The gross income of the company in 1870 exceeded $3,000,000, principally from the city. The extortionate profits earned by Tweed through this concern may be approximated from a bill of $10,000 paid for supplies to one of the city's bureaus. For this $10,000 the city received six reams (3,000 sheets) of foolscap paper; six reams of note paper; two dozen pen holders; four ink bottles; one dozen sponges; three dozen boxes of rubber bands.

The Boss was also a newspaper publisher. His paper was *The Transcript*. It was a struggling morning paper late in 1869 when Tweed took it over. The Boss engaged one of his Republican editorial friends, Charles E. Wilbour, to manage it. Editor Wilbour held at least three city jobs simultaneously. He was stenographer in the Bureau of Elections at $3,000 a year; stenographer in the Superior Court at $2,500 annually, and Examiner of Accounts at $3,500. *The Transcript* was the official newspaper of the City of New York. No journal fared so well in the matter of municipal advertising.

The sight of so much money coming in so fast and furious a stream turned Tweed's head. He began to grow arrogant. Until the early part of 1870, Tweed, in all his crooked dealings, played square with his fellow corruptionists. But now he began to forget, as thieves eventually do, the tradition that has it that honor must prevail among them. At a conference with Connolly the two agreed, at Tweed's suggestion, that they cut in half the proportionate shares of the loot which should go to the Elegant Oakey and Sweeny, and divide the shares of their two thieving partners between themselves. Accordingly the orders went out to Woodward and Watson, and from that time on Sweeny and Hall, when each received what they thought was twenty per cent of the loot, received but ten per cent.

The Elegant Oakey, whose share of the loot was always paid over to James Sweeny, a brother of Peter B. Sweeny, or to Hugh Smith, on at least one occasion protested to Tweed that he was not getting what he considered a fair division, and threatened to refuse to sign, as Mayor, any more bills until a reckoning was made. The Boss persuaded the Elegant One that he was in error. Sweeny never grumbled. He took what his brother James gave him—James did the collecting for brother Peter—and said thanks.

On the eve of the spring election, held on May 17, when a

new Board of Aldermen was to be chosen, the Citizens' Association, of which Peter Cooper was president, indorsed the Tweed ticket with: "A new state of things has been inaugurated. The Democratic leaders are pledged to good government and progress, and the Association has full confidence that these pledges will be kept. It was feared by many when the present session of the Legislature opened that our local government would not be improved; but happily these fears have not been realized. On the contrary, most satisfactory changes have been inaugurated, encouraging the hope of results most beneficial to the city."

The Boss may be pardoned, when, in the early Summer of 1870, he began to assume the grand manner in public. The city fawned upon him and his Ring. They were, to use the language of Tilden, "accepted as rulers of the Metropolis" who added: "The general public had acquiesced in the general disposition to try them again. The whole press assented. Nearly everybody began to make relations with them." Here and there an artful editor, with a foreboding of an explosion which would blast The Ring and reveal its frightful iniquity, was placing on the record—as Tilden himself had done—an innocuous attack on the powerful Ring which, if the occasion arose, could be distorted into the semblance of a courageous assault on Tweed.

Toward the end of the summer Taylor, one of the three directors of *The Times*, and Tweed's partner in the New York Printing Company, died. The Boss soon realized that he had lost a powerful friend, for within a few days of Taylor's passing, on September 20, *The Times* let loose its first editorial attack in its historic crusade. That editorial opened with: "We should like to have a treatise from Mr. Tweed in the art of growing rich in as many years as can be counted on the fingers of one hand. It would be instructive to young men, both as an example and a warning. . . . You begin with nothing and in five or six years you can boast of your ten millions. How is it done? We wish Mr. Tweed or Mr. Sweeny or some of their friends would tell us. The general public say there is foul play somewhere. They are under the impression that monstrous abuses of their funds, corrupt bargains with railroad sharpers, outrageous plots to swindle the general community, account for the vast fortunes heaped up by men who spring up like mushrooms."

And there was considerable more of the same mild sort in the two columns of type which bore the head: "The Democratic Millennium." Exactly thirteen days later the tone changes and there is talk of thievery, and of unnamed Republican leaders who made possible the thefts of The Ring. Another thirteen days and we find *The Times* on October 16th naming four Republican leaders, including "Mr. Nathaniel Sands, the Mr. Facing-Both-Ways of the day." This editorial struck at the very root of The Ring: "All the notoriously corrupt Republicans ought to have been kicked out of the party long ago. While Republicans in the rest of the State have been striving to do their duty, these Tammany hirelings have only been anxious to find an opportunity for betraying our camp into the hands of the enemy. If the system which had nurtured them had been abolished some time ago, this great City would not now be at the mercy of reckless plunderers, Governor Hoffman would not have been enabled to pack the Bench with dishonest judges, and Mr. James Fisk would not insult public decency every day at the expense of the Erie shareholders."

Nast now had more than an ally. He had a leader. Nast had erred in not making his cartoons less partisan. And Jones, in directing Jennings to attack the leaders of his own party without whose aid the thefts of Tweed and his gang could not have been perpetrated, not only lent additional strength to *The Times* editorials, but robbed Tweed of the opportunity of retorting that a disgruntled Republican editor was assailing him. As the days rolled by, the attacks increased in invective. Thieves, robbers, and plunderers were now being pinned on The Ring by the unfettered pen of the brilliant Englishman.

Tweed paid little heed to these attacks. What was one newspaper? It was a Republican sheet, and the crusade could be ascribed to its partisanship, and to Connolly's withholding of payment for advertising. It was at least a talking point. If it should get dangerous, it could be bought.

The Boss was more concerned in the State and municipal elections that were impending than in the cartoons of Nast or the editorials of Jennings. He renominated the Elegant Oakey for Mayor, and his man Hoffman for Governor. Hoffman's reëlection was as certain as Hall's. And Tweed left nothing undone to make the majorities of both such as would commend them to the Democrats of the State and Nation two years hence, when he planned to advance the Elegant Oakey to the Governorship, and Hoffman to the Presidency.

There was one line of attack adopted by *The Times* that Tweed decided to meet. This was the constant demand that Comptroller Connolly throw open the books of his department. If this were done the corruption of The Ring would at once be disclosed. Six of the leading men of the city were appointed a Committee of Investigation. John Jacob Astor was chairman of the Committee. Moses Taylor and Marshall O. Roberts, two other multi-millionaires, were also on the committee. The others were George K. Sistaire, Edward Schell, and E. D. Brown. Here were men, the citizens had every reason to believe, who could not be induced to aid any corrupt Ring. Their report was anxiously awaited by the people.

Toward the beginning of the last two weeks of the campaign Republican leaders, who were not in the pay of Tweed, believing that *The Times* had made such inroads as were likely to cause trouble upon The Ring with its daily attacks, appealed to President Grant to send Federal troops to protect the polls on Election Day. The President was told that Tweed controlled the Metropolitan Police and a majority of the Republican election inspectors. Under these conditions, it would be impossible to have a fair election if Tweed saw the count going against him. On October 25 the first of the troops were ordered to New York, the Eighth United States Infantry. These and other troops were concentrated in the forts in the harbor. Two warships, the U.S.S. *Guerriere* and the U.S.S. *Narragansett*, were anchored in the East and North Rivers. And orders were issued by President Grant to Major General Shaler, commanding the First Division, New York State National Guard, to hold himself in readiness to support the

United States Marshal and the regular forces "in the enforcement of the Election Laws . . . if the Marshal shall deem such aid necessary."

Tweed had had a canvass made of the city before the first of these orders was issued by President Grant, who no doubt looked upon New York as part of the unreconstructed South. The survey revealed that the Democrats would carry the city by at least three to two. Tweed's only task now was to prevent some of his followers from getting drunk on Election Day and destroying ballot boxes in Republican strongholds. And on October 27, when thousands of Democrats met outside their clubhouses in the teeming rain, all wearing red shirts out of tribute to Tweed's start in politics through *Americus Fire Engine Company No. 6*, they were handed torches and individually warned to go to the polls on November 8, vote, and then return to their homes. There must be no clash between citizens and troops.

The Mecca of all these Democrats who braved the rain on this particular Thursday night was Tammany Hall. Conservative estimates placed their number at 40,000. Every man of the marching thousands carried a lighted torch. Never before, and never since—save in a Presidential year—has any political demonstration approached this torchlight parade in magnitude. The caption of *The Herald* story read: "The Democratic Host—Fifty Thousand Torches and Red Shirted Democrats in Line." Former Governor Seymour was on the platform and made a speech. Fernando Wood was also there to talk. He, like Seymour, had been won back to the fold by Tweed. And The Boss, while the enthusiastic throng was filing into the hall, sat beaming over all, flanked on one side by August Belmont, and on the other by James Fisk, Jr. The Prince of Erie's presence on the platform was an occasion of general comment, for his stanch Republicanism was common knowledge. Every one in the audience knew his jovial countenance.

When Tweed rose from his seat beside Fisk, the audience cheered their idol, continuing their frenzied demonstration long after he had extended his hand for silence. He said:

"Democrats and fellow citizens: I need not say that we are pleased to see so many of you here to-night, who think with us that the time has at length arrived when the great City of New York must put forth all her energies and all the vitality of her system to overthrow the despotic sway under which we have groaned for eleven years. (Applause.) We feel the time has arrived, by the scenes in the streets, and by what we read in the telegraphic reports from day to day, and in which the great City of New York is sought to be disfranchised, the popular voice not respected, and all power exerted to subject her to the immense power of the Federal government.

"Those who were born here upon the soil, and those who have sworn allegiance to the country, feel that to be respected we must unite in every part, and with one accord denounce and frown down all attempts at mob violence, or anything which shall have a tendency to intimidate those who are entitled to vote, and against any endeavor to prevent access to or egress from the polls upon Election Day. (Cheers.) We know our rights, we know our power, and we have over ourselves entire control, and hope that no act of violence will mar that day. (Applause.)

"We know and feel that although an aggressive hand is upon us, yet we must, by a judicious exercise of law and order, which is our only protection, show that it is a law-abiding, and as all the world knows, a well governed city. (Great applause.)"

Before he sat down, Tweed placed the name of August Belmont in nomination for chairman of the meeting. The old custom of letting the people choose the chairman had not yet passed out. Every one in the room seconded the motion. Then The Boss surrendered the gavel to Belmont.

Scattered among the audience, Tweed had placed claques which started a demonstration for the Prince of Erie. Their continued demands for a speech from the Republican financier were heeded.

Fisk proved himself no mean mob orator. His speech was far from brief. He began by saying that he knew every Democratic leader, mentioning "my friend Mr. Tweed, and my friend Mr. Sweeny." The audience cheered him frantically when he announced that henceforward, he would abjure the doctrines of the Republican Party and embrace the faith of

Tweed and Sweeny, and, more than that, he would see that every one of the 25,000 men working under him on the Erie Railroad voted the Democratic ticket.

Up and down the platform paced Fisk, as his tongue grew more and more unrestrained under the intoxicating effects of public applause. After professing his new-found political faith, Fisk said:

"And I will be most happy—if you don't think it will tamper with your morals—if you will come up to the Opera House, one by one, and inform me what the duty of a good faithful Democrat is (Voice: 'Give us free tickets and we will.' Great laughter and applause.)"

Some of the Republican papers carried portions of Fisk's speech, but none this reference to President Grant and some of the members of his official family and the disastrous Black Friday of the preceding year:

"A great deal has been said and written regarding transactions between myself and the Executive Magistrate of this country. Perhaps he was all right, and I all wrong. I am certain of one thing: that the Republican Party and many of the heads of departments were perfectly willing to join us [Fisk and Gould] in speculations. . . . They misled me; but only through my misplaced confidence in them. . . . I went forth to do my business with the Chief Magistrate or with his officials, as with other business men. . . . I had no confidence in those Republicans going speculating in Wall Street, and I don't want any more of that. . . ."

Fisk, now athirst for the plaudits of his intensely sympathetic audience, won his next laugh with his prophetic: "So far I have had no political aspirations. I am something like Horace Greeley, and if I am ever elected at all, I shall be elected to stay at home."

The Democratic papers properly called this meeting a great rally. Meanwhile *The Times* continued demanding that Comptroller Connolly make public a statement of the city's finances. On November 7—the day before Election—the results of the investigation of the city's financial condition by the Committee headed by Astor were published in the newspapers. This report was the most perfect piece of whitewashing conceivable. These six men, all heavy taxpayers—The Ring could have made them pay heavily in increased assessments if Tweed so willed it—certified that they had examined the condition of the finance department of the city, that the office was thrown open to them, and that they had inspected the account books, securities, and other records, including the data relating to the sinking fund, and gave it as their opinion that the entire debt of the city would be liquidated within twelve years if the policies of Connolly were continued. And just over their honorable names appeared:

"And we further certify the account books of the department are faithfully kept, that we have personally examined the securities of the department and sinking fund and found them correct. We have come to the conclusion and certify that the financial affairs of the city under the charge of the Comptroller are administered in a correct and faithful manner."

The slightest examination of the records would have disclosed the payment of more than $15,000,000 in fraudulent claims in the first few months of the year.

The Astor Whitewashing Committee could also have found that Watson, the County Auditor, had so little fear of detection, he made out one voucher for $66,000 to a fictitious character with the weirdly exotic name of Phillippo Donnoruma, and that the droll fellow who received the check Anglicized the name to Philip Dummy. Another wholly imaginative creditor was T. C. Cash. He was paid $64,000. They would have found had they looked, a check for $35,000 which the plunderer to whom it had been made out had raised to $135,000. These were but a few of the lesser crimes which Astor and his Committee could have found had they been only half-honest with the city.

There was no violence at the polls. Hoffman was reëlected Governor, and the Elegant Oakey was again chosen Mayor. Hall's opponent was Thomas A. Ledwith, a Police Court Justice, who not only received the Republican vote, but the support of the Young Democracy. Ledwith's vote was 46,392.

The Elegant Oakey polled 71,037, a majority of 24,645. The vote for Governor in the city was: General Stewart L. Woodford, 34,472; Hoffman, 86,561, a majority for Tweed's candidate of 52,089. It required no expert analysis of the returns to reveal that a reaction against The Ring had set in. Hoffman's majority exceeded Hall's by more than 15,000.

After the victory of November 8 nothing was too good for Tweed, in the eyes of Judge Shandley, whose inventive mind was charged with devising means of keeping The Boss constantly before the public in the most favorable light. Shandley suddenly thought of a novel idea. He submitted it to Tweed's friends high in public office, from the Elegant Oakey down. The result was the organization of the "Testimonial Association of the City of New York." Shandley was president, and Bernard Smythe, Receiver of Taxes, treasurer. Mayor Hall was chairman of the Board of Trustees. Sweeny, and Connolly, of course, were on the Board. In December, these worshipers of Tweed announced their intention to erect a statue to The Boss. This was done through a circular, elaborately engraved by the American Bank Note Company, reading in part:

"The association has for its object the erection of a statue of Senator, The Honorable William M. Tweed, in consideration of his services to the Commonwealth of New York. If the project meets your approbation, be pleased to contribute to the fund established for its accomplishment.

"Subscriptions should be forwarded to Bernard Smythe, Receiver of Taxes, office 32 Chambers Street. Acknowledgment will be made through the medium of the press and by a receipt signed by the President and Treasurer."

The attacks of *The Times* had roused some of the newspapers to a sense of their duty to the public. *The Tribune*, whose managing editor was Whitelaw Reid, was the first to join the procession. Then *The Evening Post*, where Charles Nordhoff held a like position, followed the trail that Nast had opened. Nordhoff assailed the proposal to erect a statue to

The Boss. But no more effectively than obscure Thomas
McCue, who lived among the poor of the lower West Side at
82 Carmine Street. McCue sent nine cents to *The Sun* with the
following letter:

"Inclosed you will find 9 cents, my contribution toward the erection of a statue of Honorable W. M. Tweed. I send this for the
purpose of showing my appreciation of the man who for the last
ten years has defrauded the public, more especially the poor man,
out of millions of dollars, so that his image may always remain to
the public gaze for generations to come. I want to show the man
who has increased our taxation, and deprived the poor man of his
hard earnings. Then their children may point their fingers and say
it was he who drove my father to destruction by the enormous rents
we had to pay."

This was one of the few occasions when Charles A. Dana's
journal displayed any antagonism toward Tweed during the
early months of the crusade of *The Times*.

After the letter of McCue was printed, Tweed gave $1,000
to each of the fifteen members of the Board of Aldermen, Republicans and Democrats alike, to purchase coal for the poor
of their wards. Judge Shandley, although still active in raising funds for a statue to Tweed, started a subscription to
provide Christmas dinners for the needy, and to supply them
with food during the Winter. Shandley took the list to Tweed.
The Boss signed his name and opposite put down—$5,000.
"Can't you make it more?" asked Shandley. The Boss added
another cipher to his contribution, making it $50,000.

Tweed's henchmen on the newspapers wrote maudlin praise
of The Boss's generosity. And four days after Christmas,
this editorial by Jennings, headed: "Some Stolen Property
Returned," appeared:

"The other day, Mr. Tweed devoted to the 'relief of the poor'
$50,000, out of the $75,000 which he and Sweeny robbed the
public of by means of a single day's *Transcript*. When a man
can plunder the public at the rate of $75,000 or $80,000 a day, it
does not cost him much of an effort to give a few odd thousand
dollars to the 'poor'. Who, in fact, have done so much as Tweed

and his cronies to make people poor? Who has worked so systematically to reduce many a hard working family to poverty? Having created their destitution, the Tweed Gang now contemptuously fling a bone to them to stop their mouths. . . .

"The proposal to raise a statue to Mr. Tweed is simply part of the Christmas mummeries which The Ring have been carrying on for a week or two past. . . .

"Let us if possible have one of Sweeny to match it, and let them both be flanked by effigies of Moses Taylor and John Jacob Astor. It will be a very appropriate gallery of worthies, a collection of New York's greatest men—and the public will doubtless gaze upon it with affectionate admiration. . . .

"If you ask why it is that so many people 'stick up' for Tweed and his Gang, you have your answer in what is now going on. These rascals know that they must share their plunder if they would be kept in their present positions. . . . By way of cajoling the 'working classes' they distribute among them a part of their superfluous riches. Few pause to ask where this money originally came from, or how many have been made poorer in order that it might be raised. Bought newspapers cry out 'how generous'. . . .

"We live in an age—or at least a community—which takes men like Tweed and Sweeny, and Connolly and Sands, and Moses Taylor and John Jacob Astor, and James Fisk, Jr., to be types of all that is noble and admirable in our species. It is therefore eminently proper that we should have a statue of Tweed at every street corner. No doubt Washington was removed from City Hall Park to make room for Tweed—a change which affords a vivid illustration of the two periods in our history represented by the two men. . . . "

Stories were now buzzing round that Jennings had been discharged from the London *Times* for untruthful writing and unnamed offenses. This indictment of Jennings was as untrue as the accusation circulated by Tweed's whisper squads against Nast. Of him it was said that he had fled from Germany to escape military service. Nast was a child of six when he landed in New York.

One of the practices of corrupt politics is to destroy the reputations of those who stand between public plunderers and their loot. Sometimes money is the medium used. More often the purpose is accomplished with the expenditure of little more than breath.

CHAPTER XXVIII

THE double inaugurations of New Year's Day, 1871 over—
Hall was again sworn in as Mayor, and Hoffman as Governor
—Tweed began to move fast to silence *The Times*, by purchase,
or otherwise. Those daily tirades from the tireless pen of
Jennings, while they could not affect Tweed's hold on the party
locally, would affect his standing with the Democrats of
the Nation. That would spell defeat of his plan to make Hoffman President. If Taylor were only alive! The very fact
that he and the deceased director of *The Times* were partners
in his corrupt printing company would, in itself, have forced
Jones and Jennings to think twice before attacking him. They
had no proofs of his guilt, or that of any of the other members
of The Ring. They just suspected that he, and Hall, and
Sweeny, and Connolly were corrupt, and let drive at them. It
was one thing to call a man a thief, but it was something else
again to prove him one. No evidence of his corruption could be
obtained without access to the books of the Comptroller's office.
And only one man ever saw those books besides Connolly. This
was Jimmy Watson, the County Auditor. And Jimmy was a
sharp lad. How he must work, looking after most of the accounts himself! He trusted nobody else. But then, he was
well paid for it. A small-salaried clerk who lived in a mansion
and had his own stable adjoining.

The Winter of 1871 was a good season for sleighing. From
New Year's Day on, Watson was out in a speedy cutter on the
roads in Yorkville and Harlem. There was less traffic there,
and there were few ruts in the roads. On Tuesday evening,
January 24, after dining with his wife and two children at their
splendid home on the northeast corner of Forty-second Street
and Madison Avenue, Watson, heavily muffled in furs, climbed

351

into a sleigh at the curb, took the reins from his coachman, and in a second the high-spirited team was speeding up Fifth Avenue. North for a good six miles. Then a split of champagne at Berthold's. And back in the bracing night air.

As they started back, Watson let his coachman take the reins. He had observed in driving that the road was rough. In places there were deep ruts from the runners of sleighs. It was better that Townsend drive. He was always careful. They had not gone far when Watson heard Townsend shouting. He was tugging for very life on the right rein. A horse leaping on them? It must be a horrible dream. Then all became dark.

Later Townsend told how he was driving slowly down Eighth Avenue, well over on the right side of the road. When they reached One Hundred Thirtieth Street, a horse, attached to a sleigh coming toward them, suddenly turned out of the proper track, dashed across the road, in between Watson's horses, breaking the neck yoke, knocking down the off horse, and rearing over the dashboard, came down with one hoof on Watson's forehead. The other hoof knocked Townsend out of the sleigh. Townsend had tried to turn west into One Hundred Thirtieth Street, but a deep rut in the road rendered his efforts futile.

Watson was unconscious but a few seconds. Townsend, as he lay in the snow, dazed, heard him calling. The coachman helped his master out of the sleigh, and at his order, assisted him back to Berthold's road house. There a police surgeon bandaged Watson's torn forehead.

Two days later Tweed heard that Watson was in bad shape. He hurried from Albany. When he learned how serious Watson's condition was, The Boss placed trusted men inside the house, day and night, to prevent any of his enemies from visiting the dying man. There must be no deathbed confession heard by unfriendly ears. A week after the accident Watson died. The daily papers said that he left his family well-provided for, some accounting for his wealth by saying that he had been fortunate in Wall Street. Others hazarded no explanation.

There was a strong streak of superstition in Tweed. Taylor died in September and immediately *The Times* began its attacks upon him. Now Watson was dead. They must get hold of *The Times*. That might undo the effect of Taylor's death. Even with Watson lying dead Jennings continued his attacks.

Tweed, however, could turn to *The Sun* for consolation. The week of Watson's end, one of Dana's editorial writers made a counter-attack on Jennings. "The decline of the *New York Times* in everything that entitles a paper to respect and confidence has been rapid and complete. Its present editor, who was dismissed from the London *Times* for improper conduct and untruthful writing, has sunk into a tedious monotony of slander, disregard of truth, and blackguard vituperation. Poor Mr. Jones and the other proprietors should understand that while the public admires a fearless, independent, truthful, and candid journal, such as *The Sun* is, they are bored and repelled by mere ill-nature and tiresome repetition of venomous slander."

This would wake up Jones! This is what the respectable *Sun* thought of the attacks upon Tweed. Slander! Disregard of truth! Blackguard vituperation! And the remedy? *The Sun* had it: "Let *The Times* change its course, send off Jennings, and get some gentleman and scholar in his place, and become again an able and high-toned paper. Thus it may escape from ruin. Otherwise it is doomed."

It was out at last. Jennings was not a gentleman. He was not a member of any of the select clubs in New York or London. Not having a title, he should have come over here as an M.P., rather than return to get this honor. Louis John Jennings, late M.P., would instantly have been recognized as one of the ruling class. Then, with propriety, he could have attacked Astor, Tweed, or anybody else.

Jones, as he and Jennings carried on the fight, could not help wondering what had come over the fire-eating Greeley. He and Raymond had worked beside the old man in the beginning of *The Tribune*, and before *The Times* was even thought of in their youthful imaginations. What was keeping him so meek now, when he had an opportunity of hurling his favorite epithets at the most villainous gang that ruled a city? Money? No. Political ambition? That could account for stranger things.

Connolly named Stephen C. Lyons, Jr., to succeed Watson. Lyons had been County Bookkeeper. Another in whom Connolly placed his faith was Matthew J. O'Rourke. To him was given Lyons' place. O'Rourke had been military news editor on one of the newspapers, and came well recommended. There was nothing to be feared from O'Rourke. About the time these changes were made, O'Brien, whose term as Sheriff had ended some five weeks before, called on Connolly and asked that a friend of his, one William Copeland, be given a job. The erstwhile leader of the Young Democracy had returned to the fold. He was one of the Board of Trustees of the association that was raising funds for the erection of a statue to Tweed. So Copeland was placed in charge of a set of books.

There was considerable criticism of the proposal to raise an enduring bronze of The Boss, who put an end to the undertaking on March 13, when he wrote: "Statues are not erected to living men, but to those who have ended their careers, and where no interest exists to question the partial tributes of friends." The following day Judge Shandley said that for some time it had been the thought of the sponsors of the statue project to abandon it and erect "a grand charitable institution, bearing Mr. Tweed's honorable name" . . . to pass on to future generations "the fame of that statesman, philanthropist and patriot."

The town was now agog with the tale that Tweed, aided by Peter Cooper, Moses Taylor, Fisk, Gould, Cyrus W. Field, and the Elegant Oakey had about completed the final arrangements for taking over *The Times*. Sweeny, it was reported had acted as the agent of the group in its dealings with Jones. On March 28 Jones made a public denial of ever having offered to dispose of his holdings in *The Times* to Sweeny or anybody connected with him.

"I am aware," continued Jones, "that Mr. Nathaniel Sands, Secretary of the Citizens' Association, has been for some time actively engaged in the effort to purchase or otherwise silence this journal in the interest of his Tammany employers. But believing that the course which *The Times* is pursuing is that which the interests of the great body of the public demand, and that it would be a base betrayal of the public to turn aside from that course until an honest government and an incorruptible judiciary are restored to the community, no money that could be offered should induce me to dispose of a single share of my property to the Tammany faction, or to any man associated with it, or indeed, to any person or party whatever, until this struggle is fought out. I have the same confidence in the integrity and firmness of my fellow proprietors, and believe that they will decline to sell their honor to a corrupt clique at the instigation of 'Republicans' who are as unprincipled as their employers.

"Rather than prove false to the public in the present crisis, I would, if necessity by any possibility arose, immediately start another journal to denounce those frauds upon the people which are so great a scandal to the city, and I should carry with me in this renewal of our present labors the colleagues who have already stood by me through a long and arduous contest."

It was a long and arduous contest. One cannot but marvel at Jones' zeal. Tweed was scoring heavily against him. Jones' most stalwart ally, Charles Nordhoff, lost his job as managing editor of *The Evening Post*, for his attacks on The Boss. Nordhoff was not discharged outright. Those things are never done that way. He was given a long vacation with pay with the understanding that he was to find another place in the meantime. William Cullen Bryant was owner and publisher of the paper. The poet was then in his seventy-sixth year. Attempts have been made to shoulder on Isaac Henderson all the odium involved in the disgraceful treatment of Nordhoff. Henderson had an unsavory reputation, known to Bryant, as far back as 1865. In July of that year, Parke Godwin, who owned one-third interest in *The Post*, addressed the poet a letter reviewing certain war contract scandals of which Henderson was the center. Part of Godwin's letter reads:

"Admitting him [Henderson], however, to be wholly innocent, his position before the public has become such that it is
a source of the most serious mortification and embarrassment
to the conductors of *The Evening Post*. We cannot brand a
defaulter, condemn peculation, urge official economy, or get
into any sort of controversy with other journals, without having the charges against Henderson, which nine-tenths of the
public believe to be true, flung in our faces. Not once, but
two dozen times, I have been shut up by a rejoinder of this sort.

"Mr. Nordhoff has felt this, in his private intercourse as
well as in a public way, to such an extent that he has told me
peremptorily and positively that he would not continue in the
paper if Mr. Henderson retained an active part in connection
with it. Now it seems to me that if there were any feeling of
delicacy in Mr. Henderson, any regard for the sensitiveness
of others, any care for the reputation and independence of the
paper, he would be willing to relieve us of this most injurious
and unpleasant predicament.

"I will add that I am not satisfied with his management of
our business affairs; he gives them very little of his attention,
though he pretends to do so; he is largely and constantly engaged in outside speculations, in grain, provisions, etc.; and
in one instance, as our books show, he has given himself a
fictitious credit of $7,000 which was irregular."

Here we have a picture of Nordhoff as well as Henderson.
We have also here a cross-cut view, ugly, but true, of the
journalism of the day, for Henderson was left in his place of
trust where he proved of service to the cause of corruption
in 1871.

With the honest Nordhoff out of the way, *The Evening Post*
rushed to the defense of Tweed, Sweeny, Hall, and Connolly,
ingeniously explaining that Connolly could not show the books
of the finance department because the Aldermen alone possessed that power, and implied that *The Times* and *Harper's
Weekly* were actuated by dishonest motives in their attacks on
Tweed.

Jones and Jennings found solace in the soft-pedalled support
they received from Greeley. He was keeping the faith, but in

his own erratic way. If the making of a huge woodcut cartoon were not so tedious a process, and *Harper's Weekly* could but come out daily! Jones could not quite understand this change in Greeley. He knew him when both had the fire of youth in their hearts. He had spurned an offer to become his partner, accepting instead, the business managership of *The Tribune.* Anyway, he was confident Greeley could not be suppressed like Bryant. Better an editor-politician than a poet-editor.

When Tweed and his Ring learned that *The Times* could not be bought, they caused to be passed through the Legislature a bill which Governor Hoffman signed. This most infamous measure gave to the local Appellate Division of the Supreme Court—two of the three, Barnard and Albert Cardozo, were owned body and soul by Tweed—the power to adjudge any critic of Tweed or his Ring in contempt of court and to send him to jail. The measure was not worded that baldly, but that was its effect.

When this bill was introduced, we find Tilden becoming his old self again, and dashing madly to Albany to protest against passage of the measure.

The legislative session of 1871 was short, as sessions in New York State go. The adjournment *sine die* was April 21. Two weeks before this date, Jimmy Irving, one of Tweed's Assemblymen from New York, made a wanton and unprovoked assault on Smith M. Weed, a Republican member from Clinton County. Part of the attack occurred in front of the Speaker's rostrum, in full view of the House. Tweed's Speaker, Billy Hitchman, was presiding. Weed took refuge in the Clerk's Room. Irving, a typical plug-ugly, followed Weed and struck him under the eye, opening the cheek to the bone. Weed, a lawyer was physically Irving's inferior in height and weight, as well as in years. The blow knocked Weed down. In falling, his head struck against a door jamb, inflicting another ugly wound. Irving, who was probably drunk, attempted to visit more punishment on his victim, but was restrained by other members.

The Assembly this year consisted of sixty-five Democrats and sixty-three Republicans. Although this was a numerical majority of two, in practice, it was a bare constitutional majority, as sixty-five votes were required to pass any measure.

The entire House was incensed at Irving's conduct. There were unscrupulous fellows in the body, but they had their own sense of fairness. Alexander Frear, Tweed's spokesman on the floor, told The Boss of what had happened. Tweed ordered Irving's resignation. Irving resigned the next day. Three days later, before any formal action was taken on this, a Committee of Investigation reported to the Assembly that "had Mr. Irving remained a member of this House, he would have deserved the severest punishment in its power to submit."

This report, which recognized the resignation of Irving, was unanimously adopted.

From New York City there came the thunders of Horace Greeley to the Republicans to refuse to pass the Tax Levy bill and four or five other New York City measures sorely needed by The Ring. The Republicans solemnly covenanted in caucus to oppose all these measures.

In the emergency Tweed did what we would expect of him. He bought a Republican Assemblyman to replace Irving. The price was $100,000. The Republican who fell for this temptation was Orange S. Winans, of Dunkirk, Chautauqua County. When he first voted with the Democrats there were cries of "Traitor!" "Sold out!" "Shame!" and the like from the Republican seats.

This was Saturday, April 15. On the following Monday, on the editorial page of *The Tribune* appeared:

"For Sale or To Let for Business Purposes—a Member of Assembly. Rent, for the season, $100,000, or will be sold cheap for cash. Possession as soon as the Tax Levy and Election Bills are passed, the present lessee having no further use for the property. Inquire of William M. Tweed, Albany, or O. S. Winans, on the premises."

Winans' father-in-law prevailed upon his daughter to leave Winans. His neighbors ostracized him. He fled from his desolate home. What happened to him is apocryphal. One account had him a drunkard in a Western State, and another that he had committed suicide.

When the session ended, Tweed began to think of other things. There was *The Times*. It kept pounding away at him. Jennings and Jones daily branded him a thief. A young man was coming up from the South to marry one of his daughters. The Boss did not want him to see these editorials of Jennings.

Tweed had no fears for himself. On April 6 his enemies had held a meeting in Cooper Union and had enlisted the services of Henry Ward Beecher. Several bigwigs spoke there. And what had they accomplished? Stories the next day in the newspapers and then a little talk for a few days, and thereafter silence.

On May 31, Tweed's daughter, Mary Amelia, was married in Trinity Chapel on West Twenty-fifth Street, off Broadway. The ceremony was solemnized by Dr. Price, now stooped and gray, the same gentle servant of Christ whom Tweed first met when he took Mary Jane Skaden to the altar where Price ministered.

The lavish wedding presents! They pleased Tweed, and yet they caused him great pain when *The Herald*—generally with him whole-heartedly, but at times taking a fling that was intended to be harmless—published the entire list of gifts and commented editorially on them. Tweed had given her $25,000. His friends had sent her forty silver sets, and diamonds such as queens might envy. True, they were, in all, worth $700,000, but why need Bennett say so in the way he did? But then he had to say something occasionally.

"The wedding presents, displayed in a grand show-room, were glorious to behold. They represented in cash seven hundred thousand dollars—a display of wedding presents unsurpassed by the collection of the celebrated Oviedo diamond wedding, or of any occasion of the kind, we dare say, since the marriage, two or three years ago, of a daughter of the Khedive of Egypt, and completely eclipsing the jewelry presents to the British Princess Louise, on the occasion of her union with the heir of the great Scottish Duke of Argyll. Seven hundred thousand dollars!"

And the day after the wedding Tweed made out a check for his son—Richard M. Tweed—for $7,500. This sum represented the rent of the largest hotel in the city, the Metropolitan, Broadway near Prince Street. Tweed had spent more than half a million dollars in overhauling the place. So far it was all outgo.

Independence Day in New York City would not be complete without a celebration in Tammany Hall. There was the usual packed auditorium, and the Grand Sachem, following tradition, presided. But the address of Tweed on this occasion lacked the note of victory that is inseparable from the day. The Boss spoke extemporaneously. There was an undertone of gloom in his brief speech, which we reproduce:

"FRIENDS AND BRETHREN: In accordance with our time-honored custom, the Tammany Society has assembled here to-day for the purpose of keeping alive the patriotic fires which caused the organization of the institution. We are gratified to see so many of our fellow citizens among us—gratified to find that the interest the Tammany Society has striven to protect, to advance, and to organize, meets the approbation of so many.

"In these great and perilous times, standpoints must be taken. The Tammany Society proposes to be governed by those rules which have made powerful all countries that have followed them.

"We propose that the interests of one shall be the interests of all. We propose to carry on a strictly economical government, and to wrest if possible, the National Government from the hands of those who now, in our opinion, are betraying it, and trying to crush out all principles of equality, liberty, and toleration. (Applause). We propose to recognize the right of the governed to choose who shall be their governors. We propose to let the issues of the past die; to strike forward into a bright and noble career (applause); to once more place the Federal Government in the hands of those who have always conducted it in a manner satisfactory to the country. From the formation of the government, except for a brief time, the Democratic Party has been in the ascendency, and while in the ascendency what was the result? Commerce thrived, shipyards were filled with workingmen. Our ships, built by Americans, covered the ocean. Our manufacturing interests were protected. It is not necessary to occupy your attention longer, except to say that the present condition of those interests is the result of the action of those who now govern us. Commerce is paralyzed. Where before the ocean was studded with ships of American building, sailed by American captains, owned by American owners, and manned by American crews, what now does the register show? No increase, none whatever, but a falling off, a great diminution! We propose to take the government from those who now hold it, and to go forward as we did before, steadily advancing, steadily promoting, steadily increasing the welfare and prosperity of all. (Applause.)"

This was the speech of a weary man who had a foreboding of impending disaster.

On the day that Tweed's daughter was married, Matthew O'Rourke, who had succeeded Lyons as County Bookkeeper when the latter was promoted to County Auditor following Watson's death, resigned from the city employ. For little more than a month, O'Rourke vainly went from one newspaper to another with his package of dynamite under his arm. These documents were far from conclusive, and they represented only a fraction of The Ring's stealing. But they were proofs of guilt.

Copeland, for whom O'Brien had obtained a job in Connolly's office, had also made copies from the books disclosing most of the frauds of The Ring. These were placed in the possession of his master, former Sheriff O'Brien, who, it was testified, offered them to The Ring for an unnamed price. O'Rourke gave this testimony. All that O'Brien demanded was the payment of $350,000 which he claimed the county owed him. What was $350,000 out of the treasury to Tweed? O'Brien was far from an exemplary type. The records tell an ugly story of this lieutenant of Tilden. O'Rourke unquestion-

ably believed what he related under oath, but he was the victim
of guileful men.

One night, in the first week of July, O'Brien called at the
office of *The Sun*. He had Copeland's transcripts of the
books of the finance department revealing the corruption of
Tweed and The Ring. He told an editor what he had. His
proofs of The Ring's corruption were declined. The explanation since made is that Dana was not there. O'Brien then
visited the office of *The Times*, opened the door of Jennings'
office, and observed that it was a warm evening.

"Yes, hot," replied Jennings.

"You and Nast have had a hard fight."

"Have still."

"I said you have had it," repeated O'Brien, as he laid a
mass of papers on Jennings' desk. "Here are the proofs of
all your charges—exact transcriptions from Dick Connolly's
books. The boys will likely murder you when they know
you've got 'em, just as they've tried to murder me."

Two days or so later O'Rourke came to *The Times*. He
showed his documents to Jennings. O'Rourke's evidence disclosed that ten old stables, rented by The Ring for a pittance,
had been sublet to the county as armories at an annual rental of
$85,000, and that, although they had never been used by troops,
the county had paid out $436,064 for alleged repairs. Then
there were other fraudulent repair charges totaling $941,453.86
for ten armories that were in use. Here were figures tending
to prove the theft of nearly $1,500,000 from the taxpayers.
But this was only a small part of the armory frauds. In the
thirty months The Ring had been in existence, $2,940,473.70
had been paid out on account of armories. Less than ten per
cent of this was a fair charge.

The actions of O'Rourke, closely patterning those of O'Brien,
in first offering the proofs of corruption to other newspapers
than *The Times*, reveal the cold, calculating, political genius of
Tilden. O'Rourke, as we know, was a newspaperman. Had
he followed his natural instincts, he would have gone immediately
to Jones. The fearless editor of *The Times* had staked his
reputation and his property in making the accusations that

were daily published in his paper. As yet he had not a scintilla
of evidence of wrong-doing. He was out on a limb. O'Rourke
and O'Brien were the only men who could save the situation
for him. Tilden could have had the proofs of guilt published
in *The World*. That would not have served his purpose, as it
was widely known that Manton Marble, owner of this paper,
was Tilden's inseparable companion. We are familiar with
Tilden's motives in wishing to destroy Tweed without his own
identity being disclosed. And his object in preferring the
publication of the charges in a Democratic journal, or in a
paper less prominently associated with the Republican Party
than *The Times*, is apparent.

Tweed soon learned that *The Times* had proofs of his guilt
in its possession. Comptroller Connolly, then worth $6,000,-
000, was appointed an emissary to deal with Jones. Every
man has his price. What transpired between Connolly and
Jones is thus descibed by a writer in *Harper's Weekly*:

"A tenant in the same building (the Times building) sent for
Mr. Jones to come to his office, as he wished to see him on an important matter. Mr. Jones wènt to the lawyer's office, and, being
ushered into a private room, was confronted by Comptroller
Connolly.

" 'I don't want to see this man,' said Mr. Jones, and he turned
to go.

" 'For God's sake!' exclaimed Connolly, 'let me say one word
to you.'

"At this appeal Mr. Jones stopped. Connolly then made him
a proposition to forego the publication of the documents he had
in his possession and offered him the enormous sum of five million
dollars to do this. As Connolly waited for the answer, Mr. Jones
said:

" 'I don't think the devil will ever make a higher bid for me
than that.'

"Connolly began to plead, and drew a graphic picture of what
one could do with five million dollars. He ended by saying:

" 'Why, with that sum you could go to Europe and live like
a prince.'

" 'Yes,' said Mr. Jones, 'but I should know that I was a rascal.

I cannot consider your offer or any offer not to publish the facts in my possession.' "

Two attempts were made to bribe Nast at this time. A lawyer of his acquaintance made the first offer. Nast had considerable talent as a painter. He was informed that some unnamed rich men wanted to send him abroad to study under European masters. Nast politely ended the conversation. The following Sunday the bribe assumed a definite form. An officer of the Broadway Bank, the chief depository of The Ring, visited the cartoonist at his home and said that he had heard Nast had been made an offer to go abroad for art study.

"Yes, but I can't go," replied Nast. "I haven't time."

"They will pay you for your time. I have reason to believe you could get one hundred thousand dollars for the trip."

"Do you think I could get two hundred thousand?"

"Well, possibly, I believe from what I hear in the bank that you might get it. You have great talent. You need study and you need rest. Besides, this Ring business will get you into trouble. They own all the judges and jurors and can get you locked up for libel. My advice is to take the money and get away."

"Don't you think I could get five hundred thousand dollars to make that trip?"

"You can. You can get five hundred thousand dollars in gold to drop this Ring business and get out of the country."

"Well, I don't think I'll do it," laughed Nast. "I made up my mind long ago to put some of those fellows behind the bars, and I'm going to put them there."

"Only be careful, Mr. Nast," said the banker on leaving, "that you do not first put yourself into a coffin."

On July 8, *The Times* began the publication of transcripts from Connolly's books. First appeared the armory frauds which O'Rourke had copied, and then the equally madly extravagant prices for furnishings and labor for the new court house from January 1, 1869. Andrew J. Garvey, plasterer for The Ring, was paid $138,187 for two days' work. Garvey, who was called The Prince of Plasterers by *The Times*, had a total bill of $2,870,464.06, which had been paid. Jennings, satirizing the shouted charity of The Ring, suggested Garvey give the odd six cents to the poor. To Tweed's New York Printing Company a single item of stationery netted $186,-495.61. Thermometers for the Court House were charged at $7,500. Three tables and forty chairs cost the taxpayers $179,729.60. The firm which supplied this, James H. Ingersoll and Company, whose head was a chairmaker, and a boyhood friend of Tweed's father, received a total of $5,691,144.26 for furniture for this temple of justice. The Ring carpenter, George S. Miller, was paid $360,747.61 for one month's work. Lumber worth $48,000 cost the taxpayers $460,000. John H. Keyser received $1,149,874.50 for repairing plumbing and gas light fixtures in the Court House. His total charges aggregated nearly $3,000,000. All save one of these swindlers were unknown to the people at large. Keyser, The Ring's plumber, was noted for his philanthropy. He was a trustee or director in several charitable organizations.

After nearly two weeks of daily publication of the proofs of these monstrous frauds, with names, dates, and amounts, the apathy of the press is best illustrated by the zeal, one moment hot, the next cold, of Greeley. On July 22 speaking of *The Times* exposé, *The Tribune* said:

"We do not indorse it neither do we discredit it. We are not in possession of facts that would warrant us in making such charges. If it be justified by facts Messrs. Hall and Connolly ought now to be cutting stone in a state prison. *The Times* deserves the thanks of the community."

Two days later, *The World* called attention editorially to the refusal of Connolly to pay an advertising bill to *The Times* back in 1868, suggesting that this accounted for the attack on The Ring.

Another forty hours passed and Greeley shouted:

"Mr. Connolly! Will you use your great official power to recover for the people of New York the millions whereof they have somehow been defrauded since you were chosen and paid by them to watch the door of their treasury? Do not excuse yourself—but try!"

Greeley's conscience was being aroused. *The Post* was also feebly reëchoing the hue and cry raised by Jennings and Jones. Bryant's journal had left the ranks of the unrepentant Magdalens of the press a few days before *The Times* began publishing the proofs of corruption. Greeley inquired pertinently of the respectable merchant, Smith Ely, Jr., one of Tweed's Democratic associates on the bi-partisan Board of Supervisors, to tell what he knew of the exorbitant bills or claims passed while he was a member of it. For nearly ten years had the respectable Smith Ely, Jr., been Supervisor by grace of Tweed.

On July 29, *The Times* exhausted the damning documents provided by O'Brien and O'Rourke. The entire series of articles were published in a special supplement, in English and German, for many citizens of German birth read only their native tongue.

The day before the last of these articles appeared the infamy of the controlled newspapers was typified by an editorial in *The World* accusing *The Times* of "a reckless attempt to shake and undermine the city credit, block the wheels of municipal machinery, and introduce a reign of anarchy."

It mattered little now what Tweed's newspaper supporters printed, for the people had ceased to believe them, and it required no canvass to reveal that The Ring had lost considerable popular support. Part of the lost ground was due to the cowardly order of Mayor Hall directing James Kelso, Superintendent of Police to forbid the Orangemen's Parade on July 12. This order was issued after formal permission had been given by the police to several Orange Lodges to parade. Here we see the Elegant Oakey, one-time member of the Know-Nothings, pandering to the prejudices of an ignorant minority of this same group which he had sworn to hate. In Jersey City and other communities in the Metropolitan area where the Roman Catholics of Irish origin were as numerically strong as in New York, the Orangemen paraded on the anniversary of the Battle of the Boyne without molestation. Only in New York were threats of mob violence made when it became known that the minor-minority of Protestant Irish would march to the strains of "Croppies Lie Down." An Orange Lodge in a republic is as anomalous as *The Imperialist* with whose short life we are familiar yet as deserving of the protection of the law as a gathering of the Sons of the Revolution. The rescinding of the permit to the New York Orangemen to parade provoked a storm of protest. On July 11 Governor Hoffman hurriedly left the Capitol, and issued a proclamation reading in part:

"I hereby give notice that any and all bodies of men desiring to assemble and march in peaceable procession in this city tomorrow, the 12th inst., will be permitted to do so. They will be protected to the fullest extent possible by the military and police authorities. A military and police escort will be furnished to any body of men desiring it, on application to me at my headquarters (which will be at Police Headquarters in this city) at any time during the day."

The Roman Catholic priests had previously appealed to their flocks not to molest the Orangemen.

Some one hundred and sixty members of Gideon Lodge of Orangemen took advantage of the Governor's proclamation. Four regiments of the National Guard, including the Ninth, of which James Fisk, Jr., had been elected Colonel in the preceding year, were ordered to escort them from their lodge room in Lamartine's Hall at Eighth Avenue and Twenty-ninth Street, to Cooper Union at Eighth Street and the Bowery. The other regiments were the Eighty-fourth, Sixth, and Seventh.

Police Inspector Walling, who had charge of the police assigned to aid the militia in preserving the peace, thus describes what happened immediately after the procession started:

"The line of march was down town, and beyond some shouting and hissing nothing of any moment occurred until Twenty-sixth Street was reached. There a dense crowd, including many women, had collected. It was with the greatest difficulty that my men could clear the way for the Orangemen, who were obliged to come to a halt. At Twenty-fifth Street, Captain Joseph

Petty found it necessary to order the men under him to charge the rioters, driving them towards Seventh Avenue. Stones and other missiles were now thrown from the housetops, not a few of which struck members of the Ninth Regiment, who were in position at Eighth Avenue and Twenty-fifth Street.

"Suddenly a shot was fired from a window near the corner of Twenty-fourth Street. Other accounts say that the shot came from one of the soldier's rifles, which was accidentally discharged. However that may be, that shot was most certainly the signal for the horrible scene which immediately followed."

The generally accepted version is that the first shot was fired from a tenement house. This is Walling's. The bullet blew off the top of the head of a private in Company K of Fisk's regiment. The slain soldier was Henry C. Page, manager of Fisk's temple of opera bouffe. Instantly the men of the Eighty-fourth Regiment grew panicky. Without orders, they fired into the crowds on the sidewalks. The Sixth and Ninth Regiments followed suit. The Seventh alone, made up largely of veterans of the Civil War, kept their poise. The fusillade was short. One of the first volleys was fired into a platoon of policemen at the corner of Twenty-sixth Street and Eighth Avenue. The casualties were: slain—two soldiers, one policeman, forty-six civilians including women and children; wounded—sixty-one civilians and twenty-six policemen and soldiers.

This was the first time Fisk had been under fire. He was on horseback when the panicky militiamen fired indiscriminately and without orders into the crowds on the sidewalks. Colonel Fisk dismounted and disappeared in the cloud of smoke. And his regiment, minus its Colonel with the rest of the escort of the Orangemen, resumed their march within a few seconds after panicky firing ceased. Afterwards it was learned that Fisk had fled into a saloon on Eighth Avenue between Twenty-fourth and Twenty-third Streets, escaped through a rear door, scaled several fences, and found shelter in a house on Twenty-third Street. There he doffed his Colonel's uniform, and took a cab to a North River pier where he boarded an Erie tug. The next heard of him he was safe in Long Branch, New Jersey.

A contemporaneous ballad, entitled "The Flight of Fisk," which appeared in *Harper's Weekly*, contains these somewhat fanciful verses:

> "A New Departure now he ruled—
> How blest to make a ride of it;
> A passing cab contained Jay Gould!
> And so he got inside of it.

> "Thence to the Hoffman House they **drove**;
> But as the mob still harried him,
> To Sandy Hook, our downy cove,
> A steamer quickly carried him.

> "At last, supported by his friend,
> His wits beclouded, waxy, dense,
> Long Branch he reached, the happy end
> Of all his morning accidents."

Said one commentator of the Orange Riot:
"Write on the tombstone of Wednesday's victims: 'Murdered by the criminal management of Mayor A. Oakey Hall.'"

All The Ring were to suffer for it. The Elegant Oakey had acted in this instance without consulting The Boss. Connolly, who controlled the St. Patrick's Mutual Alliance, which was largely a paper organization, although few save Connolly knew it, had been the Mayor's adviser.

CHAPTER XXIX

TWEED saw the approaching storm. He was intensely superstitious. He believed that things happened in threes. There
was the death of Taylor, which robbed him of an advocate
on the directorate of *The Times.* Then the rut in the Harlem
Road which held Watson's sleigh while a frenzied horse dealt
a mortal blow to this agent of The Ring. And last there was
the tragic Orange Riot. He felt himself at bay—with Fate.
Only thus can we account for his loss of temper—the only
time in his career—when being interviewed by a representative
of the press. He was being pressed on the disclosures in *The
Times.* "Well," he responded, with a half snarl, "what are you
going to do about it?"

The Boss now began, slowly and secretly, to transfer his real
estate holdings to his son Richard. Similar disposition was
made of other tangible property.

The Elegant Oakey was responding to inquiries concerning
The Ring with flippant puns. Let us quote one: "Counts at
Newport at a discount." Once he sneered at *The Times:* "It
is clear, from the history of *The Times* and its delayed public
meeting, that honest and intelligent persons do not believe what
The Times has charged upon the city government."

The "delayed meeting" was held in Cooper Union on Monday night of September 4. William F. Havemeyer presided.
He and other speakers stressed that one of The Ring, Comptroller Connolly, had recently admitted that the debt of the
city and county, which had been $34,407,047.91 on January 1,
1869, had increased in thirty months to $100,955,383.33.
This known increase, with the revenue of $72,547,112.11 in the
same period, showed that The Ring had at least paid out
$139,005,447.53 in two years and six months. Judge James

Emott analyzed the figures, and reviewed the frauds as made known by *The Times*, indicating the theft of some $15,000,000.

All dwelt on the fact that no one as yet knew how much The Ring had stolen. No estimate has ever placed it less than double that sum. A conservative figure is $45,000,000, although O'Rourke later calculated that in taxes arbitrarily reduced by The Ring for money and in return for favor, and by the issuance of bonds at extravagant rates of interest—many of the issues were disposed of to syndicates abroad—the city lost $200,000,000 in the thirty months that The Ring flourished.

At one point in Emott's speech he said:

"Gentlemen, there is no denial of these fraudulent payments and there is no fabrication of their amount. Now what are you going to do with these men?"

"Hang them!" answered a man on the floor.

Resolutions had been drafted, and were presented by Joseph H. Choate, who as he advanced to the center of the stage, with the program for the prosecution of The Ring, exclaimed:

"This is what we are going to do about it!"

This response to Tweed's defiant snarl brought the audience to its feet, cheering even more wildly than it had when one of its number had proposed that Tweed and his fellow culprits be hanged.

These resolutions demanded the repeal of the Tweed charter, and declared that "the credit of the City of New York and the material interests of its citizens will demand that they (Hall, Connolly, and Tweed, who comprised the Board of Audit), quit or be deprived of the offices which they have dishonored and the power which they are abusing." The resolutions, which were unanimously adopted, empowered the chairman to appoint an executive committee of seventy to carry out the objects of the meeting, including the recovery of "whatever sums of money have been fraudulently or feloniously abstracted."

The suggestion of hanging, voiced at the Cooper Union meeting, had been voiced in written and spoken word for a month or more. *The Nation* had proposed the forming of a

Vigilance Committee late in August. Instantly *The World* protested against the public suggestion of the lynching. "Lynching," answered *The Nation*, on September 2, "is, however, here a question-begging term. What we say is that, in our opinion, Hall, Connolly, Tweed, Barnard, and all the class to which they belong, and of which Louis Napoleon was the most conspicuous member, fear no penalty for their misdeeds except a violent death. They are indifferent to public opinion and have matters so arranged that the prison pen has no terror for them, and a natural death they calculate upon. But the prospect of a violent death, which would suddenly stop their champagne, knock the satin sofas from under them, shut out the velvet carpets from their view, cause their fast horses to vanish into thin air, and launch them into the cold unknown would terrify them exceedingly; and such a death, we repeat, a large and growing body of respectable citizens think they ought to die—first and foremost, in order to stop their thieving and rid the community of them, and secondly, to prevent an unwholesome influence on public and private morals of the spectacle of the peaceful close of their career in the enjoyment of their stealings."

The night following the Cooper Union meeting nine leading citizens met and considered the formation of a Vigilance Committee. These men included John Cobert, one of the largest real estate owners in the city; R. A. Hunter, a banker; James Whitten, a life insurance company president; George W. Benster, former Judge, and Joseph Hazlen, a noted lawyer and a man of wealth. Speaking to the suggestion that hanging to lamp-posts be resorted to, Hazlen said:

"Where else can you turn for a remedy? They hold everything within their grasp. Every head of Department in our City is their creature. Every employé of our government is their slave. Fifteen thousand hirelings, who never perform work, and indeed who have no work to perform, are on the City pay-roll, as a praetorian guard around the Chief Boss, to do any act or deed he may command. Can you stop this waste of your money? Can you draw back the hands that are now plunged up to the armpits in the Treasury? Can you stop

Tweed, can you stop Connolly, can you stop Hall, can you stop Sweeny, can you stop the coterie of favorite contractors all dripping with the wealth that they have stolen from you and from me? Can you go to the Grand Jury, which is filled with their tools? Can you go to the District Attorney, who is their pliant servant? Can you obtain protection from the police, who are these men's bodyguard? Can you call upon the Governor of the State, who extols the virtues of Tweed, the purity of Hall, the brains of Sweeny and the charming simplicity of Connolly? Can you, in fine, appeal to our Courts? If so, where? Get an order from some honest Judge —Barnard will vacate it. Get another—Cardozo will vacate it. Get a third, and Ingraham will 'modify' it. Appeal, and the General Term will, in turn, sustain Barnard and Cardozo and Ingraham—who compose the General Term! Appeal in such case to the Court of Appeals, and by the machinery of the Courts in the City that appeal will be hampered and delayed, and long before the case will reach that tribunal, the City will be in financial ruin."

Judge Benster, older than the rest, acknowledging "the array of damning facts" presented by Hazlen, pleaded for calmness, saying:

"While I cannot gainsay much that has been urged by him, I am still a believer in the irresistible force inherent in our legal and political system. Whatever way, under God, we may be rescued, it must be by the law, or we will only add to our disgrace, not to say worse. At all events, let us first have recourse to the law, before even a whisper is heard that men of thought and education and high standing in the community have lost faith in the efficacy of our institutions."

While this meeting of these prominent New Yorkers was not public property at the time, all the town talked of the suggestion in *The Nation*. A staff man of *The Sun* called on Tweed who "looked quite delighted when he saw *The Sun* reporter. His bright eyes sparkled when he said, in his cordial, frank manner, 'How are you? Glad to see you.'" Then this dialogue ensued:

"Did you read *The Nation?*"

"No."

"You know they are going to have you hanged?"

"He's an infamous liar. The man that wrote that knows he told a lie, and he wouldn't dare to tell me so to my face. (After a pause.) I was born in New York and I mean to stay here, too."

"You don't seem to be afraid of a violent death. Are you?"

Tweed stamped his foot and he answered: "Well, if they want me to come, I'll be there. That's all I have to say about it, I'll be there, I'll be there, sir (with a smile)."

Three days after the Cooper Union mass meeting, Tilden, still in the background, evened his score with Tweed. He did more than that, although it was not apparent at the time. He made certain the destruction of his ancient enemy.

No mere lawyer, concerned solely with a presentation of a case, conceived the carefully plotted moves of the drama that was enacted on September 7, 1871, in the Supreme Court.

Tilden was one of the advisers of the Committee of Seventy appointed at the Cooper Union meeting. One of the members of the committee was John Foley. There were sixty-nine others, but none had so pronouncedly an Irish name as this wealthy fountain pen manufacturer. Tweed's great strength lay in those of Irish lineage. So Foley was selected as a member of the Committee of Seventy, to bring a taxpayer's suit in his own name, against the city, which in effect prohibited the Mayor and all his subordinates from raising any moneys by taxation and forbade the payment of another cent of the city's funds to any one. And to make a still greater appeal to the Irish, Foley had three counsel, with unmistakably Irish names: Robert H. Strahan, Francis C. Barlow, and G. C. Barrett.

No commonplace intriguer selected the Judge who was asked to grant Foley's application for this sweeping injunction. The Judge was George G. Barnard, the servile, avaricious tool of Tweed.

Barnard granted the restraining order sought by Foley. Tweed might well exclaim: *"Et tu Brute?"*

Both Tilden and Tweed were agreed that Barnard granted

this injunction—which was so sweeping that it restrained the payment of daily wages to the laborers employed by the city —because he believed that it would make him Governor.

This betrayal of The Ring by Barnard, was such a shock to Tweed that for a time he feared that he would go mad. "My brain was threatened," Tweed confessed. At times his disordered mind gave way to hysterical outbursts. Now and then he contemplated suicide. Once he declared publicly that if he were twenty-five years younger he would kill the editor of *The Times*. Tweed, analyzing Barnard's motives in granting the injunction, said:

"We owe to Barnard all our trouble. That fellow was seized with the idea that he would be made Governor of New York by the action he took at the time. Nobody else could see how it was to come about, but Barnard thought he saw it, and he said: 'If there is no law or precedent for this injunction, I will make one.' So he put the injunction upon us, and in the straitened condition of our credit, which was so extended on every side, it broke us. You see our patronage had become so enormous and so costly that the injunction, which might not have troubled us at any other time, destroyed all our power to raise money from the banks or elsewhere and left us strapped."

This injunction was granted by Barnard immediately after argument had been made by Foley's counsel. Knowing Barnard as we do, this summary action in so important a proceeding, can be explained only on the theory that he had been promised the Democratic nomination for Governor. There was only one man capable of making good such a promise. This was Tilden. His name was bandied freely in talk of political trades. He was now the political leader of the Democrats of the State, chairman of the party's State Committee, and the outstanding figure in the fight against The Boss. Tilden's man, O'Brien, the former Sheriff, with his fraudulent bill of $350,000 against the city, immediately after the injunction, induced Tweed to buy half of this claim for $20,000 in cash and a mortgage of $128,000 with interest on one of Tweed's properties. And Connolly bought the other half of O'Brien's bill against the taxpayers. The assignment to Tweed of half of O'Brien's claim was executed before a notary on October 20. Part of the consideration involved was a promise made by one of O'Brien's friends that O'Brien "could control Tilden to the extent of having him let up on Tweed." The Boss, grasping at straws, believed this falsehood. Tilden was then planning to run for the Assembly from O'Brien's district, the 18th of New York. This singular proposal was first made to William O. Bartlett, one of Tweed's counsel, who indignantly refused to entertain the offer. Tilden's object in seeking a seat in the Assembly, where he had sat as a young man back in 1846, was to be on the floor to direct the fight in the Legislature for the enactment of measures of reform needed to achieve the aims of the Committee of Seventy. Aiding Tilden in this fight at the Albany end was the brilliant Chemung County lawyer, David Bennett Hill. These two future Governors of New York did signal service at Albany. In the Metropolis, Tilden relied chiefly on the untiring labors of Charles O'Conor, whose Parian bust adorns the Appellate Division of the First Judicial Department. It was a master stroke to enlist the aid of the venerable O'Conor. No one could ascribe other than the highest motives to any act of this great jurisconsult. Tweed's adherents could call Foley a meddling reformer, and Tilden a self-seeking politician, but no one could question the motives of a gray-beard who came from an honorable retirement to be of unselfish service to the people.

Not alone for his legal attainments was O'Conor selected, but because of his antecedents. His father was Thomas O'Conor, journalist, friend of Thomas Addis Emmet, brother of the immortal Robert. Emmet, later Attorney General of New York State, was one of the Directorate of the United Irishmen which had promoted the Irish revolution of '98. The two friends came to New York within a year or so of one another, and continued their Irish revolutionary activities. Had there been another lawyer, not of Irish extraction, the equal in all things of O'Conor, Tilden would have chosen O'Conor. The Committee of Seventy realized that a sweeping victory at the polls could not be effected if racial and religious prejudices were ignored by it.

Tweed's term as State Senator would expire on December 31. He realized it would be necessary for him to return to Albany, and to effect the reëlection of Democrats and Republicans whom he could rely on to checkmate the legislative moves of Tilden and his allies. He was nominated on Wednesday, September 20. The following afternoon, at the office of the Commissioner of Public Works, Tweed received a delegation representing the Central Tweed Club, recently organized. Randolph Guggenheimer was chairman of the delegation. Mr. Guggenheimer voiced the club's "great regret over the assaults on Tweed and assured him of their utmost confidence." Tweed, in response, said:

"Gentlemen: . . . An opportunity like this is the only one I have to make known exactly how I feel about certain matters about which there is a great deal of talk and rumor. The press has been full to running over of late with charges against my official character. I here distinctly state that I am fully prepared to meet any and all charges against me. . . . I am perfectly indifferent to all this howl that is being made about me in the way it is being made. . . . If the people who are making it want to prove that they are right, I repeat again that all they have to do is to prefer their charges in court, and then I will meet them. The sooner they do it the better I will like it and the stronger they make them the better will I be prepared to meet them."

That same night Tweed formally accepted the nomination which was tendered to him in Tweed Plaza before an assemblage of twenty thousand cheering adherents. In acknowledging the applause which greeted him when he appeared upon the platform, "Mr. Tweed took off his little Scotch tweed cap and made his bow to the boisterous and noisy multitude." He was now in the heart of the old East Side, less than half a mile from where he was born, but several miles from his mansion on Fifth Avenue and 43rd Street. Said Tweed:

"At home again amidst the haunts of my childhood and scenes where I had been always surrounded by friends, I feel

I can safely place myself and my record, all I have performed as a public official plainly before your gaze. The manner in which I have been received to-night has sent a throb to my heart, but I would be unjust to myself and unjust to those who have seen fit to entrust me with office if at times like these, when to be a Democrat, when to hold a public office is to be aspersed and condemned without trial, traduced without stint, there was not felt to be engraven on my heart the proud satisfaction that as a public officer, I can go to the friends of my childhood, take them by the hand, take them in a friendly manner, and saying to them, 'There is my record,' and finding that it meets with their approval.

"Reviled and traduced and maligned as a man has seldom been, I point proudly to my record of the past, which is open to the scan of all, and I court full, open and impartial investigation into all the official acts of my life. (Cheers.) My friends say, 'Why do you not reply to these newspaper attacks?'—an attack that is in one paper to-day, in another paper to-morrow, and one more the day after that. I have only one reply—no man can ever reply to a newspaper and find that one reply is the last. The proper place, the true place, the only place where a man's character can be vindicated from attacks like those made upon me is before a competent, a proper and legal tribunal. I have stated to my multitudinous opponents and traducers that I am ready at any moment to go forward and meet them. but while they stand behind the mighty engine of popular power—the press— no man single-handed, no man can have the temerity, no man, I say, can be just to himself and stand outside those who are inside of the press to vindicate himself from its attacks.

"My public life is before my constituents and my party. I am able to face my accusers in the only manly way in which those can be met who traduce us. Gentlemen, I place myself in your hands. I accept your nomination of Senator. I expect my friends to stand by me and resent the revilings that have been placed upon me. My majority last time was a mere 22,000 majority. I expect this time 30,000, and must be satisfied with no less. Gentlemen, I thank you for this

CHARLES O'CONOR

JOSEPH H. CHOATE

magnificent manifestation of regard and trust, and for your
agreeing with me as to the course I have pursued with my
traducers and revilers. I am glad to see so many of you here,
and for the good feeling you have manifested, as I have endeavored to show you the way in which I meet the charge of my
calumniators. I shall now give way to those to whom eloquence
is their forte. I trust my political life has been such as to meet
your approval, and I assure you that for the future I shall try
to deserve your approval."

One of the speakers at this meeting was a former Confederate
Colonel, John R. Fellows. Colonel Fellows, later honored with
the office of District Attorney, was then one of the assistant
county prosecutors. His colleague in that office was Tweed's
son and namesake. Let us listen to Colonel Fellow's frenzied
attack on the editor and managing editor of *The Times:*

"This man Jennings, who boasts of beating Tammany Hall,
why, there is nothing in the wide world that he has beaten, with
one exception, and that is his wife; he has beaten his wife
(cheers and laughter)—and the criminal courts of our city
have the proofs of it to-day. (Cheers.)

"Who, too, is George Jones, the publisher of *The Times?*

"Why, he went around with his printing account to the
leaders of Tammany Hall and the Department of Finance
in the City Hall begging to be prostituted to the corporation
for the small sum of $13,000. Well, the Tammany leaders
did not think his seduction worth the price, and the very day
that he was taken off the Tammany pay-rolls George Jones
set up for a political martyr."

Fellows' tongue was as truthful as it was clean. Jennings
had been arrested several times, but in each instance the
charges were trumped up by The Ring. But then the gallant
Colonel Fellows had to live.

Tweed's speech on this occasion reveals his broken spirit.
He knew then, although unwilling to admit it even to himself,
that he could not stay the hand of Fate. Barnard's desertion
had steeled him against anything that possibly could happen.
It was well it did, for three days before this meeting Connolly,
like Barnard, turned traitor. Connolly had been in secret con-

ference at Tilden's home in Gramercy Square with Havemeyer, who presided at the Cooper Union meeting, and agreed to carry out the plan outlined by Tilden. Connolly thought that by capitulating to Tilden he would be saved. Tilden had discovered an obscure provision in the law which empowered the Comptroller to name a Deputy to exercise the powers of his office for a limited period. Tilden asked Connolly to remove one of his Deputies, and deputize Andrew H. Green, one of the Committee of Seventy, to act as Comptroller for four months. This was done on Monday, September 18.

This second betrayal of The Ring proved more of a shock to the Elegant Oakey than to Tweed. The report quickly spread that Hall had gone crazy, and had torn handfuls of hair from his head. Hall was too distracted to write a letter. His chief clerk, Charles O. Joline, wrote a brief note to all heads of departments informing them that the Mayor did not recognize Connolly as Comptroller or Andrew H. Green as Acting Comptroller. Simultaneously Hall appointed the Civil War hero, General George B. McClellan, Democratic nominee for President in 1864, as Comptroller. McClellan promptly declined the dubious honor.

Hall made no further attempts to disturb the situation in the Comptroller's Office because of the appearance in the afternoon papers of an opinion rendered by Charles O'Conor that Connolly had acted legally in appointing Green his Deputy and conferring on him all the powers of the Comptroller. Tilden had made the request for an opinion from this recognized leader of the State bar, and thus explained his purpose: "The freedom from doubt of the law was no security. The moral support of his [O'Conor's] great legal name, affirming the validity of Mr. Green's possession, was necessary. Mr. O'Conor's opinion saved that day."

Hall, Tweed, and Sweeny next considered obtaining from one of the judges who still remained faithful an injunction restraining Green from acting. Tilden had word passed to these tools that if they dared grant such an order, a public disclosure would be made that would inflame the city. This had the desired effect. The presidents of ten of the largest banks called on Acting Comptroller Green and offered to support him in every way. Several prominent citizens offered to constitute themselves a corps of Vigilantes in case of need. Armed guards were placed round the office of the Comptroller. Tweed and Hall and Sweeny had a quiet chuckle at this, for in the week past, some 3,500 vouchers in the Comptroller's office had been purloined and burned in the furnace of the City Hall. It was the Elegant Oakey who suggested it.

We need no further evidence than this to know that the reason of the Elegant One was also temporarily tottering, for the Broadway Bank, which The Ring favored, had duplicates, in one form or another, of the burned vouchers. He had forgotten this. Tilden put one of the ablest accountants of the day in the offices of the bank, and it was not long before the proofs of the corruption of Tweed and his associates were in the hands of Tilden. On October 17, O'Conor was named Special State Attorney General to bring civil suits against Tweed and others to recover the moneys they had stolen.

A week later criminal proceedings were instituted by Tilden on behalf of the Committee of Seventy. Tilden swore to the complaining affidavit to which was attached a list of one hundred and ninety county vouchers showing that $6,312,541.37 had been fraudulently taken from the city treasury. The crime charged was deceit and fraud. Supreme Court Justice W. L. Learned signed the warrant, which was delivered to Sheriff Matthew Brennan, one of Tweed's political supporters. The writ directed that Tweed be held in $1,000,000 bail.

Tweed was in his private office in the Department of Public Works all Friday morning waiting to be arrested. A few minutes before noon a *Times* reporter called on Tweed. The Boss "quietly greeted the reporter and invited him to a chair close beside him." When Tweed was asked if he had heard that the warrant had been issued for his arrest he replied that he had. Then ensued this interview:

Reporter—Are you waiting for it now?

Tweed—I am.

Reporter—What will be your course of action?

Tweed—I shall give bail here on the spot.

Reporter—Is your bail bond prepared?

Tweed—I am prepared.

Reporter—You know that the charge against you is that the Board of Audit has fraudulently audited fictitious claims, and that a large percentage of the amounts paid has been appropriated by you.

Tweed—I have heard so.

Reporter—What have you to say about that?

Tweed—The papers have not been served on me yet. I can say nothing.

While this interview was taking place Wheeler H. Peckham, one of the associates of Tilden and O'Conor, gave the order of arrest to Sheriff Brennan. "At quarter past one the Sheriff left his office by the private door and called upon William M. Tweed, Jr., taking with him Mr. Judson Jarvis, the Arrest Deputy. Jay Gould was in waiting, and after a few minutes' conversation the four proceeded to the Department of Public Works. . . . As the Sheriff passed up the stairs, the crowd closed in behind him, jostling and pushing him to the door of Tweed's office." We are still quoting from *The Times:*

"Good morning, Mr. Tweed," said the Sheriff, pleasantly.

"Good morning," was the quiet response.

After a moment's pause the Sheriff said: "Mr. Tweed, I have an order for your arrest."

"I expected it," was the reply, "but not so soon. However, I have my bail ready, and you can take it here if you will."

Jay Gould qualified in the sum of $1,000,000, Terence Farley, Edmund Kelly, and Benjamin P. Fairchild each put up surety for $300,000 each, and our old friend, Hugh Hastings, rounded out the second million with $100,000. When real estate is offered as security in New York State, double the amount of the face of the bail bond is required.

Tweed was nominally under arrest while the bail bond was being executed. While this was being done he announced to newspapermen that he would be able to prove his innocence and was not worrying. The arrest over, Tweed devoted all his energies to the campaign, for not only was he anxious to be reëlected State Senator, but he wanted a majority of dependables from the city in both branches of the State Legislature. He knew that money would buy a sufficient number of Republican legislators to block any move Tilden could make in Albany. There were a number of candidates for the various courts in whom Tweed had more than a passing interest. These, too, he wanted elected.

The most desperate contest of all was being waged in his own Senatorial district. Here, carrying out the racial and religious appeal program, the reformers had nominated O'Donovan Rossa, who to his generation represented what Thomas Addis Emmet and Thomas O'Conor represented to an earlier one. Rossa, who had drilled his fellow countrymen in anticipation of the uprising of 1867, had been released a few months before from an English jail. He had been a prisoner since 1865 on charge of treason. Rossa made comparatively few speeches in Tweed's Senatorial district. Most of his campaigning was carried on in other parts of the city, speaking whenever there was a colony of Irish.

The most popular man of German birth in the city was the Union veteran, General Franz Sigel. He was nominated by the reformers for Register. He made his appeals chiefly in the German sections. He was elected by a majority of 28,117. All the reform candidates who had the benefit of a city-wide vote were also elected. Only two of Tweed's Aldermen were successful, and a majority of the reform candidates for Assistant Aldermen were also victorious. Of the twenty-one Assembly districts in the city the reformers carried fourteen. Only one of the five Senatorial districts in the city was lost by the Committee of Seventy. This was Tweed's. Here all sorts of thuggery and election frauds were committed. The official count of this stolen election gave Tweed a majority over O'Donovan Rossa of nine thousand, some thirteen thousand less than he polled two years before.

This rout of The Ring at the polls revived the faith of those who had their misgivings of the capacity of the people to rule. In New York, a majority of the citizens who were of foreign birth, possessing little more than the clothes on their backs and the scant furnishing of their homes, made possible the defeat of candidates of a corrupt bi-partisan machine. The people needed only a leader. They had found one in George Jones.

Tweed had aged noticeably during the campaign. After Election Day he had the appearance of a man approaching sixty. His actual years were forty-eight.

CHAPTER XXX

AFTER the election The Committee of Seventy began to seek indictments. Some of the underlings of The Ring sought safety in flight. Sweeny's brother James was the first to leave. He was followed by Sweeny himself, who had resigned his office as President of the Park Board six days before election. Peter joined brother James in France. J. H. Ingersoll, who made millions for The Ring with his fraudulent furniture bills, also took French leave. Andrew J. Garvey, the Prince of Plasterers, fled. Elbert A. Woodward, Tweed's collector, also departed. These last three had been named in the same warrant with Tweed.

On November 20 Connolly made a formal resignation of his office to the Elegant Oakey, who like Connolly, was now playing with the Committee of Seventy. Hall appointed Green Comptroller. Connolly and Hall had deserted Tweed. Sweeny had fled. Tweed could console himself with the thought that he had betrayed no one.

Connolly, after making his capitulation to Tilden, walked with lighter tread. He no longer feared arrest or indictment. He had been a big help to the reformers. Without the possession of his office they could not have traced the payments to Tweed. After he resigned Connolly, from force of habit, daily visited his office.

On November 24 Genet was arrested, charged with the theft of material from the Harlem Court House at East One hundred twenty-first Street, near Third Avenue, which he used in building his home a few blocks away, at One hundred twenty-sixth Street and Fifth Avenue, and for fraudulently certifying a bill of one of the contractors on the court house. This unworthy descendant of Citizen Genêt and a daughter of

George Clinton, the first Governor of New York State, was released on $4,000 bail. After his conviction, Prince Hal escaped through the connivance of Sheriff Brennan and a deputy, who served thirty days in jail for letting him slip through their fingers. Five years later Genet surrendered himself, submitted to punishment, and died shortly after his release from prison.

The day after Prince Hal's arrest Connolly, as usual, found himself in the old office he had vacated five days before at the request of Tilden. While he was chatting with Tilden, Sheriff Brennan entered and tapping Connolly on the shoulder, announced that he had a warrant for his arrest.

"Mr. Tilden!" exclaimed Connolly. "I'm arrested."

"No," said Tilden, with feigned surprise. "What is the bail, Sheriff?"

"One million dollars."

Connolly had more than six millions of the loot intact. But to have put up part of it would have meant its loss, as an attachment would be brought against it by O'Conor. He must find some friends. But no Jay Goulds came to Connolly's rescue, so he went to Ludlow Street Jail.

On December 15 the Grand Jury returned an indictment against Tweed. The fallen Boss was arrested the following day. Judge Gunning S. Bedford held him without bail. While he was on his way to the Tombs, Judge Barnard, whose injunction was primarily responsible for the crash of The Ring issued a writ of *habeas corpus* sought by one of Tweed's counsel. This writ was served on Tweed's custodians at the entrance of the Tombs. When he was brought before Barnard bail was fixed in the sum of $5,000. It was furnished.

On December 18 the Grand Jury returned two indictments against Tweed alleging forgery in the third degree. On the same day an indictment charging grand larceny was presented against him. Two days later he resigned as director of the Erie Railroad, and all his other private and public offices, save one, that of State Senator. On December 29 Tammany elected August Schell, Grand Sachem, in place of Tweed. Charles O'Conor supplanted Connolly; Tilden was chosen to succeed Sweeny, and Honest John Kelly in place of Hall.

Other new Sachems elected included former Governor Seymour and August Belmont. Tilden was in the saddle.

On December 31, 1871, Connolly offered bail, which had been reduced to $500,000. It was accepted by Sheriff Brennan. Connolly was released from Ludlow Street Jail on New Year's Eve, and immediately thereafter took ship to France.

On January 6, 1872, Tweed's friend, Colonel James Fisk, Jr., was shot down in the Grand Central Hotel by Edward S. Stokes. Four shots had been fired at the Prince of Erie as he ascended the stairs from the lobby of the famous old hostelry.

"For God's sake, will anybody save me?" exclaimed Fisk. One of the bullets had struck him in the right arm, and another in the abdomen. To a servant who reached his side Fisk pleaded that Tweed and Jay Gould be immediately summoned.

Stokes, a scion of a wealthy family that had made millions in metals, was little more than thirty. He had made considerable money in oil. When he met Fisk and Gould he owned a Brooklyn refinery. Fisk, keeping within the law, stole Stokes' property. Stokes revenged himself by stealing Fisk's mistress, Josie Mansfield. Fisk then had Stokes arrested on a trumped-up charge of embezzling. Stokes spent a night in the Tombs, and was honorably discharged as a victim of malicious prosecution. Ensued series of suits and counter-suits, and threats to publish the love letters of the Prince of Erie, which Stokes possessed. These suits ended, apparently, six months after the unjustifiable arrest of Stokes, when an arbitrator held that Stokes' claim of $200,000 against Fisk over the refinery was null and void, but awarded Stokes $10,000 for the night he spent in the Tombs. Fisk agreed to pay this if Stokes would surrender Fisk's love letters. Eight days before *The Times* began its publication of the proofs of the frauds of Tweed, Hall, Connolly, and Sweeny, Stokes addressed the following letter:

"Hon. Peter B. Sweeny:

"Dear Sir:—Mr. Buckley informed me of your desire to have

possession of Mr. Fisk's letters, approved, &c. I herewith send them all to you.

"Yours respectfully,

"E. S. Stokes."

Sweeny, as we know, was a member of the Board of Directors of the Erie Railroad, and was acting as one of Fisk's counsel in this *affaire du cœur*.

But Stokes still possessed Fisk's former mistress. In a jealous rage, Fisk published an unsupported affidavit of Miss Mansfield's discharged butler. This manifestly false testimony, accusing Stokes and Miss Mansfield of conspiring to blackmail Fisk, was the flimsy pretext of an indictment against Stokes. The spurned lover then published the servant's statement. Immediately Miss Mansfield had Fisk arrested for criminal libel. This case was pending when Stokes, temporarily insane from the persecutions of Fisk, shot him.

Frederick Lane was one of the first to reach the side of the dying man. Lane was still a member of the Executive Committee of the Erie Railroad with Fisk, Gould, and Tweed. Fisk, in his Colonel's uniform, lay in state in the opera house which bore his name, a guard of honor from his regiment standing watch at his bier. Stokes was sentenced to be hanged in the courtyard of the Tombs. The Court of Appeals ordered a new trial, at which Stokes made the dramatic charge in open court that his prosecution had been inspired by the Tweed Ring. This mob appeal had its effect. The jury returned a verdict of manslaughter. Stokes was let off with a sentence of four years in Sing Sing.

While we have left us a picture of Jay Gould shedding tears as he stood beside the rosewood coffin with its gold handles, we have a record of public mourning by Tweed, who, without show, paid his final tribute by visiting the opera house that night before the Ninth Regiment, their band playing the "Dead March in Saul," followed their slain leader to the train that took him back to his childhood scenes amidst the hills of Vermont.

While O'Conor was working in New York City against The Ring, Tilden and David Bennett Hill were moving to purge the courts of Tweed's judges. Cardozo, before filing the report of the investigators on which the impeachment proceedings were based, resigned from the Supreme Court bench. Barnard, who first played with the reformers and gave the injunction which broke the backbone of The Ring, was the first to be removed. Judge John McCunn, of the Superior Court, was also deposed. Immediately after he heard the verdict, McCunn returned to his home and died there three days later of a broken heart. One of the mourners at his funeral was Charles O'Conor. It was in O'Conor's office that McCunn, a friendless and penniless youth, read law.

Tweed was the only member of the Senate who did not vote on these impeachments. There was a gentlemen's agreement that no proceedings would be taken against him by the Senate pending the outcome of the charges against him provided he did not embarrass his old colleagues and hirelings by taking his seat.

While Tweed was having his own troubles, he found some satisfaction in the removal of Barnard. Three more indictments were returned against the fallen Boss before the Committee of Investigation of the Legislature had organized. These were handed up on February 3, making a total of six true bills, each charging a felony.

The Elegant Oakey, who had also played with the reformers, was privately worrying while he made a public show of unconcern. He had been arrested on an indictment charging him with neglect of duty. Still he held on to his office as Mayor—he remained brazenly in the City Hall until the end of his term. There was talk of a duplicate charge, which would have served no other purpose than a second appearance and pleading to the same offense. He wrote a whining letter to Tilden entreating that this not be done. "To press one now," wrote Hall, "is only to wound the feelings of my very interesting family by arousing fresh (and doubtless, at this partisan pitch, cruel) newspaper criticism, and without accomplishing any better oblation to justice (either to me or the people as the case may prove) than could be attained with existing pleading."

But Fate was kinder to Hall than to Tweed. At the first of the Elegant Oakey's trials he escaped because death claimed one of the jurors. At the second, the jury disagreed. A third panel acquitted him.

Oakey was ever inspired by his love for the dramatic. At his last trial he rose and personally challenged a juror because they were personal friends.

In October, on the 17th, two more indictments were returned against Tweed. One of them recited fifty-five separate offenses, and each was the basis of four separate counts.

Adjournments had been granted almost without number since the first of the eight indictments was found the preceding December. Friends told him to flee. Not he. He knew that he would not be called up to stand trial, but he was resolved to be there at the scratch. He had seen juries packed where men were penniless. He had millions. And who, with his flair for politics, would leave the country with such an exciting and eccentric campaign as the Presidential campaign of that year afforded?

Greeley was the candidate for President of a small group of the Republicans who could not endure the corruption of the Grant Administration and of the Democratic Party. A stranger double-bed would be hard to imagine. This was the election to which Tweed had been looking forward. Hoffman, whom he had cast for the rôle of President, was preparing for his exit from public life. Nominated by the Democrats, or rather by Tilden, for Governor, was Francis Kernan, of Utica, who also had the indorsement of the faction known as the Liberal Republicans. Kernan's selection was a piece of political chicanery conceived for the sole purpose of bulwarking Tilden's position in New York City. On November 3, there appeared in *The World* what purported to be an interview with Tilden. No reporter ever asked the three brief questions, or recorded the long-winded responses—one of them consists of nearly one thousand five hundred words. It was a lawyer's brief, not a newspaper man's interview. After Tilden sets forth three reasons why Kernan was nominated, he says that here are reasons enough, and good ones, but not all. Then

Tilden's imaginary interviewer asked: "What were the others? The Republican newspapers say that one was that Mr. Kernan is a Catholic, and that you advised his nomination on that account." Whereat Mr. Tilden says there is not the slightest truth, or resemblance to truth in that story. And then he drags in Charles O'Conor—saying, quite truthfully—that he had sought both these men for advice and aid when *The Times* began its exposé of the stealings of The Ring, and then added:

"Now it happened that both of these gentlemen are born within this State; that they are both sons of exiles, for the sake of liberty, from Ireland; that they are both of the Catholic religion. Mr. Kernan's creed had nothing more to do with my desire for his nomination for Governor than it had with my seeking his coöperation, or Mr. O'Conor's coöperation in the reform measures."

And then followed much of the spirit of the old Tilden, of the Tilden of seventeen years back, who cast away an election to the State Attorney Generalship to denounce the Know-Nothings.

Tilden, who supported Greeley made no reference in this interview to the candidacy of Charles O'Conor, who had been nominated for President by the Straight-Out Democrats. This was a faction of the Democratic Party which refused to accept Greeley. O'Conor's running mate was John Quincy Adams, a Republican. Neither had been consulted when they were nominated and made no campaign, although they did not decline the honor. The Prohibitionists entered a national campaign for the first time this year. James Black of Pennsylvania headed the Dry ticket. The popular vote was:

Grant	3,597,070
Greeley	2,834,079
O'Conor	29,489
Black	5,608

New York State went heavily Republican, John A. Dix being elected Governor over Kernan. In the city the reformers again put up their own candidates for Mayor, and other local offices, and elected most of them. William F. Havemeyer succeeded the Elegant Oakey, defeating Abraham Lawrence, one of the Committee of Seventy, whom Tammany had named for Mayor, and ex-Sheriff James O'Brien, who emulating the example of Fernando Wood, had a Democratic Party of his own, named like Wood's, after the hall the O'Brien Democrats met in—Apollo Hall. Havemeyer defeated Lawrence by more than 8,000 votes, and his plurality over O'Brien exceeded 22,000. Greeley carried the city by 23,000. Greeley, his health shattered by the arduous campaign, his defeat, and the death of his wife, died on November 29. He carried only six States: Georgia, Kentucky, Maryland, Missouri, Tennessee, Texas.

CHAPTER XXXI

TWEED was placed on trial on January 7 before Judge Noah Davis in the Court of Oyer and Terminer. Defending him were some of the most noted men at the bar, including David Dudley Field, one of the counsel of the Erie Railroad, and John Graham, without a peer in trying a criminal case. There were other veterans, and three young lawyers, known only to the profession. One of these was Elihu Root, at that time twenty-eight years of age. Wheeler H. Peckham, one of the Committee of Seventy, was in charge of the prosecution, although the prosecutor of record was the District Attorney, Benjamin K. Phelps, who, like the trial judge, had been elected on the anti-Ring ticket. The two principal witnesses were Tilden and Garvey, the Prince of Plasterers, who had returned from hiding under promise of immunity if he would turn State's evidence. Garvey, with a straight face, said that he fled to Europe because he feared assassination at the hands of The Ring. Tweed's face went red with rage at this wanton perjury. At recess he followed Garvey into an ante-room of the court and said something *sotto voce* to the man he made a millionaire. A reporter inquired of Garvey what Tweed had said. "His language was blasphemous," answered Garvey who observed the Third Commandment while scornful of the Eighth.

Judge Davis gave the case to the jury on the afternoon of January 30. The jurors were locked up for the night, having failed to agree by a reasonable hour. The following morning at ten o'clock, Tweed, seated at his counsel's table, looking the most unconcerned man in the room, watched the jury file in. The jury had disagreed.

The next day, Tweed summed up his sentiments thus: "I

am tired of the whole farce. No jury will ever convict me."
Tweed was himself again.

Four more indictments against Tweed were returned within the next three weeks. On July 3, Tweed suffered the most severe blow that had yet befallen him. He lost his mother. She was in her eighty-first year. There was seldom a week slipped by that he did not visit her at the old home at 237 East Broadway. It is said that the shame that had befallen her son had been successfully kept from her. She was buried beside her husband in the family plot in Greenwood.

Tweed went to California for a rest. While there, friends wrote him not to return to New York, advising him that the Committee of Seventy had hired private detectives to prevent tampering with the jury at a second trial, which was scheduled for the Fall. It was common belief that Tweed had packed the first jury. Ignoring these advices, Tweed returned to face the music.

Again Judge Davis presided. Again the omnibus indictment with the fifty-five specific offenses charged, each consisting of four counts, was the presentment to which Tweed pleaded not guilty. The case was called November 5. It took nine days to select the twelve jurors. Then it was revealed to the court by detectives of the prosecution that they had seen Police Captain Walsh speak privately with Tweed, and that thereafter, as the jurors were going out for luncheon, Walsh accosted E. H. Lubry, Juror No. 8, and held a five minutes' conversation with him in the hall, and that then the Police Captain returned to the room where Tweed was having a midday repast. These detectives also informed the court— which Lubry had not revealed in his examination to test his fitness to serve—that the juror had been the barber of one of Tweed's colleagues. Lubry was censured by the court and excused. The actual trial took only four days. The same facts, but in briefer form, were presented. Again Tweed was not put on the stand. Again the jury was locked up over night. This time the verdict was guilty on two hundred and four of the two hundred and twenty counts in the indictment.

Tweed seemingly took his conviction as he did the disagree-

ment at the first trial. This time the bored expression was
assumed. Wednesday was the day of the verdict. The following Saturday morning was set for sentence. Before he entered
the court Sheriff Brennan took Tweed's hand. "I hope you will
bear up, Bill." he said. Tweed sighed: "Ah, I have tried to
bear up, Matt. I never thought though it would come to
this."

The courtroom was packed as Tweed took his seat at the
counsel table. There were surging, buzzing crowds in the
corridors. Not until his chief counsel, John Graham, approached, did the weary face brighten. Presently Judge Davis,
stern and serious, ascended the bench. After he had over-
ruled the various motions made by counsel for the defense,
Lyman Tremain, on behalf of the People, demanded judgment.
A fine of $250 or a year in jail, or both, was the penalty an-
ticipated by Tweed's counsel. Tremain in asking for the
imposition of sentence, observed that the jury had found
Tweed guilty of two hundred and four of the two hundred and
twenty counts in the indictment, and that as some of them
were grouped because of the nature of the payments of moneys
to which they related, the defendant stood liable to fine and
imprisonment for only one hundred and two distinct offenses.

Tweed and his counsel sat up. What did the prosecutor
mean? That Tweed was liable to a cumulative sentence of
one hundred and two years and a fine of more than $25,000?
Tremain did not leave them in doubt, for he immediately
added: "It is for the court to say, whether for humanity's
sake, or for any other reason, all the offenses should be treated
as one."

Graham argued against this contention of the prosecution,
recalling that the State, in its opening address to the jury,
had conceded that the maximum punishment was one year,
and that the jury must have so believed, or they would not
have brought in a verdict which would have permitted the
imposition of a sentence of one hundred and two years.
Graham then made an eloquent plea for mercy that moved
every one in the room. His last sentence he could not finish:
"Your honor, we are taught, from the time we enter this world,

to ask for mercy; and those prayers which we put up in our own behalf must teach us to render deeds of mercy to—" Graham was now sobbing audibly, his body heaving convulsively with each sob. Tweed buried his face in his hands. Spectators shared their emotions.

Tremain now rose, and tried to respond. His lips quivered but no word came from them for several seconds. He began to argue the law of the case, but his heart controlled, and reacting to his emotions, he cast aside logic and turning to Graham said:

"Far be it from me to ignore those innermost reasons which must sway us in a case like this. I cannot but feel, and I am sure my associates feel with me—indeed, all must feel—how terrible is the position of this man, who has been so high and who has fallen so low. He is now drinking the bitter waters of humiliation. The spell is broken. God knows we do not feel glad at our position here to-day. Would it were otherwise!"

Then addressing the Court, Tremain, who had now perfect control of himself, continued:

"The law has placed in your hands the responsibility of the matter. The case is one of international interest and attracts the attention of the whole world. We now leave to you the question of what shall be meted out to the prisoner as an impartial and just penalty."

As Tremain finished, the audience, which a few moments before wept with Tweed's counsel, now audibly murmured its approval of his opponent.

Judge Davis imposed a cumulative sentence of twelve years and a fine of $12,750.

Tweed did not pay the $12,750 fine, nor serve the twelve years. He spent a little more than a year in the County Penitentiary on Blackwell's Island, and paid $250, the Court of Appeals ruling that while an indictment might contain any number of counts, no punishment in excess of that prescribed for one offense could be inflicted.

This action had been anticipated by Tilden and O'Conor, and during Tweed's imprisonment a law was enacted enabling the State to bring suit for moneys stolen from public treasuries. So when the disgraced Boss was released on January 15, 1875, he was rearrested on a civil action wherein the State, as plaintiff, sought to recover $6,000,000 of loot that had been directly traced to him. Bail was fixed in the unheard of sum of $3,000,000.

Jay Gould did not rush to Tweed's aid to furnish this bond. He did not dare. Tilden was now Governor, having been inaugurated fifteen days before the release of his old foe. And for Tweed to have put up the money would have meant its certain loss, as there would be that much to attach in the event of judgment, which was as certain as his conviction. Tilden was the man of the hour. He had been elected directly because of The Ring disclosures. For one to have spoken ill of him now would have been to attack the idol of the shouting crowds. So Tweed was committed to Ludlow Street Jail in default of surety of $3,000,000 cash or double that princely sum in real estate.

Tweed's confinement in the debtors' prison was purely nominal. He left the jail almost every afternoon in a closed carriage, accompanied by the two keepers, and when one of the upper sections of the city—then sparsely settled—was reached, the prisoner of State would alight, and take a walk for a mile or more. On the way back to the jail the party would stop at Tweed's home where dinner would be served. This continued for nearly a year.

At noon of December 4, 1875, Tweed, with his son William M. Tweed, Jr., in the custody of Warden Dunham and Keeper Hagan drove, as usual, to the upper end of the Island. This time their destination was the furthermost extreme, and on the return trip they stopped in Central Park where Tweed and his son, the Warden and Keeper at a respectful distance, walked for fifteen minutes, and then reëntered the carriage, which was driven to Tweed's mansion at the southeast corner of Forty-third Street and Fifth Avenue. It was now dark. Dunham and Hagan sat in the drawing room while Tweed went to the second floor to talk with his wife. Five minutes later, according to Dunham's story, he looked at his watch.

It was then about 6:20 o'clock. Dunham now turned to young Tweed, who sat beside them, saying that it was time to go, and to call his father. A few minutes later former Assistant District Attorney Tweed informed the two keepers that his father was not upstairs. Hagan rushed upstairs and failed to find their prisoner. Dunham rushed to the front door, looked up and down the block, but saw no signs of Tweed. The carriage was still at the door. Within ten minutes Dunham reported the escape, with this story, to the police.

High ranking police officials discredited this. They believed that Tweed had been gone for hours—probably since noon—before his escape was reported by Dunham. Two days later $10,000 reward was offered for the delivery of the escaped prisoner to William C. Conner, Sheriff of the City and County of New York. Broadsides announcing the reward, with a photograph of Tweed pasted on the upper left-hand corner—this was before the time of half-tones—were sent to the police chiefs of every city in the country and in Canada. A description of the fugitive from a copy in the possession of the New York Historical Society, follows:

"He is about fifty-five (*Sic!*) years of age, about five feet eleven inches high, will weigh about two hundred and eighty pounds, very portly, ruddy complexion, has rather large, coarse, prominent features and large prominent nose; rather small blue or grey eyes, grey hair, from originally auburn color; head nearly bald on top from forehead back to crown, and bare part of ruddy color; head projecting toward the crown. His beard may be removed or dyed, and he may wear a wig or be otherwise disguised."

In the next few weeks Tweed was reported in various parts of the world. He was in Savannah, Georgia; Dallas, Texas; Havana, Cuba; London, England; Hamilton, Ontario. At no time was he any very great distance from New York Police Headquarters for six months, less a week, after his flight. Just where is as much in the realm of doubt as his movements on the afternoon and early evening of his escape. He is placed in concealment at Bayside, Long Island; and Cos Cob, Connecticut, and Weehawken, New Jersey. Everything points to the last-named community. A carriage from his home would cover the distance to the Weehawken Ferry at the foot of West Forty-second Street in a few minutes. His destination was Spain, with which this country had no extradition treaty at the time. Some little visited part of New York Harbor would be the ideal hiding place. Tweed never revealed the manner of his escape, which cost him $60,000.

On May 29, 1876, Tweed, shorn of his beard, and wearing a wig, boarded the schooner *Frank Atwood*, which rode at anchor in the Lower Bay, off the Jersey Coast. Here is another circumstance in favor of Weehawken as Tweed's temporary retreat. A few days later Tweed landed at St. Augustine, Florida, where he was joined by a man believed to be the young Southerner, who married his daughter when nearly all New York groveled at his feet. The pair sailed in a small fishing smack to Santiago, Cuba. When their passports failed to disclose the visé of the Spanish Consul at St. Augustine, the fugitive and his companion were thrown into prison. Here let us leave them to return to the States.

The Democratic National Convention in 1876 met in St. Louis. On June 27 Tilden was nominated for President. In the following issue Nast had a cartoon in *Harper's Weekly* linking Tweed and Tilden in unholy fashion. Nast, like Greeley before his flirtation for the Democratic Presidential nomination, thought that "every one who choose to live by pugilism, gambling, or harlotry, with nearly every keeper of a tippling house, was politically a Democrat." This woodcut of the man who started the fight on Tweed, pictures the fallen Boss as a brute in prison stripes, lifting two small boys off their feet with his left hand, while his right hand, clenching a club, is upraised menacingly. The caption reads:

"TWEED—LE—DEE AND TILDEN—DUM."

Beneath the title is printed: "Reform Tweed: 'If all the people want is to have somebody arrested, I'll have you plunderers convicted. You will be allowed to escape; nobody will be hurt; and then Tilden will go to the White House, and I to Albany as Governor.' "

The background of the cartoon shows a wall, covered with signs, mostly bitter partisan attacks on Tilden, such as "It takes a thief or one who has associated with thieves to catch a thief"; and "Reward to all public thieves who have enough and can stop others from cheating and stealing." This last was a reference to Tilden's pardoning of J. H. Ingersoll, shortly after he had been convicted and sentenced to five years and seven months for his complicity in the looting of the city. Ingersoll, who had stolen millions, was given his freedom in return for turning State's evidence.

This cartoon, however, served a good purpose, for although a grotesque Tweed, the face, as all of Nast's faces, was more of a portrait than a caricature. One of the patrons of *Harper's Weekly* was Don Benigno S. Suarez, of Madrid, a friend of Alvey A. Adee, then Secretary of the American Legation in Spain. When, in the month of August the cable—the Atlantic Telegraph it was called—laid by the brother of Tweed's chief counsel, carried the message of Hamilton Fish, Grant's Secretary of State, that Tweed had sailed on the Spanish brig, *Carmen*, from Santiago, on July 27, and to arrest him on the arrival of the ship, Adee sought his friend Don Benigno. The American Consul, not knowing Tweed, had him released from the Cuban jail after he had been imprisoned seven weeks. And when the authorities at Vigo received the Don's copy of "Tweed-le-dee and Tilden-dum" with the bare orders to seize Tweed and detain him, they gathered from the cut that the fugitive was a kidnaper.

When the *Carmen* reached Vigo, Tweed, disguised as a common sailor, was found scrubbing a deck. The Spanish soldiers recognized him from the Nast cartoon. He was placed in a cell in the fortress to await the arrival of the U. S. S. *Franklin*, Admiral David Glasgow Farragut's old flagship. Escorted by thirty soldiers in gaudy red and yellow uniforms, their rifles and helmets flashing as they passed the street lamps, the prisoner was marched to the wharf. This imposing guard was led by the High Sheriff of Vigo, in all his robes of office, who with much pomp, surrendered his charge to a patrol from the American frigate. In contrast with all this ceremony was

the sorry appearance of Tweed. He was dressed in the nondescript shore clothes of a poor sailorman, a collarless linen
shirt, an old black alpaca coat, a still older brown vest, and
trousers of black and white check.

Tweed was assigned a salon adjoining the Commander's.
It was a long and stormy voyage. Tweed messed with the
officers, one of whom said on the ship's arrival in New York
on November 23: "His behavior was that of a perfect gentleman. He was always glad to see any of us when we called
on him. . . . In his habits he was very abstemious. Though
everything on the ship was at his disposal, he made no extra
demands. He did not smoke, nor did he drink, either wine
or spirits, unless when unwell. Most of the time he spent
in reading, and when urged by the Captain, on the Surgeon's
recommendation, to take an airing on deck, he availed himself
of the privilege only once. Perhaps he felt it humiliating to
walk on deck in company with an officer on guard."

Tweed gives us a possible reason for remaining in his
salon and not seeking the freedom of the deck. There was the
temptation to end it all by leaping overboard. He tells us
that he frequently contemplated suicide, but was restrained
by the thought of the additional sorrow and disgrace this would
bring upon his family. Then, too, this strange mixture had
profound religious convictions that interposed. Thus he explained: "It would have been a wicked end to a very wicked
life." Still another reason was his ill-health. He was a very
sick man and knew that he had not long to live. His intense
life, and the hounding of the past five years or more, had
told on him. Tweed had a superstitious dread that he would
die as his father had died, of heart trouble. Several times
on shipboard the *Franklin's* surgeon had prescribed sherry
and water.

Tweed when returned to the jail was no longer held as a
prisoner awaiting trial in the civil suit for $6,000,000 brought
by the State, but as a debtor to the People in that sum, judgment having been obtained against him in his absence. Reporters sought interviews with him daily. He denied himself
to all. He was very bitter toward the newspapers and their

staffs—in New York City. A member of the staff of *The Herald*, who had known Tweed well, called at the prison on December 4, the anniversary of his escape. He met with no better success. Said *The Herald* the following day on the word of a mutual friend who visited the prisoner:

"Mr. Tweed considers at present that the newspapers are treating him badly. He talks against them like an aggrieved person. He seems to have looked upon the 'corporation printing' in the light of a personal gift or bribe from himself. . . . He claims to have paid regularly the tailor's bills of one reporter and the house rent of another; to have loaned a third journalist sums ranging from $5 to $50 constantly, and now he says, 'the boys are all writing against me.' "

Tweed did not personally mind the attacks. He was thinking of the recurring blows dealt the women members of his family by these newspaper articles. He had been back in the jail eleven days when he voiced his sentiments of the press. He did not look for any quarter there, and sought none. As well seek mercy from Tilden. In the days of his power he had often humiliated Tilden by cursing and damning him in the presence of other Democratic leaders. He had found life largely a game of tit for tat. There would be a relief from all his sorrows soon. He did not need the expert advice of physicians to tell him that he had not long to live. If he had the $6,000,000 to settle the judgment against him, what would it avail him to pay it? There were other actions— criminal actions all—pending against him. After his escape an indictment charging him with conspiracy was added to the list. Only one of the fourteen indictments had been tried, leaving thirteen. In his sickness of body and soul Tweed saw in the thirteen indictments a prophecy of Fate. If he could die outside prison walls he would gladly part with all his worldly wealth!

Tweed had been back in Ludlow Street Jail about a week when on the advice of John D. Townsend, son of John R. Townsend, banker, life insurance president, and lawyer, he wrote to Charles O'Conor. Townsend, although later retained

HARPER'S WEEKLY.
JOURNAL OF CIVILIZATION

VOL. XX.—No. 1018.]   NEW YORK, SATURDAY, JULY 1, 1876.   [WITH A SUPPLEMENT. PRICE TEN CENTS.

Entered according to Act of Congress, in the Year 1876, by Harper & Brothers, in the Office of the Librarian of Congress, at Washington.

POLITICAL "CAPITAL."

The "people are in a very puzzled and despondent state of mind about the political situation, and have got beyond the point at which they look for the appearance of the ideal statesman uniting the purest motives with the highest ability. They can get the pure motives, and they can get the high ability; but somehow, owing to no matter what circumstances, to get a man who unites both into a leading place in the government is a work of such difficulty that most people have given it up as (for the present at least) a bad job, and are willing to content themselves with any man who, for whatever motive, will do good work. It so happens, too, that the work to be done at this moment is not work which calls either for the highest order of genius or the highest aspirations. A man may do it very well without being a Moses or a Washington—without, in short, being either a prophet or a hero. He has neither to lead a race out of captivity nor call a nation into existence. The task before the American politician of to-day is the simple and somewhat homely one of preventing public officers from stealing and dividing the public money, and of preventing the government from cheating its creditors; and when a man offers himself for this work, there is no general disposition to ask whether he is a statesman of the first rank, or whether his political judgment has always been sure or his "voice have always heard on the right side. In fact, they go so far as to say that to make capital in this way is a good thing to do, and they wish all politicians to engage in it. They are ready to forbear all curious inquiries into the motives or antecedents of men who will undertake to put an end to cheating and stealing. In fact, the voters of the country are sticking notices up offering the highest offices in their gift, and "no questions asked," to any body who will bring in a few plunderers of the state. Mr. Tilden has achieved his present success simply owing to his having, before any body else of his class, understood the exact nature of the situation. He perceived sooner than his competitors that the time had come to stop preaching, and to begin making arrests and drawing up indictments. He now finds, and his competitors find, that his acuteness has rendered him the highest service, and his enemies actually play into his hands."—The Nation, October 7, 1875.

IT HAS BLOWN OVER

WANTED REFORMERS OF THE TAMMANY CLASS

WANTED REFORMERS EDUCATED IN THE TAMMANY HALL SCHOOL OF REFORM.

REFORM.

REFORMED THIEVES WANTED TO TAKE CARE OF THE PEOPLE'S MONEY.

REWARD AND NO QUESTIONS ASKED.

ANYBODY WHO WILL BRING A FEW PLUNDERERS OF THE STATE TO JUSTICE (?) WILL BE REWARDED BY THE HIGHEST OFFICES IN THE GIFT OF THE PEOPLE

O.D. LORD CONVICTED, ONE OF THE CANAL RING.

TAMMANY HALL SCHOOL OF REFORM. SCHOLARS WANTED FOR REFORMERS.

REWARD TO THOSE THAT HAVE ASSOCIATED WITH THIEVES, AND GIVE STATE EVIDENCE.

TAMMANY POLICE RING

REWARD TO ALL PUBLIC THIEVES WHO HAVE ENOUGH AND CAN STOP OTHERS FROM CHEATING AND STEALING. THEY WILL BE REWARDED BY HONORABLE POSITIONS AND FAT OFFICES.

IT TAKES A THIEF OR ONE WHO HAS ASSOCIATED WITH THIEVES TO CATCH A THIEF.

TWEED-LE-DEE AND TILDEN-DUM.

REFORM TWEED. "If all the people want is to have somebody arrested, I'll have you plunderers convicted. You will be allowed to escape; nobody will be hurt, and then Tilden will go to the White House, and I to Albany, as Governor."

Tweed was arrested in Spain on a charge of kidnaping. He was recognized from Nast's "Tweed-le-dee and Tilden-dum" cartoon. The captors of The Boss could not read English. The sub-title reads: "Reform Tweed: 'If all the people want is to have somebody arrested, I'll have you plunderers convicted. You will all be allowed to escape; nobody will be hurt; and then Tilden will go to the White House, and I to Albany as Governor.'"

T<small>HIS IS</small>

THE MAN OF THE TIMES,

GEORGE JONES.

By George, but he always was flinging of stones
And kicking up shindies
Till he broke all the windies
And so got in the House
That TWEED built.

A PAGE FROM THE PAMPHLET, "THE HOUSE THAT TWEED BUILT."

by Tweed, was at this time acting merely as a friendly adviser. Townsend, a man of unblemished reputation, and long identified with civic reform, knew that in O'Conor the flames of passion and the fires of ambition had long ceased to burn. Here, if anywhere Tweed would be assured of a just hearing. O'Conor had no axes to grind. He was in his seventy-second year.

The sick prisoner dreaded the extreme humiliation that would be his if O'Conor should publicly reject his proposal to lay bare all the iniquities of The Ring and the lesser rings which preceded it, to name names, to produce checks showing the corruption of men in high place throughout the State, and in a word, to spare no one, himself least of all.

Townsend visited the venerable and venerated O'Conor at his home on Washington Heights. The old leader of the bar welcomed Tweed's change of heart, remarking: "The spectacle of Tweed upon his knees asking for mercy, and consenting to be a witness against his associates would have more effect as a preventative against future associations of like nature than would the recovery of all the money that had been stolen." On December 6, Tilden's principal aid in the prosecution of The Ring received the following:

> "Ludlow Street Jail,
> "New York, Dec. 5th, 1876.

"Charles O'Conor, Esq.,

"Sir: I take the liberty of addressing you this letter in view of the fact that your position as counsel for the State authorities is professed soley for the public good regardless of any factions or personal interest.

"Heretofore I have responded in the courts and met my troubles with every resource at my disposal. *Possibly* in the mistaken sense of duty I have stood up too long to shield others as well as myself, bearing such losses and punishments as were meted out to me in my misfortunes, and it was truly in the interests of others, more than in my own, that litigations and resistances were prolonged. Viewing the manner of my return to the Wards of this Prison, realizing the events in the City, in the State, and in the Nation which I am brought here to confront, it will not, I hope, seem to be a presumption or insincerity in me to say to you that I am indeed overwhelmed; that all further resistance being hopeless, I have now to make and only seek the shortest and most efficient manner in which I may make unqualified surrender. It is not my purpose to appeal or further resist the suits which you have against me in the name of the State or the people. I propose forthwith to place at your disposal a full surrender of all I have left of property or effects and respond at once to such examination in this connection as may assure you and the public of the good faith of the assignment as well as show the entire amount and disposition of all I have possessed as far as you wish it to be detailed.

"I am an old man, greatly broken in health, and cut down in spirits and can no longer bear my burden, and to mitigate the prospects of hopeless imprisonment, which must speedily terminate my life, I should, it seems to me, make any sacrifice or effort. During the early stage of the suits and proceedings against me, I was ready to make restitution and reparation as far as in my power. Entanglements with interests and counsels of others delayed and defeated this. I regret that now my means have become so utterly inadequate. I would not make this futile offer if I had not had some assurance through your published statements that the vindication of principle and the prospect of permanently purifying the public service was the object you have in view as being more desirable than the recovery of money. If in any manner you see fit to use me for such purposes, I shall be only too glad to respond, trusting implicitly in your high reputation and character. I ask only to make a slight reservation, not as regards myself, wherever others are concerned, and leaving my property and personal interests to be put to the fullest examination and publicity. I hope to have any matters affecting other persons restricted to your *personal* knowledge and discretion. Knowing as you do every material fact already it would be unavailing for me to withhold any details you may demand. I only ask in qualification that your more reliable judgment shall take the responsibility of publication and the use of such matters only as may be necessary for the ends you may wish to advance. For the present I have no legal counsel. I shall not employ any except to aid in the spirit of this communication, and conform to the usages of the courts.

"I send Mr. Dewey, who was at one time employed by me as my secretary. He is directed to receive any instructions or suggestions from you and to answer in detail as to my affairs.

"Very truly yours,

"WILLIAM M. TWEED."

O'Conor immediately took the letter to Tilden, who had three weeks of his term as Governor to serve. The Governor after hearing the letter read, gave his caller the shock of his life. O'Conor was not to give Tweed any assurances of freedom until after Tilden had inspected the proofs of guilt which Tweed was prepared to offer. This was more than a snub. A personal affront O'Conor would ignore if its resentment might interfere with the orderly progress of justice. But when it was coupled with an admission of what O'Conor had long suspected, that the prosecutions of The Ring were to be limited to Tweed, and that the dying prisoner in Ludlow Street Jail was to be made the scapegoat of the sins of hundreds equally guilty, this strait-laced old man, took his hat, and with a formal good-evening, withdrew from Tilden's presence and further participation in the prosecution of The Ring frauds.

O'Conor's suspicions were far from groundless. The exposé of The Ring was now more than five years old. Some of the thieves were in France with which this country had an extradition treaty. Connolly and lesser tools of Tweed were in Paris enjoying the stolen loot. Men were presiding over the destinies of several up-State cities who had made fortunes through their corrupt alliance with Tweed. There were many respectable citizens in New York who had joined hands with The Ring in looting the city. Their names were not even made public. Promise had been made when Connolly resigned, and Andrew H. Green was named Comptroller in his stead, that a complete list, showing the name of every person who had dealings with the city, and the amount of money awarded him by The Ring, would be published. Yet this was not done, and never has been done. Too many good people would be shown as participants in the wholesale looting of the taxpayers. More than $30,000,000 had been stolen by The Ring in thirty months. Tweed was sued for $6,000,000, yet no suit was brought against the Elegant Oakey. Sweeny was permitted to escape punishment after his brother James died by giving back $394,594.28 of the money he had stolen, and saying that his dead brother was the thief!

Woodward, one of the collectors of The Ring obtained a clean bill of health when he paid the tithe of his thievings, $150,387.90. The executors of the estate of Watson settled for a sum slightly in excess of $558,237. But up to the time of O'Conor's visit to Tilden, only the Watson's estate had returned any of the stolen moneys. The rest came after it became known that Tweed was ready to confess. There were two other restitutions, one from the Broadway National Bank for $227,325.00 and $22,866.78 received from E. Starkweather. Out of this aggregate of $1,353,410.96, lawyers employed to collect from The Ring were paid fees amounting to $231,690.21 leaving $1,121,720.75 net for the city. This was all the people received of their stolen millions, which Henry F. Taintor, the accountant who inquired into The Ring frauds, reported at $45,000,000 to $50,000,000 in the three and a half years beginning January 1, 1868. This was a year before The Ring proper began. O'Rourke, whose disclosures helped to dethrone The Ring, estimates that Tweed and his associates stole $75,000,000 in the thirty months of the life of The Ring. There is no support for O'Rourke's statement that the total peculations of Tweed and his associates from the beginning of 1865 to the summer of 1871 totalled $200,000,000. In this last figure O'Rourke included bond issues of which he said no record had ever been kept.

After O'Conor withdrew from the case, Tweed's offer was submitted to Charles S. Fairchild, the Attorney General of the State, who was now in sole charge of The Ring prosecutions. Fairchild lived in Albany, and owed his nomination on the Democratic ticket for the office he held to up-State friends of Tilden. Tweed specifically offered to surrender all his real and personal property then in his control, in which he was or had been interested since 1870; to produce proofs of the fraudulent character of several claims against the city aggregating $2,000,000; and to turn over canceled checks revealing payments of moneys looted from the city treasury. These proofs involved Judges then sitting on the bench, members of the Legislature, and many up-State Mayors. In addition, Tweed offered to testify in any proceeding where he was needed.

Fairchild called on Tweed late in March, 1877. Ludlow Street Jail, being built for debtors, lacks the severity of a prison for felons, and inmates are not subjected to the rigors of prison life. Their quarters are comparatively comfortable, and those able to pay for luxuries enjoy them. Daily visits are permitted, and there is no censorship of mail, incoming or outgoing, either as to contents or quantity, and all forms of reading matter may be kept by the prisoners. The average man sent to Ludlow Street Jail has been guilty usually of only one crime—being poor. Tweed's chambers consisted of two rooms. These were the quarters assigned to the Warden. For their use Tweed paid $75 weekly to this official. They were on the first floor, immediately to the left as one entered the heavy-barred door from Ludlow Street. On entering the little apartment Fairchild found himself in Tweed's bedroom. Through the window he could look out on Ludlow Street. On the sill were several pots of blooming flowers. A square grand piano stood in one corner. In the center was a small table on which the Bible and other books and papers were piled. Off this was a small chamber, used as a sitting and dining room. There was a sideboard near a window overlooking the small courtyard where Tweed took his daily walks. This window, too, was filled with geraniums and other flowering potted plants. There were several comfortable chairs scattered throughout both rooms, and the walls were covered with lithographs, engravings, and etchings. Had Fairchild visited Tweed in the days of his glory when he rented seven rooms in the Delevan House in Albany, he would have noticed how successfully Tweed had reproduced a similarity of the two rooms at the end of his regal suite—his own private quarters. All that was missing were singing canaries in their brass cages. But what prisoner of imagination could endure the constant sight of an imprisoned songster? Tweed had a volunteer in his imprisonment, Luke Grant, a Negro servant. Luke was well paid for his services. He, too, called his master "Boss." There was one thing about the place that was absent in the Delevan House—formidable, steel bars on the windows. These grim reminders of Tweed's plight were not visible from within. Cretonne curtains, richly flowered, hid them from view.

When the Attorney General departed Tweed was satisfied that he would be used as a witness in the State's suit against Sweeny for $7,000,000. Sweeny was back from France. A safe conduct signed by representatives of city and State protected him from arrest or other legal annoyance pending a discussion of possible settlement. Fairchild assured Tweed there would be no settlement, and that after he testified against Sweeny he would once more be free, shorn, it is true, of all he had. But what was that compared with the air of freedom and death outside prison walls, mourned as a repentant thief who had publicly atoned, in part at least, for the wrongs he had done?

More than a month dragged wearily by and the disease of the heart was getting worse, and diabetes, which had first shown itself when he was a prisoner on Blackwell's Island two years before, had now become acute. "Since he has been under the excitement attending his anticipation of release, his troubles have become greatly aggravated. He absolutely needs rest of mind and opportunity to obtain exercise and sunshine." This was from a letter from Tweed's physician, which accompanied a certificate dated May 10, 1877, detailing the symptoms of the prisoner's case, and ending with: "I am therefore of the opinion that he cannot recover again if the constant worriment of mind and confinement are not removed."

Tweed had no reason to doubt Fairchild's word, for the Attorney General had also assured Honest John Kelly, leader of Tammany Hall, as well as Tweed's counsel, that he would keep his promise to free Tweed. Fairchild had examined his statement, and so had Peckham and Whitney, his assistants, who on May 26 wrote the Attorney General that Tweed would be of immediate value as a witness in the Sweeny action and in a case where the city was being sued.

A week later it was gossiped that Fairchild would not keep his promise, and that a settlement out of court had been effected with Sweeny. On June 6 Townsend wrote Fairchild:

"I am just informed that you have effected a settlement in the case against Peter B. Sweeny and there is every reason to believe that the amount of money obtained was secured in a great degree by the use you have made of the Statement I furnished to you about two months since, by direction of my client, Mr. Tweed, under your promise that he should be discharged if *any use* was made of that 'Statement.' I now request the fulfillment of your agreement."

On June 12 Fairchild wrote a weasel reply to the above, herewith reproduced:

"Herewith I return to you the statement of testimony which you assert that William M. Tweed could give if he were released from imprisonment. After careful consideration I have come to the conclusion that the testimony which said Tweed could give, as shown by said statement, would not justify his release. You will also find the letter of Dr. Schirmer."

It will be observed that Fairchild here ignores any reference to his visit to Tweed in jail, or to the promise he had made to Townsend.

The summer passed and Fairchild who had probably anticipated all possible consequences, or else counted on Tilden's influence to save him, was denied a renomination on the orders of Honest John Kelly, who had Augustus Schoonmaker, Jr., of Kingston, named. Schoonmaker was elected and took office on January 1, 1878. In the interim an Aldermanic Committee was appointed before which Tweed testified to a few of the things he could tell. Much of it is already familiar to the reader. He looked better after these daily excursions from the jail, in the heart of the East Side, every inch of which he knew from early boyhood. Here in the City Hall, he first sat as an Alderman a little more than a quarter of a century ago. Tweed began his testimony before the Aldermanic investigators on September 16. The following morning *The Sun* published a letter from our crooked acquaintance, John Morrissey, attacking Tweed, and suggesting various questions to put to the witness. Tweed asked permission to reply. One of the Aldermen suggested he take no notice of it, but answer the questions of counsel for the committee.

"Must I sit here," said Tweed, "and be abused by every thief that stands on the corner who chooses to wag his tongue at me, and then be told that I can have no opportunity of defending myself? I am tied hand and foot. I am in jail. This man is in the streets, free, haunting the public houses, hotels, barrooms, and restaurants. He says he has given me one dose, and shall give me another. Then I shall give him another. This man has taken me when I am at a disadvantage, and he has sent this paper here to hurt me all it can. I shall fight back at everybody that fights me. I can't be crushed out because I'm unfortunate."

Tweed soon forgot his anger against Morrissey. When he volunteered that he put the former Assistant Secretary of State, E. K. Apgar, on the Street Department payroll, and was asked what work Apgar was doing in return for his salary from the city, Tweed smilingly responded:

"Spouting—talking—making speeches."

On another occasion, when he suddenly remembered that he had been talking at lightning speed, he paused in his recital of corruption, and addressing the press table, said:

"I must apologize to the reporters for speaking so fast, but it is my nature when I get excited. It has caused me more trouble than it has anybody else."

He had forgotten his grievance against the reporters. He was beginning to understand that George Jones had ushered in a new dawn in American journalism.

In the winter of 1877-1878 Tweed had several bad heart attacks. On these occasions his black servant never left his side at night. He was constantly under the attendance of physicians. Among them was one of the noted specialists of the day, Dr. John M. Carnochan. Several clergymen from neighboring churches called to offer him the consolation of religion. Tweed thanked them as he declined their good offices. And when each departed he would open the Bible at some favorite passage. At times he would suddenly stop reading the Book to swear like a trooper at the irrepressible Negro, who, forgetting that his master was at his devotions, would burst into boisterous song that called for a buck-and-wing accompaniment. Tweed would quickly make amends for this outburst, for he was fond of Luke, and took keen pleasure in chaffing the darky. Luke was in love with a dusky damsel who wrote him constantly at the jail, for Luke was little better than a prisoner. She thought her Luke the smartest man of their race in all New York. She did receive letters that no other Negro could write, or her sweetheart, for that matter. Tweed dictated these letters, using the biggest words in the language to the intense delight of his man. There were always two or three visitors at the dinner hour, for Tweed did not like dining alone. After Luke served the meal—if Tweed was not too ill to stay up—a quiet game of cards would round out the evening.

Tweed's appearance in the day belied his real condition. But his friends knew that his days were numbered. They moved to obtain his freedom. The Board of Aldermen, by a majority resolution, urged it. Here again partisanship entered, or perhaps fear that it might be thought they had been bribed, for six Republicans opposed his release. On March 21, 1878, Honest John Kelly, then the Comptroller, wrote to Attorney General Schoonmaker:

"I feel it to be my duty as an individual and as a public officer, to urge upon you the discharge of William M. Tweed, who is now confined in the debtors' prison in this city. My protest, as an individual, against the further detention, arises from the fact that my assurance to Mr. Tweed's counsel (Mr. J. D. Townsend) that the late Attorney-General would fulfil his promise to discharge his client should he make full confession of his misdeeds and surrender his property, more than anything else induced the confession thereafter made by Tweed and his proffer of surrender of property. Mr. Fairchild did state to me that he would discharge Mr. Tweed if he made a full confession and surrendered his property, and I did say to Mr. Townsend that he might rely upon Mr. Fairchild's statement, which he (Mr. Townsend), then said had been made to him. As a citizen I feel that the State is being dishonored by this breach of faith. As a public officer I urge his discharge, because I believe his further detention in a debtors' prison is neither beneficial to the State as an example to evil-doers nor in any sense serviceable to the city.

"There are several actions now pending against this city in which millions of dollars are involved, and it is conceded that in some of these, if not all, Tweed's testimony will be very important. I am informed by Mr. Townsend that Tweed will decline to testify as a witness unless the promise of his discharge, heretofore made him, be carried out, and no one can fairly blame him if he adheres to that determination. Had Mr. Tweed and his associates been convicted and sent to State Prison, as I believe should have been the course pursued at first against them, I would be among the last to advocate the discharge of any of them, but I conceive that neither justice nor good policy, now that such opposite course has been adopted towards the others, dictates the present treatment of Tweed."

The State had been dishonored by Fairchild's breach of faith, and Schoonmaker gave assurances to Tweed's successor as leader of Tammany Hall that he would release Tweed after the Legislature adjourned on May 15. This gave Tweed something to look forward to. But he had resolved that he would not testify in any case in which he might be called until the promise was fulfilled.

Five days after Kelly's letter had been written and published, for Honest John gave copies of it to the newspapers, Tweed was subpœnæd in a suit before Judge Potter, in the Supreme Court. The account in *The Herald* tells us that "Boss Tweed . . . looked in fine health, shook hands smilingly with old acquaintances, stepped nimbly to the witness stand."

"May I read a statement?" asked Tweed.

"Certainly," answered Judge Potter, "if it has anything to do with your appearance here as a witness."

Tweed, who had pulled a manuscript from his coat pocket, responded: "I think you will see that it has a very important connection with my being here."

Then Tweed adjusted his glasses and read: "Your Honor, before a question is put to me in this case, with all respect to the court, I must be permitted to make an explanation." He then recited the promises made to him and his counsel by Fairchild to liberate him from the imprisonment under which he had been suffering for several years past, and that on advice of counsel he would not answer any questions in any proceedings where the city or State was a party until that promise was fulfilled. "And in making this statement I wish to add that I do not wish Your Honor or the jury in this particular case to infer that I have anything to communicate or conceal which has any bearing whatever upon this question now being tried."

There was no attempt to question Tweed. The Judge, who with every other right-thinking man, felt the justice of Tweed's position, nodded, and the witness returned to Ludlow Street Jail. Men who had roundly condemned The Ring and all his associates now sympathized with him. It was evident to all with understanding that he was being made the scapegoat. Judge Davis, who had sentenced him, condemned from the bench the failure of Fairchild and Peckham and the rest of their crew in failing to prosecute others. O'Conor had publicly protested against the shameful settlements that were made with Sweeny and one or two others, whereby these stealers of millions were given immunity from all civil and criminal prosecution upon returning a small fraction of their thefts. Tweed was philosophical. He knew how those things were done. He found solace in his Bible.

Tweed celebrated his fifty-fifth birthday on April 3. A few old friends dined with him. On his right was George W. Butts, who sat next to him on a similar occasion in the old Westchester House twenty years before. Butts, who had a profitable livery business, was one of the very few who remained steadfast to the fallen Boss. April 3 fell on a Wednesday. On Friday Dr. Carnochan found Tweed's heart in a serious condition. He was also suffering from a slight attack of bronchial pneumonia. That night Luke slept on the floor beside his master's bed. To the head of the bed a string was attached. The other end of the cord was fastened to the wrist of the Negro so when Tweed needed him in the night he could summon him by jerking the string. The following

Thursday evening Dr. Carnochan remained at Tweed's bedside until eleven o'clock. When the physician departed, the patient, who was feeling comfortable for the first time in days, said: "Now, Luke, you and I can have a good sleep to-night. We need it much. I think I will sit up to-morrow, Luke, I feel so well."

Luke turned the gas low, and then with the string attached to his wrist, lay down on the floor as he had done continuously for six nights past. He had orders to give his master a draught of medicine at three o'clock. He waited until Tweed's eyes were closed and he was breathing regularly. Then he undid the string round his wrist and tiptoed out of the room to the jail office. He was so worn out that he knew if he closed his eyes for a minute he would sleep well beyond the four hours unless The Boss awakened before that time and needed him. Luke talked to the keeper, and every fifteen minutes tiptoed back to see if his patient had awakened. At midnight when the servant entered the sick room he heard Tweed breathing with difficulty. "Boss, are you asleep?" he whispered softly. "No, I am not asleep. Here, give me your hand. My heart pains me."

Luke was now at the bedside. Tweed took the servant's hand and placed it over his heart. The darky tucked his free hand under Tweed's shoulders, raised him to a sitting position, and pillowing The Boss's head on his own breast, massaged the region of the heart. In a few minutes the sick man breathed more easily. But the pain continued intense. For a full two hours Tweed remained in this position. Then, his pain relieved by the constant chafing, he lay down on the pillow.

Tweed had a fever, and while his forehead was being laved with vinegar and water, he feebly asked for something to drink. Luke made some sherry sangaree and held the glass to the parched lips. "That is too sour. Give me some beef tea." When this was proffered him he declined that, too, and asked for water.

"No, Boss," said Luke, shaking his head vigorously, "I can't give you any water. It's against the doctor's orders."

"Oh, can I not have anything?" pleaded Tweed piteously. "Do you mean—to keep me—here—to perish all alone—with you?"

"No, Boss," said Luke in a soothing voice, as he took his master's hand, "you can have anything except water." And then Luke blurted out so that it seemed like one word: "And if you insists upon it, you can have that, too."

Tweed realized that Luke was only carrying out orders, and smiled faintly as he feebly said: "No, Luke, I won't ask for any water. Give me some tea."

When Luke brewed some tea, Tweed drank it and felt better. As Luke took the cup and saucer, the patient, in a little stronger voice, said, "Lie down, Luke, and see if you can get some sleep." A moment later The Boss closed his eyes and then moaned in agony: "Oh, what shall I do! What shall I do! Give me something! Give me anything so that I can get some sleep or I shall die. I can't stand this pain!" Dr. Carnochan had left orders that if Tweed did not rest before three o'clock, he was to be given a sleeping potion. After taking it Tweed moaned, "Oh, my heart! My heart!" He had never been in such pain.

"I will send for the doctor, Boss."

"No, no. Just give me something to ease my pain. I am going to die anyway."

The voice was growing fainter. The draught was taking effect. He slept. But with the break of dawn he awakened and the pain returned. At half past eight Dr. Carnochan entered the sick room. "Oh, doctor," moaned Tweed, "I am dying. Do something for me."

The darky, who had been trying to relieve the pain by massaging Tweed's chest, burst into tears.

Tweed seized the black hand, patted it, and looked gratefully at the Negro as he said feebly: "Luke! Don't do that! Don't do that! You will make me feel bad!"

He began to sink into a stupor. Dr. Carnochan dispatched Luke for a fly blister. This revived the sufferer. One of his married daughters—the other was in Europe with her mother, Tweed having begged them to leave the country so

that they could escape humiliation of seeing the daily newspaper attacks upon him—arrived with her husband. The
couple had driven in a closed carriage from their home in
Seventy-seventh Street, just off Madison Avenue. This was
the first of Tweed's daughters to marry, and she was regular
in her visits to the jail. She was ignorant of his condition,
and greeted him as usual. As had been her custom, she suggested ice cream, and Tweed nodded. In the dim light of the
room she had mistaken the pain-distorted lips for a smile.
It was as well. She never returned with ice cream alone, for
she filled her arms with the little table delicacies he relished.
Charles Devlin, a life-long friend, who knew the end was near,
suggested that Tweed make a will. "No, I have nothing left
to settle except with my God." Then he beckoned to Dr.
Carnochan. His voice was now a low mutter. "I have tried
to do some good if I have not had good luck. I am not afraid
to die. I believe the guardian angels will protect me." He
seemed in less pain, and talked in an inaudible tone of his
confinement, and of its bad effect on his health. His breathing
was now labored. With extreme effort he gasped: "Tilden
and Fairchild—they will be satisfied now." Then he closed
his eyes. The jail was strangely still. At the foot of the
bed were grouped the Deputy Warden of the jail, Bernard
Fitzsimmons, his wife, and their daughter. Devlin, and William Edelstein, one of his many lawyers, stood at the head.
Dr. Carnochan watched his patient, who was lying on his left
side, the wan cheek pillowed on his open palm. Luke noted
this with satisfaction, for The Boss always found more quiet
in this position than in any other. Beside him was Tweed's
son-in-law, whose wife was out buying ice cream and other
delicacies for her father.

The stillness now became oppressive. Suddenly, like a thun-
derclap on the ears of the anxious group in the dimly lighted
room came a peal from the great bell in the Essex Market
tower. It was the hour of high noon. And as the last stroke
of the twelve reverberated through the prison Tweed moved his
lips for the last time. His daughter returned at this moment.
Luke was on his knees, clasping the lifeless hands of The Boss,

and sobbing convulsively. The delicacies for her father fell to the floor as she stretched forth her hands and staggered toward the bed.

Among Tweed's effects gathered up by his secretary, S. Foster Dewey, were a number of unanswered begging letters that had been received in the last days of his life. Tweed had always personally answered every one of these, and where the case seemed worthy, it was investigated, and treated according to its merits. Dewey tells us that Tweed found consolation in his last days in talking over his many charities with his old cronies. Once Tweed told them that he had been led astray by false ambition. Dewey and other worshipers of The Boss were critical of his successor in Tammany Hall, Honest John Kelly. They thought, and rightly, that Honest John should not have waited until he did to make public protest against Fairchild's broken promise. Dewey, on the day of Tweed's death, thus appraised the old and new leader of Tammany: "Tweed was not an honest politician, but a level one—Kelly is honest but not level."

The following Wednesday morning the venerable cleric, Dr. Price, who had married Tweed, and baptized each of the eight children, read the Office of the Dead before the body was taken from his daughter's home. The only politician of consequence present was Honest John Kelly. He was in one of the eight carriages which followed the hearse down Fifth Avenue, past Tweed's mansion at Forty-third Street, turning east at Washington Square, and then along Broadway to the Hamilton Avenue Ferry, at the foot of Whitehall Street. Smith Ely, Jr., who, we recall, was a member of the Board of Supervisors and an obsequious follower of The Boss, was now Mayor. He had been requested to half-mast the flag on the City Hall while the funeral cortege was passing. Perhaps the number of carriage was too few. Had there been eight hundred or eight thousand, Ely might not have denied the request. So the Stars and Stripes floated proudly from the masthead over the marble pile where Mayor Ely had often groveled in Tweed's presence.

When the ferry reached the Brooklyn shore, the little funeral procession did not halt until the Fourth Avenue entrance of Greenwood Cemetery was reached. Here it was met by twenty men, in black silk hats and white linen aprons. Tweed, too, was wearing a white apron, only his was of lambskin—the emblem of innocence. It had been presented to him when he was raised in Palestine Lodge, F. and A. M., some thirty years before.

It was the request of the contrite Tweed that he be buried by his Lodge. He knew that this was the only last honor he could count on, as behind the tiled door, hypocrisy was unknown. At the grave a Last Lodge was formed by order of R. O. Penfield, the Master, who planted a sprig of acacia to mark the place of burial of William Marcy Tweed.

THE END

BIBLIOGRAPHY

ADAMS, JR., Charles F., and Henry ADAMS, *Chapters of Erie and Other Essays*. Boston: J. R. Osgood and Company, 1871.

BAKER, General L. C., *History of the United States Secret Service*. Philadelphia: L. C. Baker, 1867.

BARNES, David M., *Draft Riots in New York*. New York: Baker and Godwin, 1863.

BARRETT, Walter, *The Old Merchants of New York City*. New York: Carleton, 1864.

BEECHER, William C., and Rev. Samuel SCOVILLE, assisted by Mrs. Henry Ward BEECHER, *A Biography of Rev. Henry Ward Beecher*. New York: Charles L. Webster & Company, 1888.

BELLOWS, Henry W., *Historical Sketch of the Union League Club of New York*. For Private Distribution, New York: The Club, 1879.

BIGELOW, John, *Restrospections of an Active Life*. New York: The Baker and Taylor Company, 1909.

BIGELOW, John, *Letters and Literary Memorials of Samuel J. Tilden*. New York and London: Harper & Brothers, 1908.

BIGELOW, John, *The Life of Samuel J. Tilden*. New York: Harper and Brothers, 1895.

BIGELOW, John, *The Writings and Speeches of Samuel J. Tilden*. New York: Harper & Brothers, 1885.

BOOTH, Mary L., *History of the City of New York*. New York: James Miller, 1863.

BRACE, Charles Loring, *The Dangerous Classes of New York*. New York: Wynkoop & Hallenbeck, 1872.

BRANN, Rev. Henry A., *Most Reverend John Hughes.* New York: Dodd, Mead and Company, 1892.

BREEN, Matthew P., *Thirty Years of New York Politics.* New York: 1899.

BROWNE, Junius Henri, *The Great Metropolis; a Mirror of New York. A Complete History of Metropolitan Life and Society, With Sketches of Prominent Places, Persons, and Things in the City, as They Actually Exist.* Hartford: American Publishing Company, 1869.

BROWNLOW, W. G., *Sketches of the Rise, Progress, and Decline of Secession.* Philadelphia: George W. Childs, 1862.

BRYCE, James, *The American Commonwealth.* London: Macmillan and Company, 1888.

COOK, Theodore P., *The Life and Public Services of Hon. Samuel J. Tilden.* New York: D. Appleton and Company, 1876.

CROLY, David G., *Seymour and Blair, Their Lives and Services.* New York: Richardson and Company, 1868.

DAVIS, Elmer, *A History of the New York Times.* New York: The New York Times, 1921.

DAVIS, Jefferson, *The Rise and Fall of the Confederate Government.* New York: D. Appleton and Company, 1881.

FOORD, John, *The Life and Public Services of Andrew Haswell Green.* Garden City, New York: Doubleday, Page and Company, 1913.

FOSTER, G. G., *New York by Gas-Light.* New York: M. J. Ivers & Co., circa 1850.

FRY, James B., Provost Marshal General of the United States, *New York and the Conscription of 1863.* New York: G. P. Putnam's Sons, 1885.

GILMORE, James R., *Personal Recollections of Abraham Lincoln.* Boston: L. C. Page & Co., 1898.

GREELEY, Horace, *Recollections of a Busy Life.* New York: J. B. Ford and Company, 1868.

HALSEY and HALSEY, *Thomas Halsey of Hertfordshire, England, and Southampton, L. I.*, 1591-1679, *With His American Descendants to the Eighth and Ninth Generations.* Morristown, New Jersey: 1895.

HALSTEAD, Murat, and J. Frank BEALE, JR., *Life of Jay Gould, How He Made His Millions.* Edgewood Publishing Company, 1892.

HOPKINS, James H., *A History of Political Parties in the United States.* New York and London: G. P. Putnam's Sons, 1900.

HUDSON, Frederic, *Journalism in the United States.* New York: Harper and Brothers, 1873.

INGRAHAM, Abijah, *A Biography of Fernando Wood. A History of the Forgeries, Perjuries, and Other Crimes of Our Model Mayor.* New York: 1856.

JONES, Willoughby, *James Fisk, Jr., The Life of a Green Mountain Boy. The Story of His Struggle from Poverty and Weakness up to Wealth and Power.* Philadelphia: W. Flint, 1872.

JONES, Willoughby, *The Life of James Fisk, Jr., The Story of His Youth and Manhood, With A Full Account of All the Schemes and Enterprises in Which He Was Engaged, Including the Great Frauds of the Tammany Ring. Biographical Sketches of Railroad Magnates and Great Financiers, with Brilliant Pen Pictures in the Lights and Shadows of New York Life.* Philadelphia, Chicago, Cincinati: Union Publishing Company, 1872.

KEHOE, Lawrence, *John Hughes, Complete Works, Comprising Sermons, Letters, Speeches, Etc.* New York: Lawrence Kehoe, 1866, London: Richardson and Son.

LEE, James Melvin, *History of American Journalism.* Boston and New York: Houghton Mifflin Company, 1917.

MACLEOD, Donald, *Biography of Hon. Fernando Wood.* New York: O. F. Parsons, Philadelphia, J. B. Lippincott and Co., 1856.

MAVERICK, Augustus, *Henry J. Raymond and the New York Press.* Hartford: A. S. Hale and Company, 1870.

McALPINE, R. W., *The Life and Times of Col. James Fisk, Jr., Being a Full and Impartial Account of the Remarkable Career of a Most Remarkable Man.* New York: The New York Book Company, 1872.

McCLURE, A. K., *Abraham Lincoln and Men of War-Times, Some Personal Recollections of War and Politics During the Lincoln Administration.* Philadelphia: The Times Publishing Company, 1892.

MEDBERY, James K., *Men and Mysteries of Wall Street.* Boston: Fields, Osgood and Co., 1870.

MYERS, Gustavus, *The History of Tammany Hall.* New York: Boni and Liveright, Incorporated, 1917.

NEVINS, Allan, *The Evening Post.* New York: Boni and Liveright, 1922.

NICHOLS, John Wesley, *The People's Candidate for President, 1872, George Francis Train.* New York, 1872.

NICOLAY, John G., and John Hay, *Abraham Lincoln, A History.* New York: Century Company, 1890.

NORTHROP, Henry Davenport, *The Life and Achievements of Jay Gould, the Wizard of Wall Street; Being a Complete Account of the Greatest Financier of Modern Times.* Philadelphia: National Publishing Company, 1892.

PAINE, Albert Bigelow, *Th. Nast, His Period and His Pictures.* New York: The Macmillan Company, 1904.

PARTON, James, *The Life of Horace Greeley.* New York: Mason Brothers, 1855.

PERRY, Bliss, *The Heart of Emerson's Journal.* Boston and New York: Houghton Mifflin Company, 1926.

REES, James, *The Life of Edwin Forrest.* Philadelphia: T. B. Peterson and Brothers, 1874.

SPRAGUE, A. P., *Speeches, Arguments and Miscellaneous Papers of David Dudley Field.* New York: D. Appleton and Company, 1884.

STAFFORD, Marshall P., *A Life of James Fisk, Jr., Being a Full and Accurate Narrative of All the Enterprises in Which He Has Been Engaged.* New York: Polhemus and Pearson, 1871.

STONE, William L., *History of New York City.* New York: Virtue and Yorston, 1872.

TILDEN, Samuel J., *The New York City Ring, Its Origin, Maturity and Fall.* New York: J. Polhemus, 1873.

TOWNSEND, Hon. John D., *New York in Bondage.* New York: 1901.

TRAIN, George Francis, *American Merchant in Europe, Asia, and Australia: A Series of Letters.* New York: G. P. Putnam and Company, 1857.

TRAIN, George Francis, [Under pen-name of Civis Americanus Sum] *In a British Jail. England Bombarded With Bastile Epigrams.* New York: The Fenian Brotherhood, 1868.

TRAIN, George Francis, *Spread Eagleism.* New York: Derby and Jackson, 1859.

TUCKERMAN, Bayard, [editor of] *The Diary of Philip Hone.* New York: Dodd, Mead and Company, 1889.

WALLING, George W., *Recollections of a New York Chief of Police.* New York: Caxton Book Concern, Limited, 1887.

VOLUNTERR SPECIAL [Pen-name] *The Volcano Under The City.* New York: Fords, Howard, and Hulbert, 1887.

WHITE, Trumbull, *The Wizard of Wall Street and His Wealth, or The Life and Deeds of Jay Gould.* Chicago: Mid-Continent Publishing Company, 1892.

In addition to the above, a succession of governmental records has been consulted—National, State, and local—as well as the newspapers of the period.

INDEX

Index

POLITICS AND PEOPLE

The Ordeal of Self-Government in America

An Arno Press Collection

Allen, Robert S., editor. **Our Fair City.** 1947

Belmont, Perry. **Return to Secret Party Funds:** Value of Reed Committee. 1927

Berge, George W. **The Free Pass Bribery System:** Showing How the Railroads, Through the Free Pass Bribery System, Procure the Government Away from the People. 1905

Billington, Ray Allen. **The Origins of Nativism in the United States, 1800-1844.** 1933

Black, Henry Campbell. **The Relation of the Executive Power to Legislation.** 1919

Boothe, Viva Belle. **The Political Party as a Social Process.** 1923

Breen, Matthew P. **Thirty Years of New York Politics, Up-to-Date.** 1899

Brooks, Robert C. **Corruption in American Politics and Life.** 1910

Brown, George Rothwell. **The Leadership of Congress.** 1922

Bryan, William Jennings. **A Tale of Two Conventions:** Being an Account of the Republican and Democratic National Conventions of June, 1912. 1912

The Caucus System in American Politics. 1974

Childs, Harwood Lawrence. **Labor and Capital in National Politics.** 1930

Clapper, Raymond. **Racketeering in Washington.** 1933

Crawford, Kenneth G. **The Pressure Boys:** The Inside Story of Lobbying in America. 1939

Dallinger, Frederick W. **Nominations for Elective Office in the United States.** 1897

Dunn, Arthur Wallace. **Gridiron Nights:** Humorous and Satirical Views of Politics and Statesmen as Presented by the Famous Dining Club. 1915

Ervin, Spencer. **Henry Ford vs. Truman H. Newberry:** The Famous Senate Election Contest. A Study in American Politics, Legislation and Justice. 1935

Ewing, Cortez A.M. and Royden J. Dangerfield. **Documentary Source Book in American Government and Politics.** 1931

Ford, Henry Jones. **The Cost of Our National Government:** A Study in Political Pathology. 1910

Foulke, William Dudley. **Fighting the Spoilsmen:** Reminiscences of the Civil Service Reform Movement. 1919

Fuller, Hubert Bruce. **The Speakers of the House.** 1909

Griffith, Elmer C. **The Rise and Development of the Gerrymander.** 1907

Hadley, Arthur Twining. **The Relations Between Freedom and Responsibility in the Evolution of Democratic Government.** 1903

Hart, Albert Bushnell. **Practical Essays on American Government.** 1893

Holcombe, Arthur N. **The Political Parties of To-Day:** A Study in Republican and Democratic Politics. 1924

Hughes, Charles Evans. **Conditions of Progress in Democratic Government.** 1910

Kales, Albert M. **Unpopular Government in the United States.** 1914

Kent, Frank R. **The Great Game of Politics.** 1930

Lynch, Denis Tilden. **"Boss" Tweed:** The Story of a Grim Generation. 1927

McCabe, James D., Jr. (Edward Winslow Martin, pseud.) **Behind the Scenes in Washington.** 1873

Macy, Jesse. **Party Organization and Machinery.** 1912

Macy, Jesse. **Political Parties in the United States, 1846-1861.** 1900

Moley, Raymond. **Politics and Criminal Prosecution.** 1929

Munro, William Bennett. **The Invisible Government** and **Personality in Politics:** A Study of Three Types in American Public Life. 1928/1934 Two volumes in one.

Myers, Gustavus. **History of Public Franchises in New York City,** Boroughs of Manhattan and the Bronx. (Reprinted from **Municipal Affairs,** March 1900) 1900

Odegard, Peter H. and E. Allen Helms. **American Politics:** A Study in Political Dynamics. 1938

Orth, Samuel P. **Five American Politicians:** A Study in the Evolution of American Politics. 1906

Ostrogorski, M[oisei I.] **Democracy and the Party System in the United States:** A Study in Extra-Constitutional Government. 1910

Overacker, Louise. **Money in Elections.** 1932

Overacker, Louise. **The Presidential Primary.** 1926

The Party Battle. 1974

Peel, Roy V. and Thomas C. Donnelly. **The 1928 Campaign:** An Analysis. 1931

Pepper, George Wharton. **In the Senate** and **Family Quarrels:** The President, The Senate, The House. 1930/1931. Two volumes in one

Platt, Thomas Collier. **The Autobiography of Thomas Collier Platt.** Compiled and edited by Louis J. Lang. 1910

Roosevelt, Theodore. **Social Justice and Popular Rule:** Essays, Addresses, and Public Statements Relating to the Progressive Movement, 1910-1916 (*The Works of Theodore Roosevelt,* Memorial Edition, Volume XIX) 1925

Root, Elihu. **The Citizen's Part in Government** and **Experiments in Government and the Essentials of the Constitution.** 1907/1913. Two volumes in one

Rosten, Leo C. **The Washington Correspondents.** 1937

Salter, J[ohn] T[homas]. **Boss Rule:** Portraits in City Politics. 1935

Schattschneider, E[lmer] E[ric]. **Politics, Pressures and the Tariff:** A Study of Free Private Enterprise in Pressure Politics, as Shown in the 1929-1930 Revision of the Tariff. 1935

Smith, T[homas] V. and Robert A. Taft. **Foundations of Democracy:** A Series of Debates. 1939

The Spoils System in New York. 1974

Stead, W[illiam] T. **Satan's Invisible World Displayed,** Or, Despairing Democracy. A Study of Greater New York (The Review of Reviews Annual) 1898

Van Devander, Charles W. **The Big Bosses.** 1944

Wallis, J[ames] H. **The Politician:** His Habits, Outcries and Protective Coloring. 1935

Werner, M[orris] R. **Privileged Characters.** 1935

White, William Allen. **Politics:** The Citizen's Business. 1924

Wooddy, Carroll Hill. **The Case of Frank L. Smith:** A Study in Representative Government. 1931

Wooddy, Carroll Hill. **The Chicago Primary of 1926:** A Study in Election Methods. 1926

The Native Americans elected their candidate. But not with Tweed's vote.

In the fall the bigotry of the spring election was forgotten in the excitement of the Presidential struggle between Henry Clay, the Whig nominee, and his Democratic rival, James K. Polk. Busts of the two candidates adorned the lintels of their respective partisans, draped with flags, and placarded with patriotic and political legends. Political clubs marched and counter-marched all throughout the month of October, and none excelled the Empire Club, overlorded by the swaggering Isaiah Rynders, crook, gambler and bruiser, whose head and body, badly scarred by bowie knives, told an eloquent tale, in their own grim way, of his gory past.

Rynders, in the spring campaign, had supported the Native Americans—it was not until ten years later that they become known as Know-Nothings—but in the Presidential election he sided with the Democrats. Rynders was openly in politics for profit. The entrance of the gangsters in New York politics was comparatively new. In 1841 the brass knuckles, shoulder-hitting and other peculiar methods of electioneering of gangdom were used systematically for the first time. Whigs and Democrats were equally culpable.

Prior to 1851, in both the Tammany and the Whig organizations, ward politics was in the control of shopkeepers and business men of the neighborhood. But with the advent of the Empire Club, the Plug-Uglies and other aggregations of knuckle-dusters and dirk-men, a change took place, and the tradesmen, the business men and the professional men were in time reduced to a negligible minority, used chiefly for window-dressing purposes and for their votes on Election Day.

On the night of November 1, the Democrats, or as they were sneeringly dubbed by the Whigs, the Loco-Focos, held a torchlight procession that set a new mark in political parades. A veracious chronicler of the day tells us that those in line for Polk, including their floats and carriages, stretched a full five miles. All the musicians and bands in the city and in nearby towns were hired for the occasion. Flags, banners and transparencies without number were borne aloft by the partisans of Polk. Torches in clusters illuminated every transparency and banner, that none of the cheering thousands along the line of march—who could read—would miss a single campaign slogan. Many of the banners demanded the annexation of Texas. Others read: Down With Coons!

Tweed marched with the rest.

Notable service was rendered Polk and the Democratic cause by a newspaper started that year. It was called the *Morning News*. It was avowedly a political journal. It was edited by a brilliant young lawyer who had been admitted to the bar three years before. He was destined to play a prominent part in Tweed's life. His name was Samuel J. Tilden.

Tweed, after casting his vote for the Polk electors, loitered around the polls. He saw both sides offering money for votes, bidding against one another. This was done openly. He went home to his bride that night, marveling at the brazen manner in which it was done. He had heard and read of these things. And some of the watchers at the polls, those who took up their positions on the curb to bargain for votes, were decent enough fellows the rest of the year. They wouldn't take money themselves, thought Tweed; they didn't look the sort; maybe— but no, they would not. Then he recalled his father-in-law's opinion of politics, and reluctantly believed it possible that these men, whom he knew, might be as bad as the others. Were they not in politics? And was not politics a corrupt game?

With his natural bent for figures, Tweed inquired of an election watcher as to the probable number of voters that would go to the polls out of the total number of 45,000 qualified voters in the city. He was informed that even in a Presidential election, when interest is keenest, there were a considerable number of stay-at-homes, and that these, when national issues were to the fore, represented about eight per cent of the total number of voters.

Tweed did some mental calculating. Eight per cent of 45,000 was 3,600. So that not more than 41,400 votes would be cast. Every one expected the vote in the city would be close, and all eagerly sought the returns in the newspapers the following day.

Tweed rubbed his eyes the day after the election as he looked at the city returns. More than 55,000 votes were reported to have been cast for Polk and Clay! This was 10,000 more than the total number of duly qualified voters in the city, and 13,600 in excess of the highest vote that would be cast, allowing for the largest possible number of stay-at-homes. What was the magic?

Tweed could not help chuckling quietly to himself when he confirmed later that the printed returns agreed with the official count, which credited the Clay (Whig) electors with 26,870 and the Polk (Democrat) electors with 28,216.

Polk, for whose electors he voted, carried the city by a comfortable margin. How it was accomplished was delightfully astonishing to Tweed. There was no magic in it. It was just plain theft. The Whigs stole in the Whig strongholds, and the Democrats in the Tammany strongholds. Ballot boxes were stuffed, incorrect tallies reported by crooked tally clerks on some of the local election boards, and the thugs of Rynders and his ilk went from one polling place to another, impersonating honest citizens who had not yet appeared at the polls. Both sides did it.

The methods of these repeaters—their work is not confined to any particular period or city—are daring almost beyond belief. Where the election boards are bribed, the repeating is done without any attempt at disguise.

The experiences of these repeaters have been the source of boisterous merriment in political gatherings for generations. One that happened during Tweed's public career involved the dignified pastor of a Dutch Reformed Church not far from his home. The reverend gentleman, whose name escapes us, was always a late voter, when he voted at all. On this particular election day the repeater, accompanied by several others, entered the polling place where the minister of the Gospel, whom we will call John Jones, had not yet put in an appearance. The repeater, as he approached the election board, was asked his name.

"Jones!" shouted the repeater, whose scraggly beard, unclean face and whiskified breath were in keeping with his battered hat and ragged overcoat.

"What is the first name, Mr. Jones?" asked the election clerk, softly, turning to the J's.

"John," snarled the repeater.

"The Reverend Dr. John Jones, pastor of the Dutch Reformed Church around the corner?" continued the inquiring election official.

"Yes, you dirty, lousy ———!" exclaimed the repeater. "Who 'n 'll else did you think I was, eh?"

The repeater was allowed to vote.

The board, of course, was fixed. The election clerk was just trying to amuse his associates on the board. He was successful. Everybody in the polling place laughed.

The policeman on duty laughed more heartily than the rest.